5

STORY & CHARACTER & FORMATION

The girls' soccer team for Saitama Prefectural High School Warabi Seinan—the weak team that was once derided as the Wallabies—is about to be reborn. Sumire Suō, a girl who has overwhelming speed as a winger. Midori Soshizaki, a defensive midfielder who was good enough to be been recruited to the national youth team. And Nozomi Onda, a midfielder who charms all who watch her. With the addition of these players and help from the new coach, the legendary Naoko Nōmi, the perpetual underdogs begin to move forward.

After the new team is formed, they have their first practice match. Their opponents: the team that stands at the peak of high school girls' soccer, Kunogi Academy. Against this unstoppable lineup of girls who played on the national youth team, the Wallabies fall behind seven points in the first half. Nevertheless, the girls' spirits remain unbroken—Onda takes center stage, and the ball starts moving around the field, coming dangerously close to Kunogi's goal.

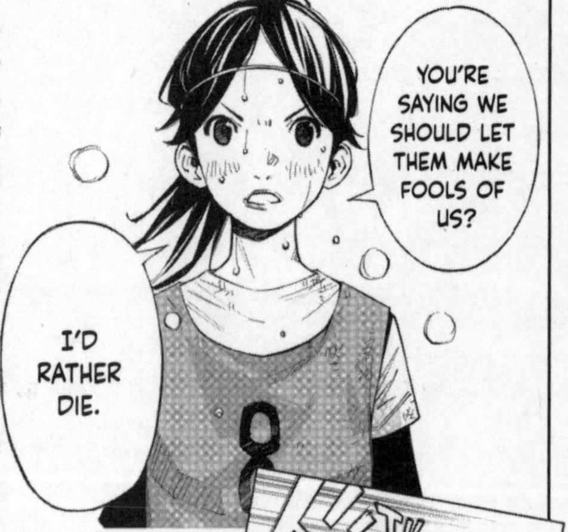
YOU'RE SAYING WE SHOULD LET THEM MAKE FOOLS OF US?
I'D RATHER DIE.

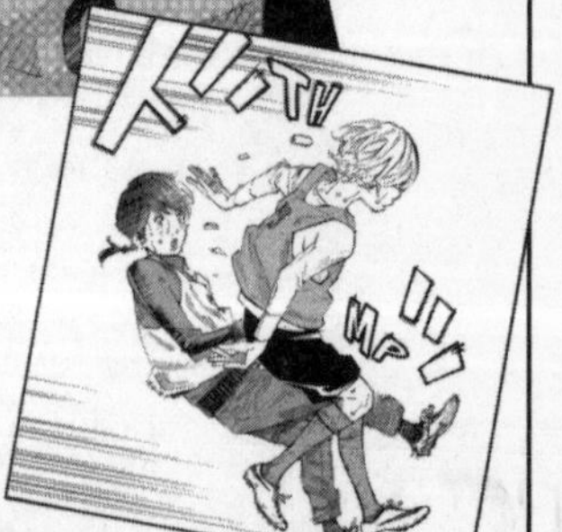

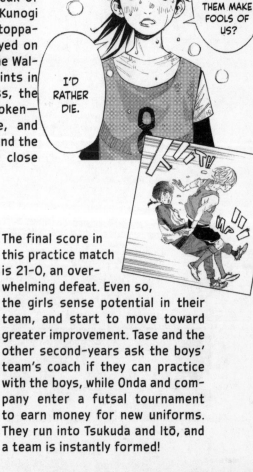

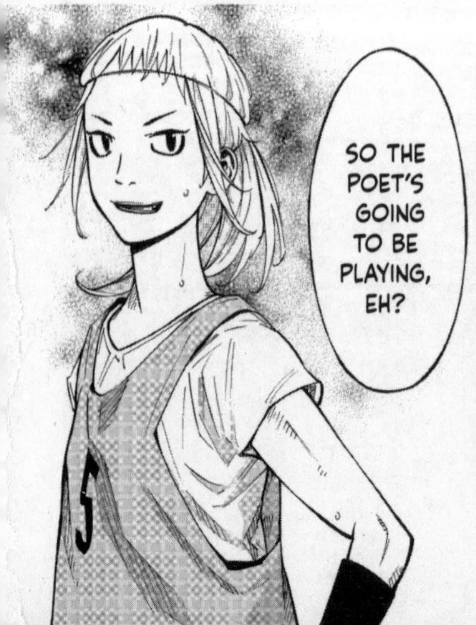
SO THE POET'S GOING TO BE PLAYING, EH?

The final score in this practice match is 21-0, an overwhelming defeat. Even so, the girls sense potential in their team, and start to move toward greater improvement. Tase and the other second-years ask the boys' team's coach if they can practice with the boys, while Onda and company enter a futsal tournament to earn money for new uniforms. They run into Tsukuda and Itō, and a team is instantly formed!

Warabi Seinan High School Formation

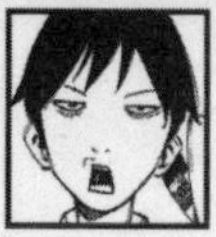

HEAD COACH: FUKATSU

A lazy sack of bones who is always reading horse racing magazines.

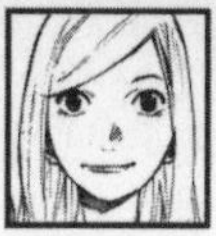

COACH: NAOKO NŌMI

A legend in Japanese girls' soccer. Has now retired and become a coach at Warabi Seinan.

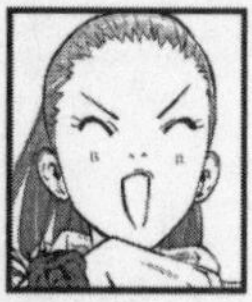

9 AYA SHIRATORI (1ST-YEAR)

The self-proclaimed center forward, who's more loud and annoying than anything else. Has an excessively high opinion of herself, but when her feet aren't involved she may actually be good at scoring?

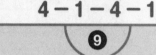

4–1–4–1

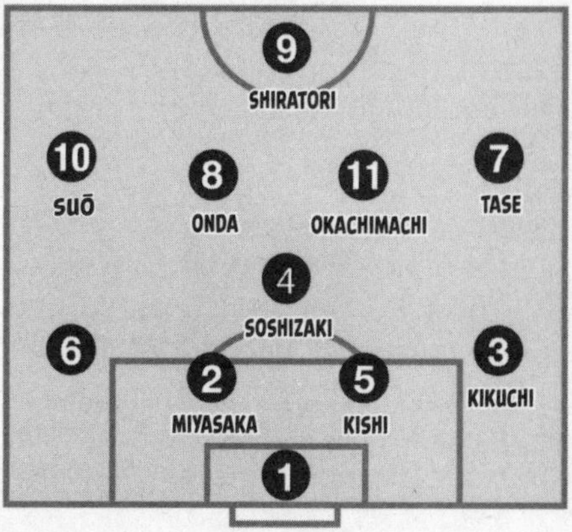
9
SHIRATORI
10
SUŌ
8
ONDA
11
OKACHIMACHI
7
TASE
4
SOSHIZAKI
6
3
2
MIYASAKA
5
KISHI
KIKUCHI
1

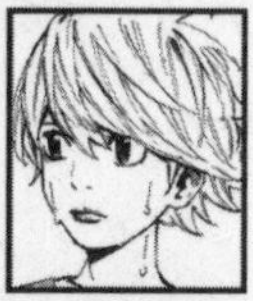

10 SUMIRE SUŌ (1ST-YEAR)

A winger with overwhelming speed. She doesn't talk much, but when she does, it isn't nice.

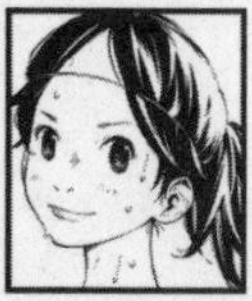

8 NOZOMI ONDA (1ST-YEAR)

A charismatic midfielder who played for a boys' team in middle school.

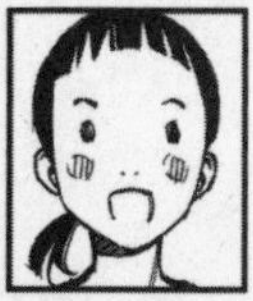

11 NORIKO OKACHIMACHI (2ND-YEAR)

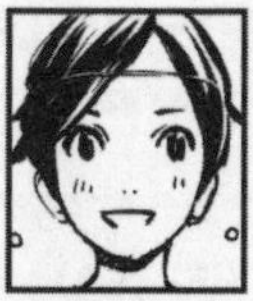

7 ERIKO TASE (2ND-YEAR)

Team captain. A kind and responsible girl who is the glue that holds this very disparate team together.

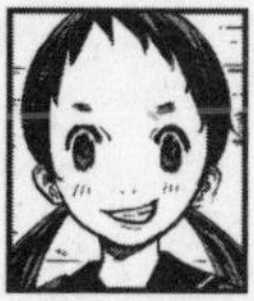

4 MIDORI SOSHIZAKI (1ST-YEAR)

Played defensive midfielder for Todakita Middle School, which was third in the nation. Surprisingly geeky.

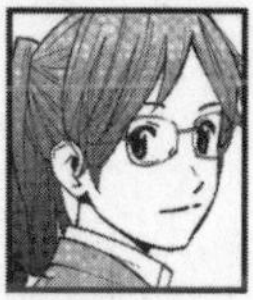

2 MAKOTO MIYASAKA (2ND-YEAR)

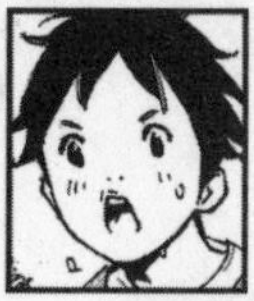

5 AYUMU KISHI (2ND-YEAR)

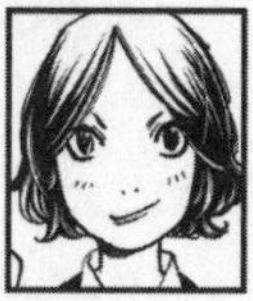

3 RUI KIKUCHI (2ND-YEAR)

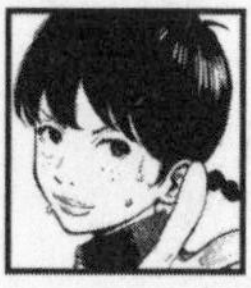

MAO TSUKUDA (1ST-YEAR)

One of Kunogi Academy's core players. A wing back who excels at offense and defense.

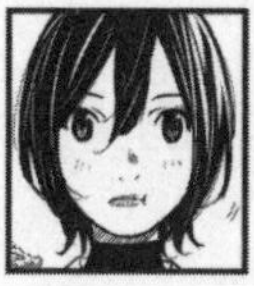

HARUNA ITŌ (1ST-YEAR)

Number 10 on Kunogi Academy's first-year team. Her technique is first-class.

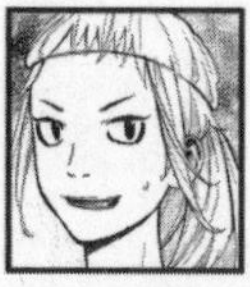

REI KUTANI (1ST-YEAR)

An athlete participating in the futsal tournament. She seems to have a history with some of the other girls...

CONTENTS

16. The Battle of High Intensity Training

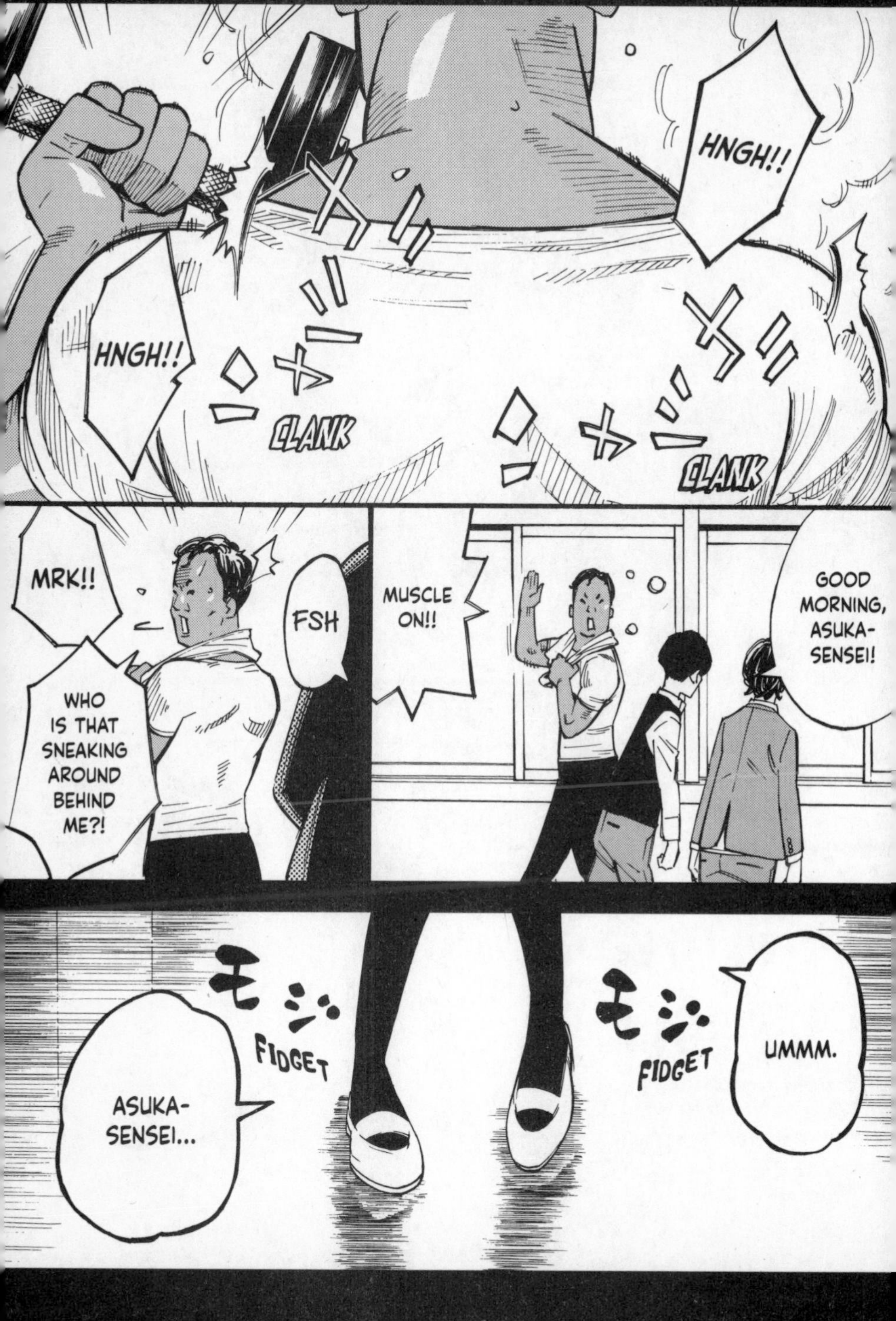
HNGH!!
HNGH!!
CLANK
CLANK
GOOD MORNING, ASUKA-SENSEI!
MUSCLE ON!!
FSH
MRK!!
WHO IS THAT SNEAKING AROUND BEHIND ME?!
UMMM.
FIDGET
FIDGET
ASUKA-SENSEI...

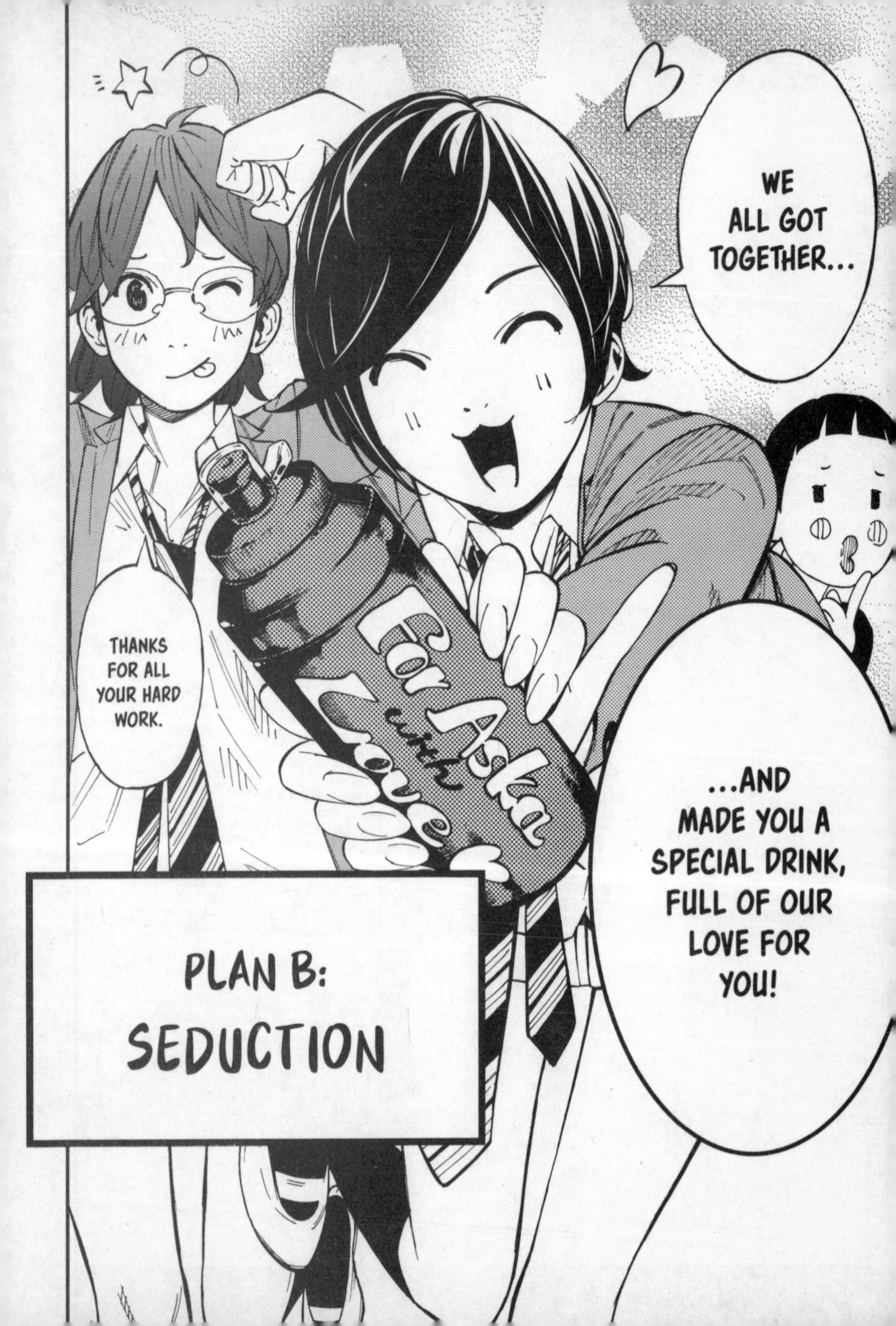
WE ALL GOT TOGETHER...
...AND MADE YOU A SPECIAL DRINK, FULL OF OUR LOVE FOR YOU!
THANKS FOR ALL YOUR HARD WORK.
PLAN B: SEDUCTION

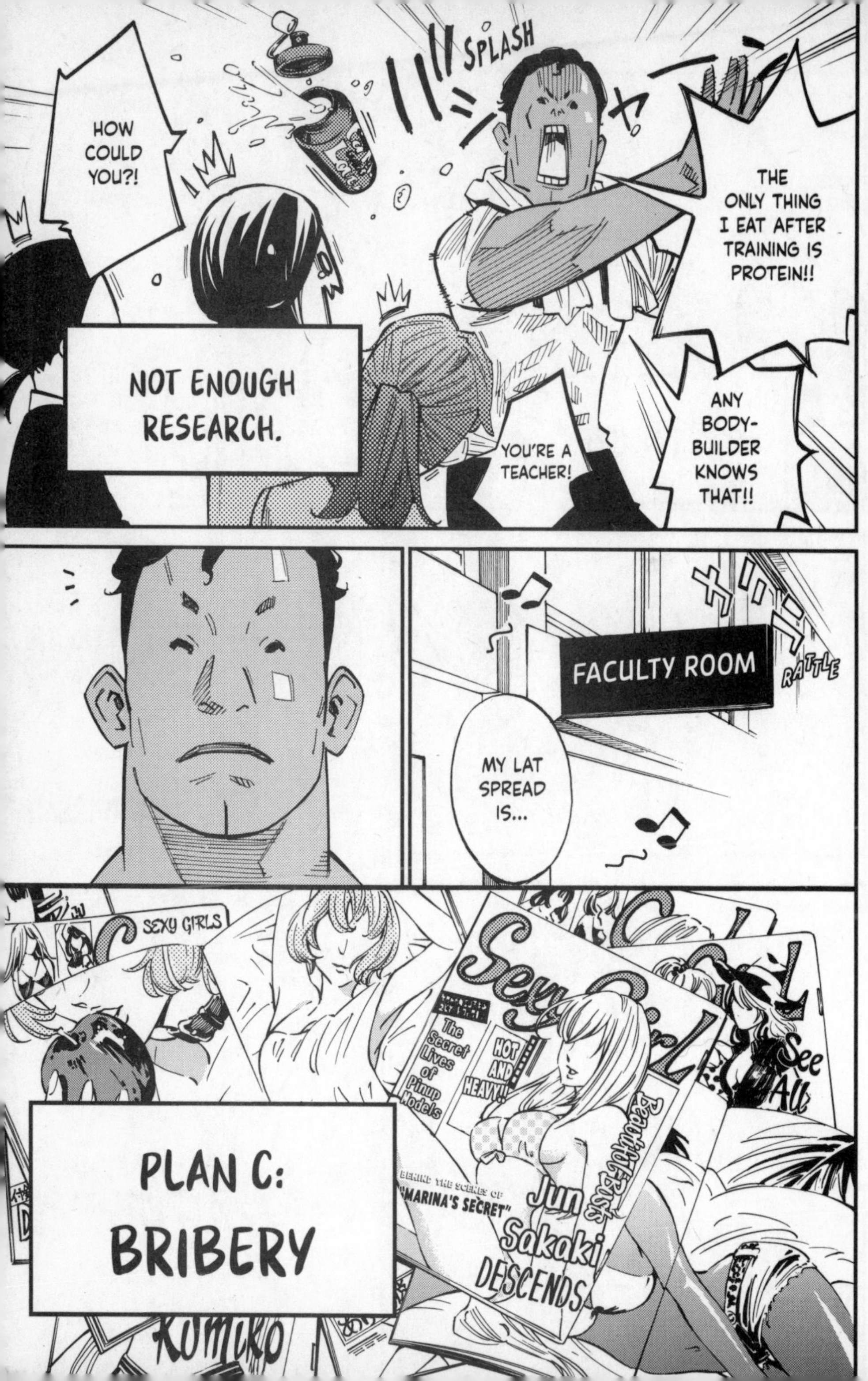
SPLASH
THE ONLY THING I EAT AFTER TRAINING IS PROTEIN!!
ANY BODY-BUILDER KNOWS THAT!!
YOU'RE A TEACHER!
HOW COULD YOU?!
NOT ENOUGH RESEARCH.
RATTLE
FACULTY ROOM
MY LAT SPREAD IS...
See All
HOT AND HEAVY!!
The Secret Lives of Pinup Models
BEHIND THE SCENES OF "MARINA'S SECRET"
Jun Sakaki DESCENDS
SEXY GIRLS
Kumiko
PLAN C: BRIBERY

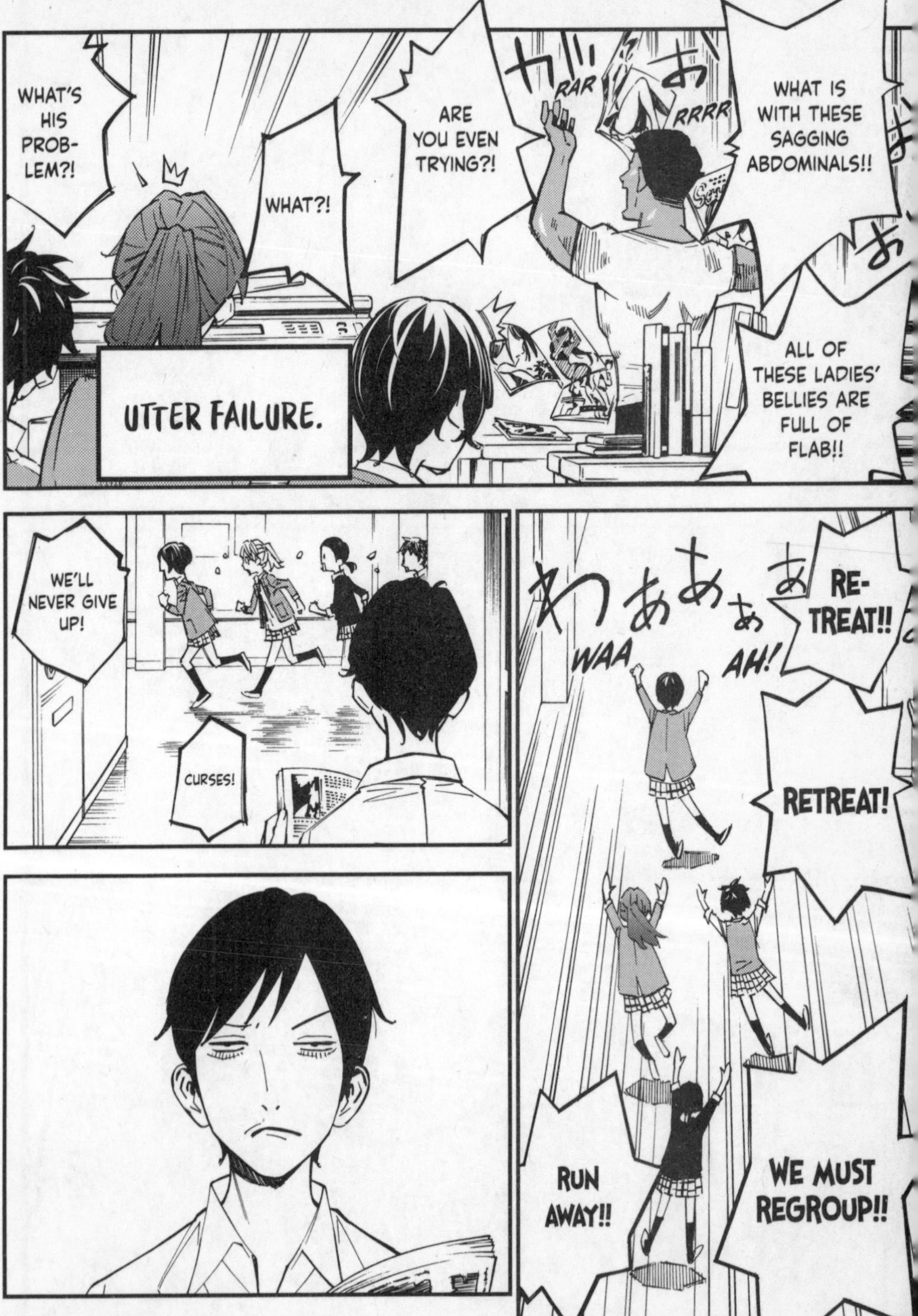
WHAT IS WITH THESE SAGGING ABDOMINALS!!
RRRR
RAR
ALL OF THESE LADIES' BELLIES ARE FULL OF FLAB!!
ARE YOU EVEN TRYING?!
WHAT?!
WHAT'S HIS PROB-LEM?!
UTTER FAILURE.
RE-TREAT!!
WAA
AH!
RETREAT!
WE MUST REGROUP!!
RUN AWAY!!
WE'LL NEVER GIVE UP!
CURSES!

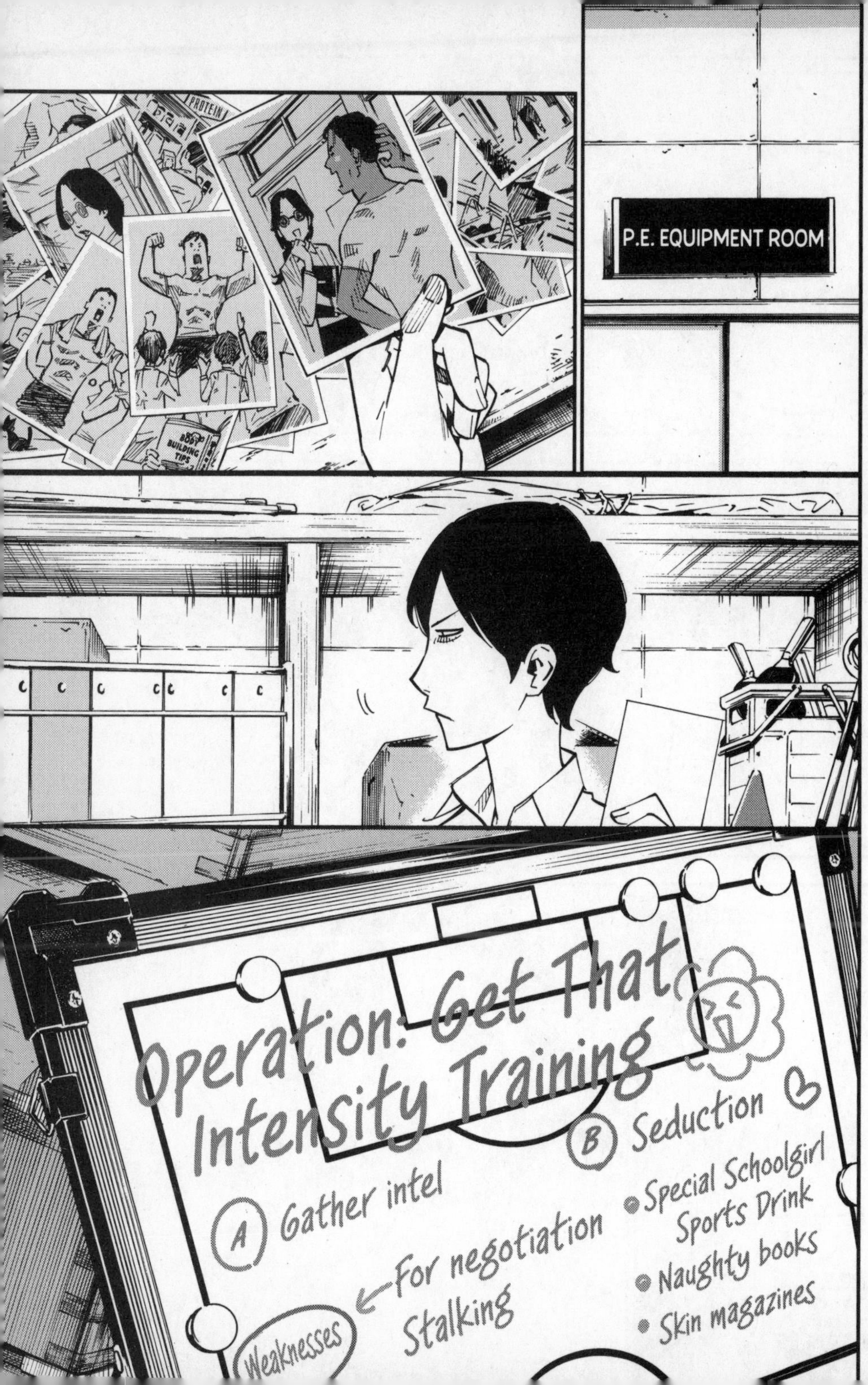
P.E. EQUIPMENT ROOM
PROTEIN
BODY BUILDING TIPS
Operation: Get That Intensity Training
Ⓑ Seduction
• Special Schoolgirl Sports Drink
• Naughty books
• Skin magazines
Ⓐ Gather intel
For negotiation
Stalking
Weaknesses

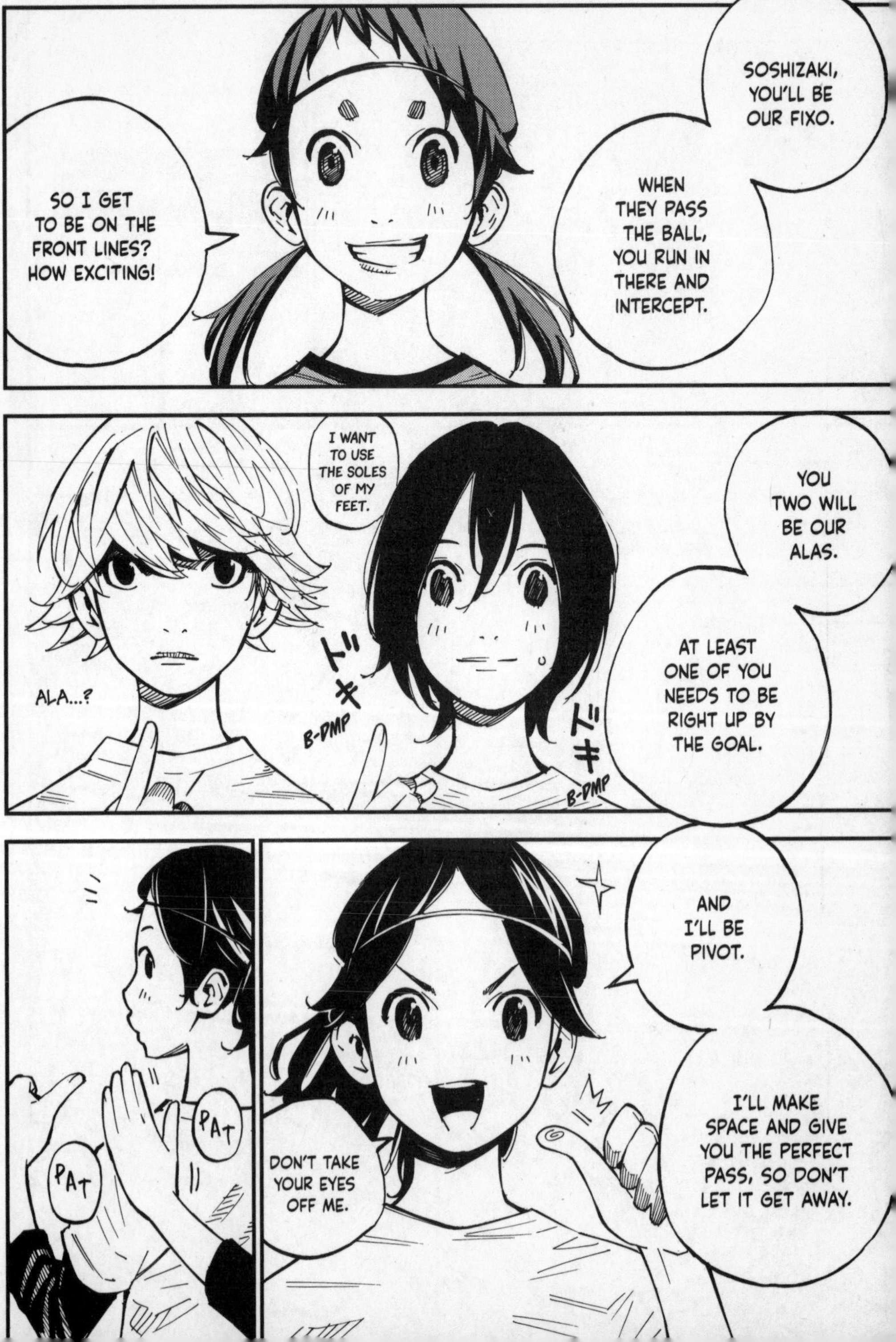
SOSHIZAKI, YOU'LL BE OUR FIXO.
WHEN THEY PASS THE BALL, YOU RUN IN THERE AND INTERCEPT.
SO I GET TO BE ON THE FRONT LINES? HOW EXCITING!
YOU TWO WILL BE OUR ALAS.
AT LEAST ONE OF YOU NEEDS TO BE RIGHT UP BY THE GOAL.
ドキ
B-DMP
I WANT TO USE THE SOLES OF MY FEET.
ドキ
B-DMP
ALA...?
AND I'LL BE PIVOT.
I'LL MAKE SPACE AND GIVE YOU THE PERFECT PASS, SO DON'T LET IT GET AWAY.
DON'T TAKE YOUR EYES OFF ME.
PAT
PAT

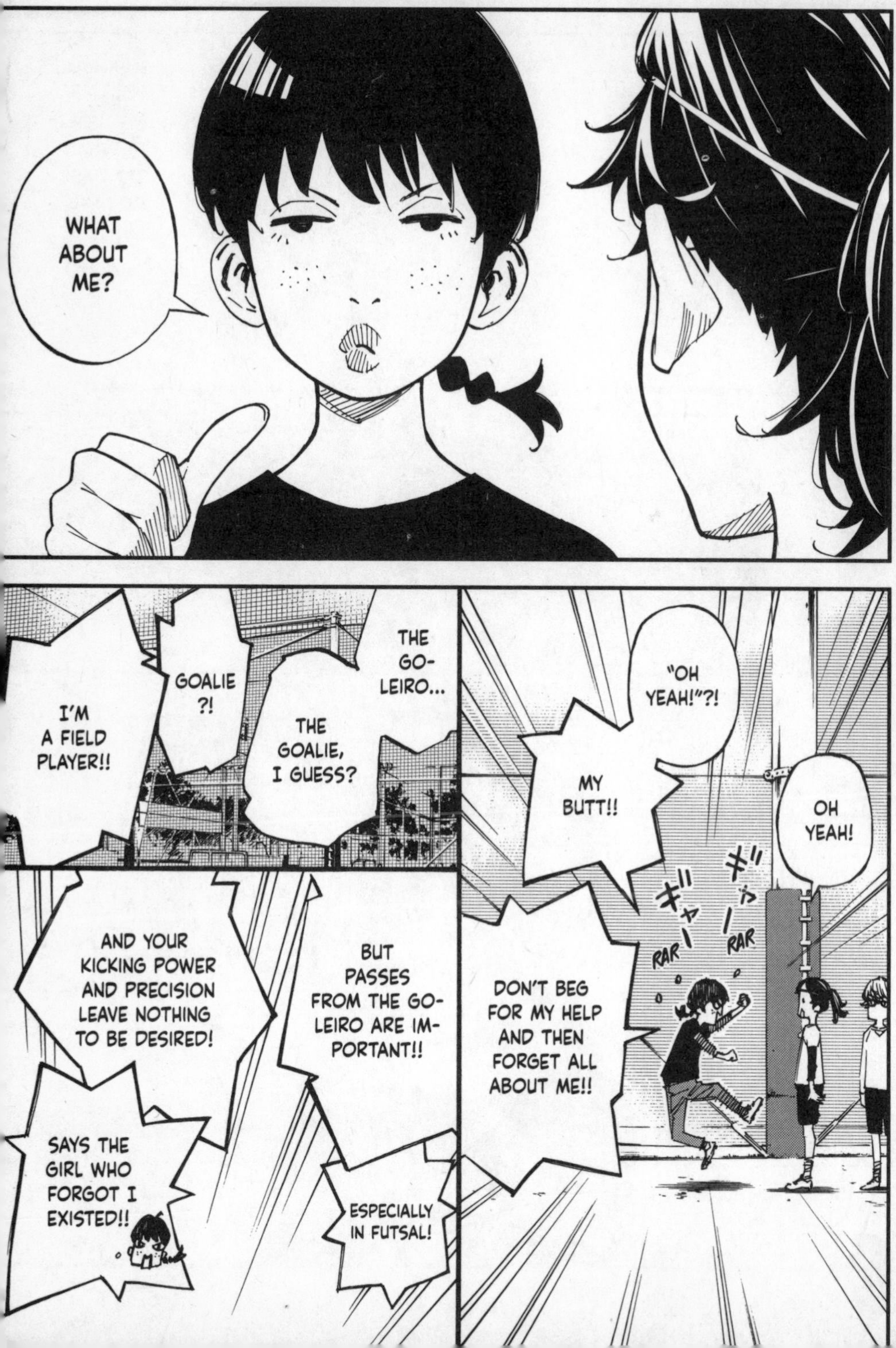
WHAT ABOUT ME?
OH YEAH!
"OH YEAH!"?!
MY BUTT!!
ギャー
RAR
ギャー
RAR
DON'T BEG FOR MY HELP AND THEN FORGET ALL ABOUT ME!!
THE GO-LEIRO...
THE GOALIE, I GUESS?
GOALIE?!
I'M A FIELD PLAYER!!
BUT PASSES FROM THE GO-LEIRO ARE IM-PORTANT!!
AND YOUR KICKING POWER AND PRECISION LEAVE NOTHING TO BE DESIRED!
ESPECIALLY IN FUTSAL!
SAYS THE GIRL WHO FORGOT I EXISTED!!

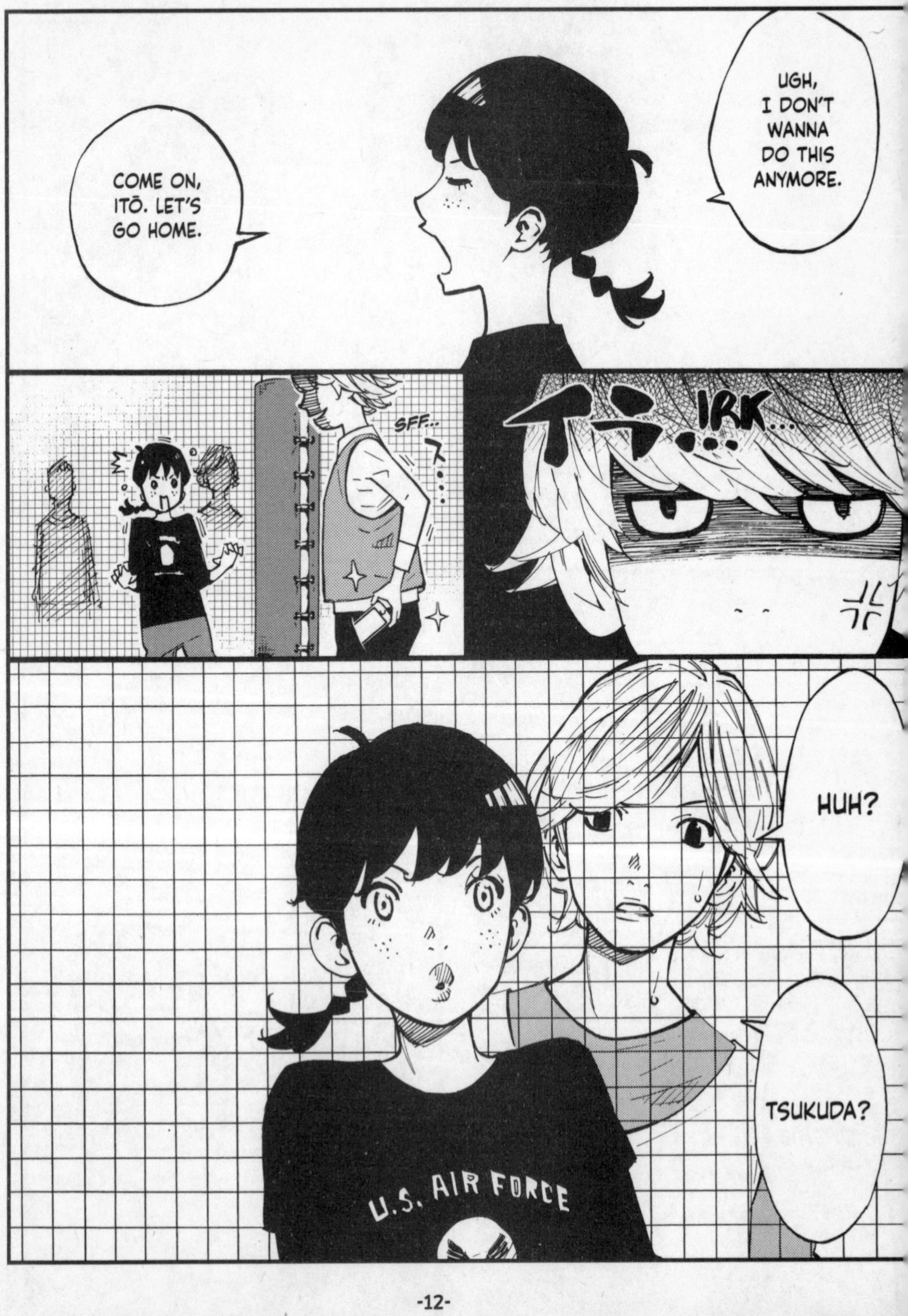
UGH, I DON'T WANNA DO THIS ANYMORE.
COME ON, ITŌ. LET'S GO HOME.
イラ...
IRK...
SFF...
ス...
HUH?
TSUKUDA?
U.S. AIR FORCE

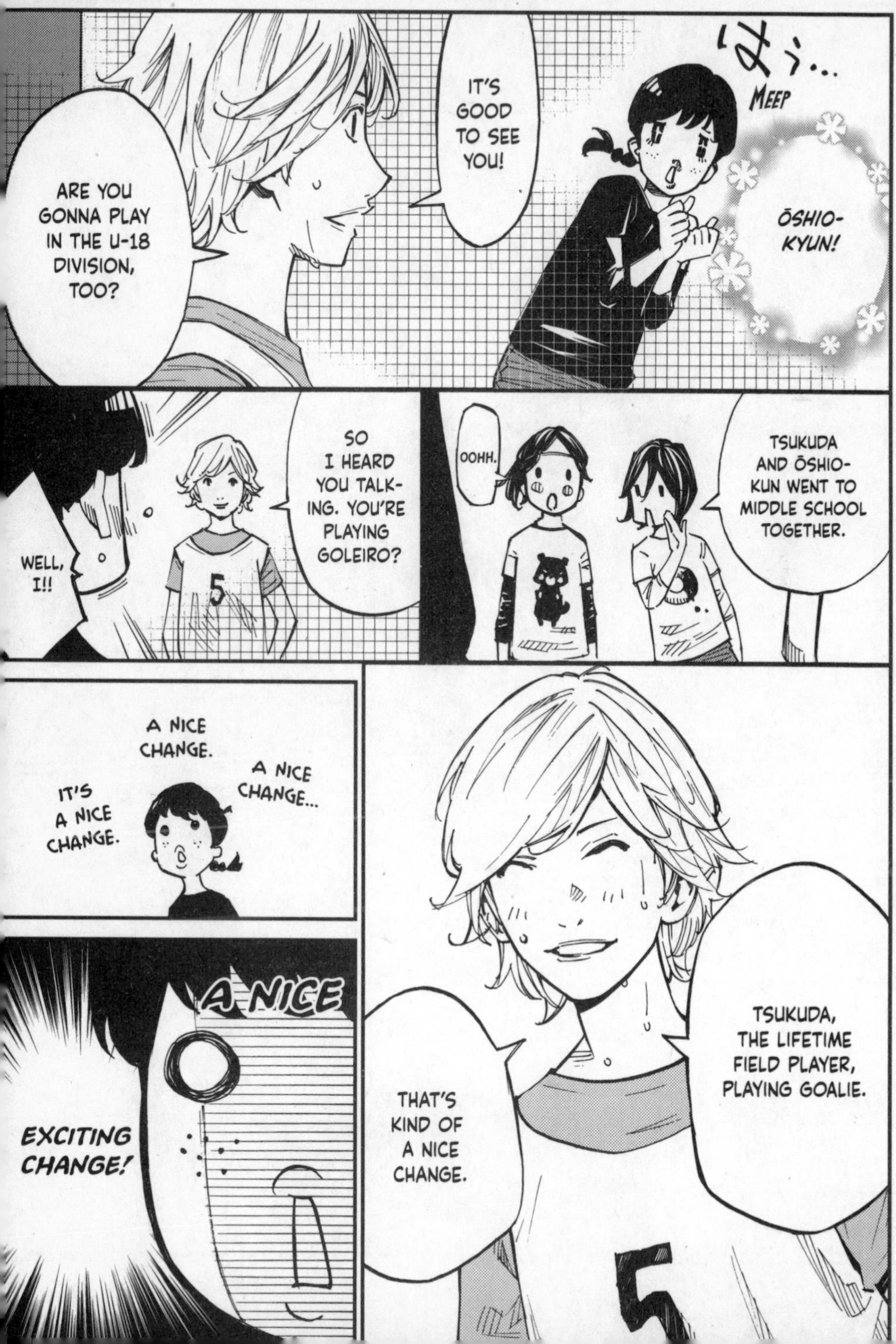
はぅ…
MEEP
ŌSHIO-KYUN!
IT'S GOOD TO SEE YOU!
ARE YOU GONNA PLAY IN THE U-18 DIVISION, TOO?
TSUKUDA AND ŌSHIO-KUN WENT TO MIDDLE SCHOOL TOGETHER.
OOHH.
SO I HEARD YOU TALKING. YOU'RE PLAYING GOLEIRO?
WELL, I!!
TSUKUDA, THE LIFETIME FIELD PLAYER, PLAYING GOALIE.
THAT'S KIND OF A NICE CHANGE.
A NICE CHANGE.
A NICE CHANGE...
IT'S A NICE CHANGE.
A NICE
EXCITING CHANGE!

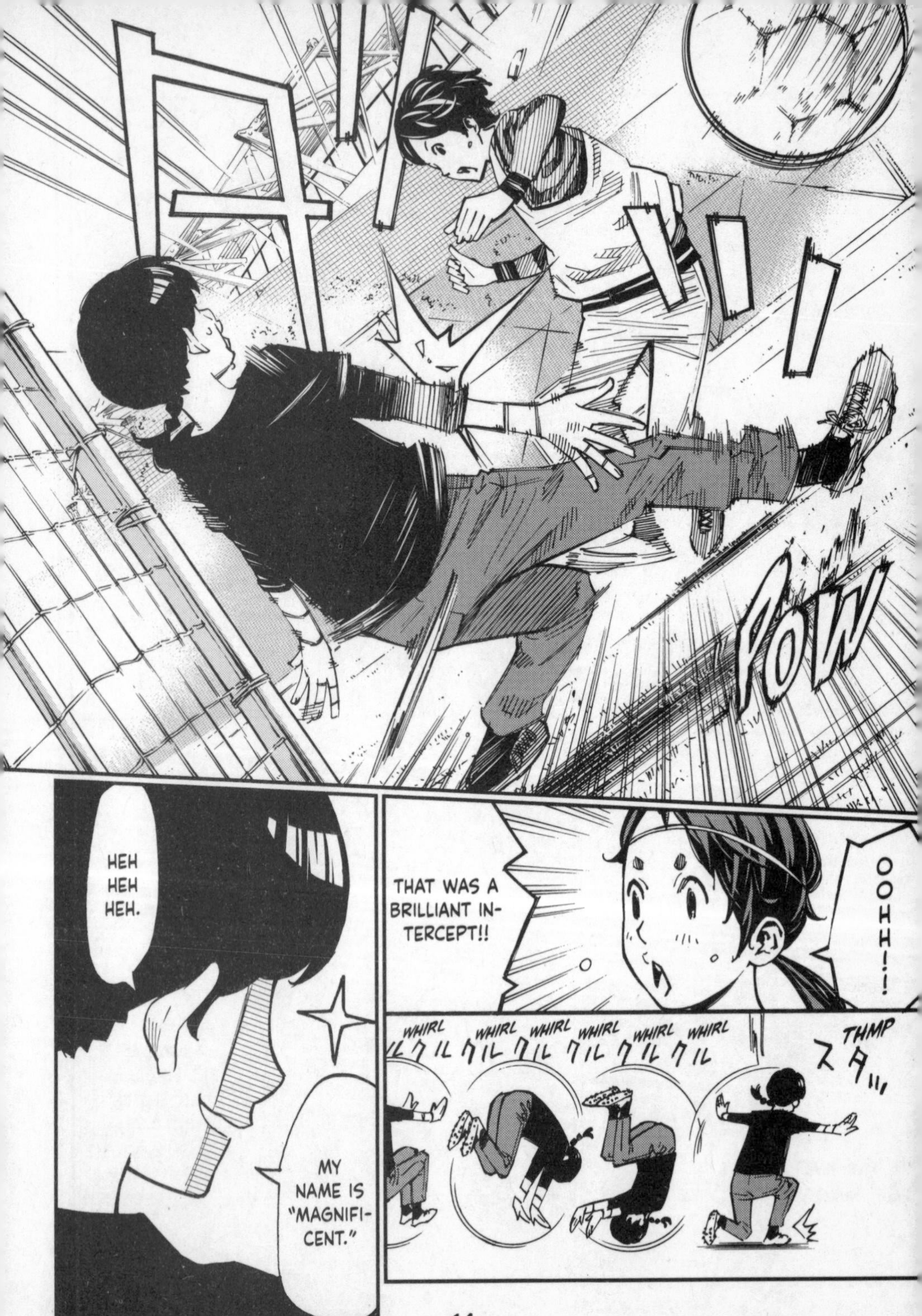
POW
OOHH!!
THAT WAS A BRILLIANT IN-TERCEPT!!
THMP
WHIRL
WHIRL
WHIRL
WHIRL
WHIRL
WHIRL
HEH HEH HEH.
MY NAME IS "MAGNIFI-CENT."

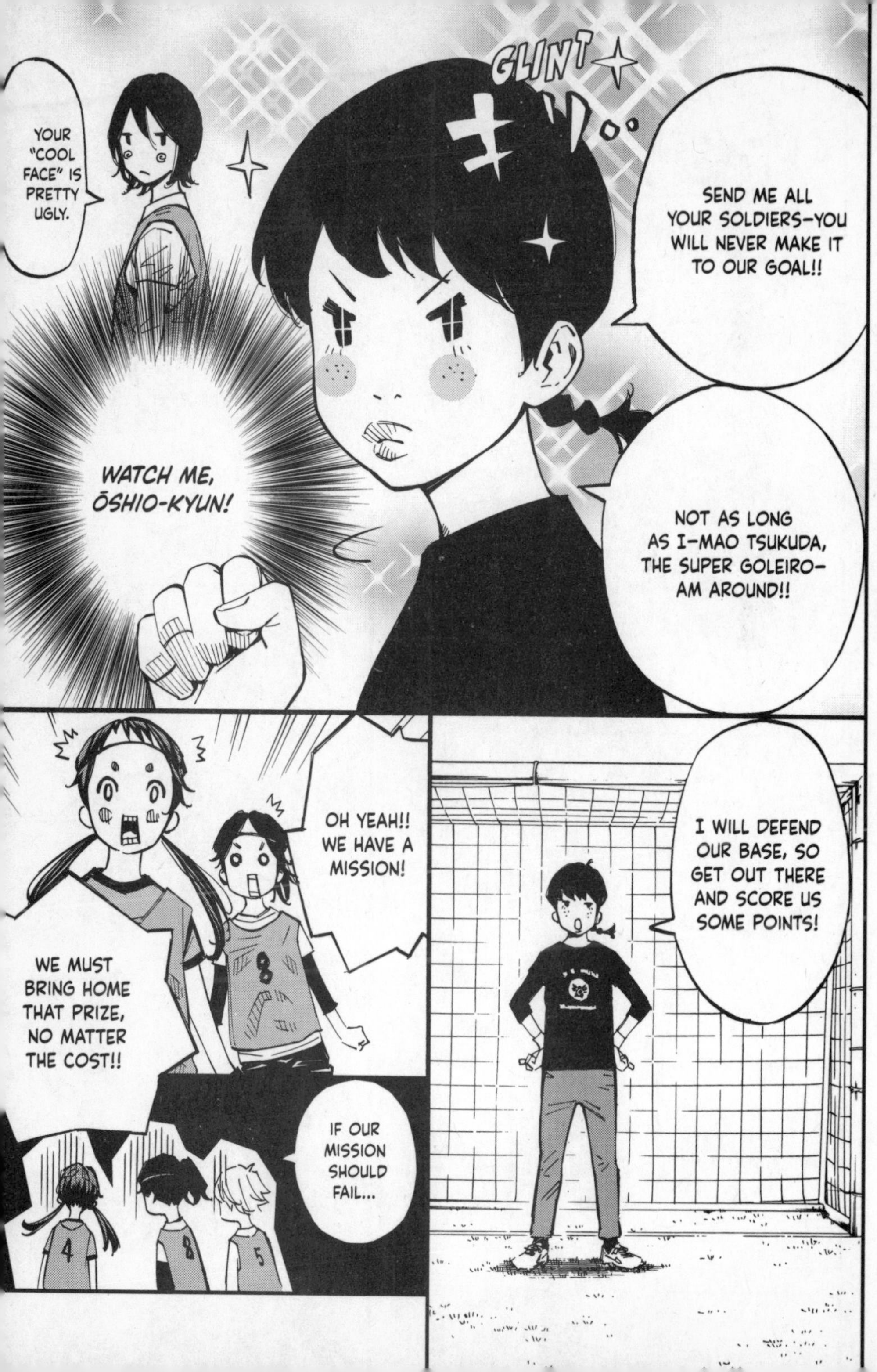
GLINT
SEND ME ALL YOUR SOLDIERS—YOU WILL NEVER MAKE IT TO OUR GOAL!!
NOT AS LONG AS I—MAO TSUKUDA, THE SUPER GOLEIRO—AM AROUND!!
WATCH ME, ŌSHIO-KYUN!
YOUR "COOL FACE" IS PRETTY UGLY.
I WILL DEFEND OUR BASE, SO GET OUT THERE AND SCORE US SOME POINTS!
OH YEAH!! WE HAVE A MISSION!
WE MUST BRING HOME THAT PRIZE, NO MATTER THE COST!!
IF OUR MISSION SHOULD FAIL...

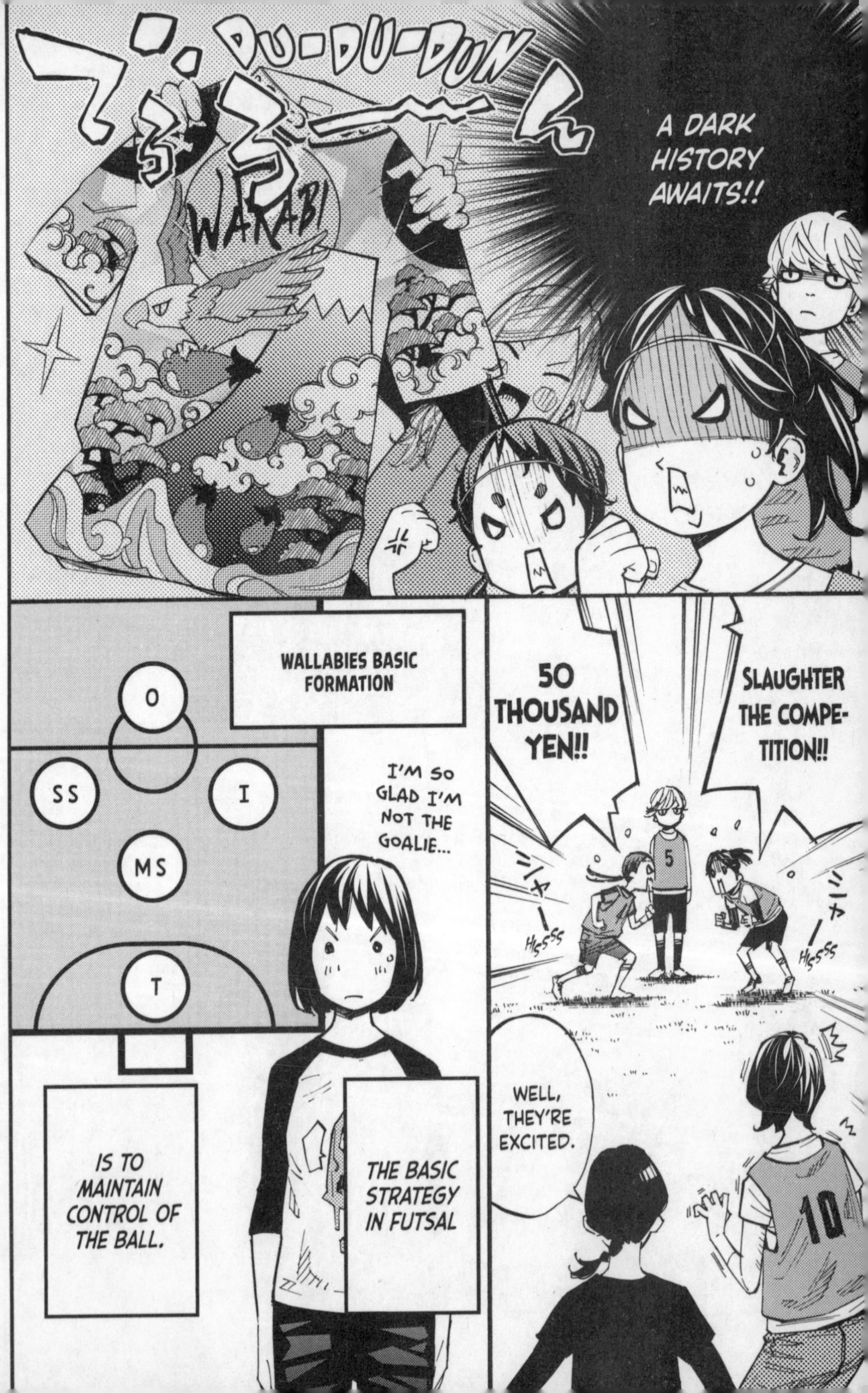
DU-DU-DUN
WARABI
A DARK HISTORY AWAITS!!
SLAUGHTER THE COMPE-TITION!!
50 THOUSAND YEN!!
HISSSS
HISSSS
WELL, THEY'RE EXCITED.
WALLABIES BASIC FORMATION
O
SS
I
MS
T
I'M SO GLAD I'M NOT THE GOALIE...
THE BASIC STRATEGY IN FUTSAL
IS TO MAINTAIN CONTROL OF THE BALL.

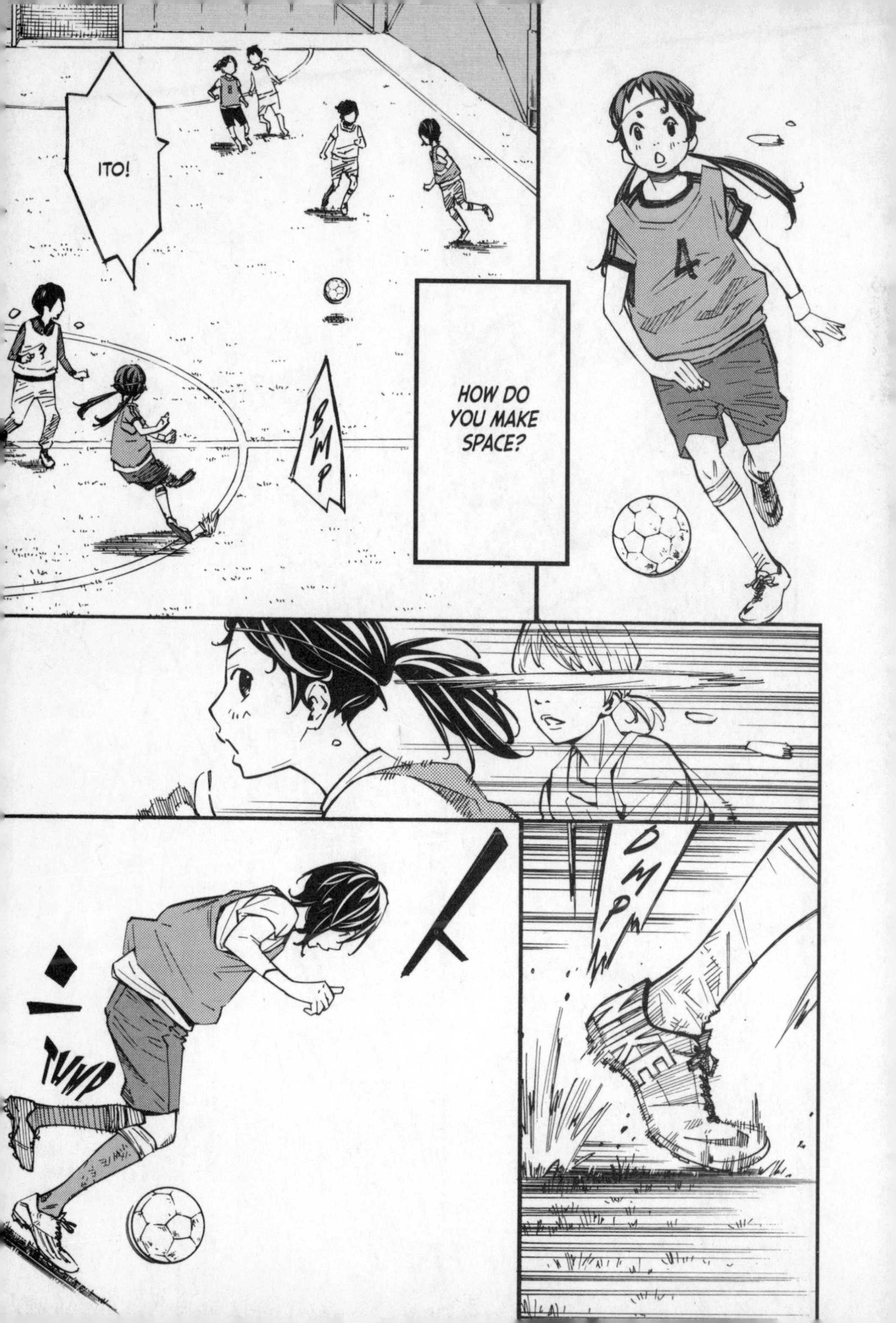
HOW DO YOU MAKE SPACE?
ITO!
BMP
DMP
TUMP

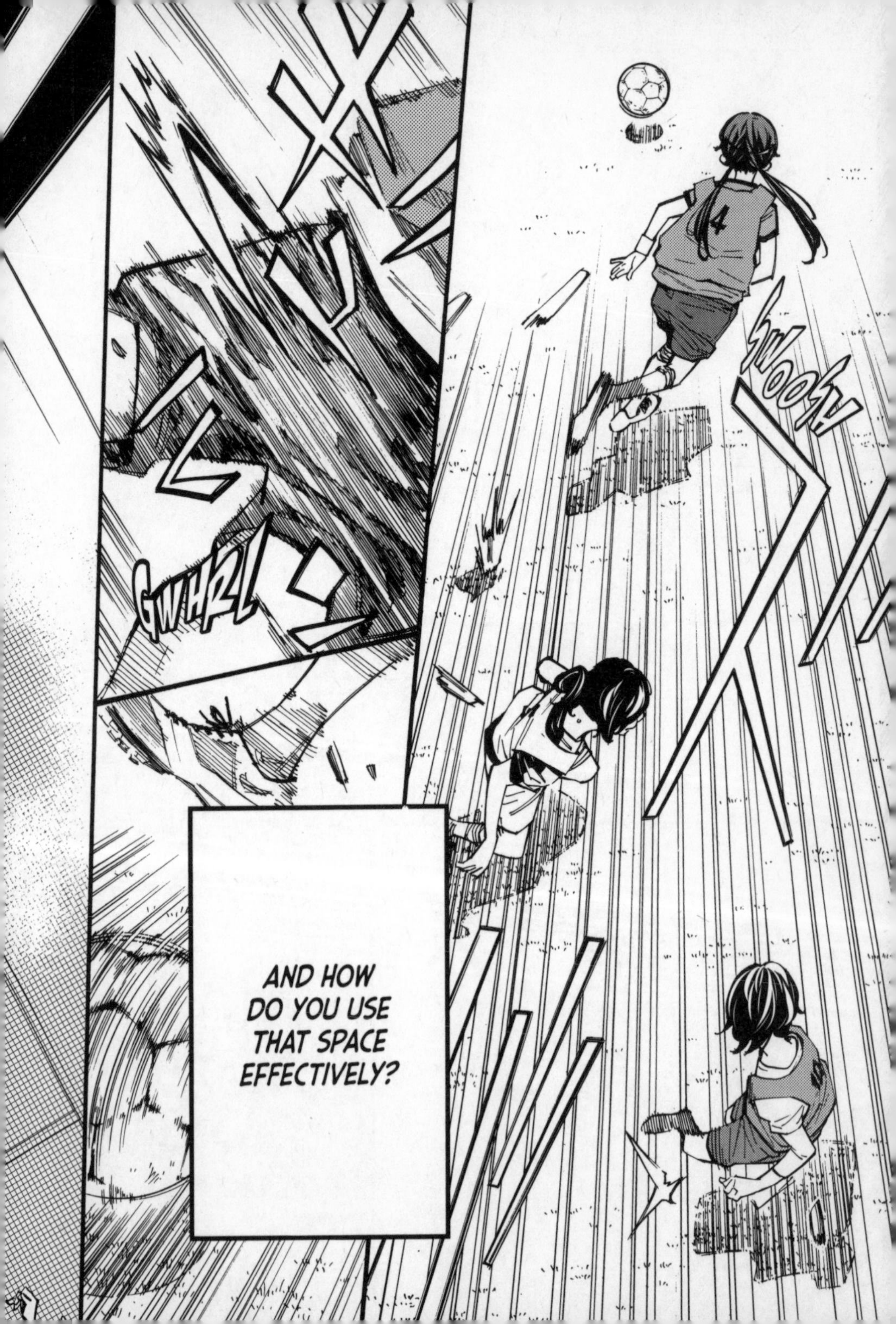
SWOOSH
GWHRL
AND HOW DO YOU USE THAT SPACE EFFECTIVELY?

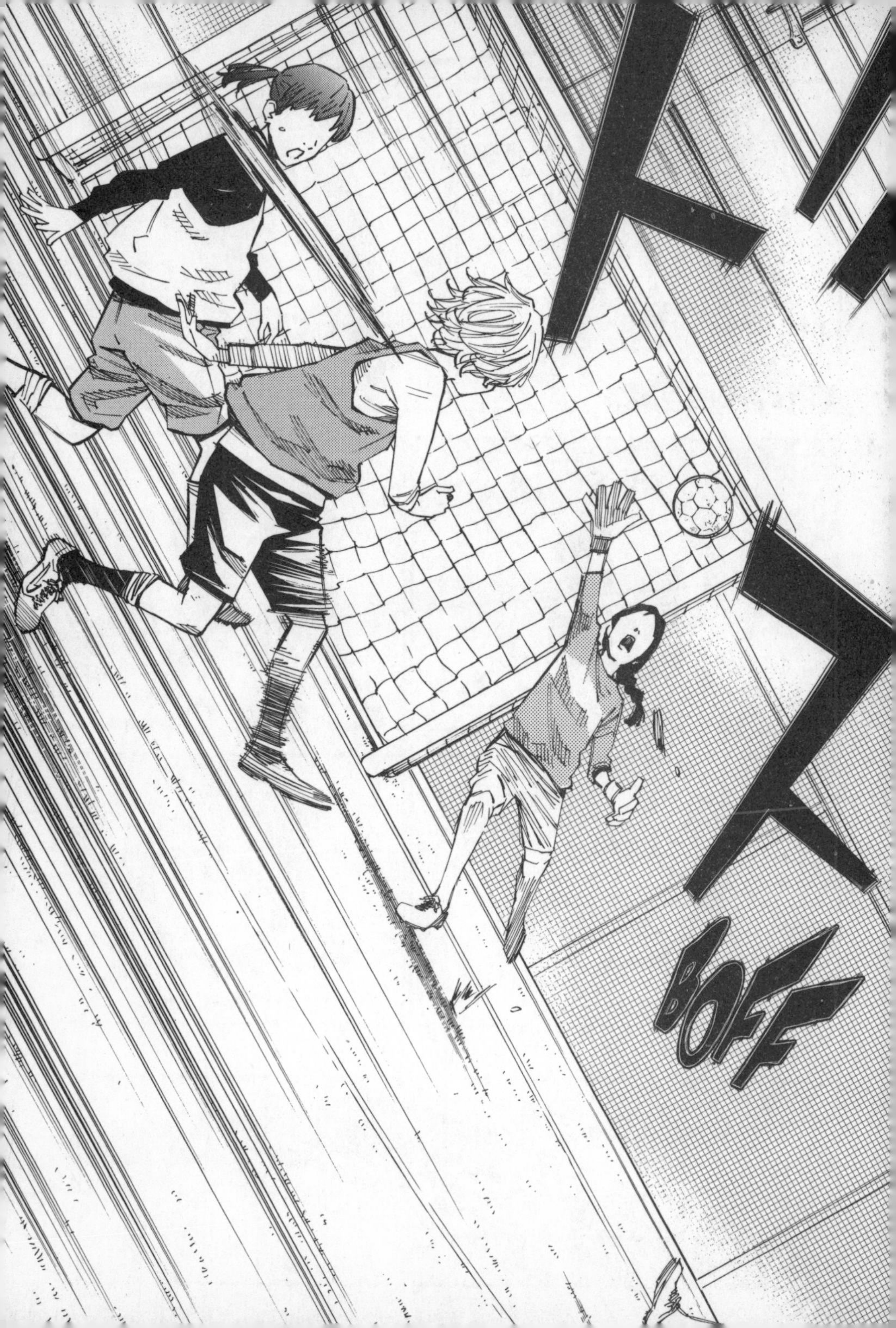
BOFF

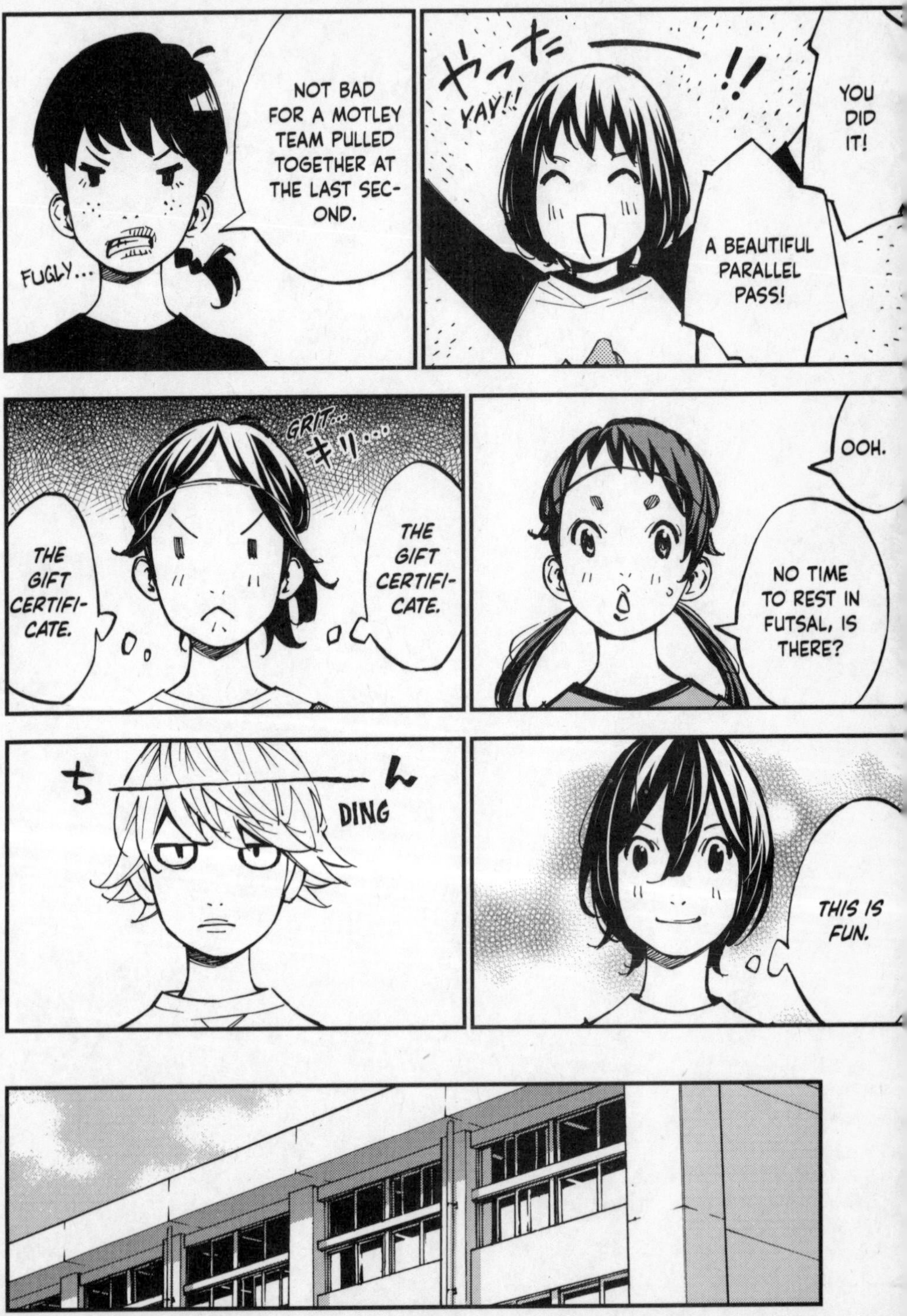
ヤったー!!
YAY!!
YOU DID IT!
A BEAUTIFUL PARALLEL PASS!
NOT BAD FOR A MOTLEY TEAM PULLED TOGETHER AT THE LAST SECOND.
FUGLY...
OOH.
NO TIME TO REST IN FUTSAL, IS THERE?
GRIT... キリ...
THE GIFT CERTIFICATE.
THE GIFT CERTIFICATE.
THIS IS FUN.
ち——ん
DING

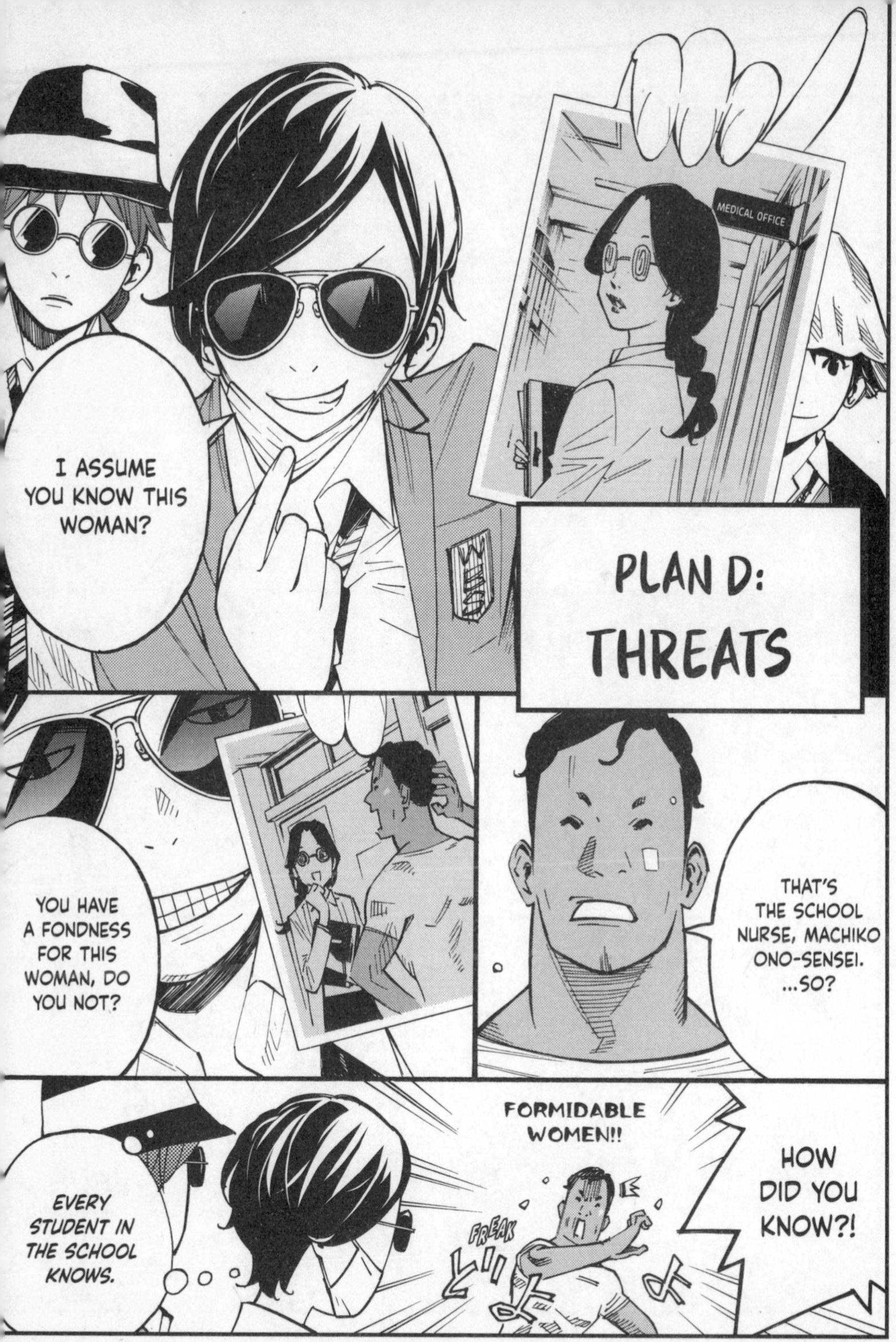

MEDICAL OFFICE
PLAN D: THREATS
I ASSUME YOU KNOW THIS WOMAN?
THAT'S THE SCHOOL NURSE, MACHIKO ONO-SENSEI. ...SO?
YOU HAVE A FONDNESS FOR THIS WOMAN, DO YOU NOT?
HOW DID YOU KNOW?!
FORMIDABLE WOMEN!!
FREAK
EVERY STUDENT IN THE SCHOOL KNOWS.

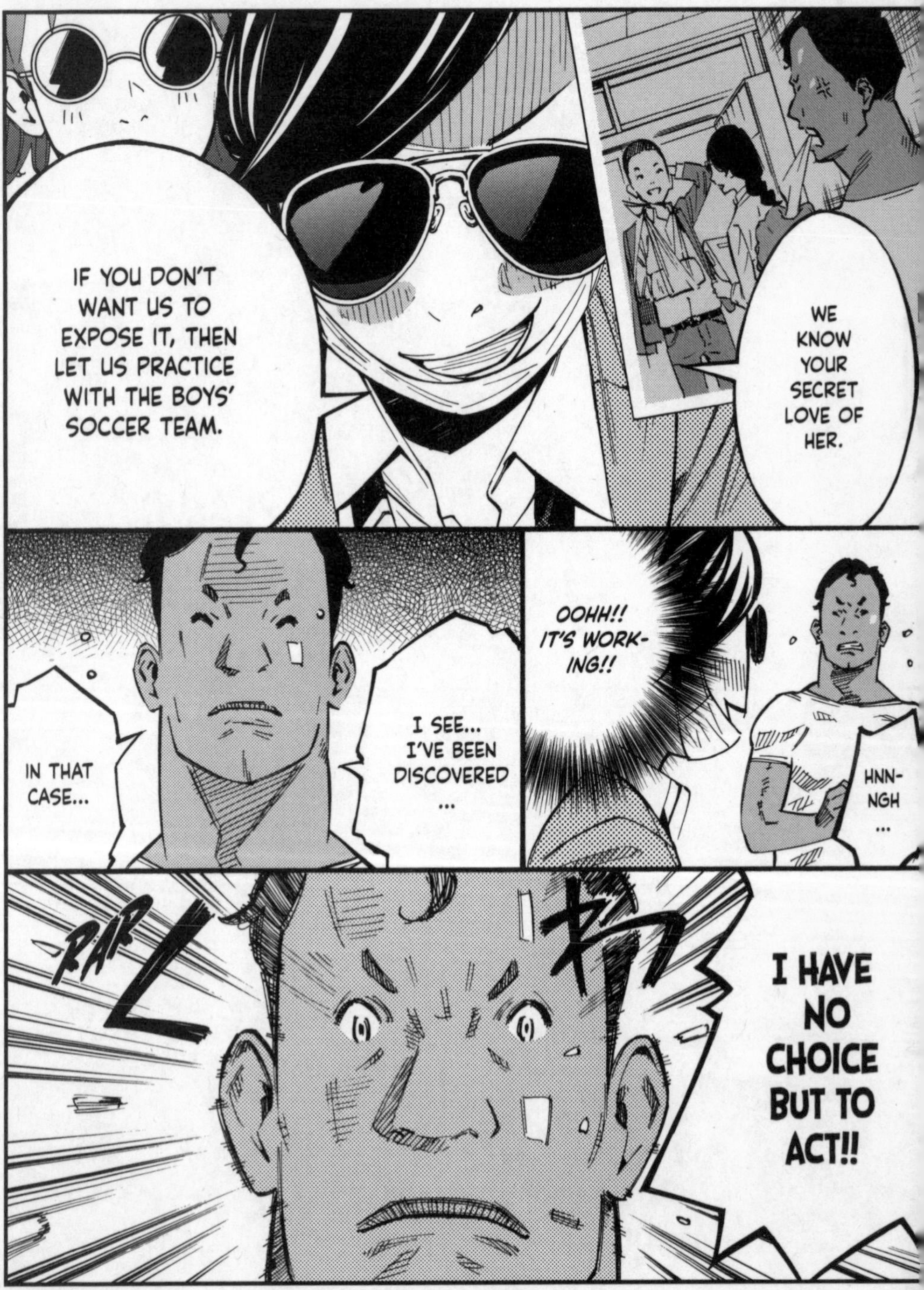
WE KNOW YOUR SECRET LOVE OF HER.
IF YOU DON'T WANT US TO EXPOSE IT, THEN LET US PRACTICE WITH THE BOYS' SOCCER TEAM.
HNN-NGH...
OOHH!! IT'S WORKING!!
I SEE... I'VE BEEN DISCOVERED...
IN THAT CASE...
I HAVE NO CHOICE BUT TO ACT!!

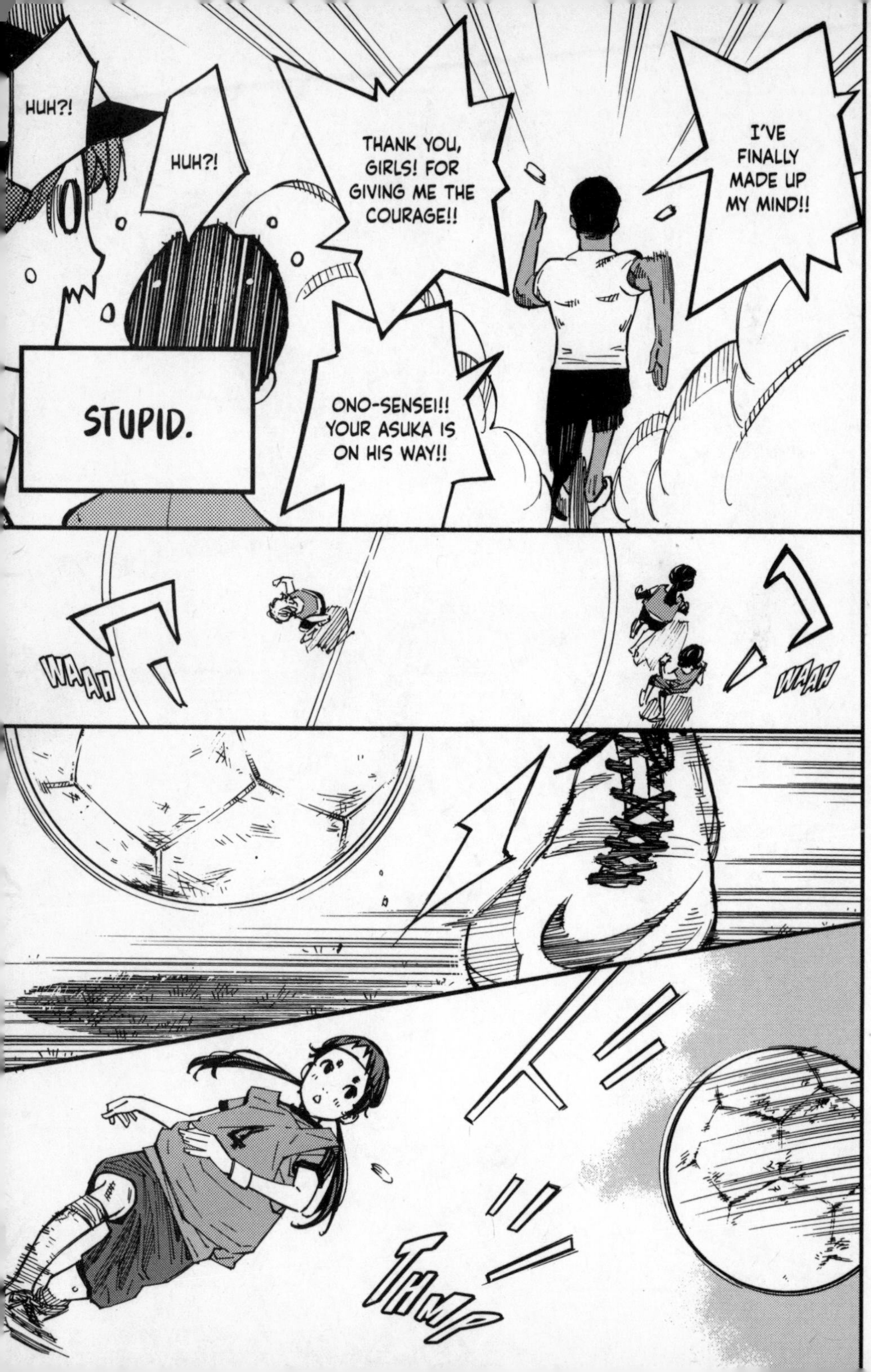
I'VE FINALLY MADE UP MY MIND!!
THANK YOU, GIRLS! FOR GIVING ME THE COURAGE!!
ONO-SENSEI!!! YOUR ASUKA IS ON HIS WAY!!
HUH?!
HUH?!
STUPID.
WAAH
WAAH
THMP

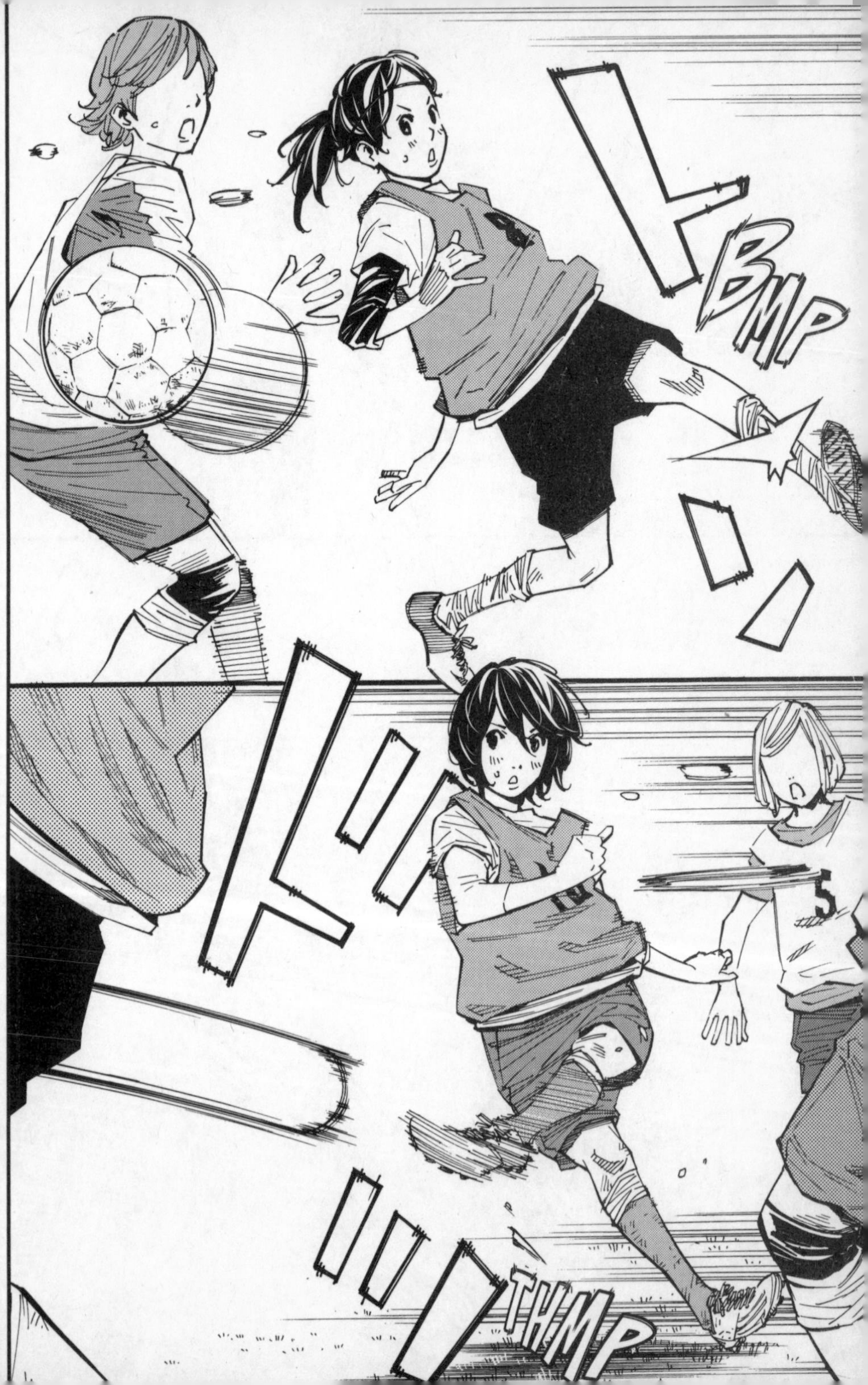
BMP
THMP

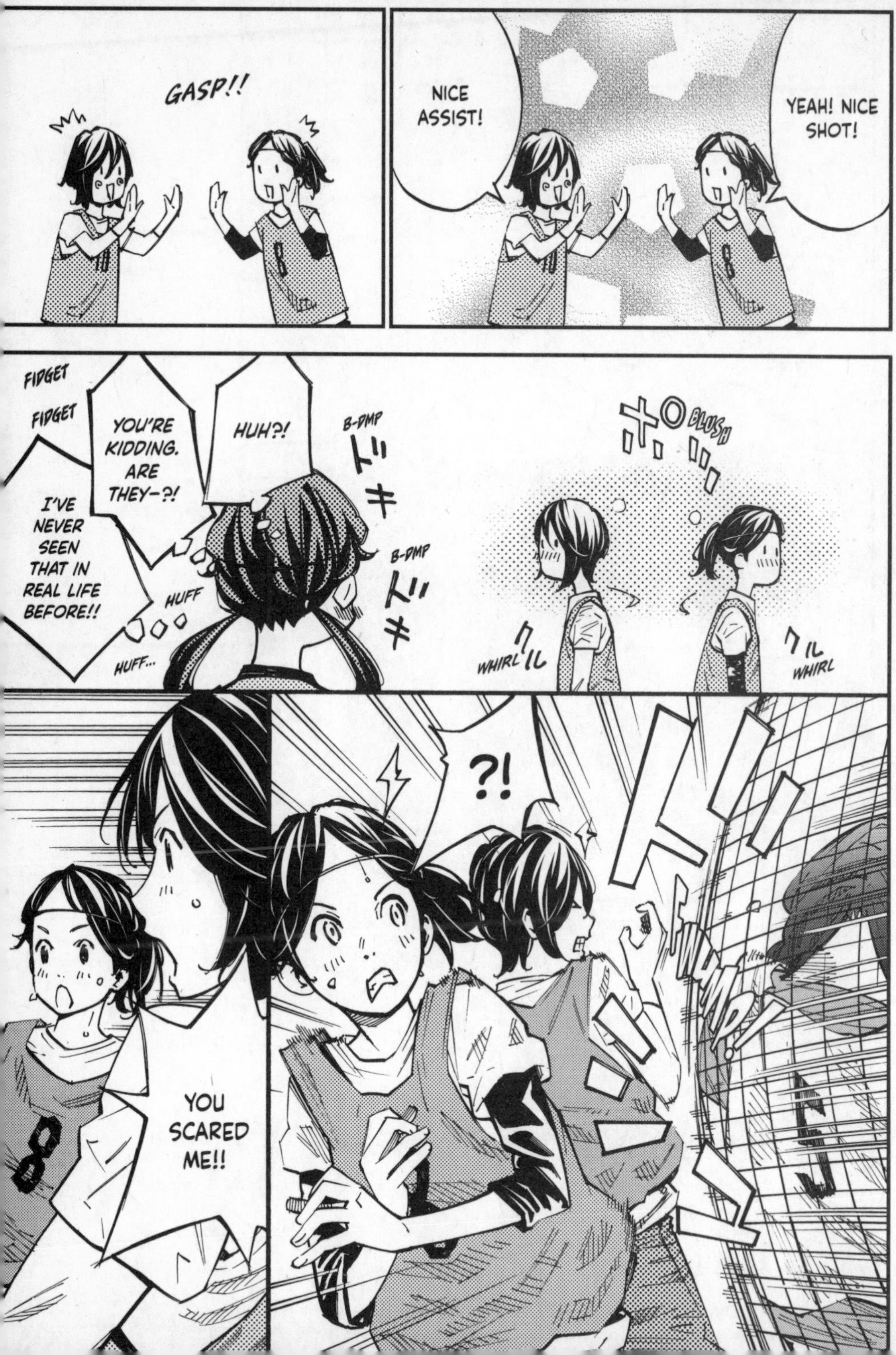
YEAH! NICE SHOT!
NICE ASSIST!
GASP!!
WHIRL
WHIRL
BLUSH
B-DMP
B-DMP
HUH?!
YOU'RE KIDDING. ARE THEY—?!
FIDGET
FIDGET
I'VE NEVER SEEN THAT IN REAL LIFE BEFORE!!
HUFF
HUFF...
?!
YOU SCARED ME!!

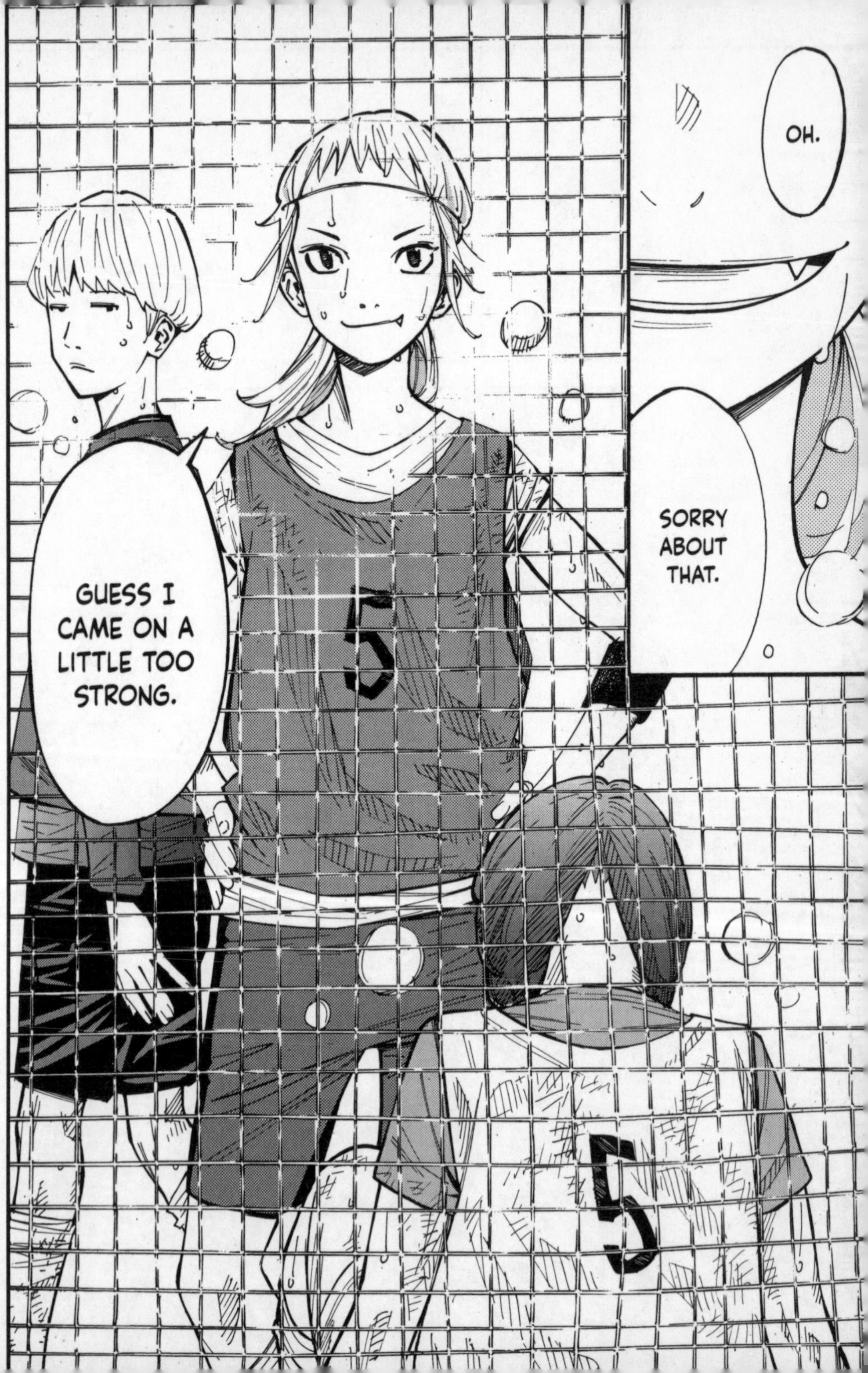

OH.
SORRY ABOUT THAT.
GUESS I CAME ON A LITTLE TOO STRONG.

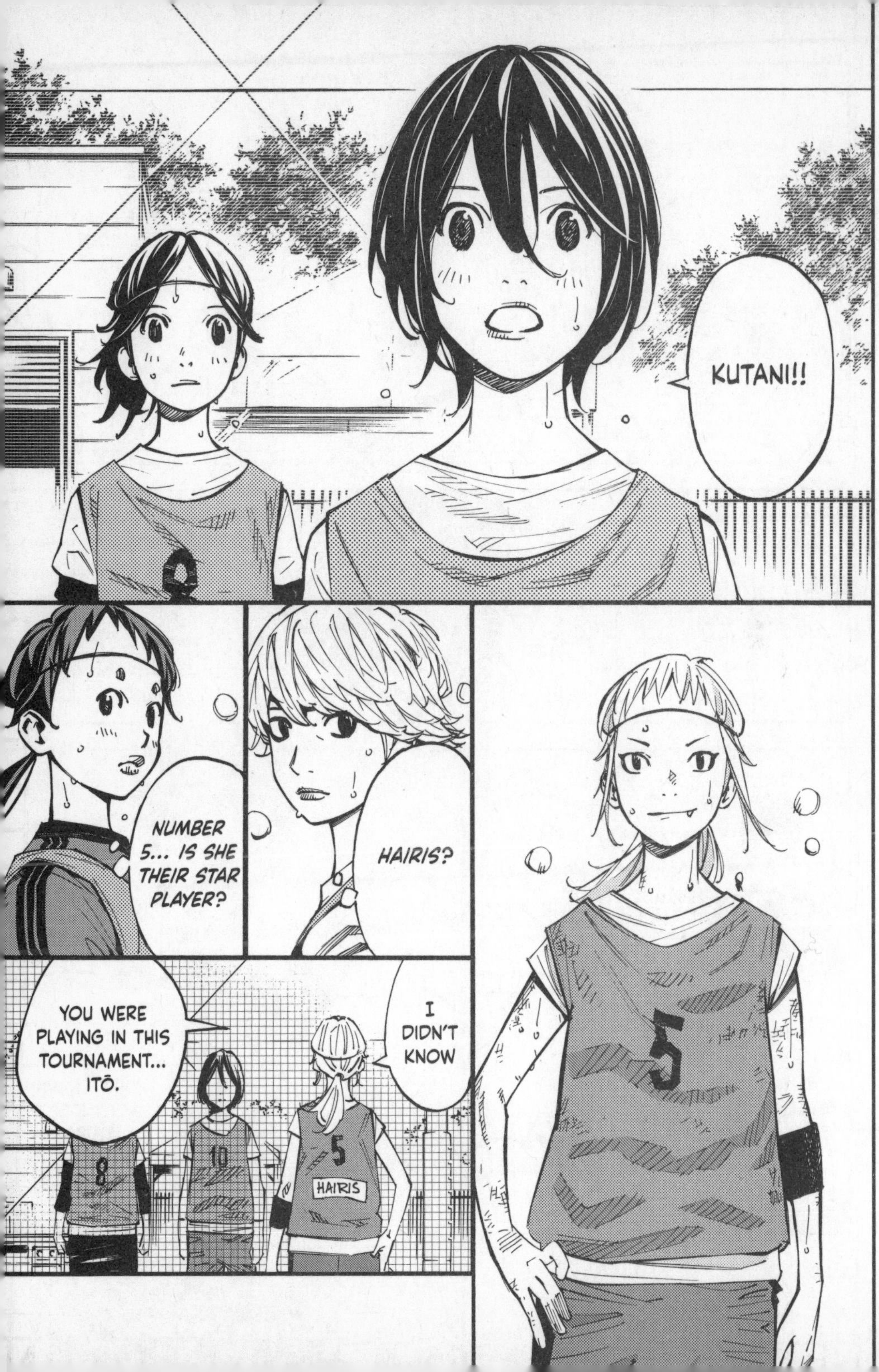
KUTANI!!
HAIRIS?
NUMBER 5... IS SHE THEIR STAR PLAYER?
I DIDN'T KNOW
YOU WERE PLAYING IN THIS TOURNAMENT... ITŌ.
HAIRIS

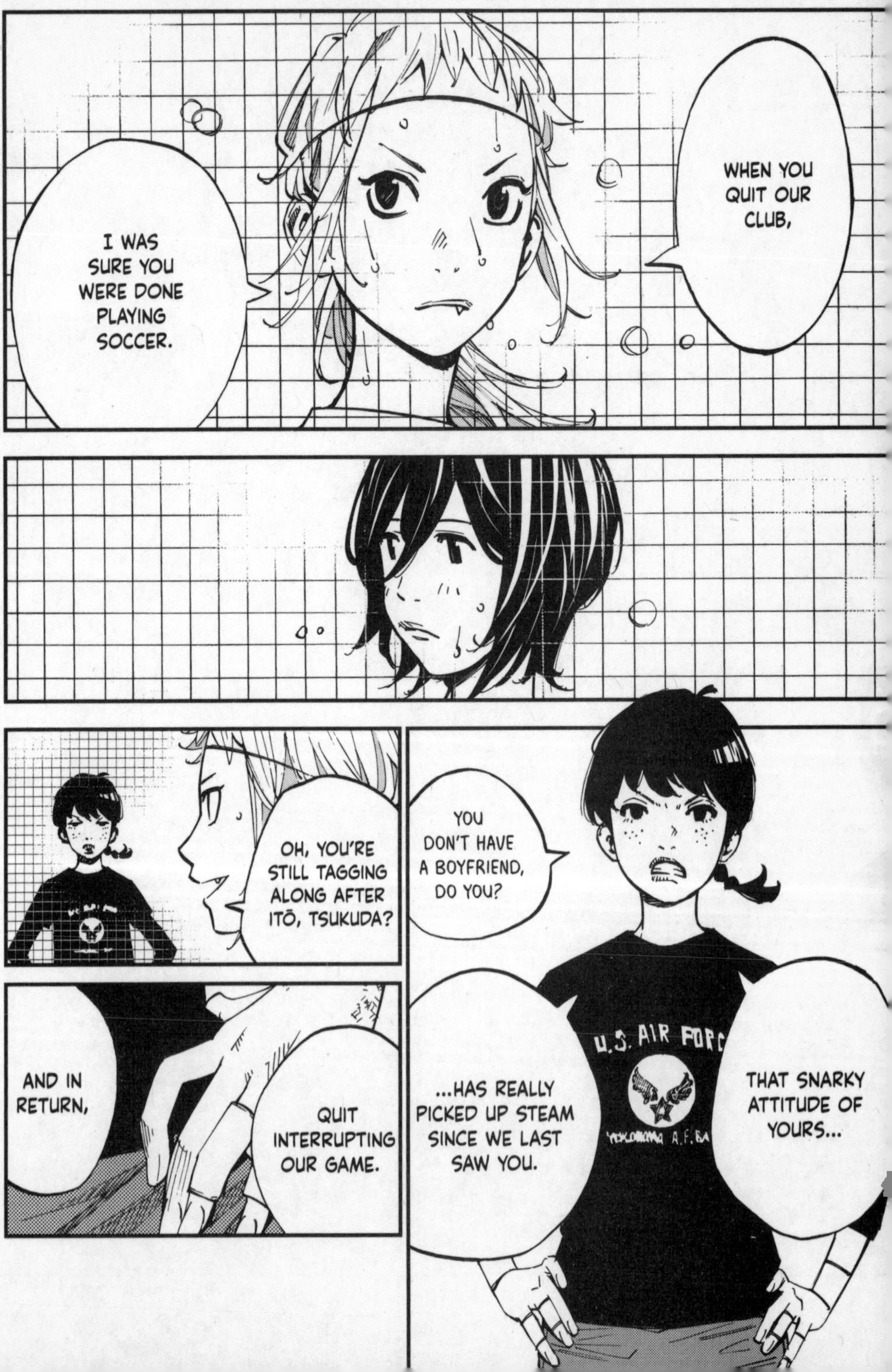
WHEN YOU QUIT OUR CLUB,
I WAS SURE YOU WERE DONE PLAYING SOCCER.
YOU DON'T HAVE A BOYFRIEND, DO YOU?
THAT SNARKY ATTITUDE OF YOURS...
...HAS REALLY PICKED UP STEAM SINCE WE LAST SAW YOU.
U.S. AIR FORC
YOKOHAMA A.F. BA
OH, YOU'RE STILL TAGGING ALONG AFTER ITŌ, TSUKUDA?
QUIT INTERRUPTING OUR GAME.
AND IN RETURN,

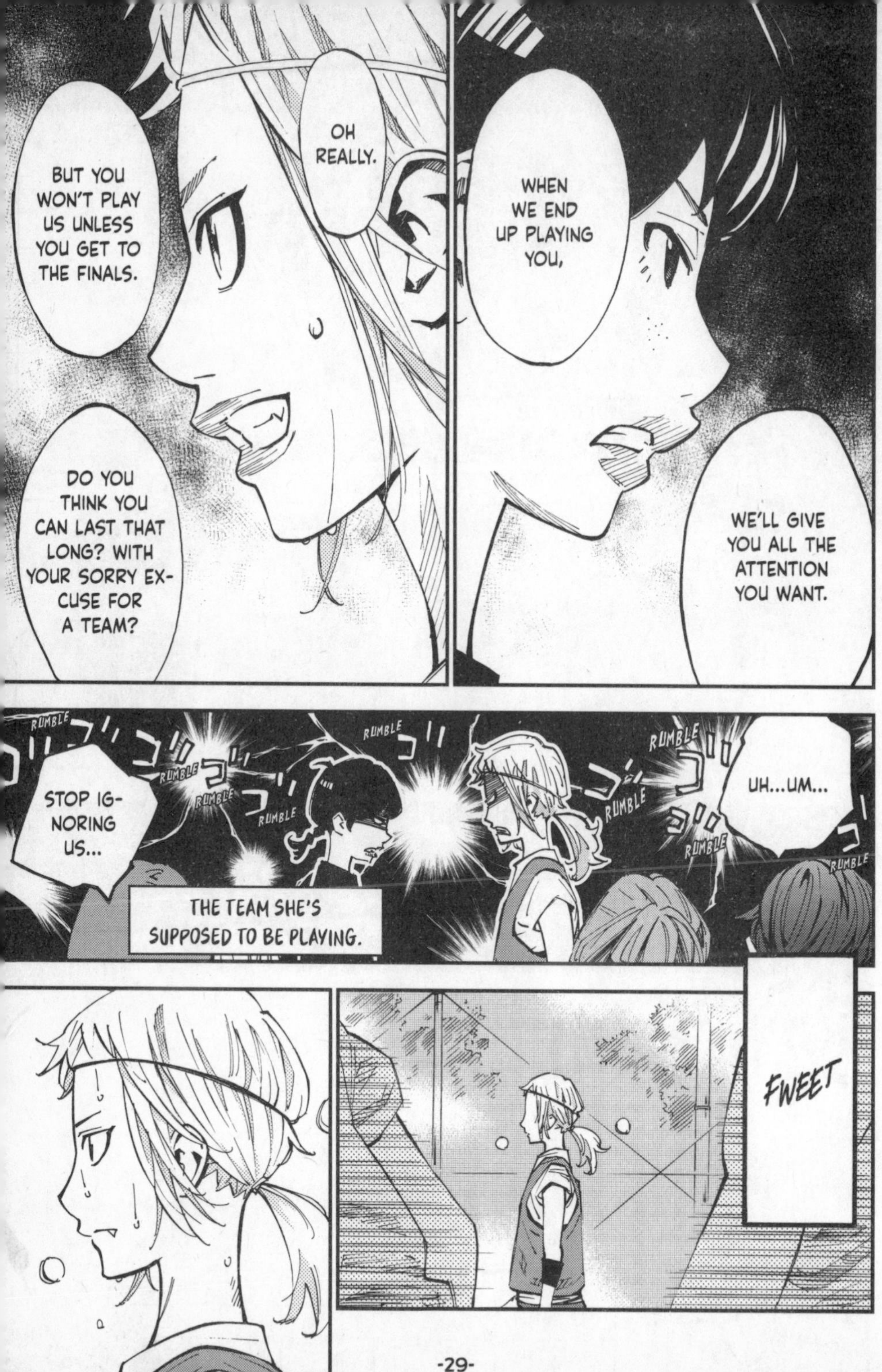
WHEN WE END UP PLAYING YOU,
WE'LL GIVE YOU ALL THE ATTENTION YOU WANT.
OH REALLY.
BUT YOU WON'T PLAY US UNLESS YOU GET TO THE FINALS.
DO YOU THINK YOU CAN LAST THAT LONG? WITH YOUR SORRY EX-CUSE FOR A TEAM?
UH...UM...
RUMBLE
RUMBLE
RUMBLE
RUMBLE
RUMBLE
RUMBLE
RUMBLE
RUMBLE
RUMBLE
STOP IG-NORING US...
THE TEAM SHE'S SUPPOSED TO BE PLAYING.
FWEET

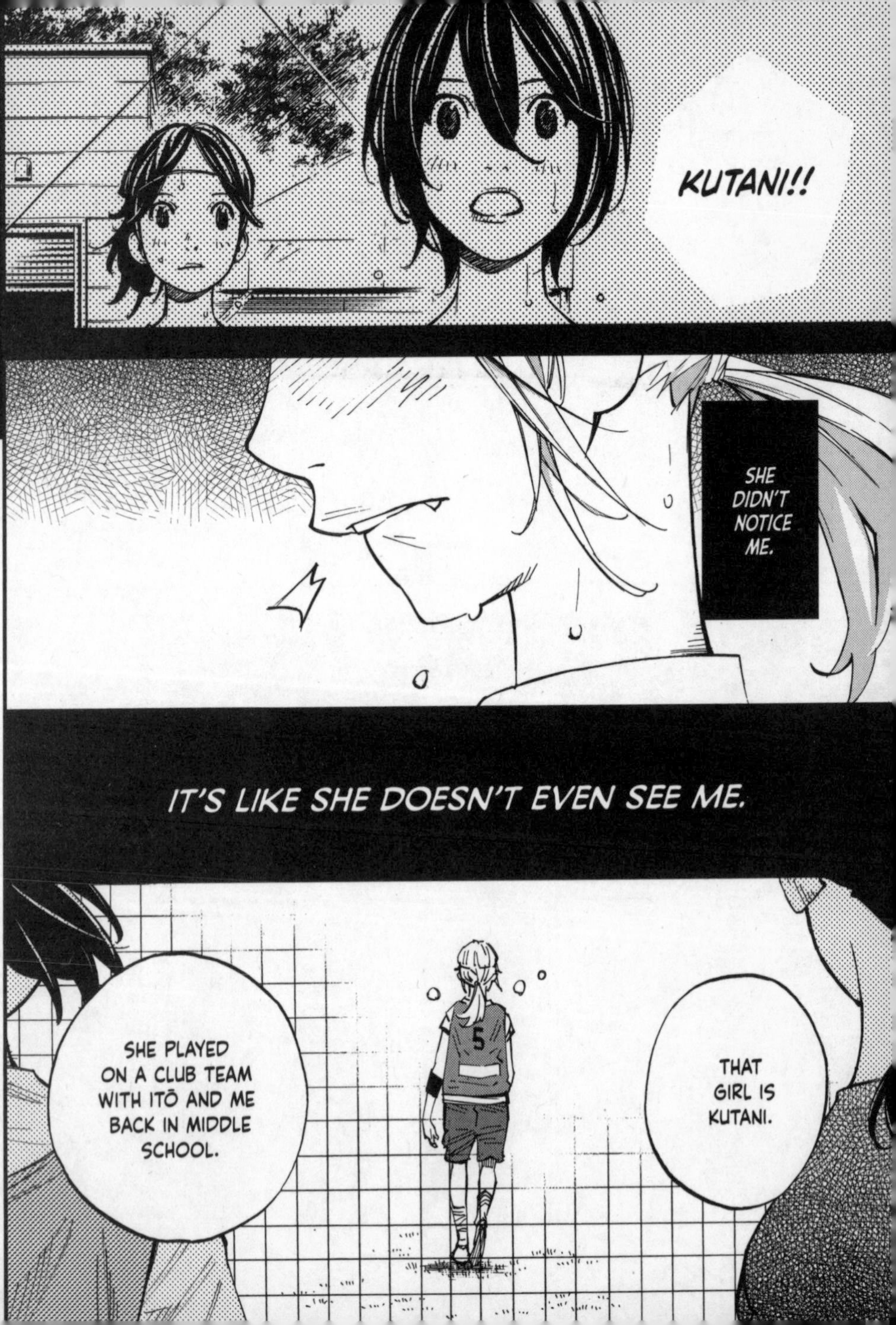
KUTANI!!
SHE DIDN'T NOTICE ME.
IT'S LIKE SHE DOESN'T EVEN SEE ME.
THAT GIRL IS KUTANI.
SHE PLAYED ON A CLUB TEAM WITH ITŌ AND ME BACK IN MIDDLE SCHOOL.

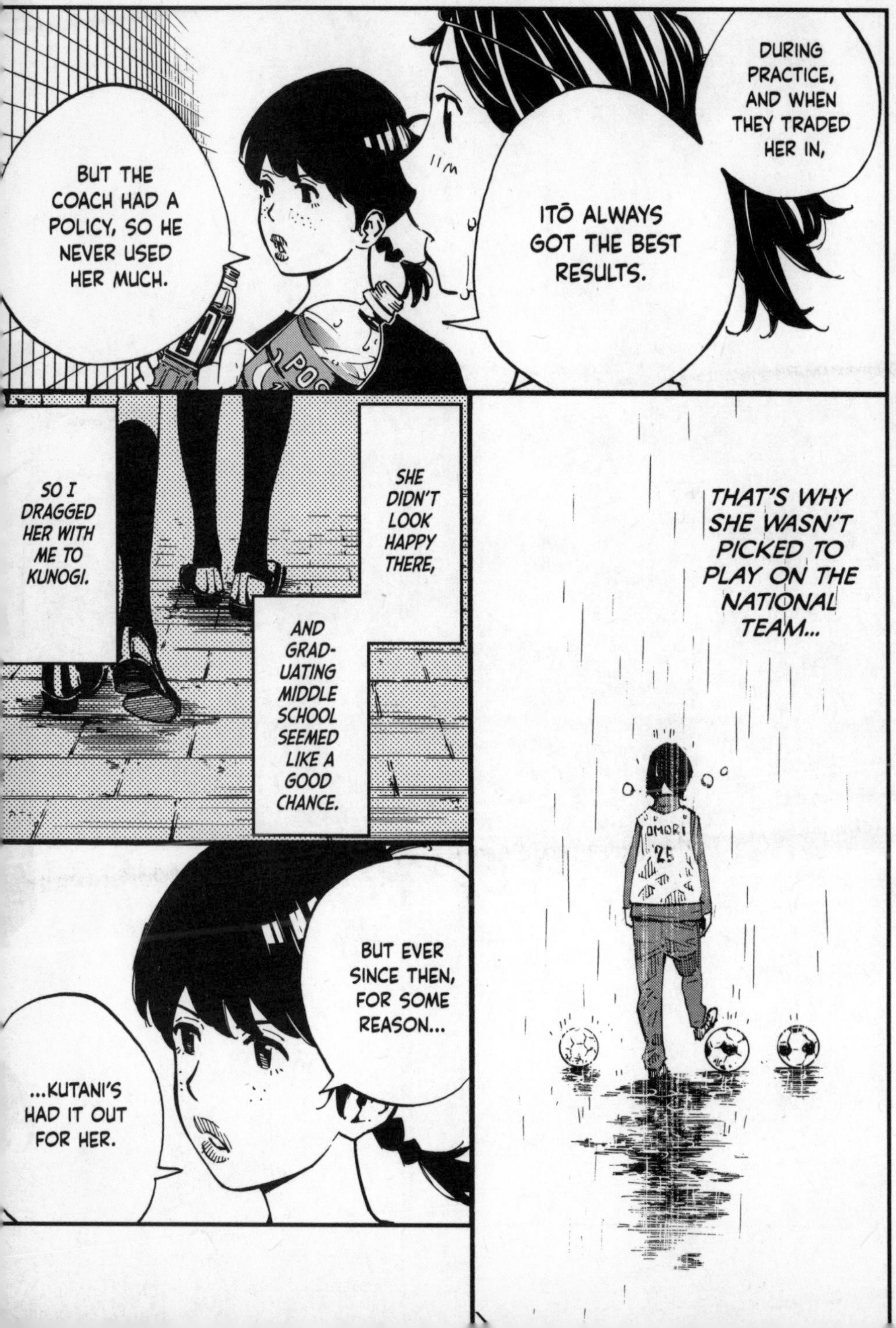
DURING PRACTICE, AND WHEN THEY TRADED HER IN,
ITŌ ALWAYS GOT THE BEST RESULTS.
BUT THE COACH HAD A POLICY, SO HE NEVER USED HER MUCH.
THAT'S WHY SHE WASN'T PICKED TO PLAY ON THE NATIONAL TEAM...
OMORI 25
SHE DIDN'T LOOK HAPPY THERE,
AND GRAD-UATING MIDDLE SCHOOL SEEMED LIKE A GOOD CHANCE.
SO I DRAGGED HER WITH ME TO KUNOGI.
BUT EVER SINCE THEN, FOR SOME REASON...
...KUTANI'S HAD IT OUT FOR HER.

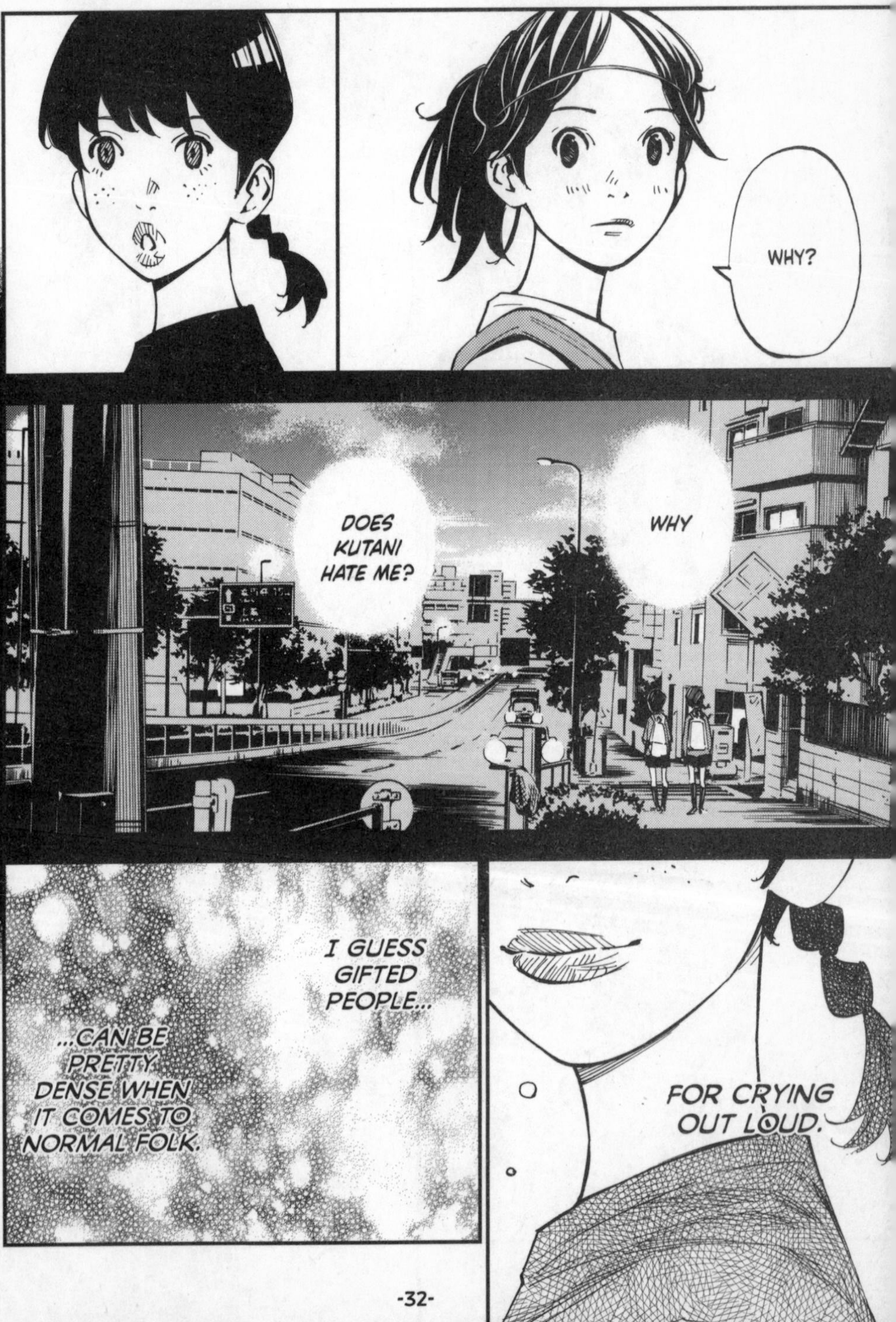
WHY?
WHY
DOES KUTANI HATE ME?
FOR CRYING OUT LOUD.
I GUESS GIFTED PEOPLE...
...CAN BE PRETTY DENSE WHEN IT COMES TO NORMAL FOLK.

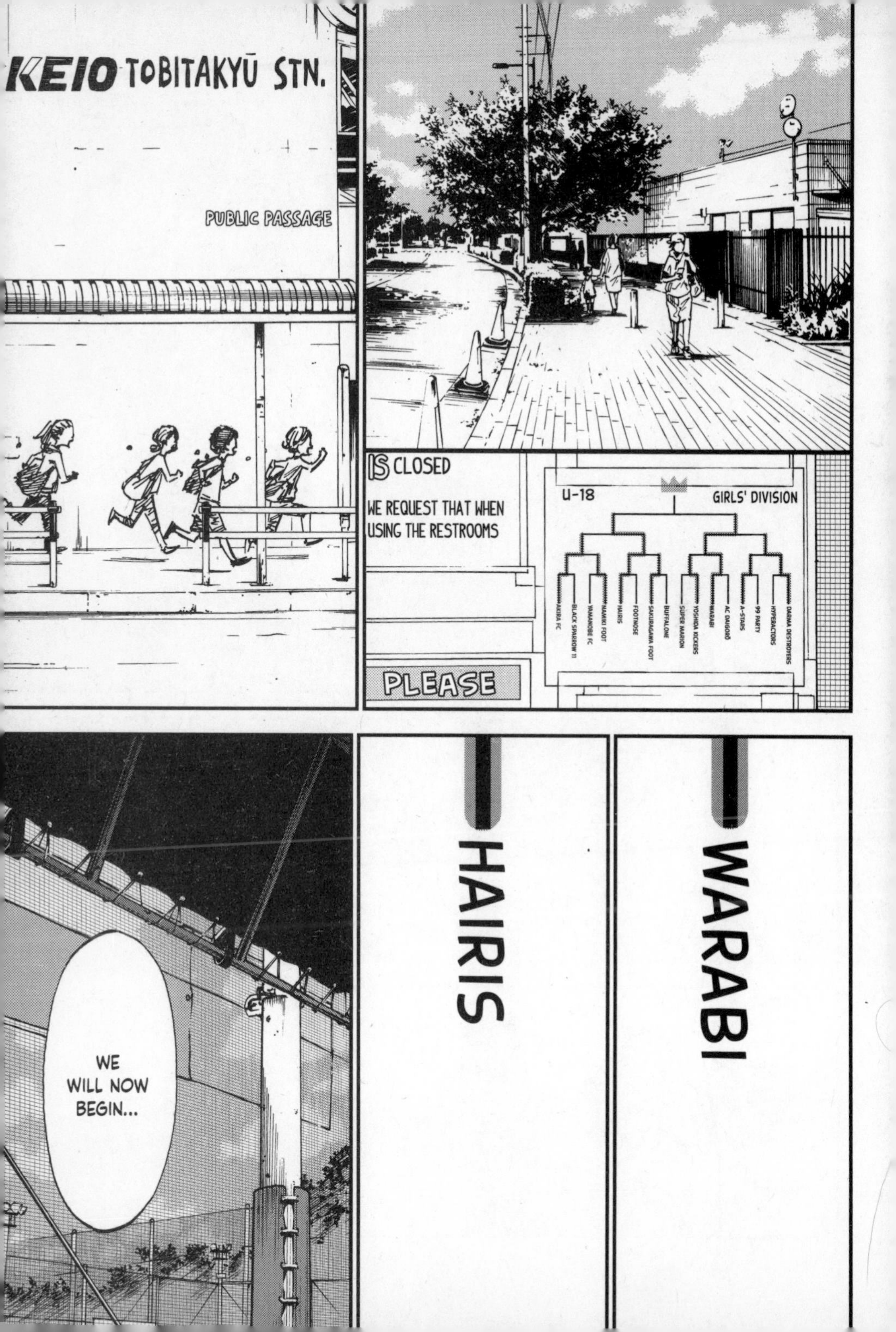

U-18
GIRLS' DIVISION
AKIRA FC
BLACK SPARROW 11
YAMANOBE FC
NAMIKI FOOT
HAIRIS
FOOTNOSE
SAKURAGAWA FOOT
BUFFALONE
SUPER MARION
YOSHIDA KICKERS
WARABI
AC DANGORŌ
A-STARS
99 PARTY
HYPERACTORS
DARUMA DESTROYERS
IS CLOSED
WE REQUEST THAT WHEN USING THE RESTROOMS
PLEASE
KEIO TOBITAKYŪ STN.
PUBLIC PASSAGE
WARABI
HAIRIS
WE WILL NOW BEGIN...

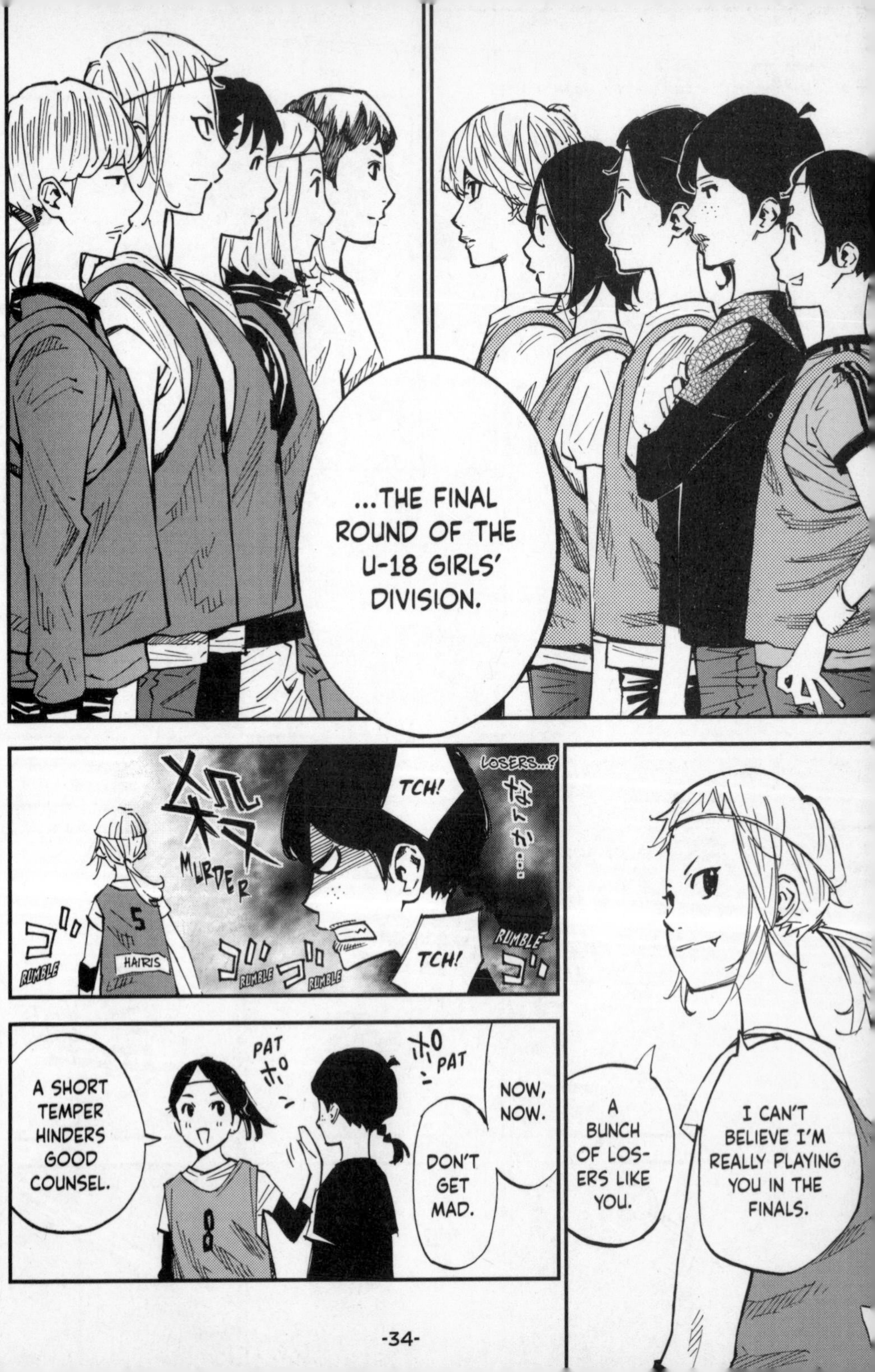
...THE FINAL ROUND OF THE U-18 GIRLS' DIVISION.
I CAN'T BELIEVE I'M REALLY PLAYING YOU IN THE FINALS.
A BUNCH OF LOS-ERS LIKE YOU.
LOSERS...?
なんか…
TCH!
MURDER
TCH!
RUMBLE
RUMBLE
RUMBLE
RUMBLE
PAT
PAT
NOW, NOW.
DON'T GET MAD.
A SHORT TEMPER HINDERS GOOD COUNSEL.

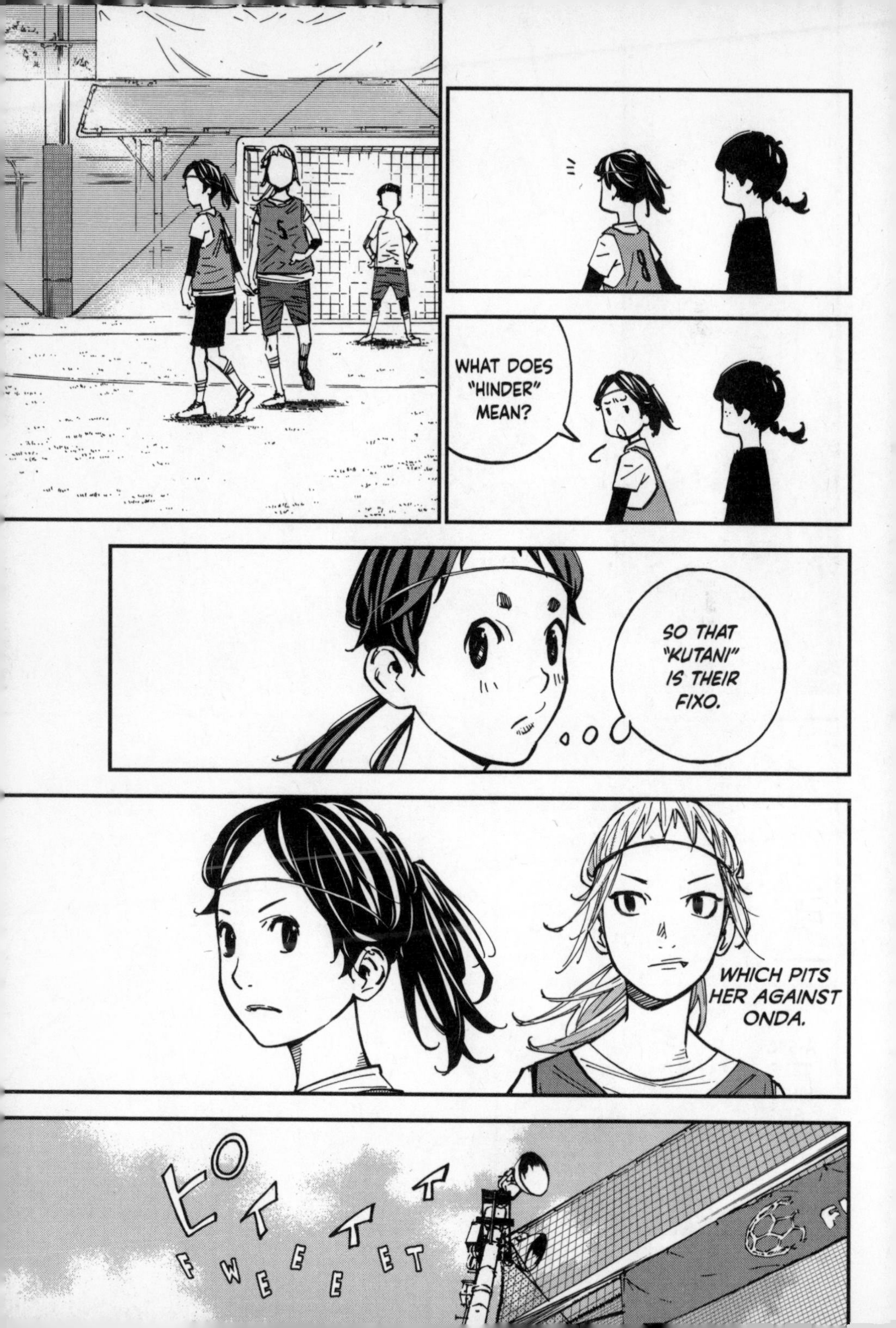
WHAT DOES "HINDER" MEAN?
SO THAT "KUTANI" IS THEIR FIXO.
WHICH PITS HER AGAINST ONDA.
ピイイイ
FWEEEET

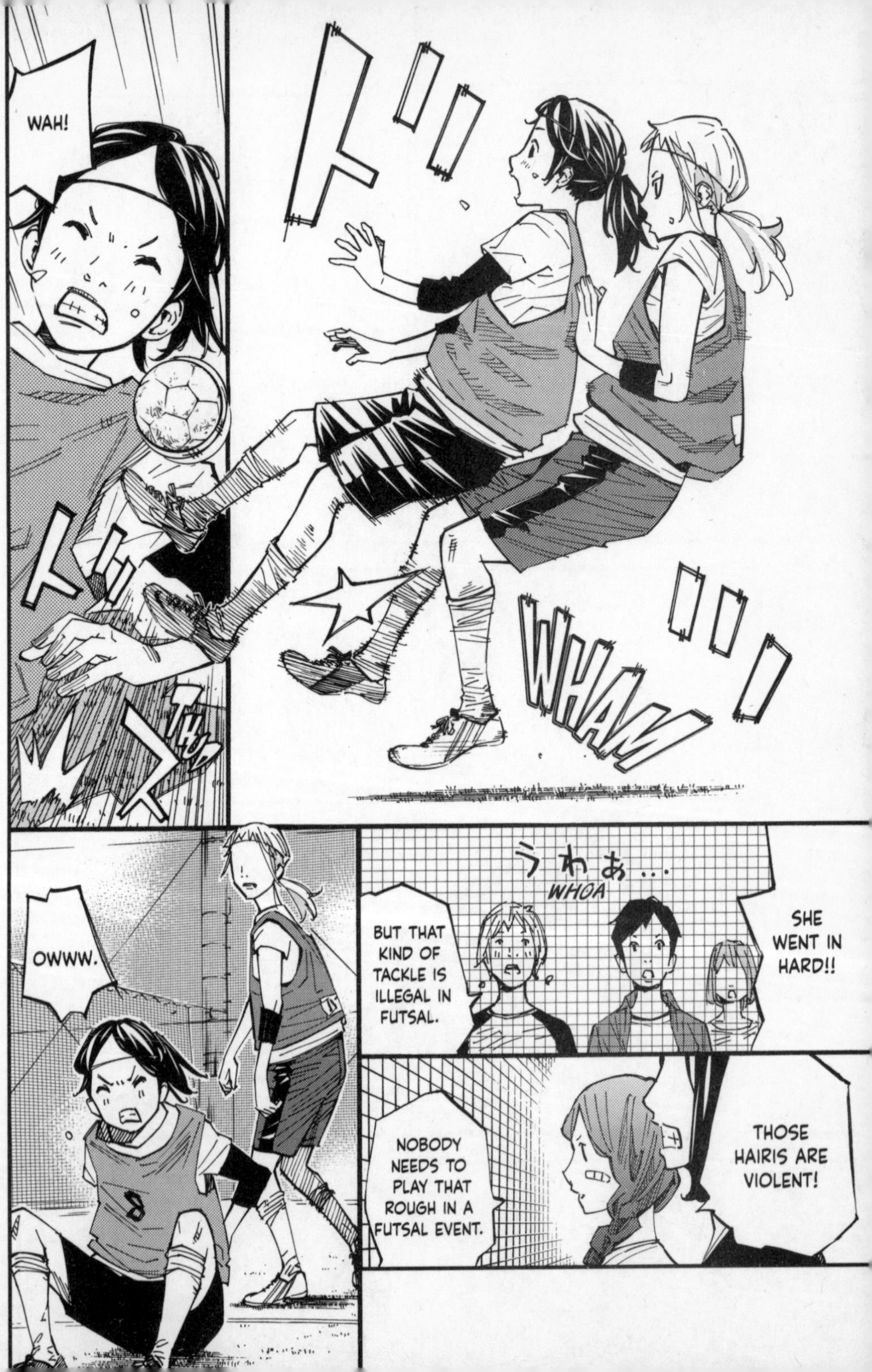
WHAM
WAH!
THUD
うわぁ…
WHOA
SHE WENT IN HARD!!
BUT THAT KIND OF TACKLE IS ILLEGAL IN FUTSAL.
THOSE HAIRIS ARE VIOLENT!
NOBODY NEEDS TO PLAY THAT ROUGH IN A FUTSAL EVENT.
OWWW.

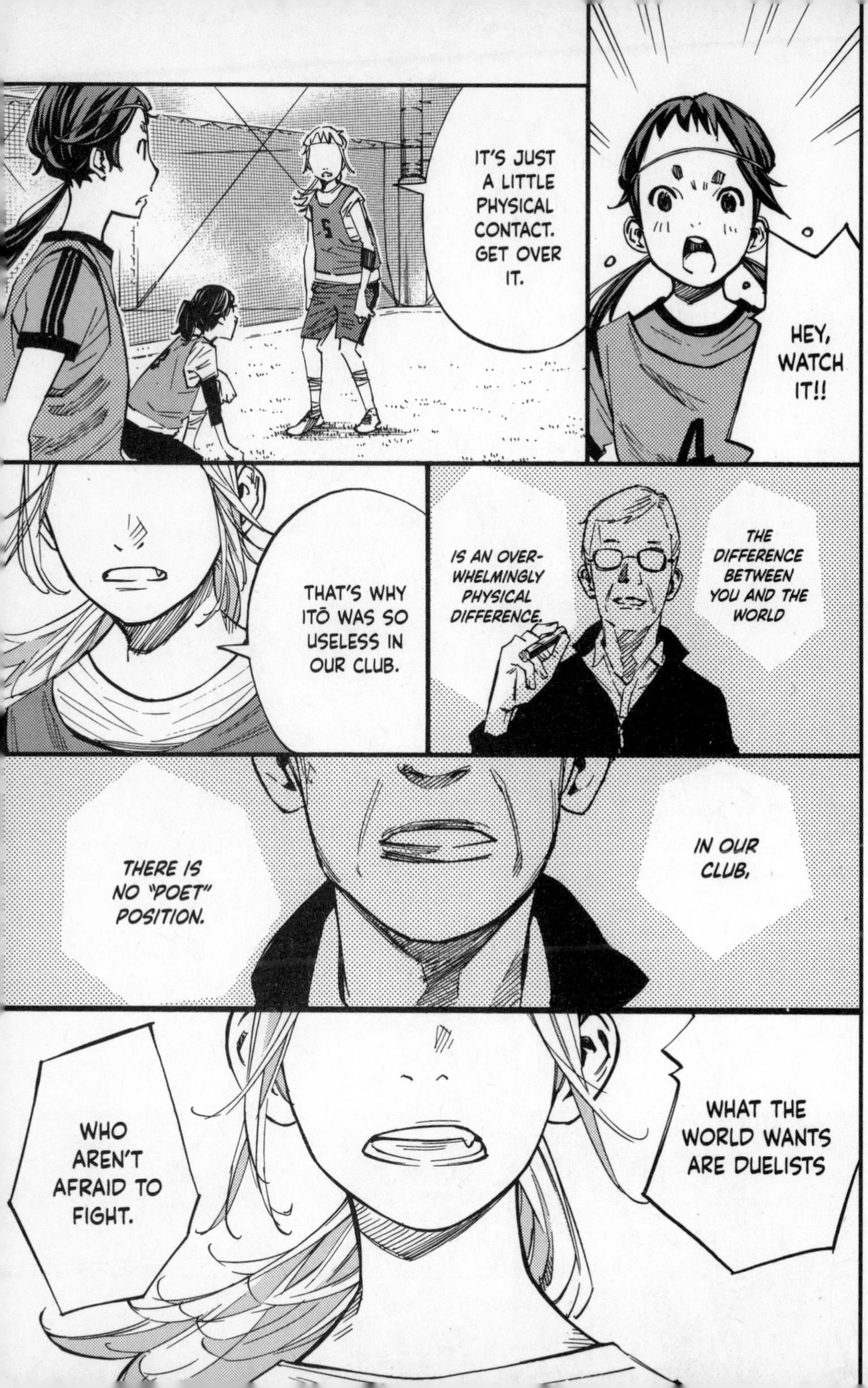
HEY, WATCH IT!!
IT'S JUST A LITTLE PHYSICAL CONTACT. GET OVER IT.
THE DIFFERENCE BETWEEN YOU AND THE WORLD
IS AN OVER-WHELMINGLY PHYSICAL DIFFERENCE.
THAT'S WHY ITŌ WAS SO USELESS IN OUR CLUB.
IN OUR CLUB,
THERE IS NO "POET" POSITION.
WHAT THE WORLD WANTS ARE DUELISTS
WHO AREN'T AFRAID TO FIGHT.

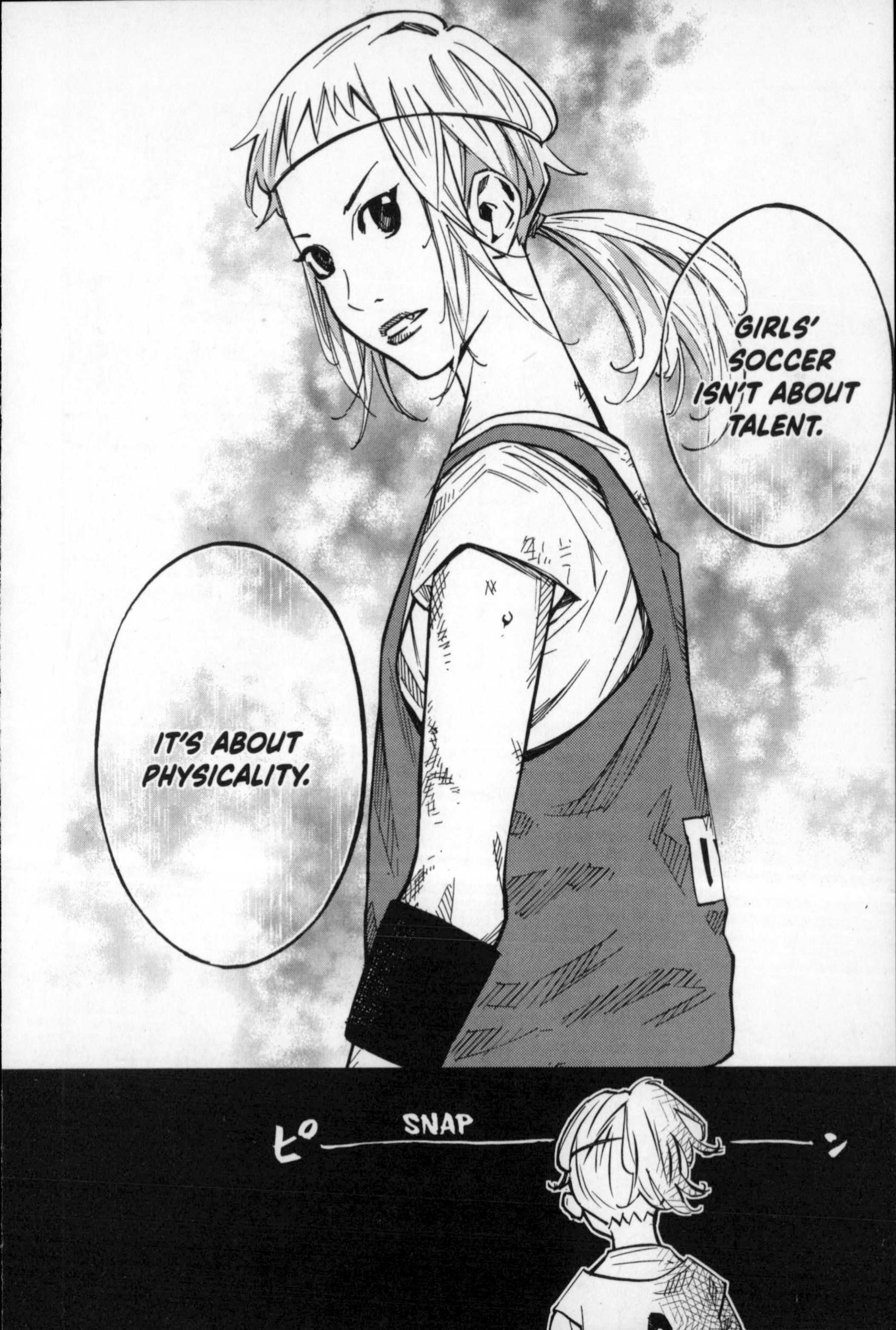
GIRLS' SOCCER ISN'T ABOUT TALENT.
IT'S ABOUT PHYSICALITY.
ピ——ン
SNAP

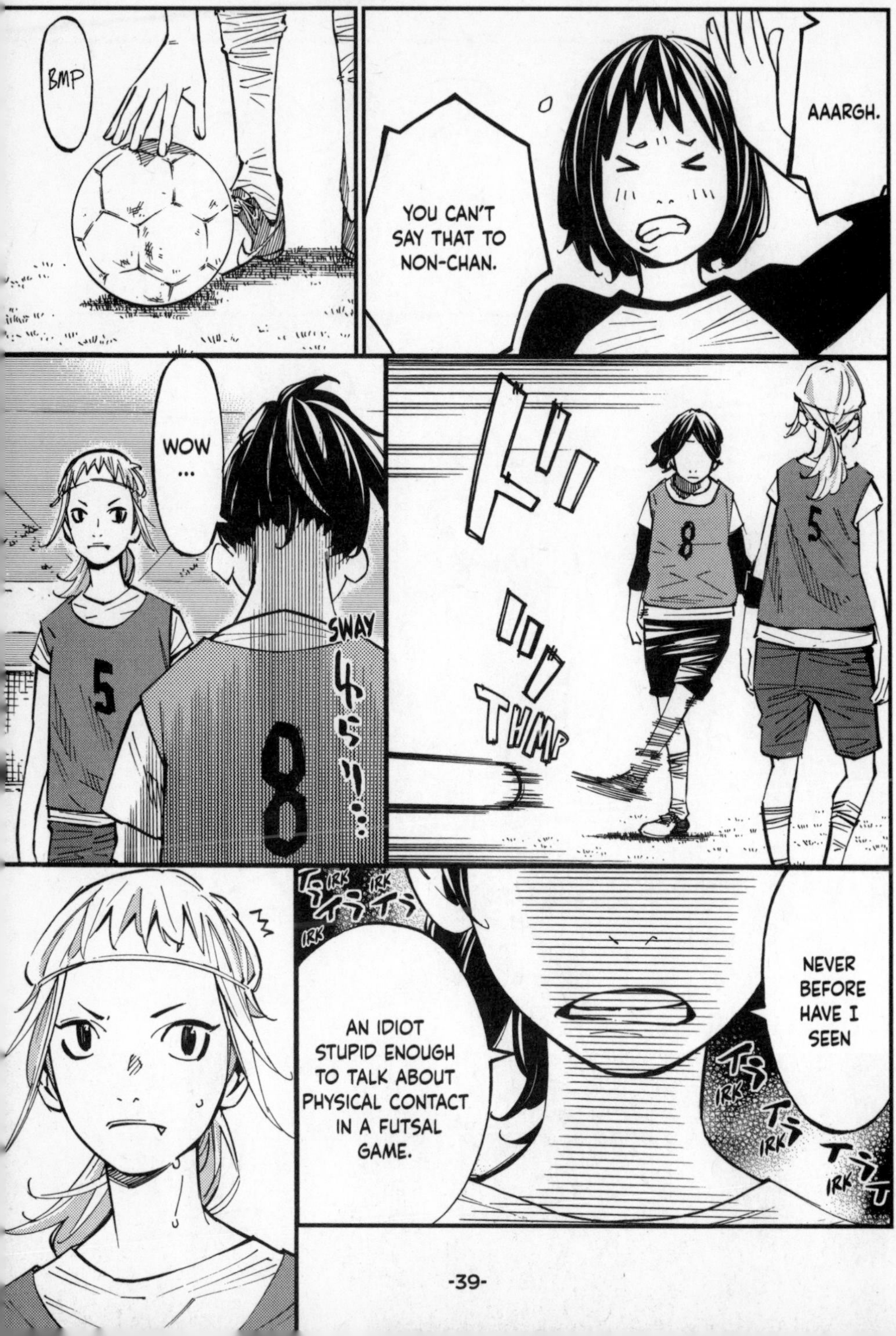
AAARGH.
YOU CAN'T SAY THAT TO NON-CHAN.
BMP
THMP
WOW ...
SWAY
IRK IRK IRK
NEVER BEFORE HAVE I SEEN
AN IDIOT STUPID ENOUGH TO TALK ABOUT PHYSICAL CONTACT IN A FUTSAL GAME.
IRK IRK IRK

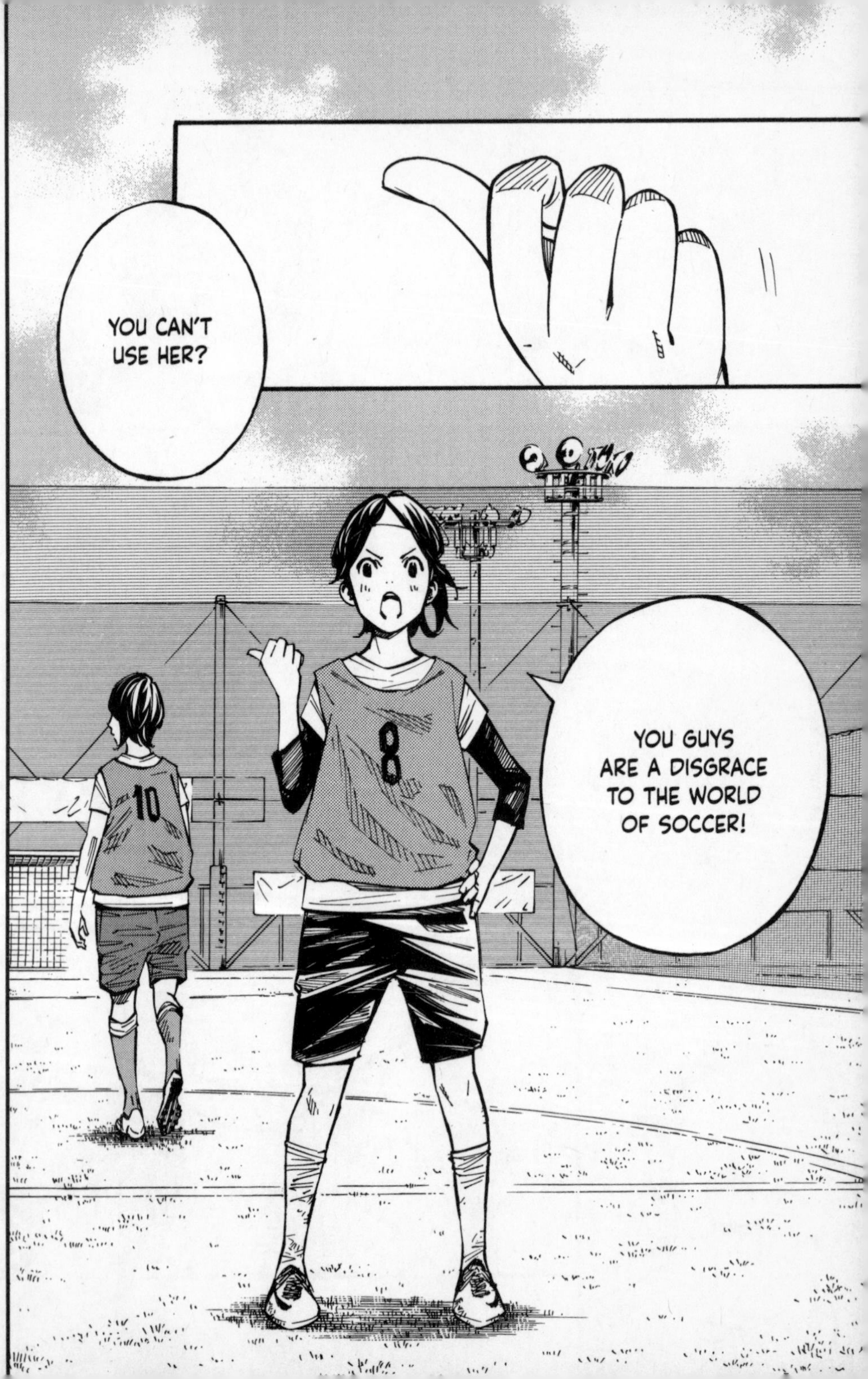
YOU CAN'T USE HER?
YOU GUYS ARE A DISGRACE TO THE WORLD OF SOCCER!

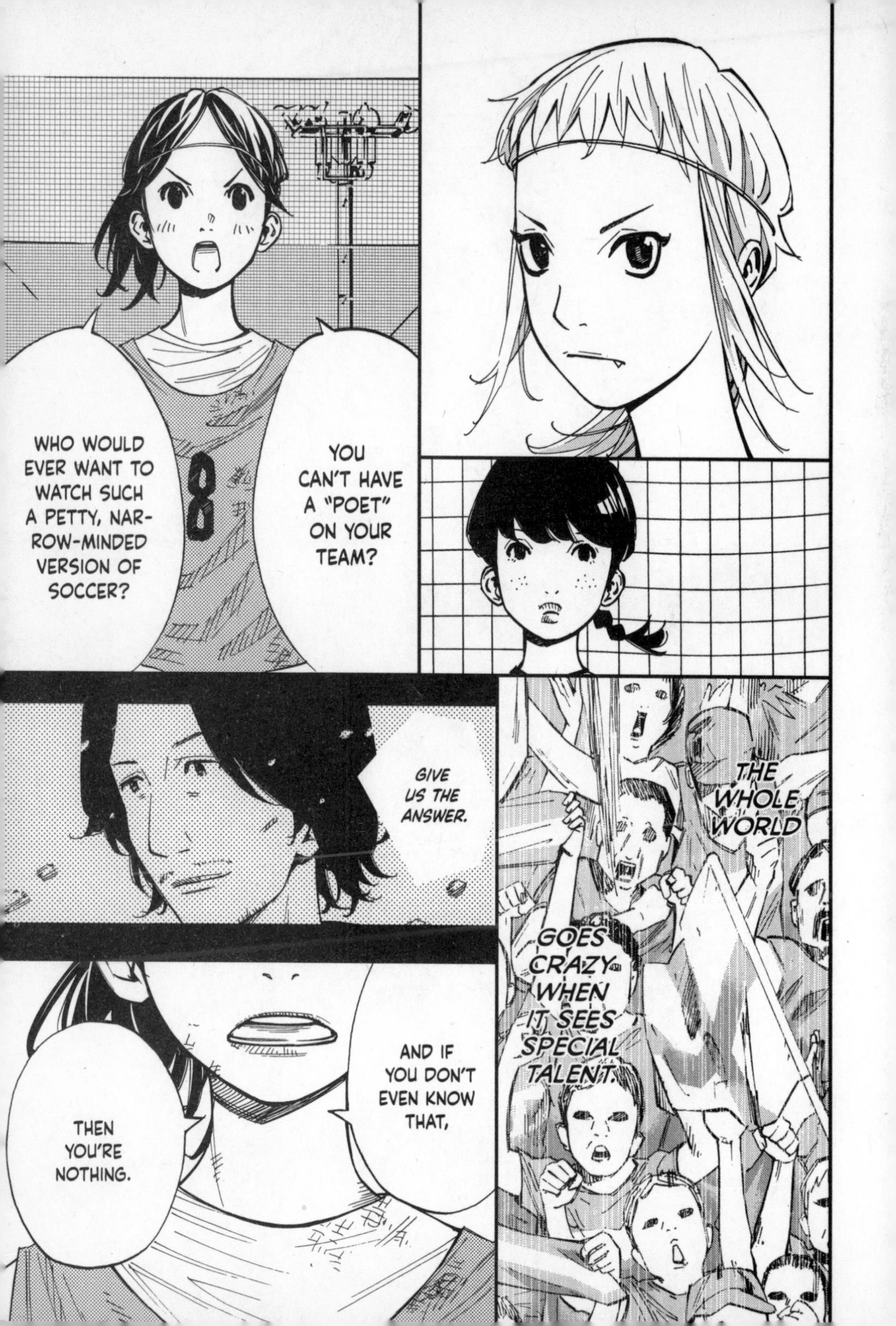

YOU CAN'T HAVE A "POET" ON YOUR TEAM?
WHO WOULD EVER WANT TO WATCH SUCH A PETTY, NAR-ROW-MINDED VERSION OF SOCCER?
THE WHOLE WORLD
GOES CRAZY WHEN IT SEES SPECIAL TALENT.
GIVE US THE ANSWER.
AND IF YOU DON'T EVEN KNOW THAT,
THEN YOU'RE NOTHING.

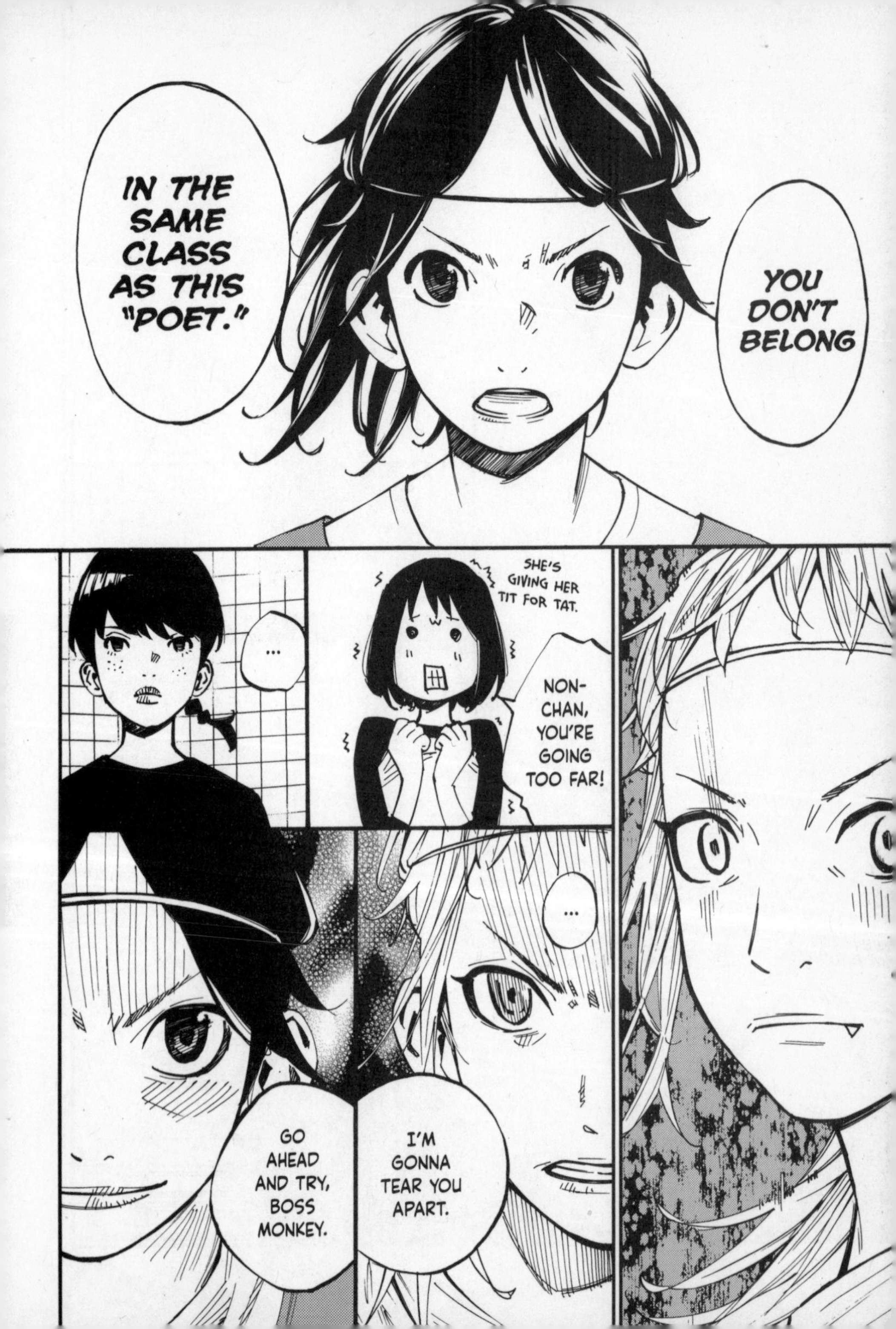
YOU DON'T BELONG
IN THE SAME CLASS AS THIS "POET."
SHE'S GIVING HER TIT FOR TAT.
NON-CHAN, YOU'RE GOING TOO FAR!
...
...
I'M GONNA TEAR YOU APART.
GO AHEAD AND TRY, BOSS MONKEY.

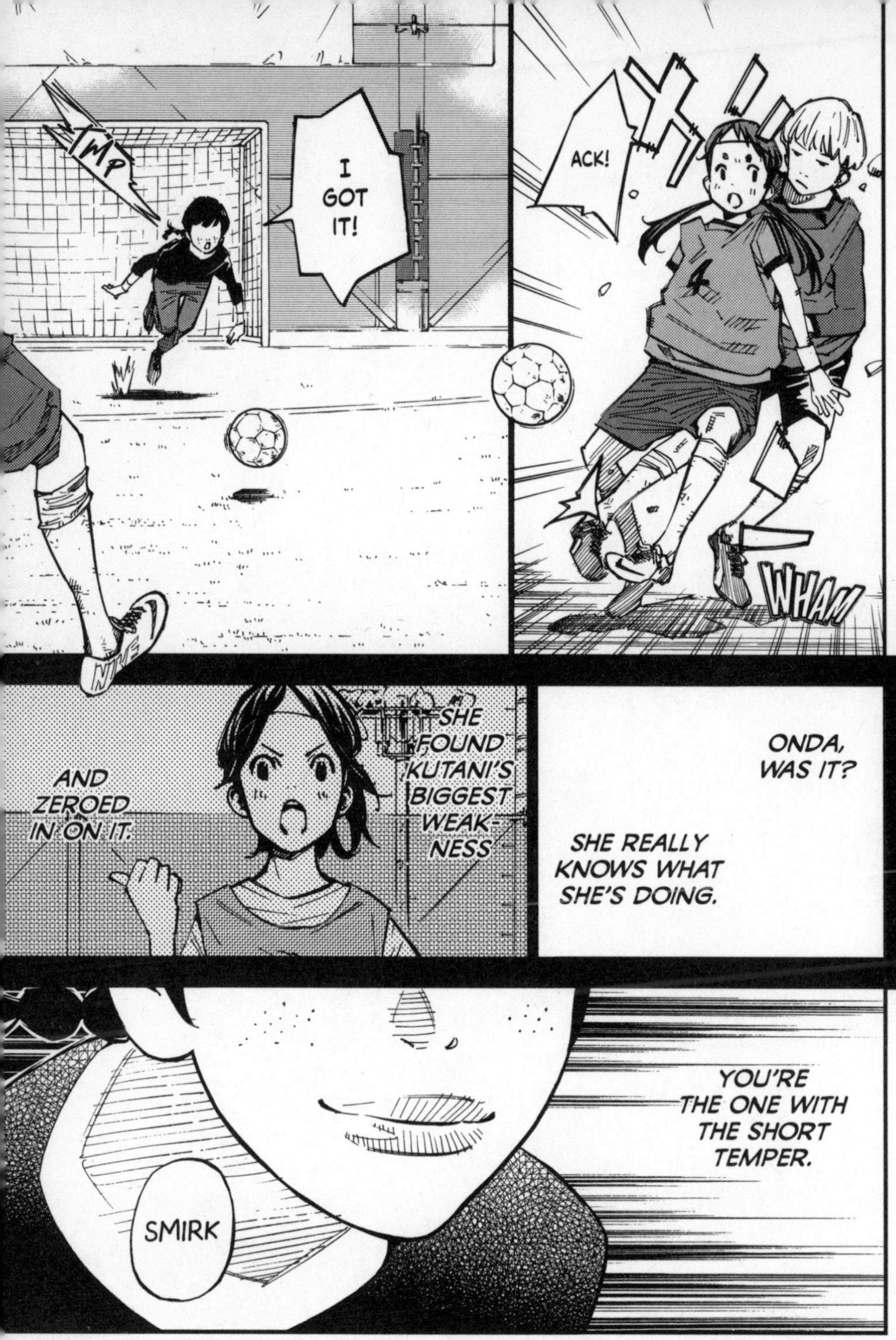
ACK!
WHAM
I GOT IT!
ONDA, WAS IT?
SHE REALLY KNOWS WHAT SHE'S DOING.
SHE FOUND KUTANI'S BIGGEST WEAK-NESS
AND ZEROED IN ON IT.
YOU'RE THE ONE WITH THE SHORT TEMPER.
SMIRK

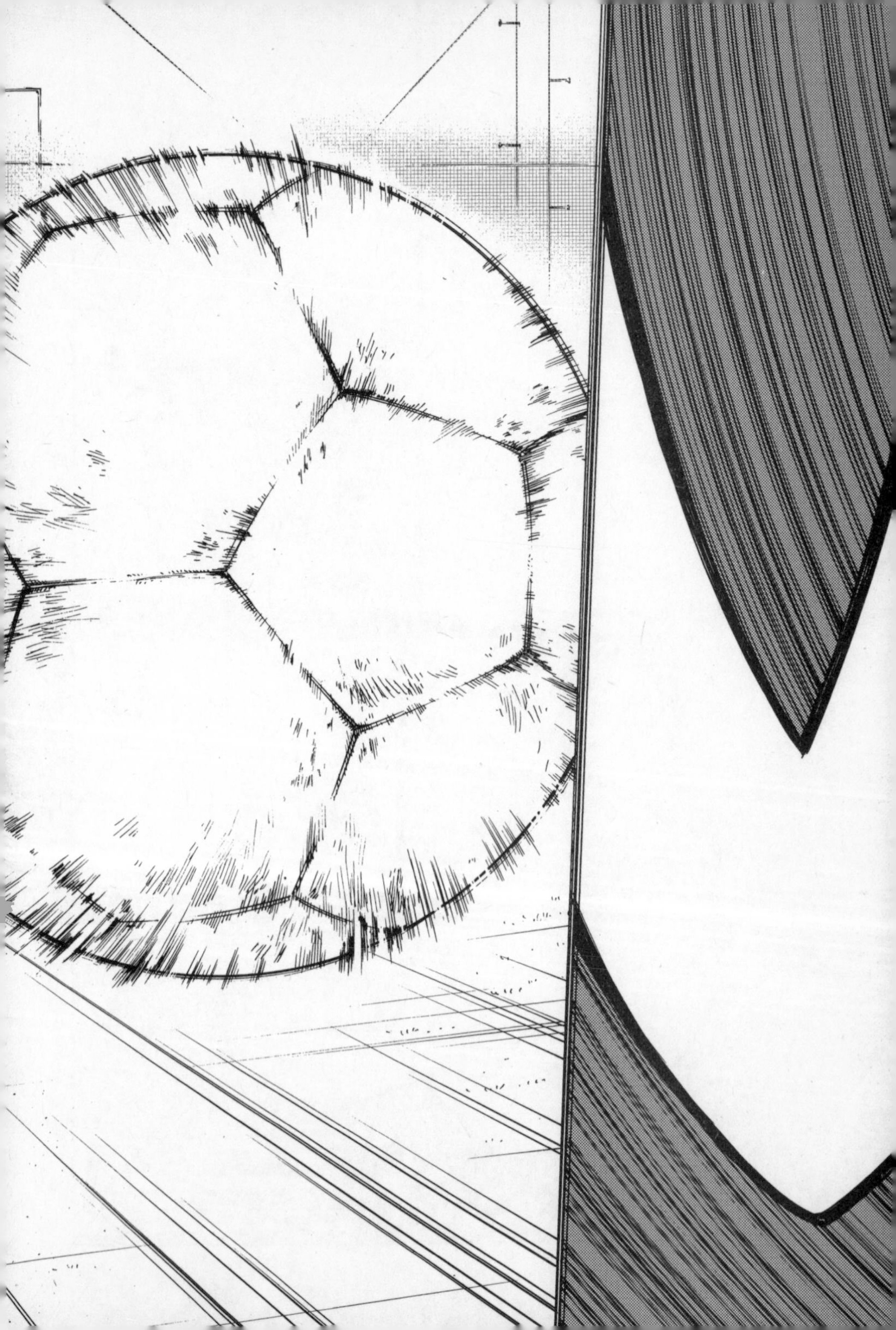

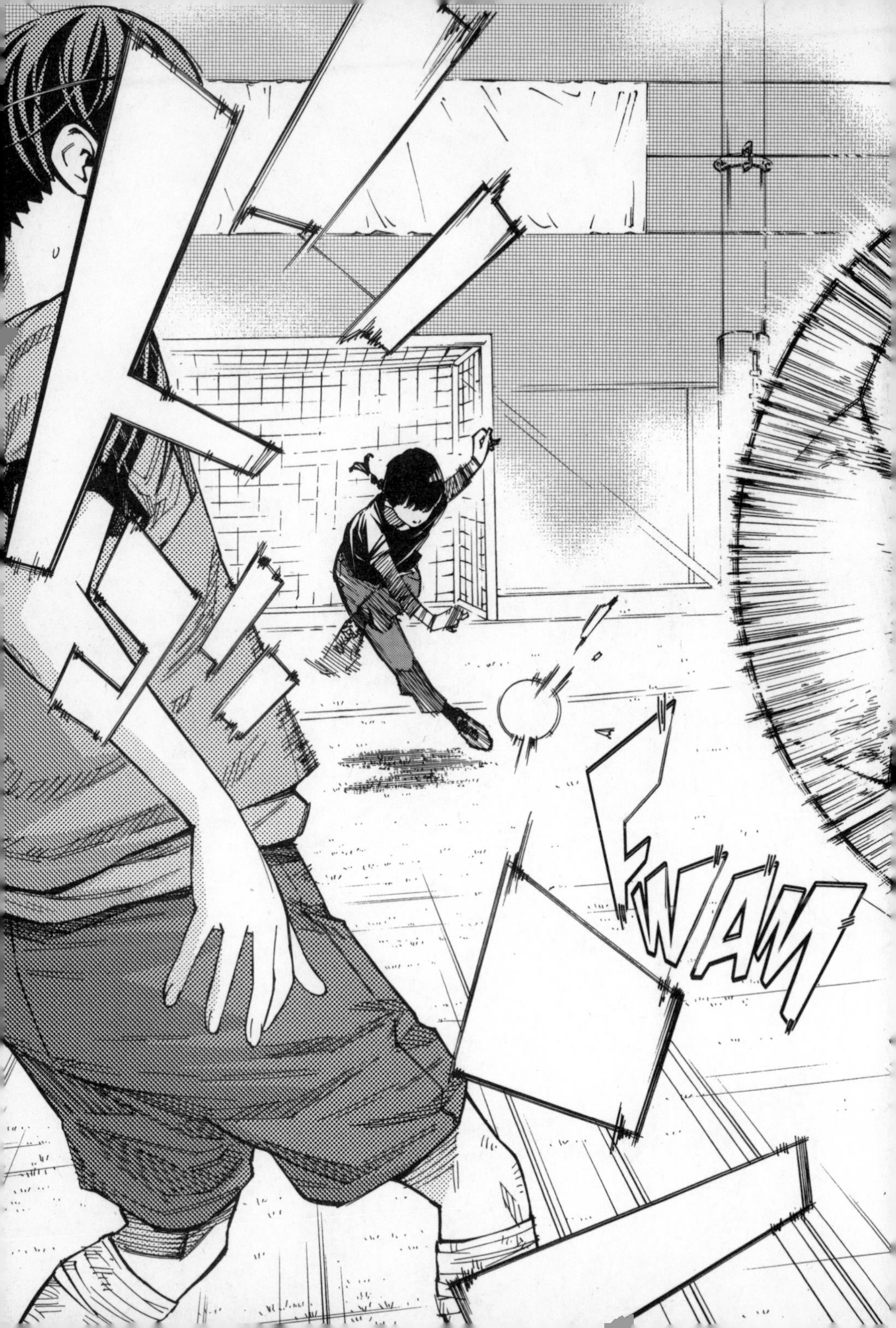
FWAM

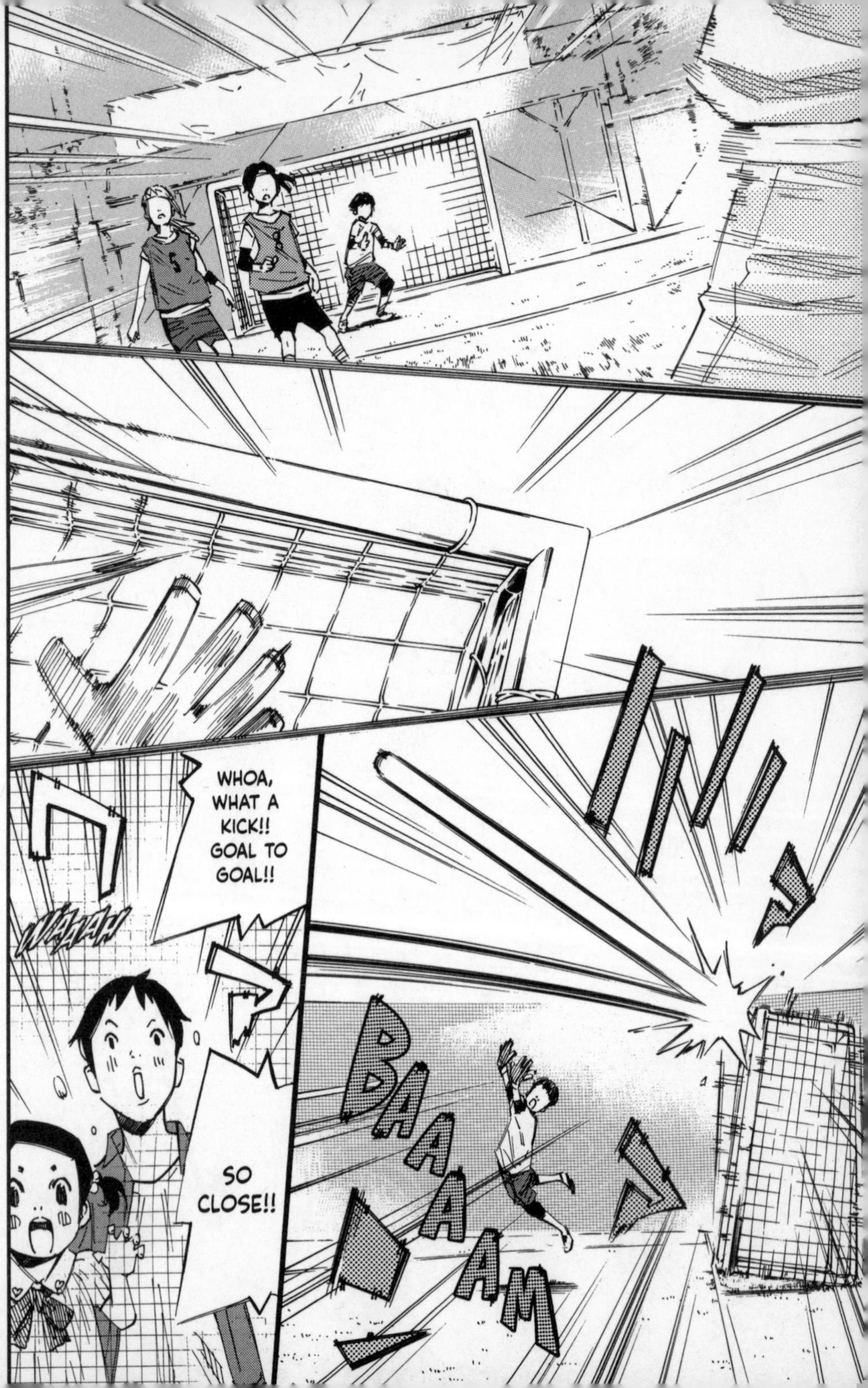
BAAAAM
WHOA, WHAT A KICK!! GOAL TO GOAL!!
SO CLOSE!!

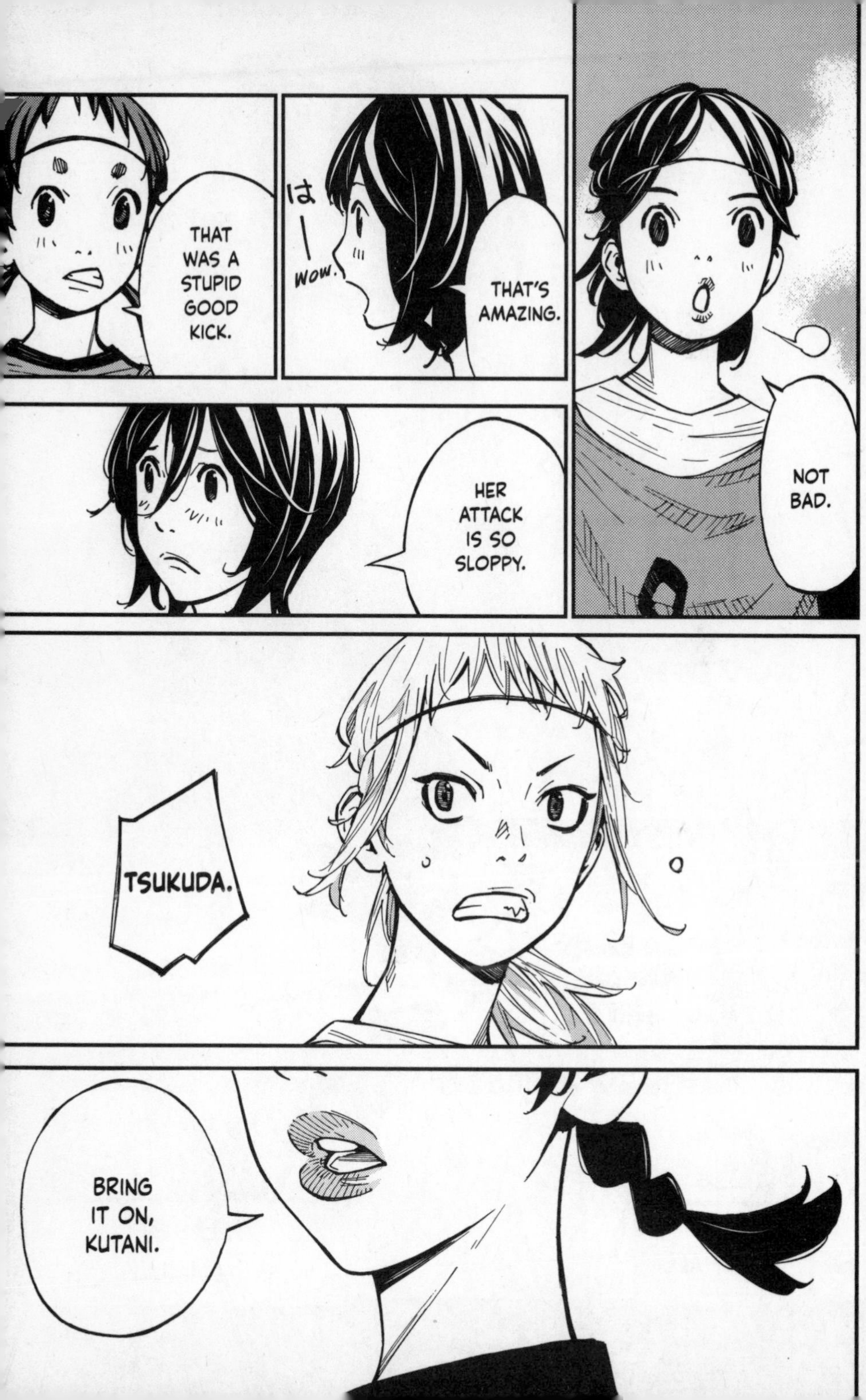
NOT BAD.
THAT'S AMAZING.
はー
WOW.
THAT WAS A STUPID GOOD KICK.
HER ATTACK IS SO SLOPPY.
TSUKUDA.
BRING IT ON, KUTANI.

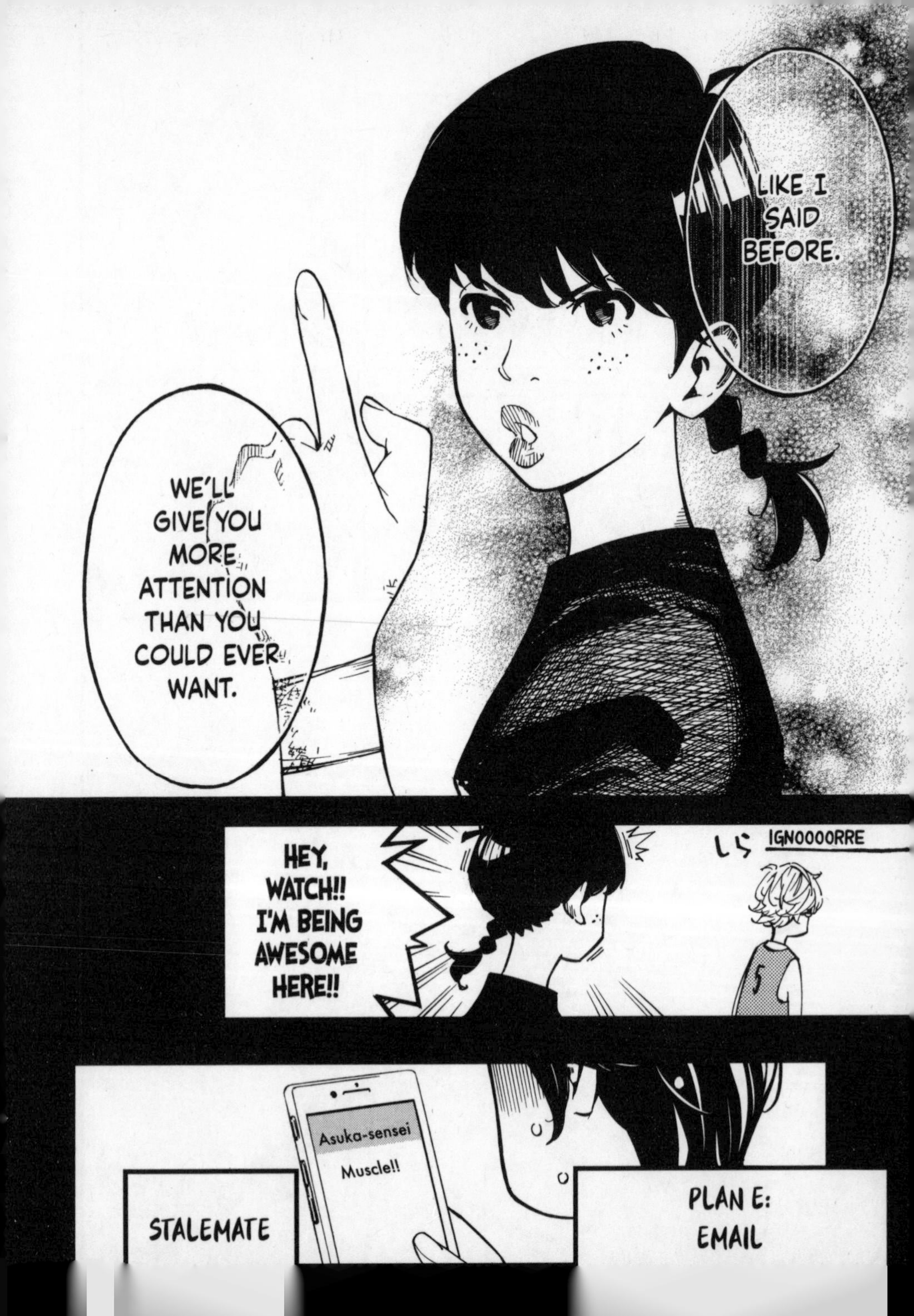
LIKE I SAID BEFORE.
WE'LL GIVE YOU MORE ATTENTION THAN YOU COULD EVER WANT.
しら IGNOOOORRE
HEY, WATCH!! I'M BEING AWESOME HERE!!
PLAN E: EMAIL
Asuka-sensei
Muscle!!
STALEMATE

Farewell, My Dear Cramer

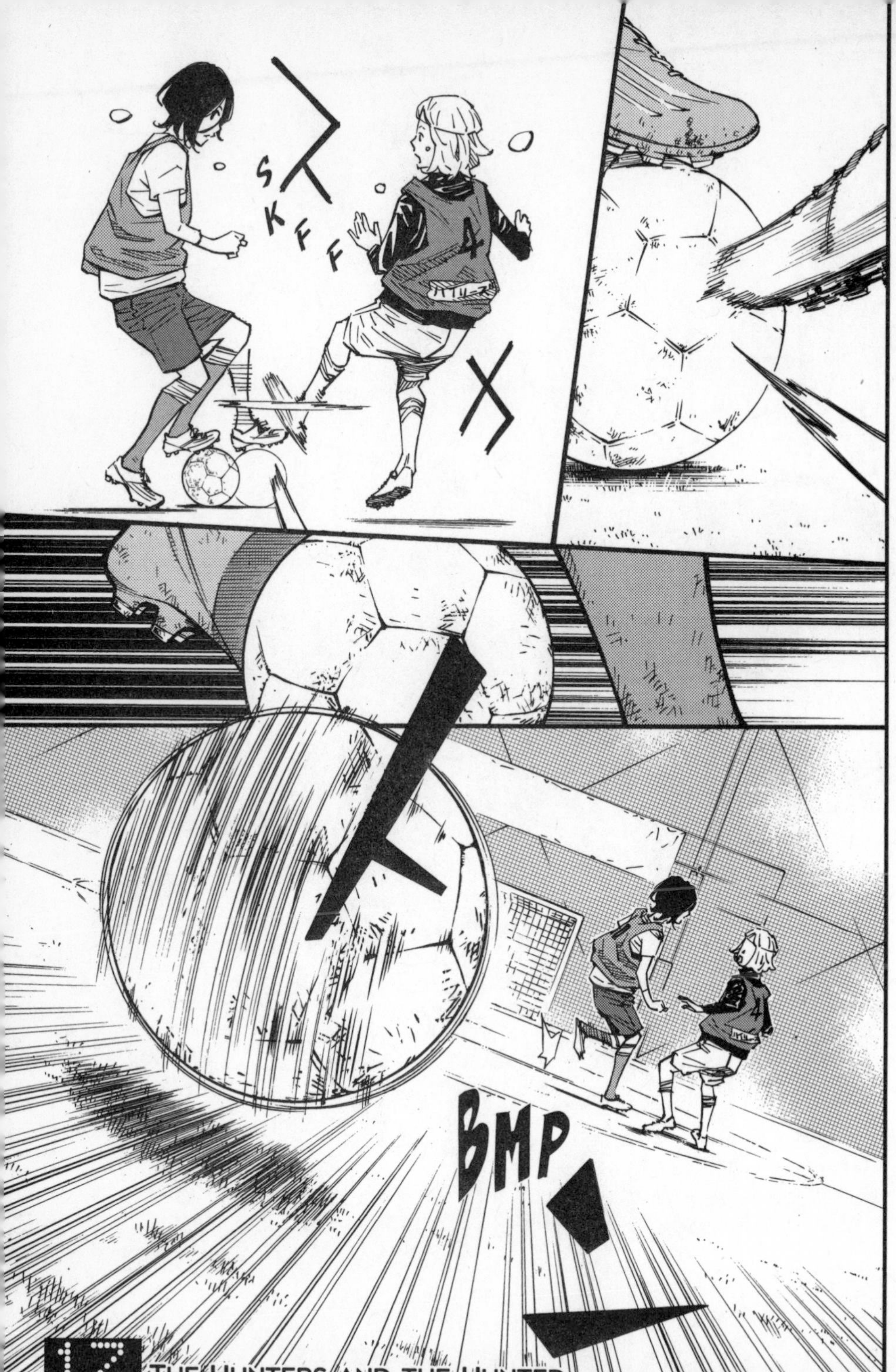
SKFF
BMP

17. THE HUNTERS AND THE HUNTED

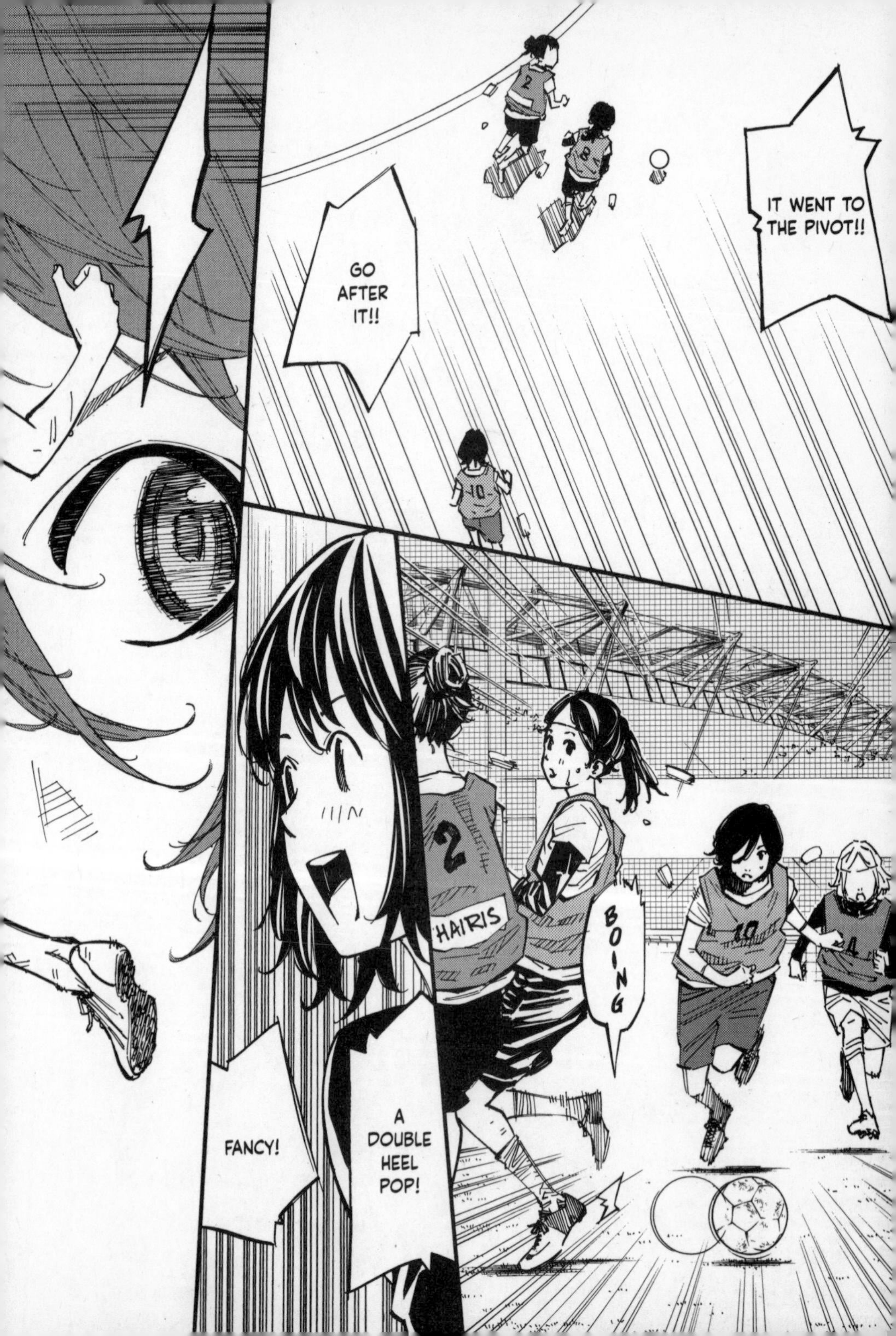
IT WENT TO THE PIVOT!!
GO AFTER IT!!
HAIRIS
BOING
A DOUBLE HEEL POP!
FANCY!

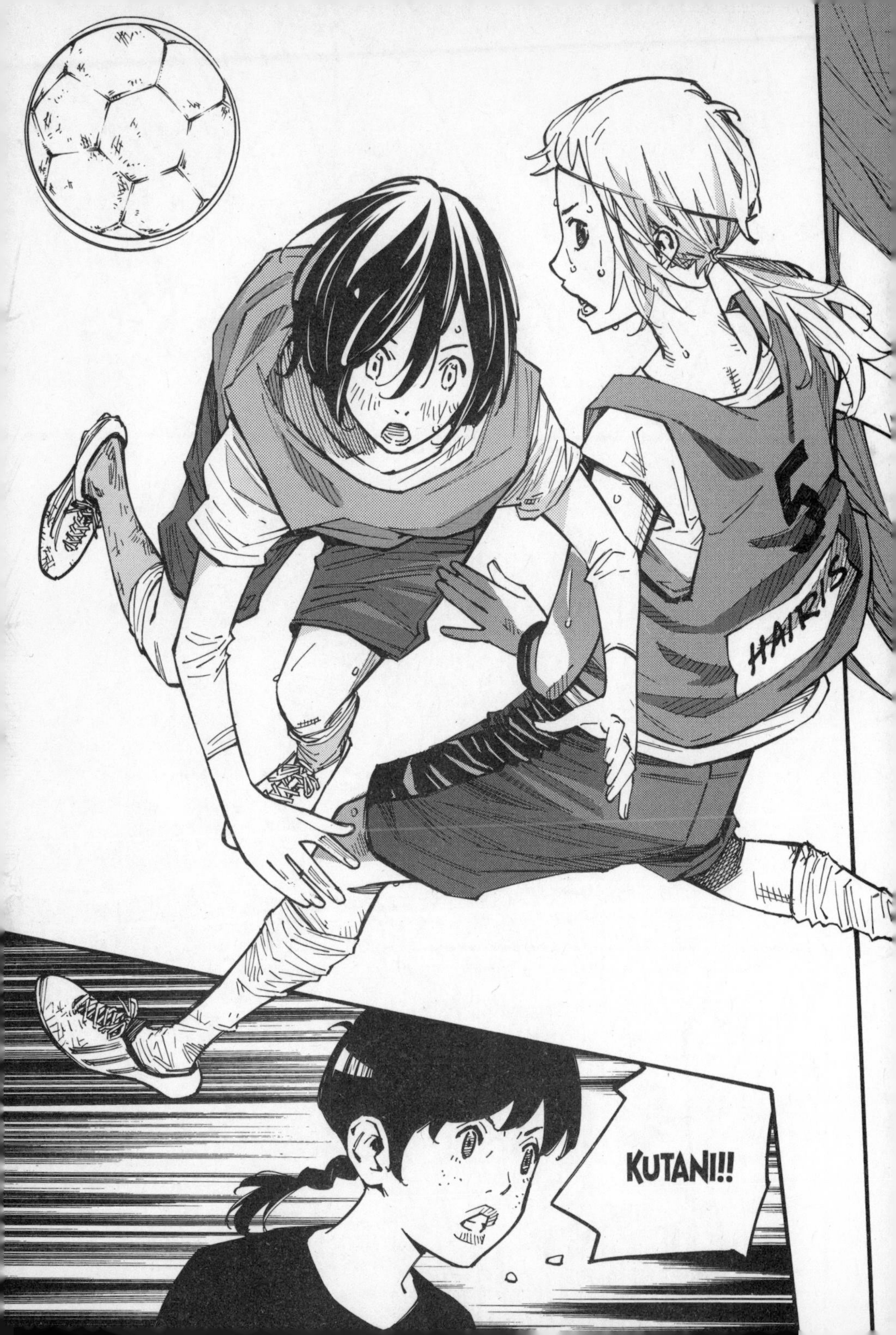
5
HAIRIS
KUTANI!!

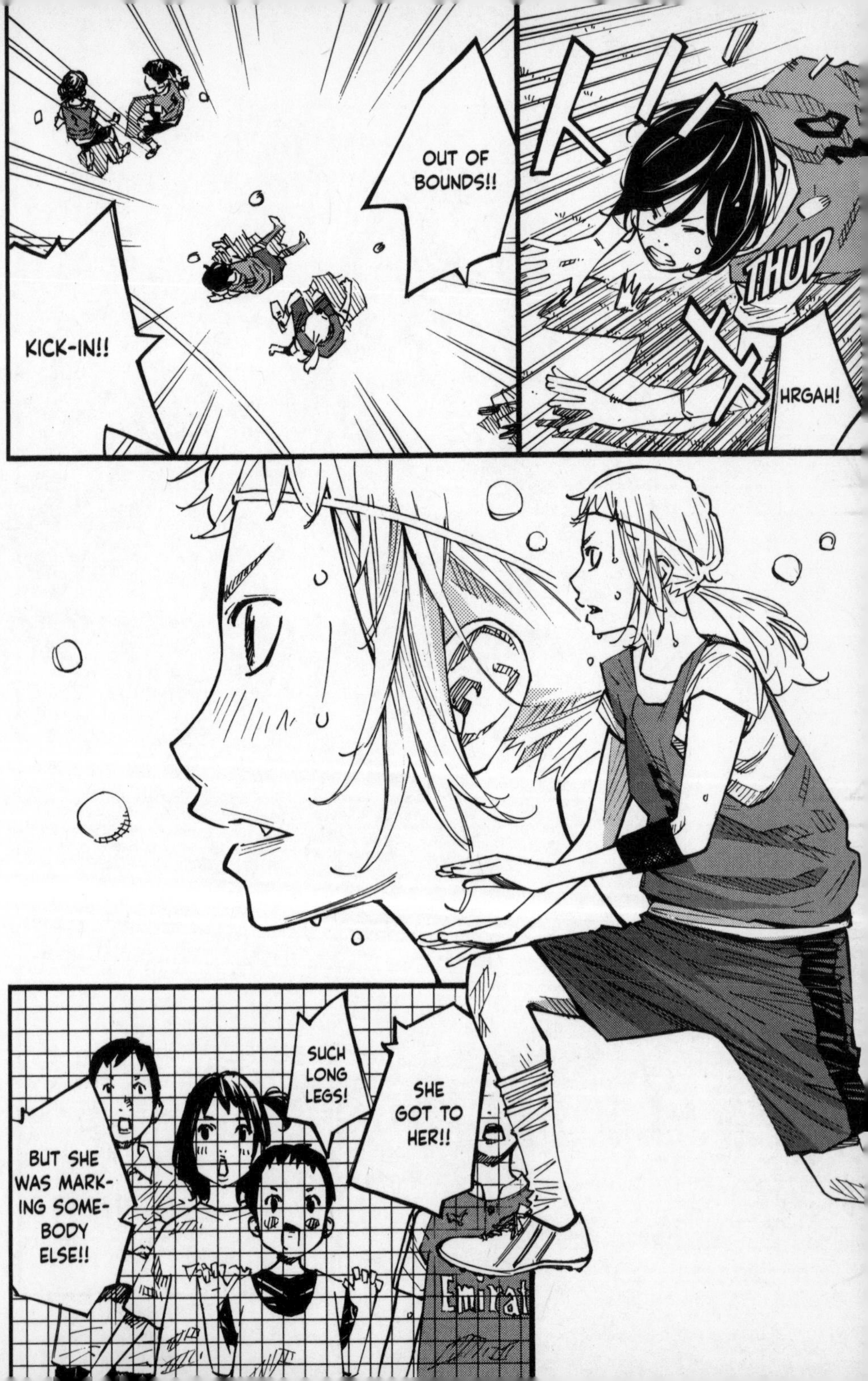
THUD
HRGAH!
OUT OF BOUNDS!!
KICK-IN!!
SHE GOT TO HER!!
SUCH LONG LEGS!
BUT SHE WAS MARKING SOMEBODY ELSE!!
Emirat

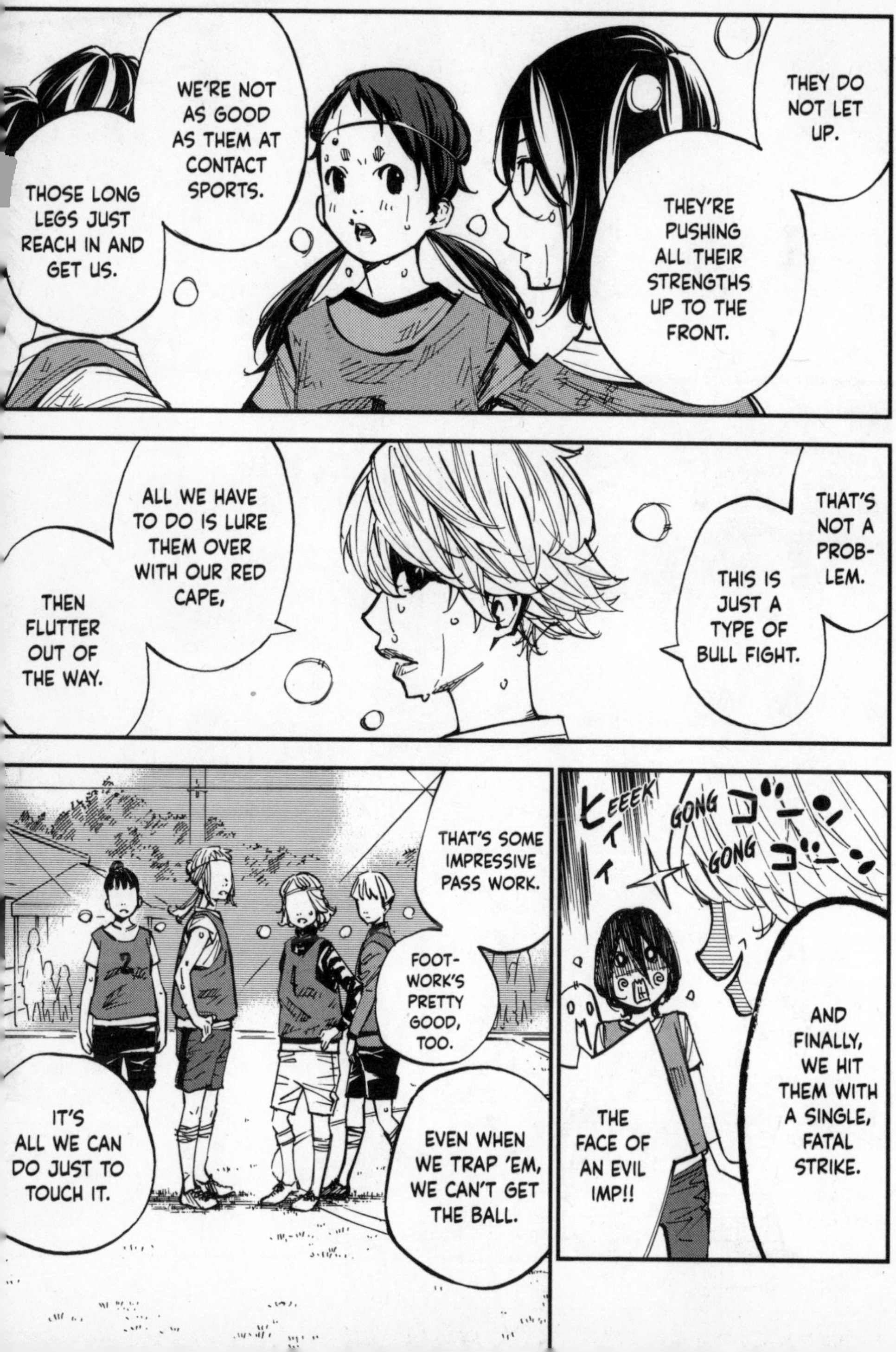
THEY DO NOT LET UP.
THEY'RE PUSHING ALL THEIR STRENGTHS UP TO THE FRONT.
WE'RE NOT AS GOOD AS THEM AT CONTACT SPORTS.
THOSE LONG LEGS JUST REACH IN AND GET US.
THAT'S NOT A PROB-LEM.
THIS IS JUST A TYPE OF BULL FIGHT.
ALL WE HAVE TO DO IS LURE THEM OVER WITH OUR RED CAPE,
THEN FLUTTER OUT OF THE WAY.
GONG
GONG
EEEK
AND FINALLY, WE HIT THEM WITH A SINGLE, FATAL STRIKE.
THE FACE OF AN EVIL IMP!!
THAT'S SOME IMPRESSIVE PASS WORK.
FOOT-WORK'S PRETTY GOOD, TOO.
EVEN WHEN WE TRAP 'EM, WE CAN'T GET THE BALL.
IT'S ALL WE CAN DO JUST TO TOUCH IT.

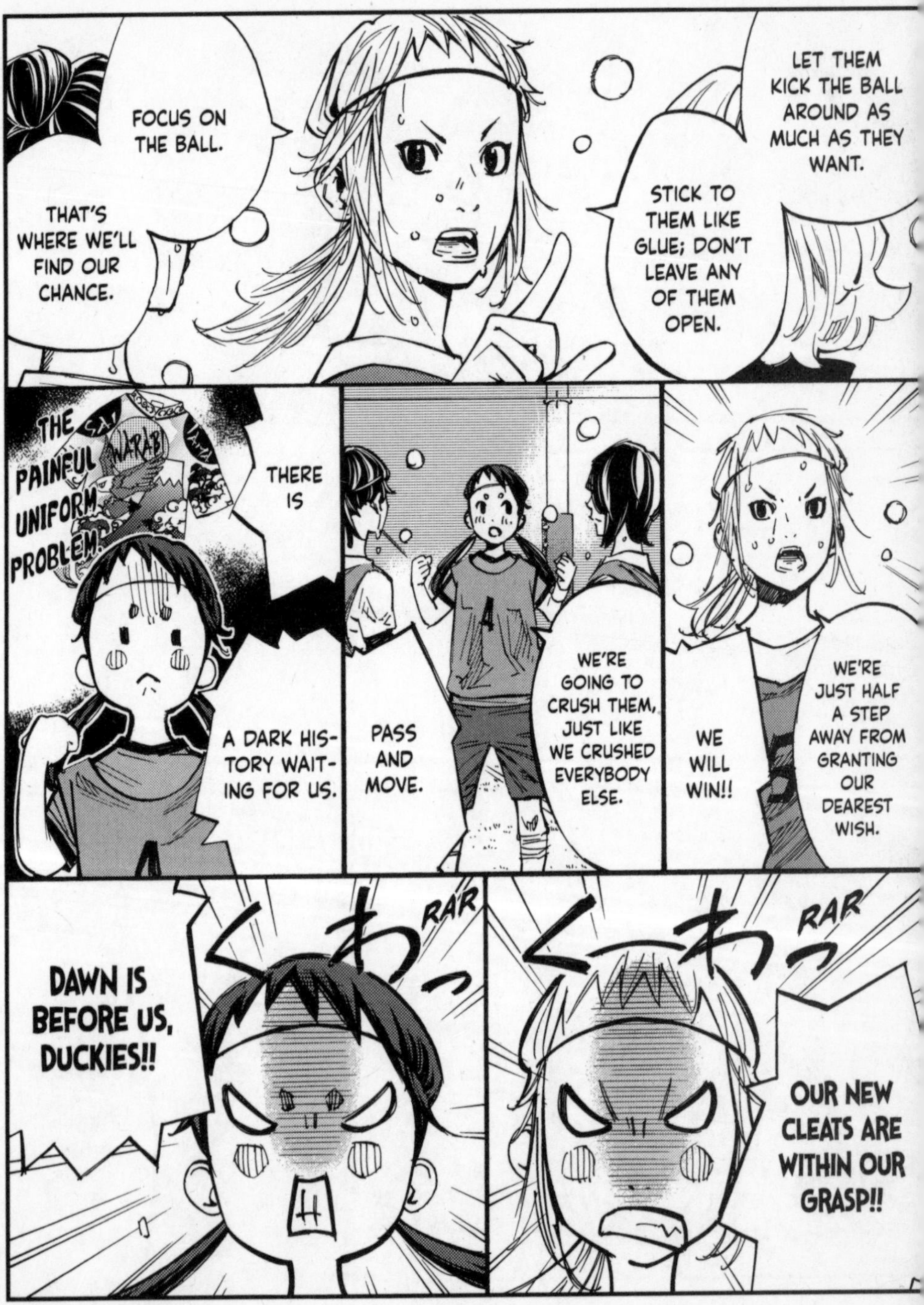
LET THEM KICK THE BALL AROUND AS MUCH AS THEY WANT.
STICK TO THEM LIKE GLUE; DON'T LEAVE ANY OF THEM OPEN.
FOCUS ON THE BALL.
THAT'S WHERE WE'LL FIND OUR CHANCE.
WE'RE JUST HALF A STEP AWAY FROM GRANTING OUR DEAREST WISH.
WE WILL WIN!!
WE'RE GOING TO CRUSH THEM, JUST LIKE WE CRUSHED EVERYBODY ELSE.
PASS AND MOVE.
THERE IS
A DARK HISTORY WAITING FOR US.
THE PAINFUL UNIFORM PROBLEM.
くわっ
RAR
OUR NEW CLEATS ARE WITHIN OUR GRASP!!
くわっ
RAR
DAWN IS BEFORE US, DUCKIES!!

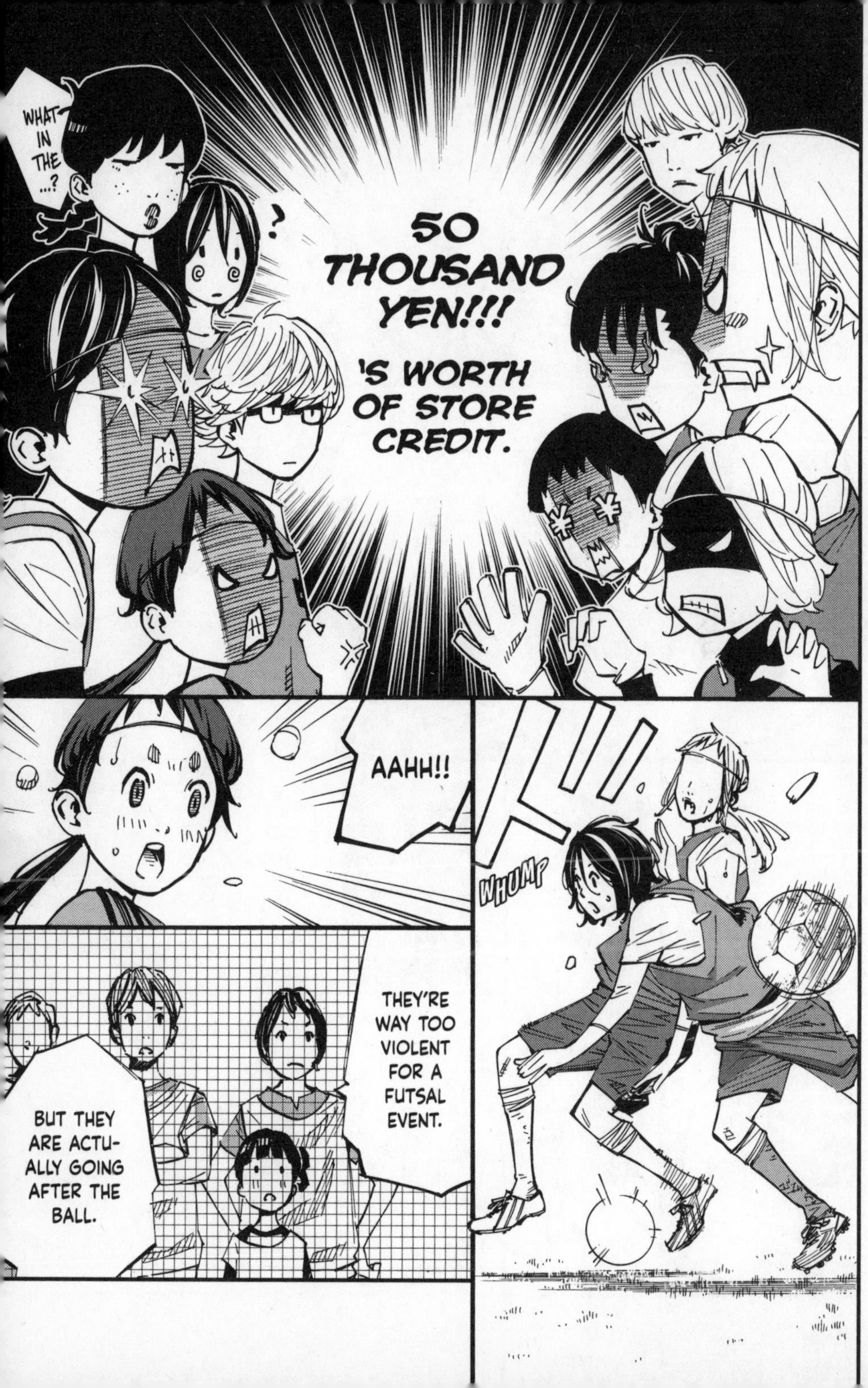
50 THOUSAND YEN!!!
'S WORTH OF STORE CREDIT.
?
WHAT IN THE ...?
WHUMP
AAHH!!
THEY'RE WAY TOO VIOLENT FOR A FUTSAL EVENT.
BUT THEY ARE ACTU-ALLY GOING AFTER THE BALL.

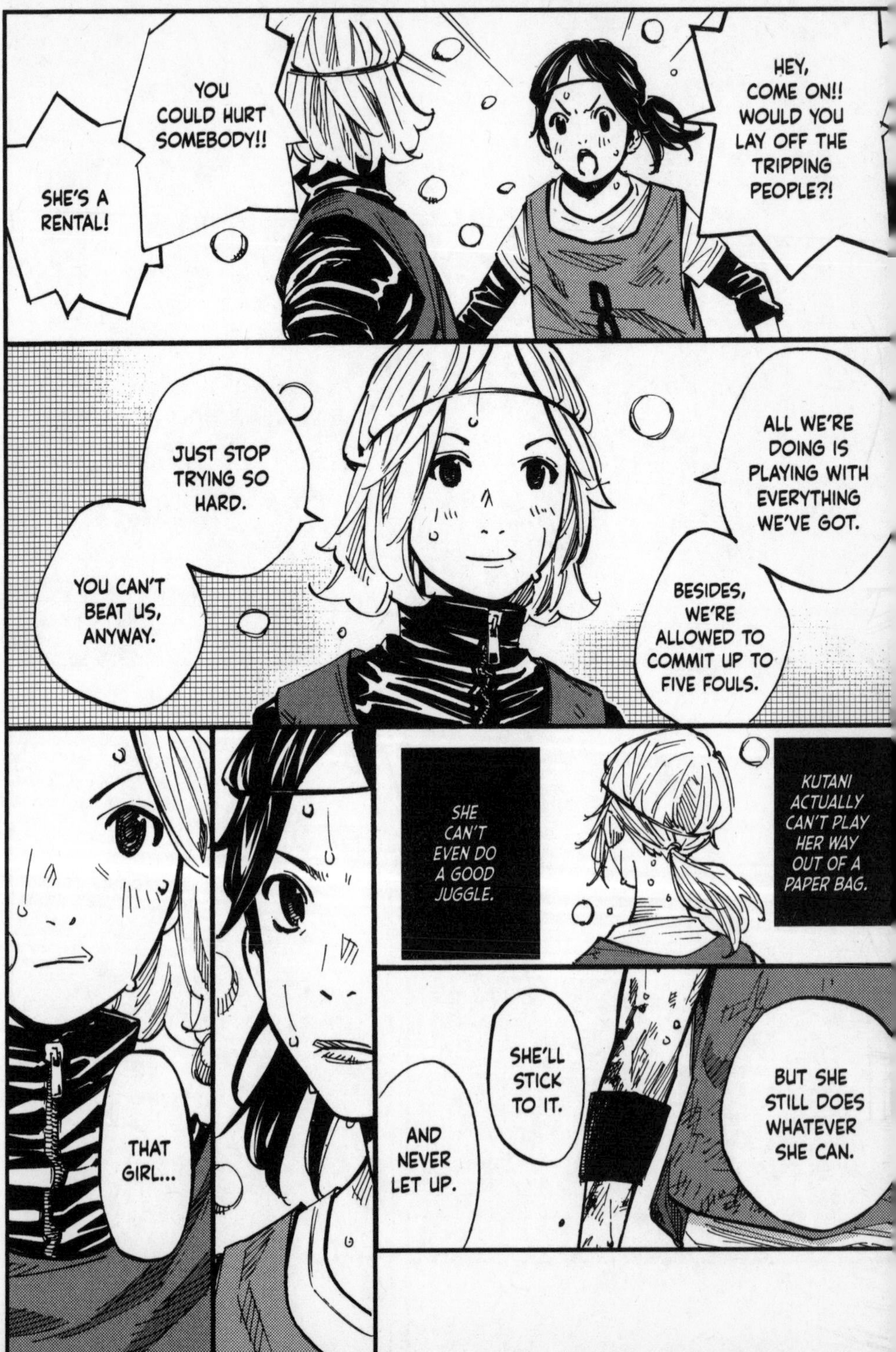
HEY, COME ON!! WOULD YOU LAY OFF THE TRIPPING PEOPLE?!
YOU COULD HURT SOMEBODY!!
SHE'S A RENTAL!
ALL WE'RE DOING IS PLAYING WITH EVERYTHING WE'VE GOT.
BESIDES, WE'RE ALLOWED TO COMMIT UP TO FIVE FOULS.
JUST STOP TRYING SO HARD.
YOU CAN'T BEAT US, ANYWAY.
KUTANI ACTUALLY CAN'T PLAY HER WAY OUT OF A PAPER BAG.
SHE CAN'T EVEN DO A GOOD JUGGLE.
BUT SHE STILL DOES WHATEVER SHE CAN.
SHE'LL STICK TO IT.
AND NEVER LET UP.
THAT GIRL...

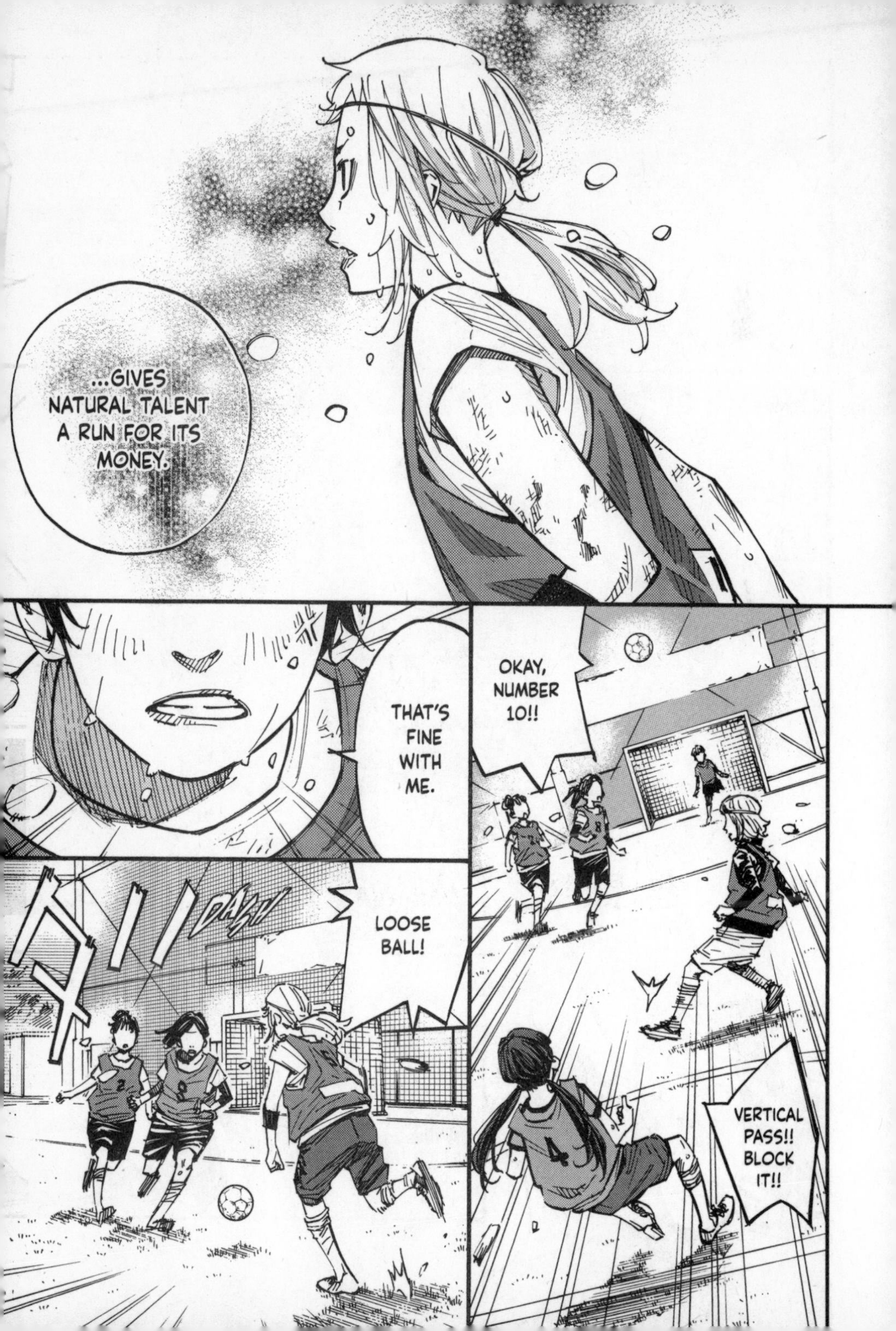
...GIVES NATURAL TALENT A RUN FOR ITS MONEY.
OKAY, NUMBER 10!!
VERTICAL PASS!! BLOCK IT!!
THAT'S FINE WITH ME.
DASH
LOOSE BALL!

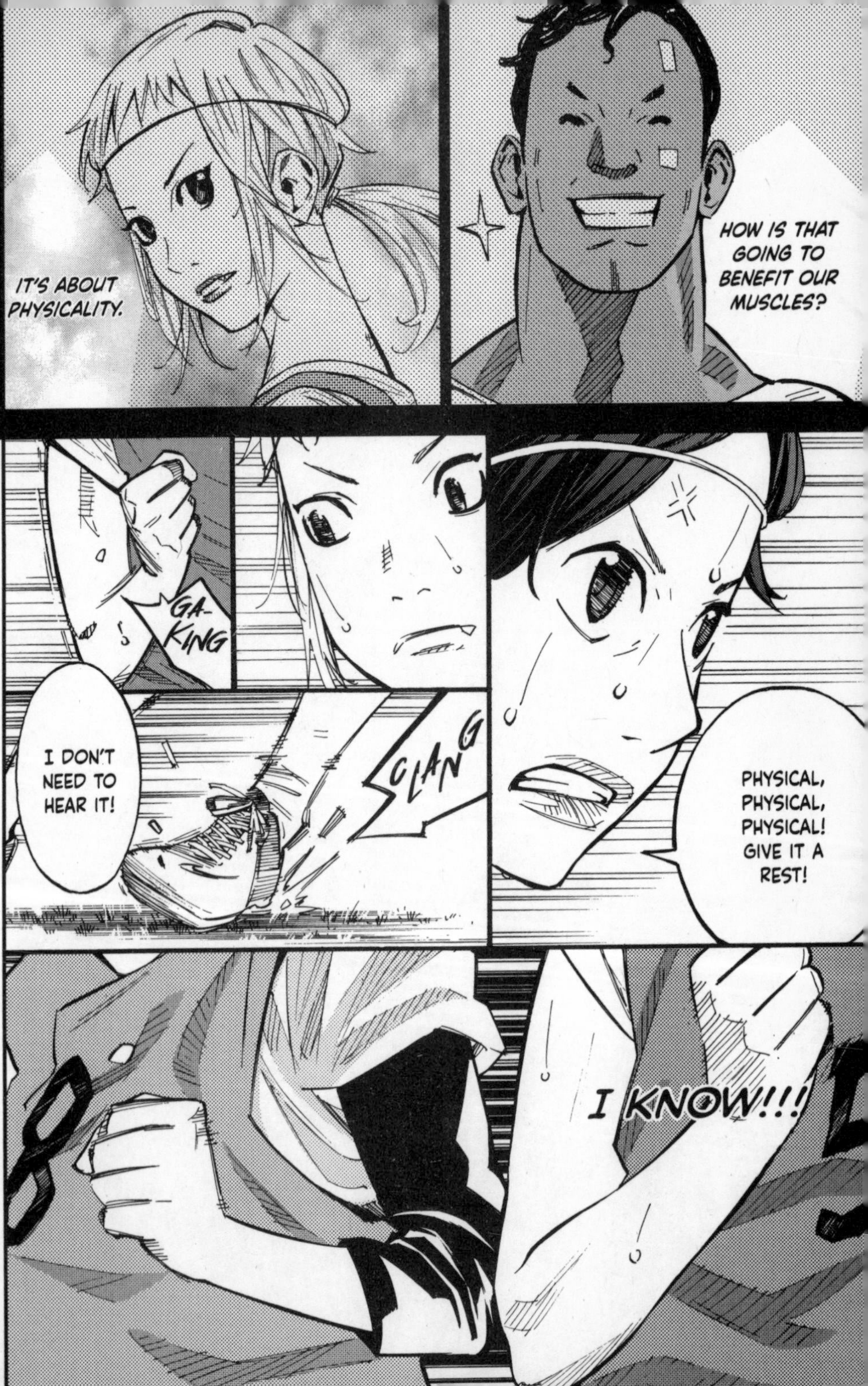
HOW IS THAT GOING TO BENEFIT OUR MUSCLES?
IT'S ABOUT PHYSICALITY.
PHYSICAL, PHYSICAL, PHYSICAL! GIVE IT A REST!
GA-KING
CLANG
I DON'T NEED TO HEAR IT!
I KNOW!!!

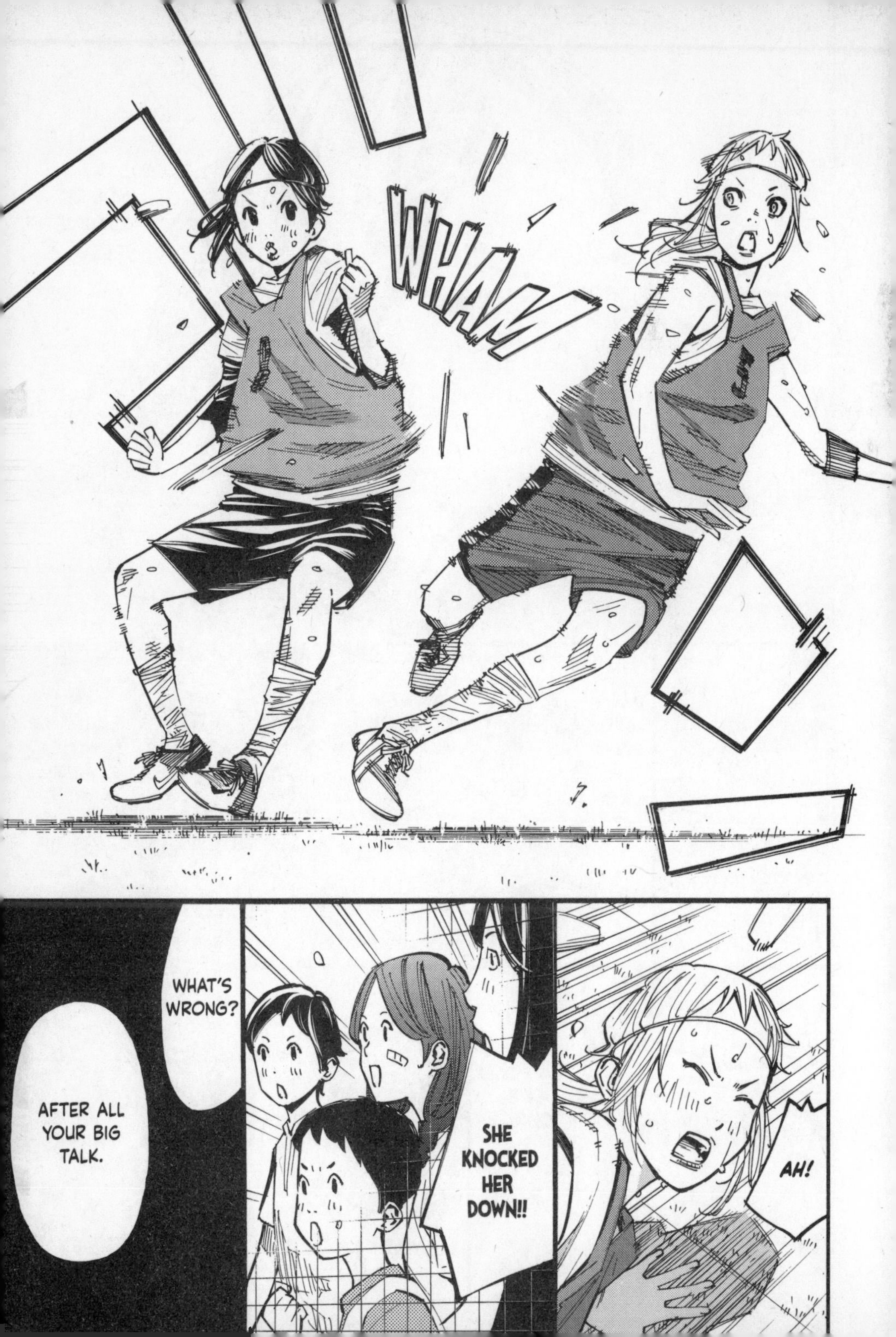
WHAM
AH!
SHE KNOCKED HER DOWN!!
WHAT'S WRONG?
AFTER ALL YOUR BIG TALK.

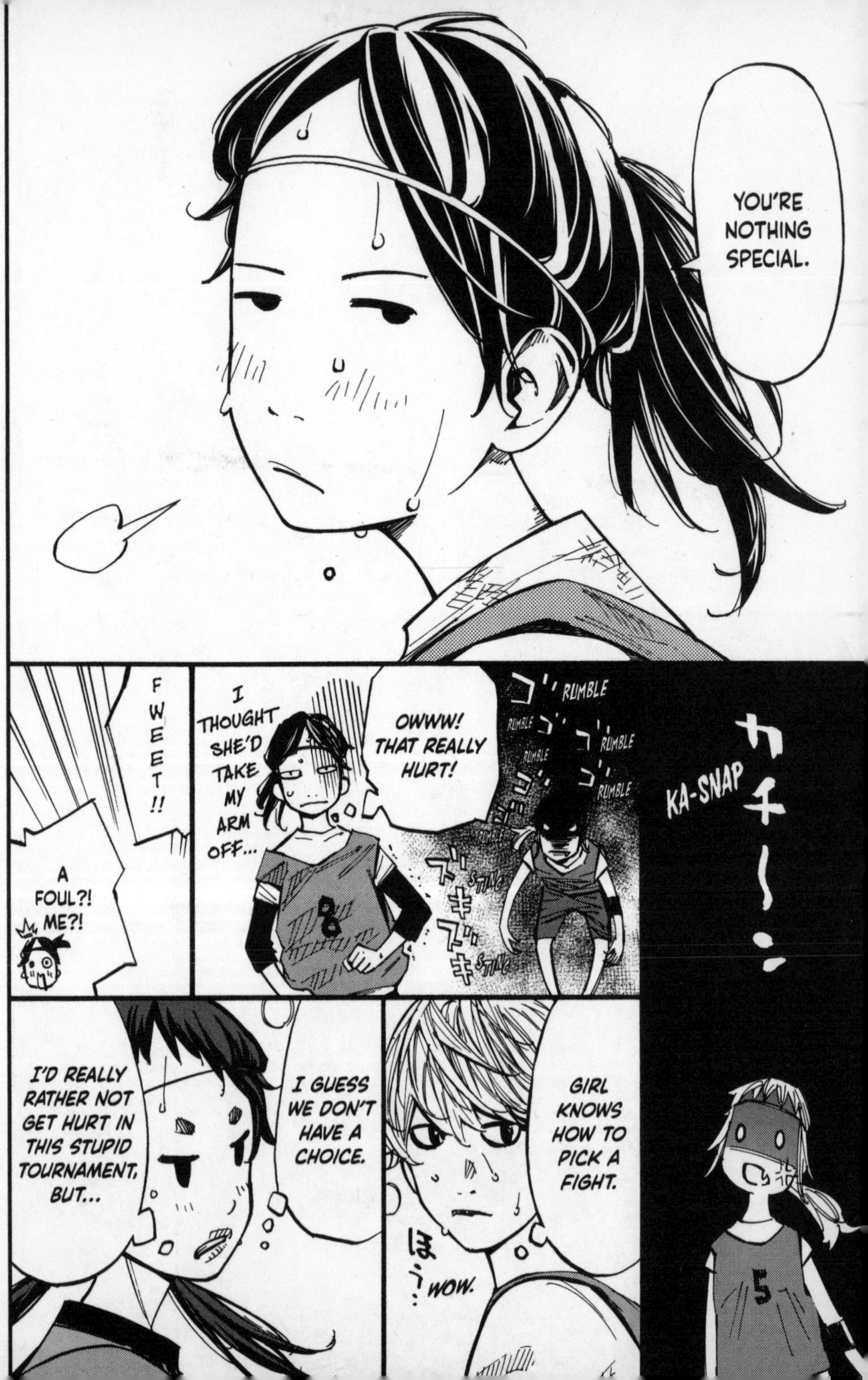
YOU'RE NOTHING SPECIAL.
カチ〜ン
KA-SNAP
ゴゴゴゴ
RUMBLE
RUMBLE
RUMBLE
RUMBLE
RUMBLE
RUMBLE
ズキズキ
STING
STING
OWWW! THAT REALLY HURT!
I THOUGHT SHE'D TAKE MY ARM OFF...
FWEET!!
A FOUL?! ME?!
GIRL KNOWS HOW TO PICK A FIGHT.
ほう
WOW.
I GUESS WE DON'T HAVE A CHOICE.
I'D REALLY RATHER NOT GET HURT IN THIS STUPID TOURNAMENT, BUT...

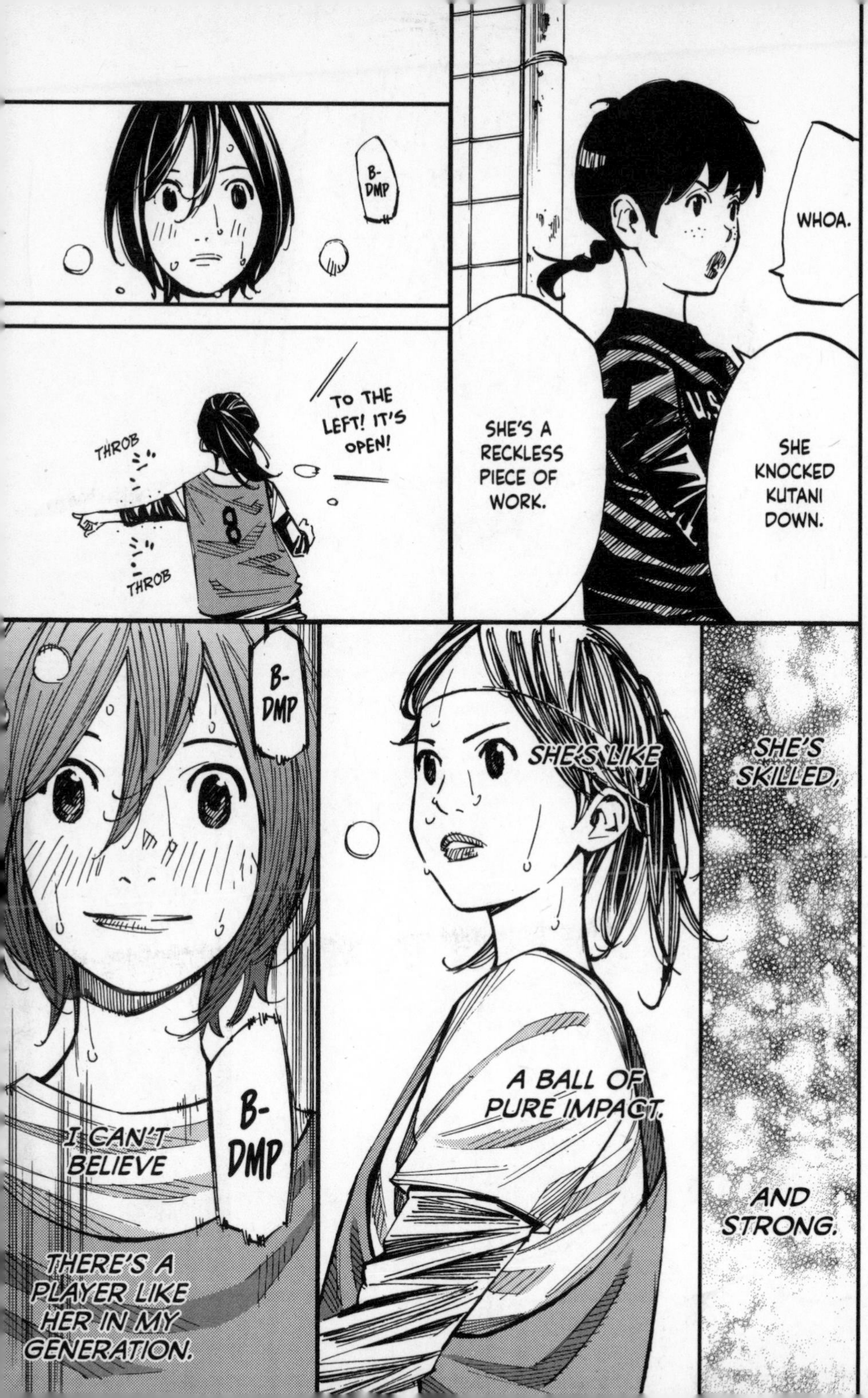
WHOA.
SHE KNOCKED KUTANI DOWN.
SHE'S A RECKLESS PIECE OF WORK.
B-DMP
TO THE LEFT! IT'S OPEN!
THROB
THROB
SHE'S SKILLED,
AND STRONG.
SHE'S LIKE
A BALL OF PURE IMPACT.
B-DMP
B-DMP
I CAN'T BELIEVE
THERE'S A PLAYER LIKE HER IN MY GENERATION.

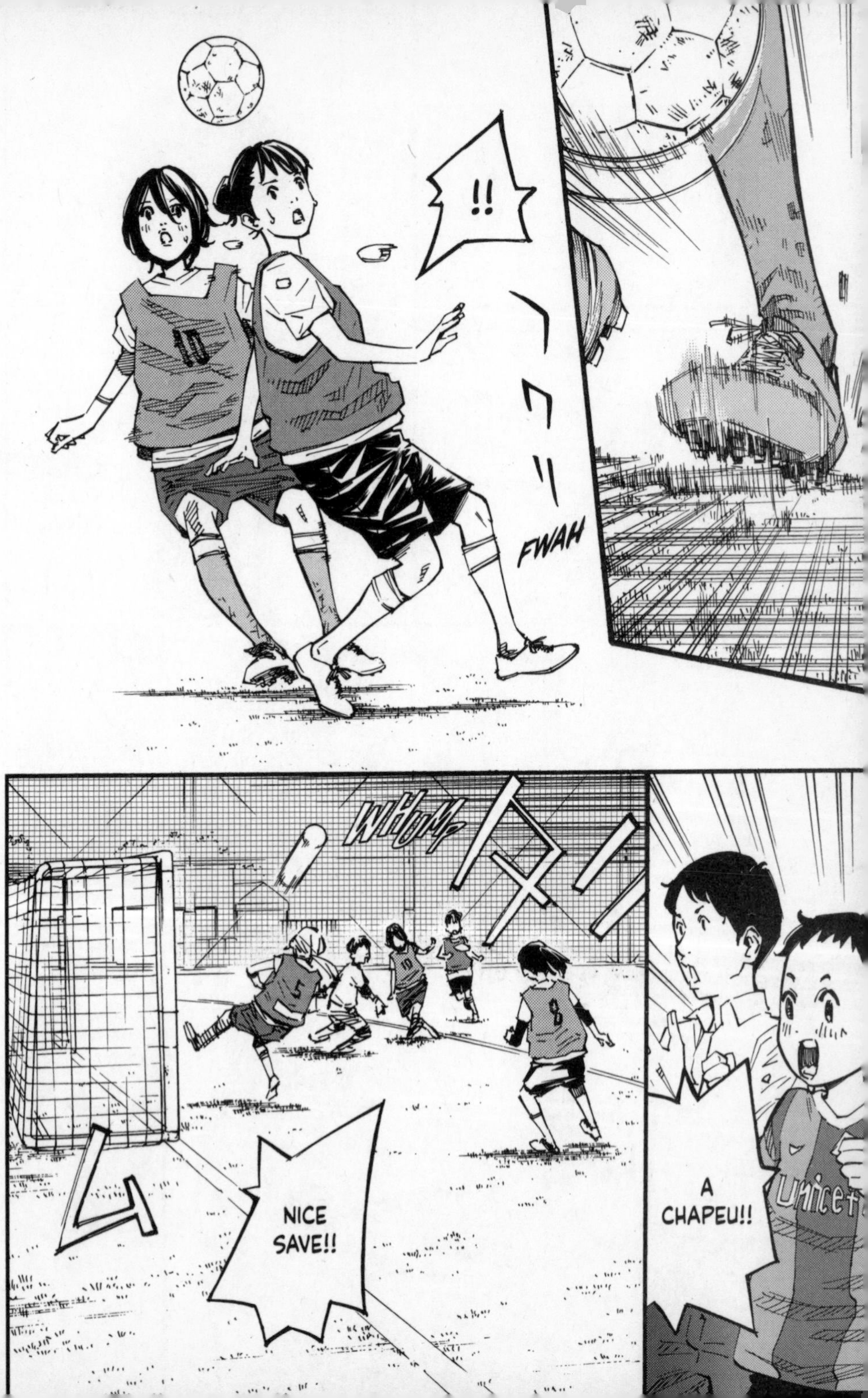
!!
FWAH
A CHAPEU!!
WHUMP
NICE SAVE!!

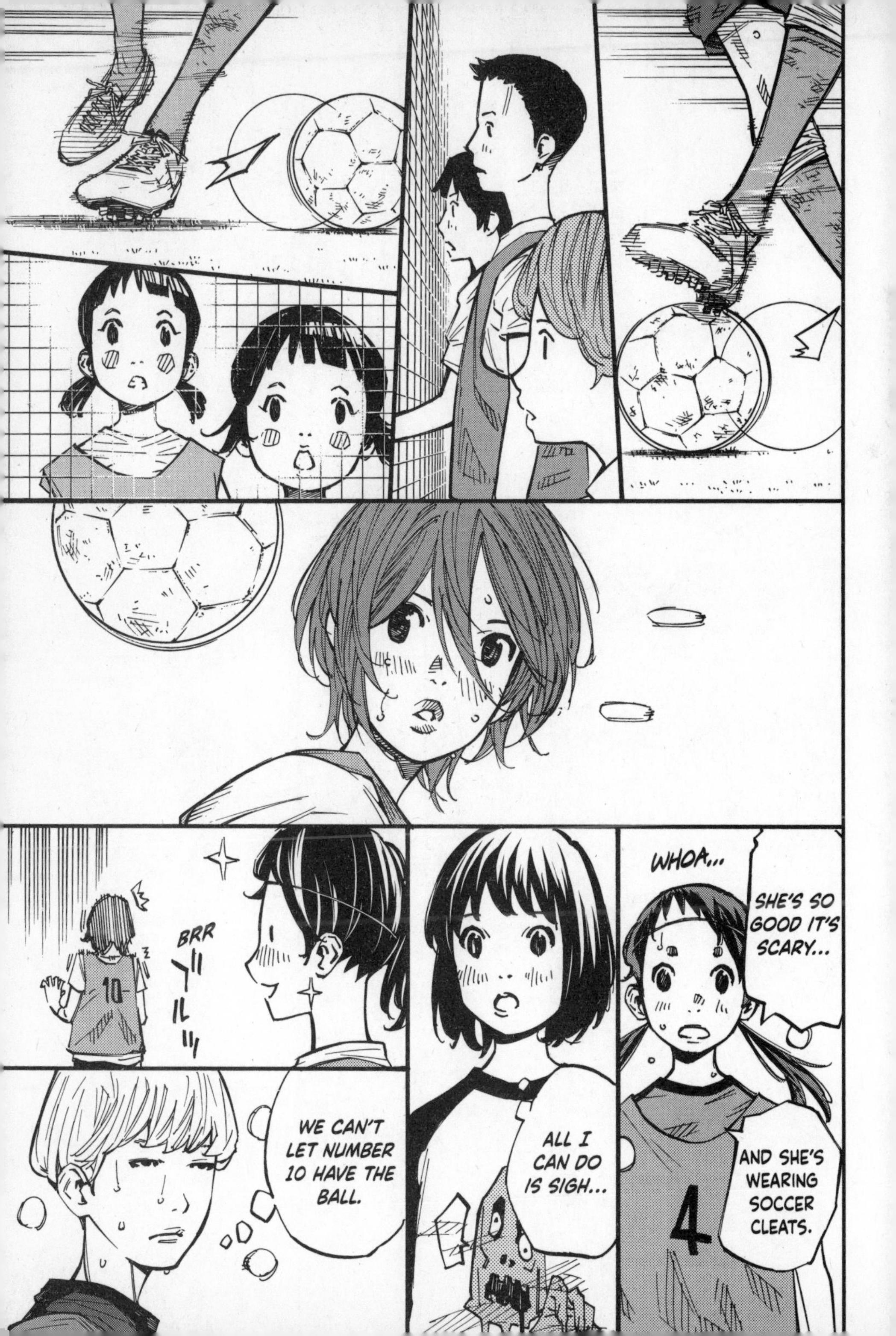
WHOA...
SHE'S SO GOOD IT'S SCARY...
AND SHE'S WEARING SOCCER CLEATS.
ALL I CAN DO IS SIGH...
BRR
ブルッ
WE CAN'T LET NUMBER 10 HAVE THE BALL.

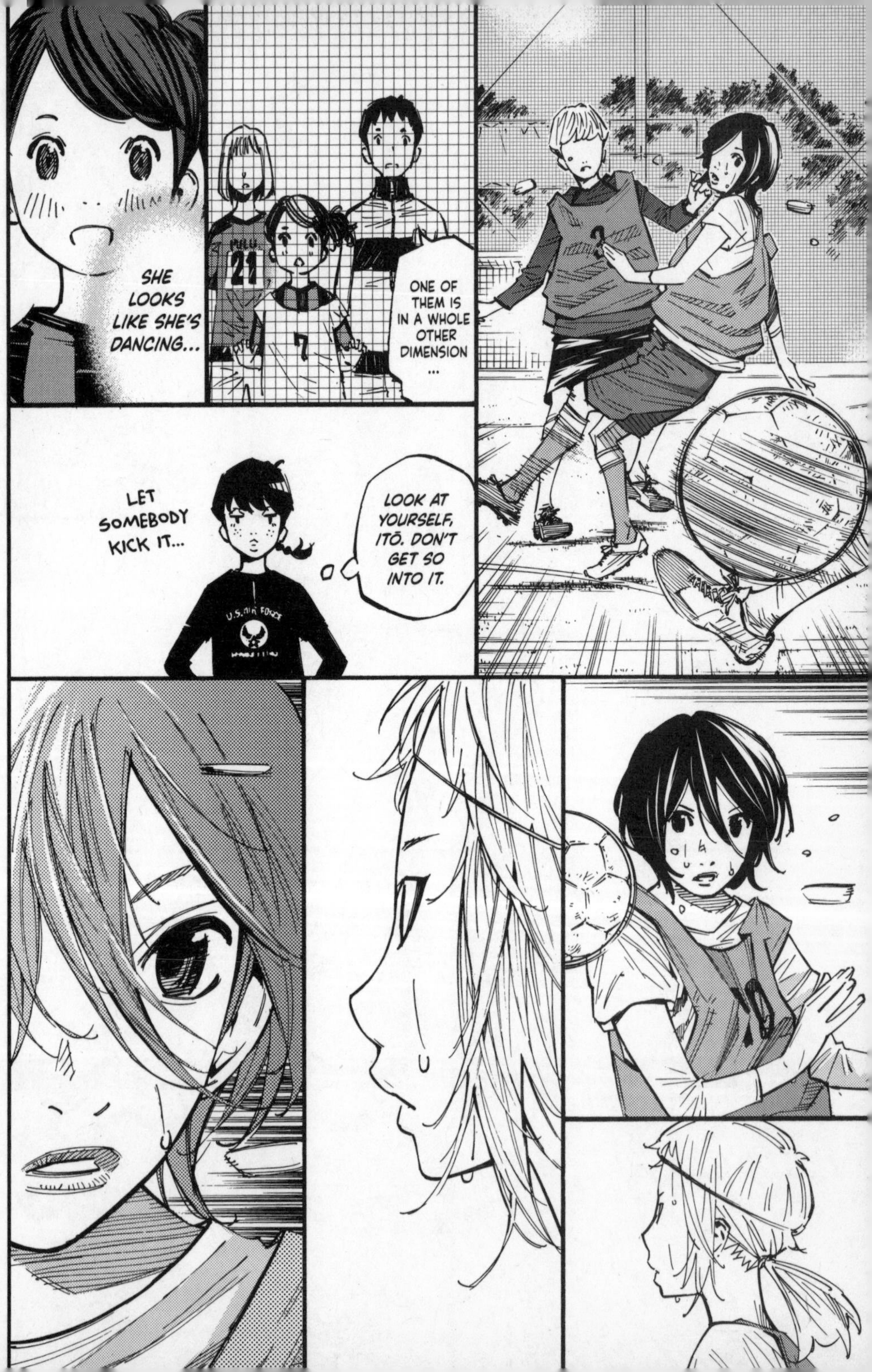
ONE OF THEM IS IN A WHOLE OTHER DIMENSION ...
SHE LOOKS LIKE SHE'S DANCING...
LOOK AT YOURSELF, ITŌ. DON'T GET SO INTO IT.
LET SOMEBODY KICK IT...

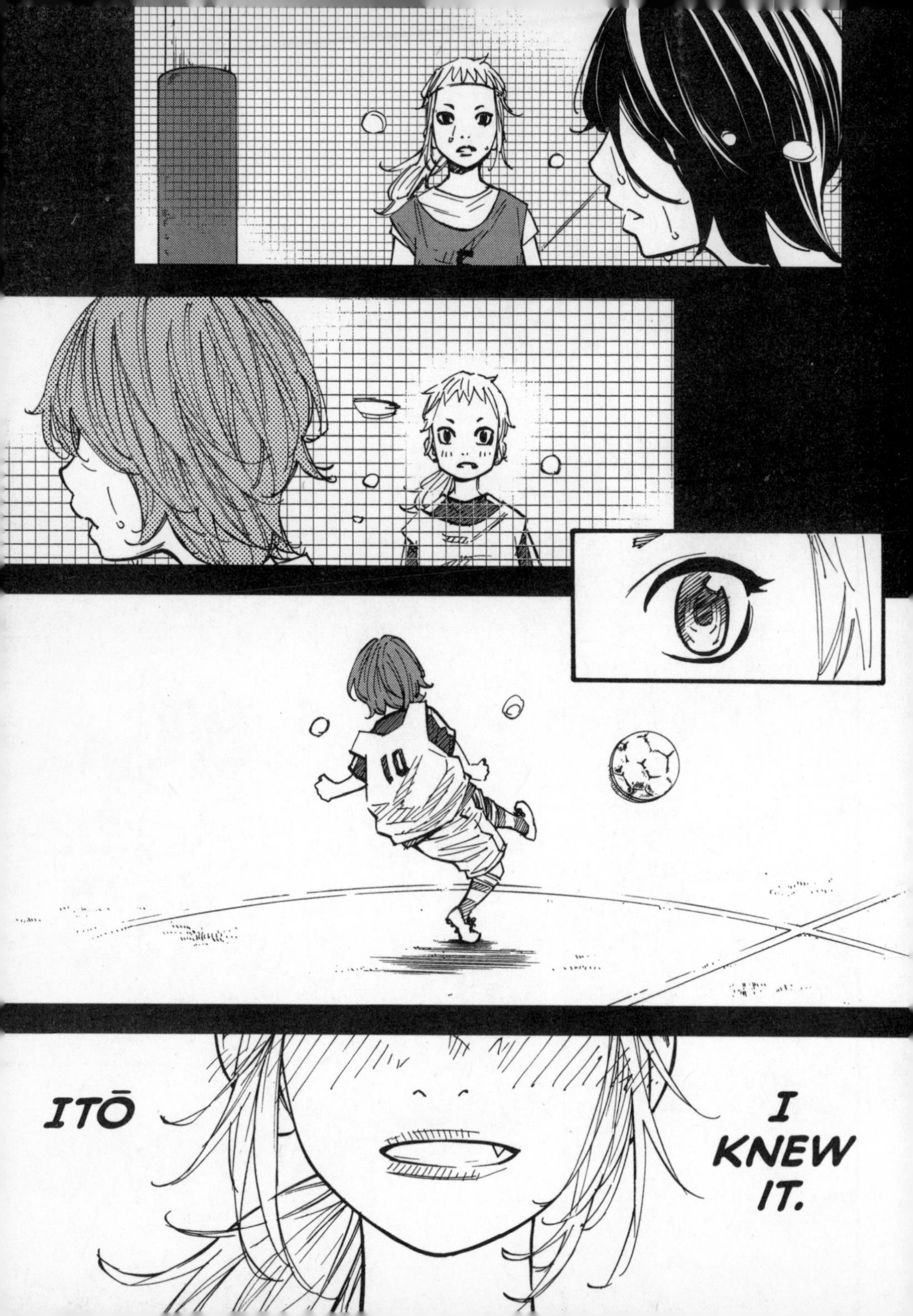
I KNEW IT.
ITŌ

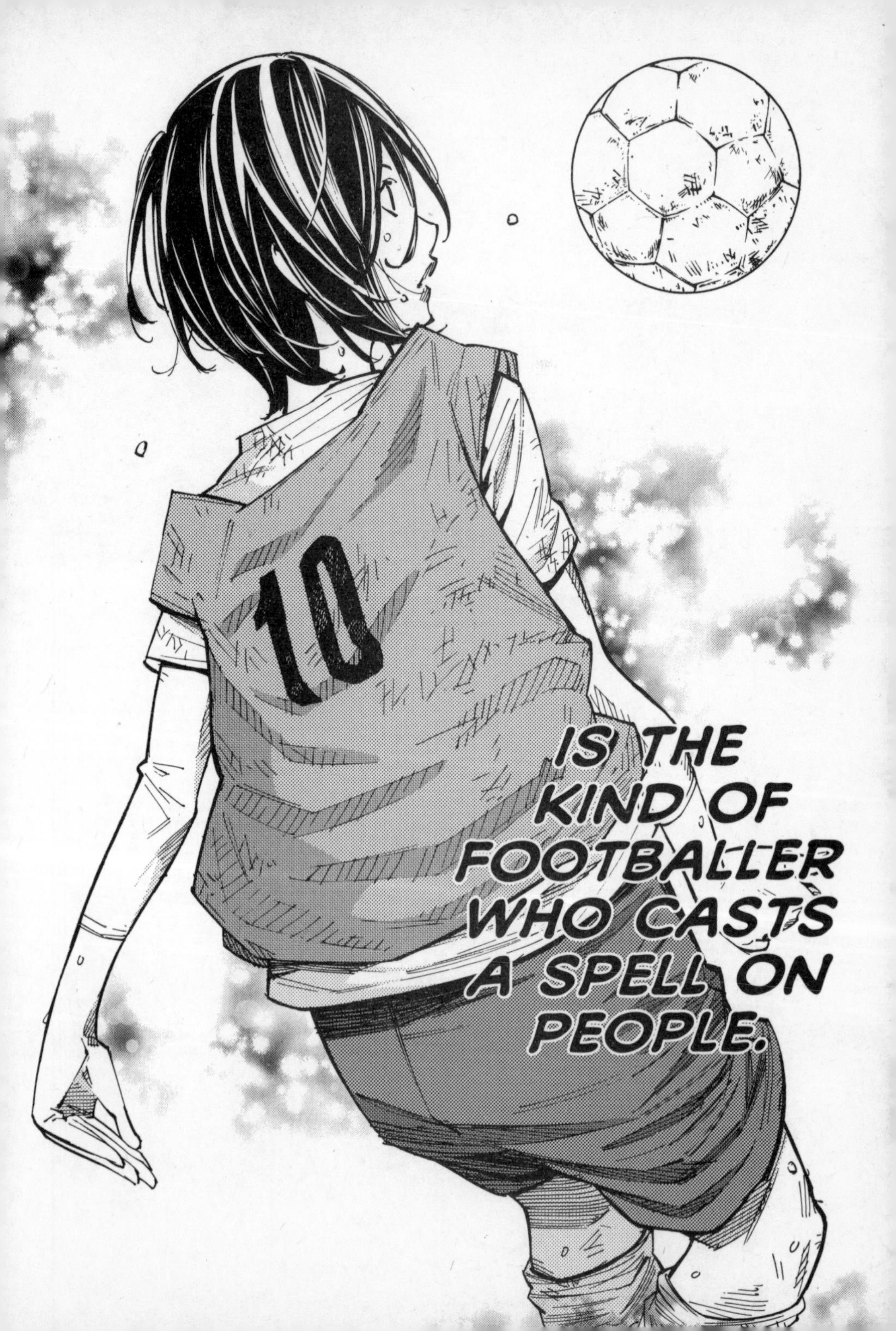
IS THE KIND OF FOOTBALLER WHO CASTS A SPELL ON PEOPLE.

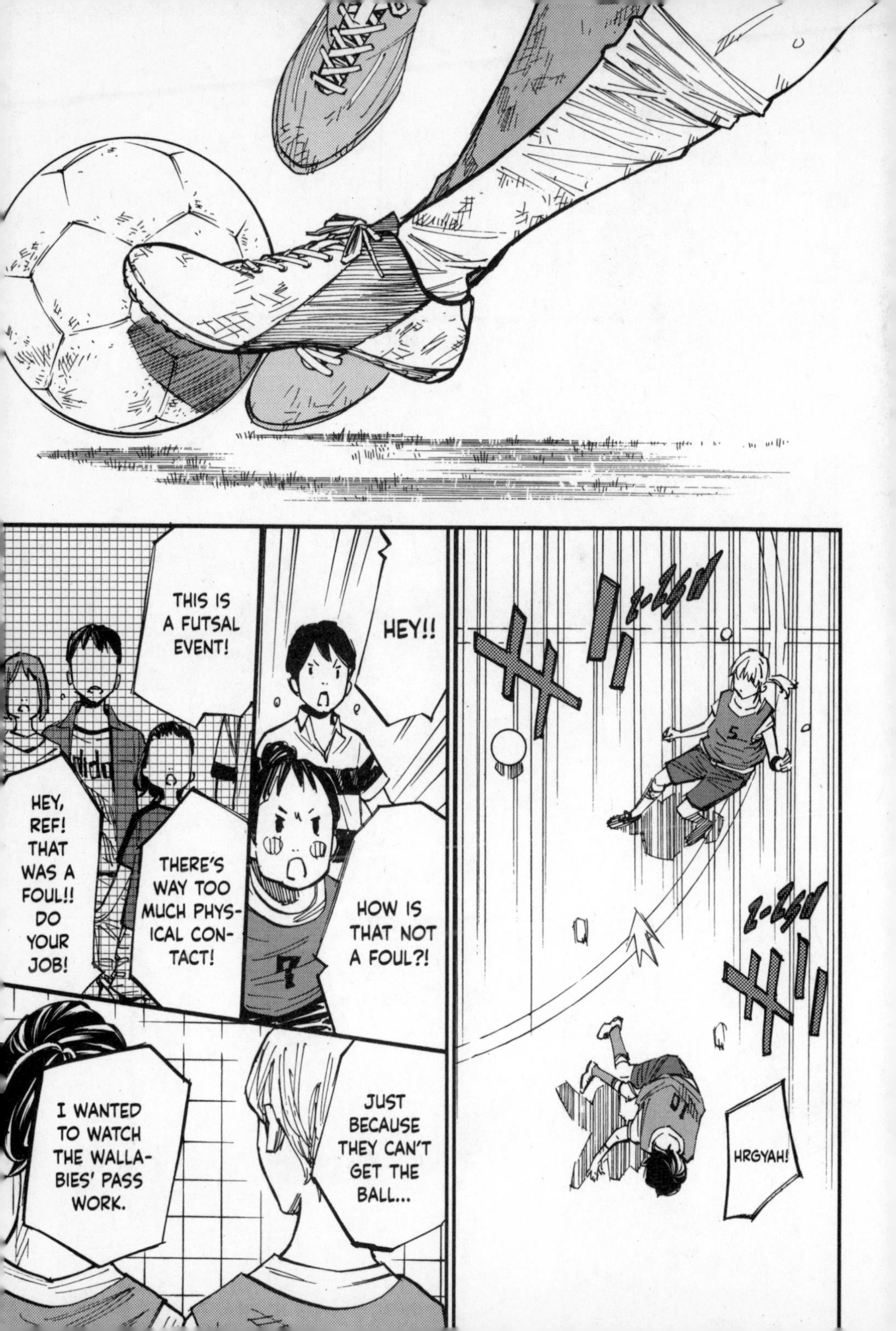
HRGYAH!
HEY!!
HOW IS THAT NOT A FOUL?!
THERE'S WAY TOO MUCH PHYSICAL CONTACT!
THIS IS A FUTSAL EVENT!
HEY, REF! THAT WAS A FOUL!! DO YOUR JOB!
JUST BECAUSE THEY CAN'T GET THE BALL...
I WANTED TO WATCH THE WALLABIES' PASS WORK.

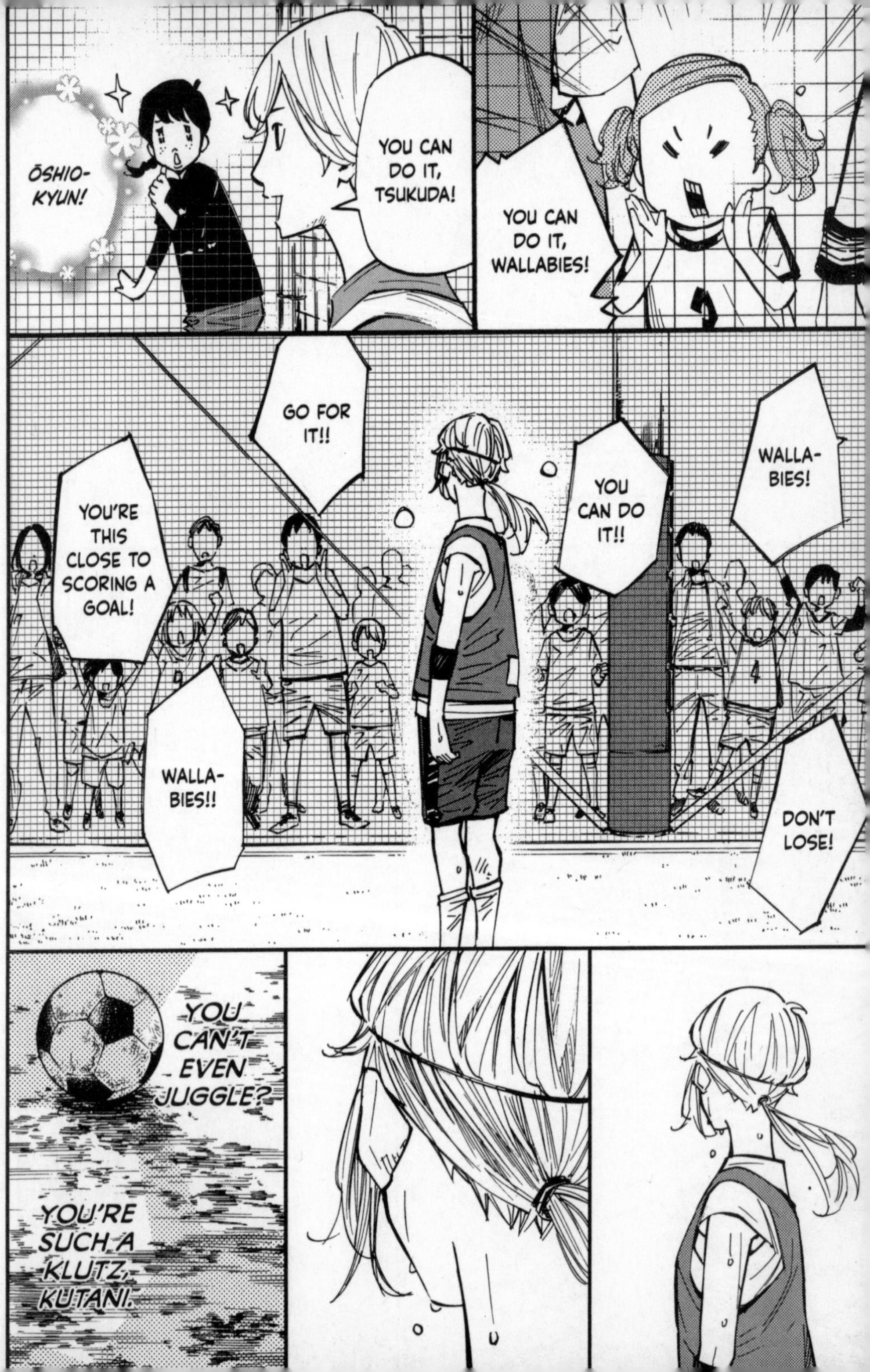
YOU CAN DO IT, WALLABIES!
YOU CAN DO IT, TSUKUDA!
ŌSHIO-KYUN!
WALLA-BIES!
YOU CAN DO IT!!
GO FOR IT!!
YOU'RE THIS CLOSE TO SCORING A GOAL!
DON'T LOSE!
WALLA-BIES!!
YOU CAN'T EVEN JUGGLE?
YOU'RE SUCH A KLUTZ, KUTANI.

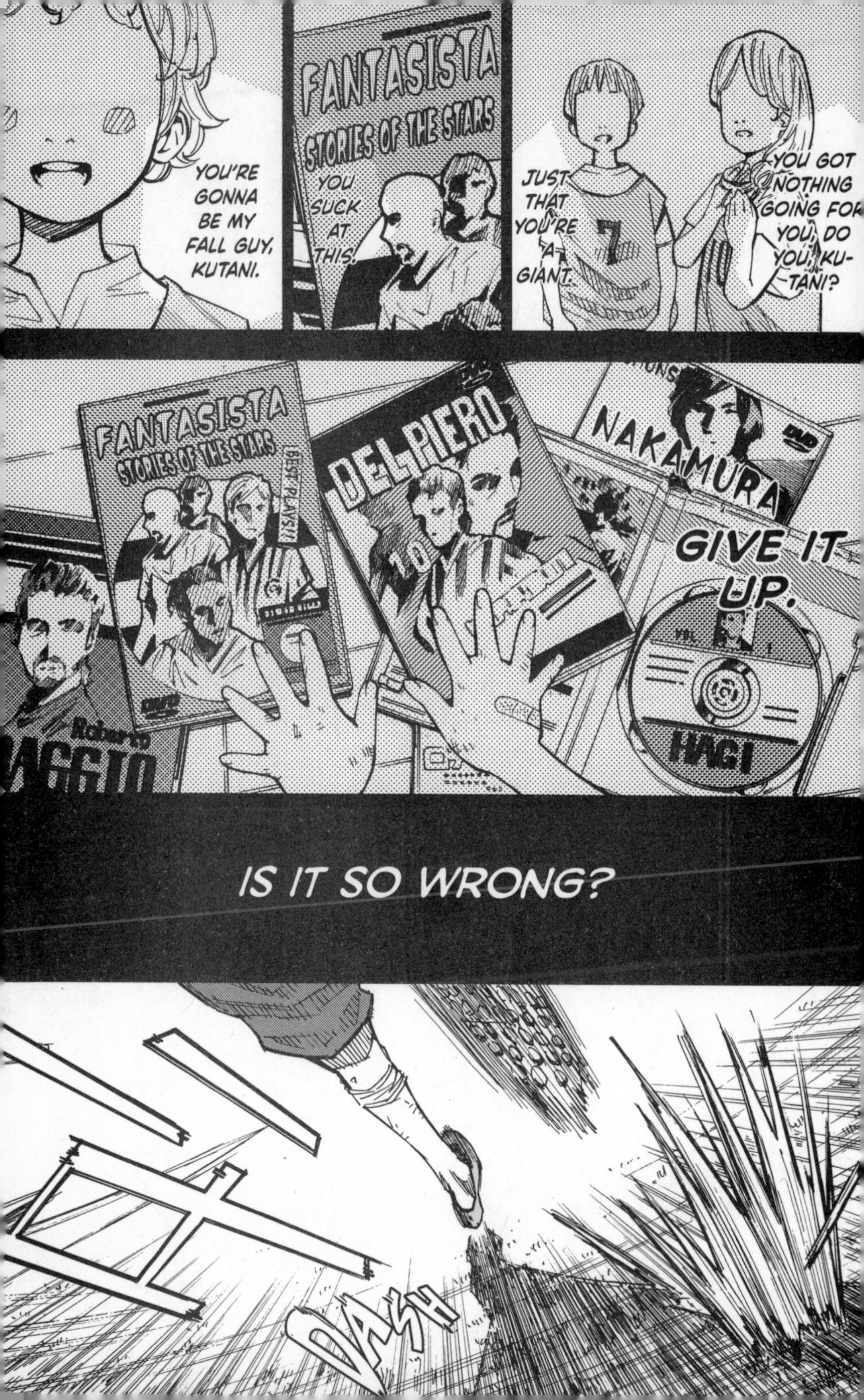
YOU GOT NOTHING GOING FOR YOU, DO YOU, KU-TANI?
JUST THAT YOU'RE A GIANT.
FANTASISTA
STORIES OF THE STARS
YOU SUCK AT THIS!
YOU'RE GONNA BE MY FALL GUY, KUTANI.
NAKAMURA
GIVE IT UP.
HAGI
DEL PIERO
FANTASISTA
STORIES OF THE STARS
BEST PLAYS!!
Roberto
BAGGIO
IS IT SO WRONG?
DASH

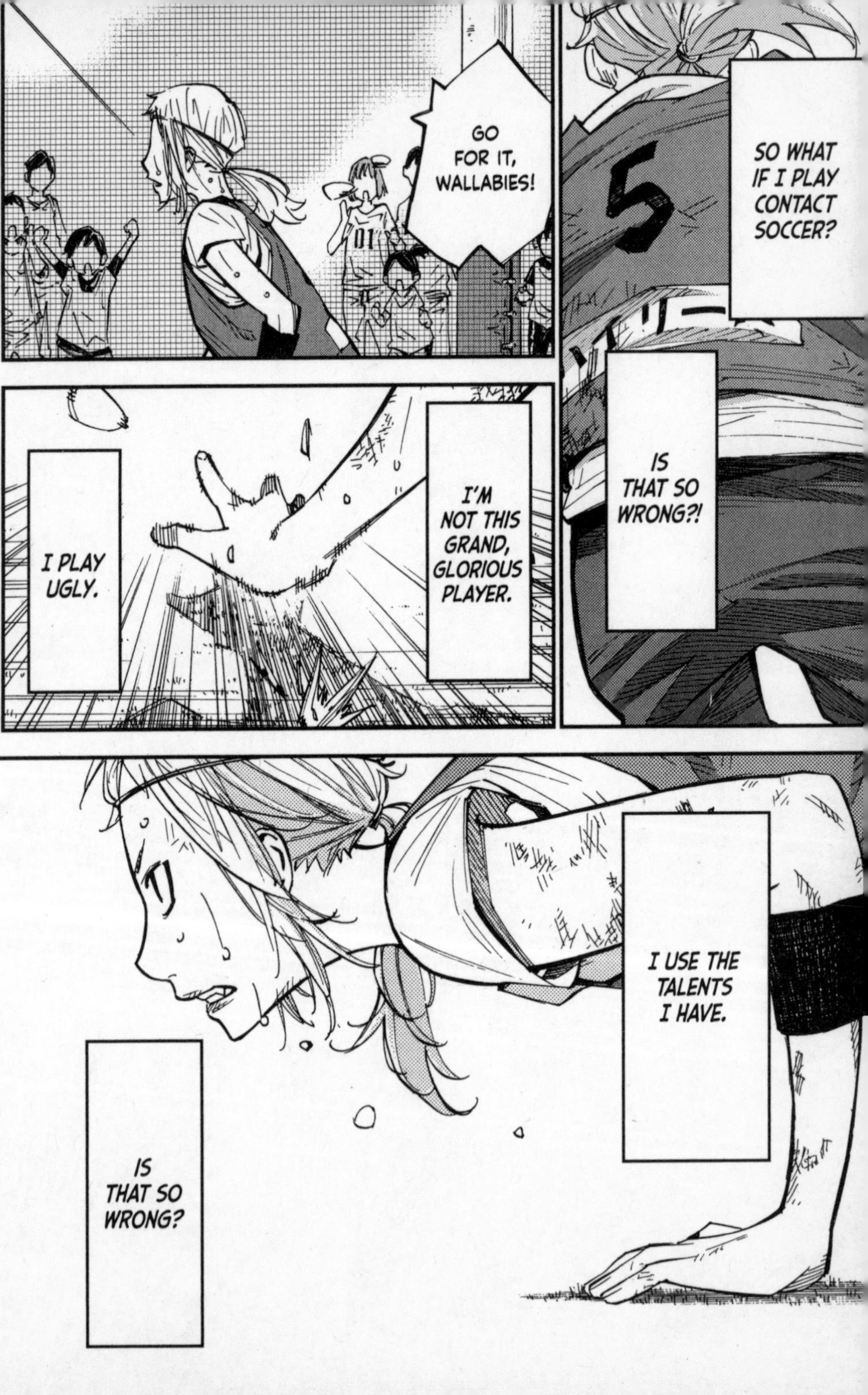
SO WHAT IF I PLAY CONTACT SOCCER?
IS THAT SO WRONG?!
GO FOR IT, WALLABIES!
I'M NOT THIS GRAND, GLORIOUS PLAYER.
I PLAY UGLY.
I USE THE TALENTS I HAVE.
IS THAT SO WRONG?

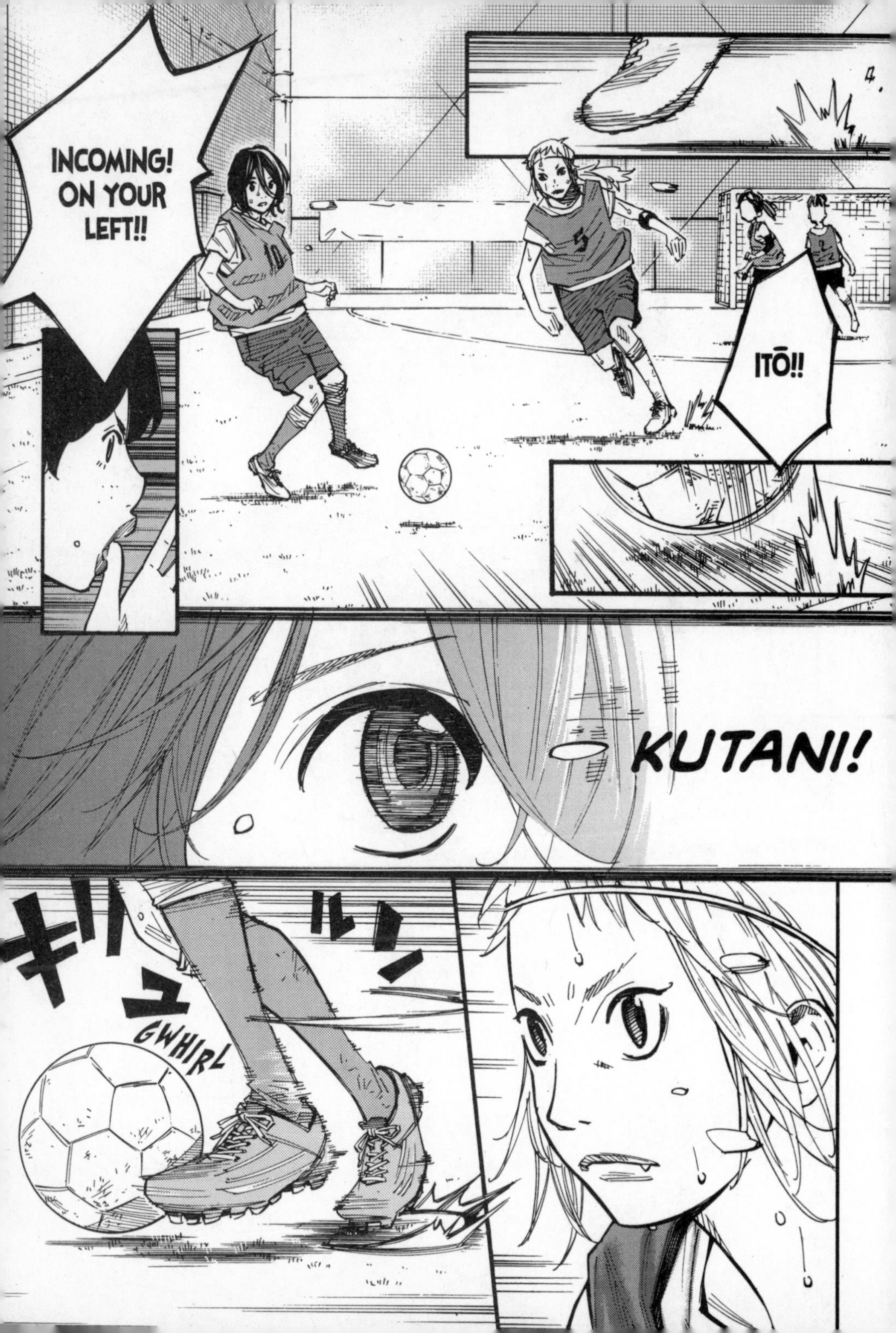
INCOMING! ON YOUR LEFT!!
ITŌ!!
KUTANI!
GWHIRL

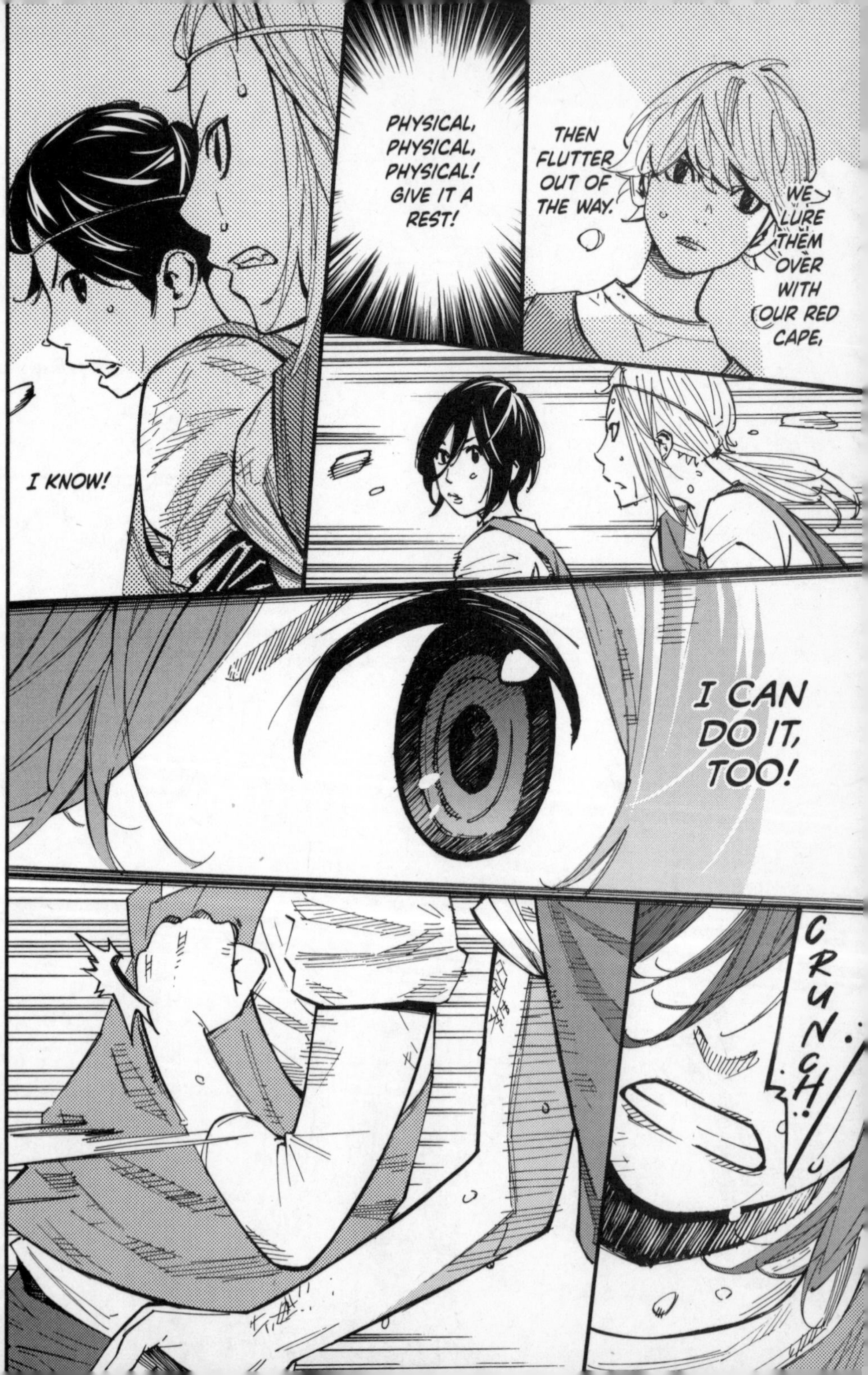
WE LURE THEM OVER WITH OUR RED CAPE,
THEN FLUTTER OUT OF THE WAY.
PHYSICAL, PHYSICAL, PHYSICAL! GIVE IT A REST!
I KNOW!
I CAN DO IT, TOO!
CRUNCH..!!

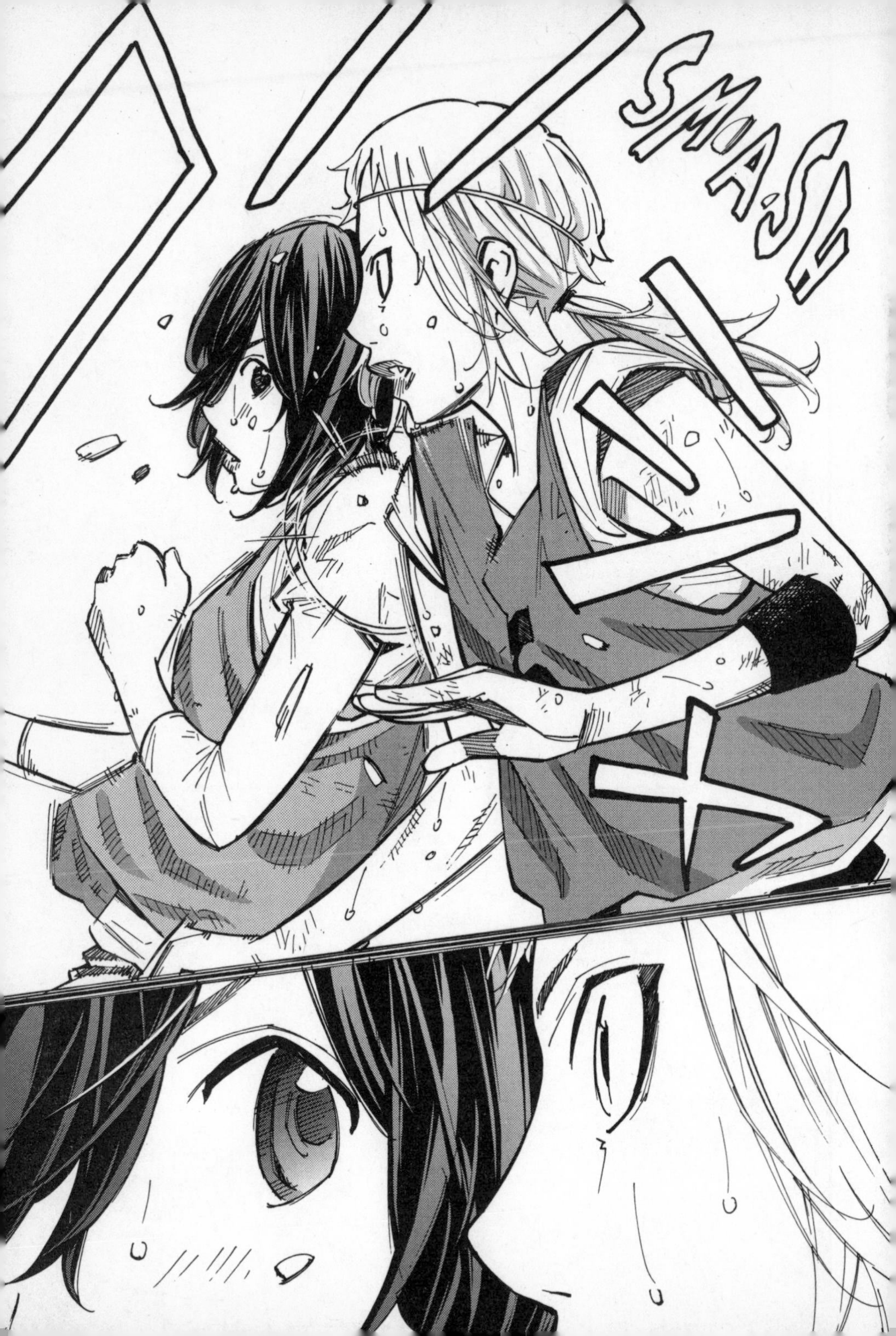
SMASH!!

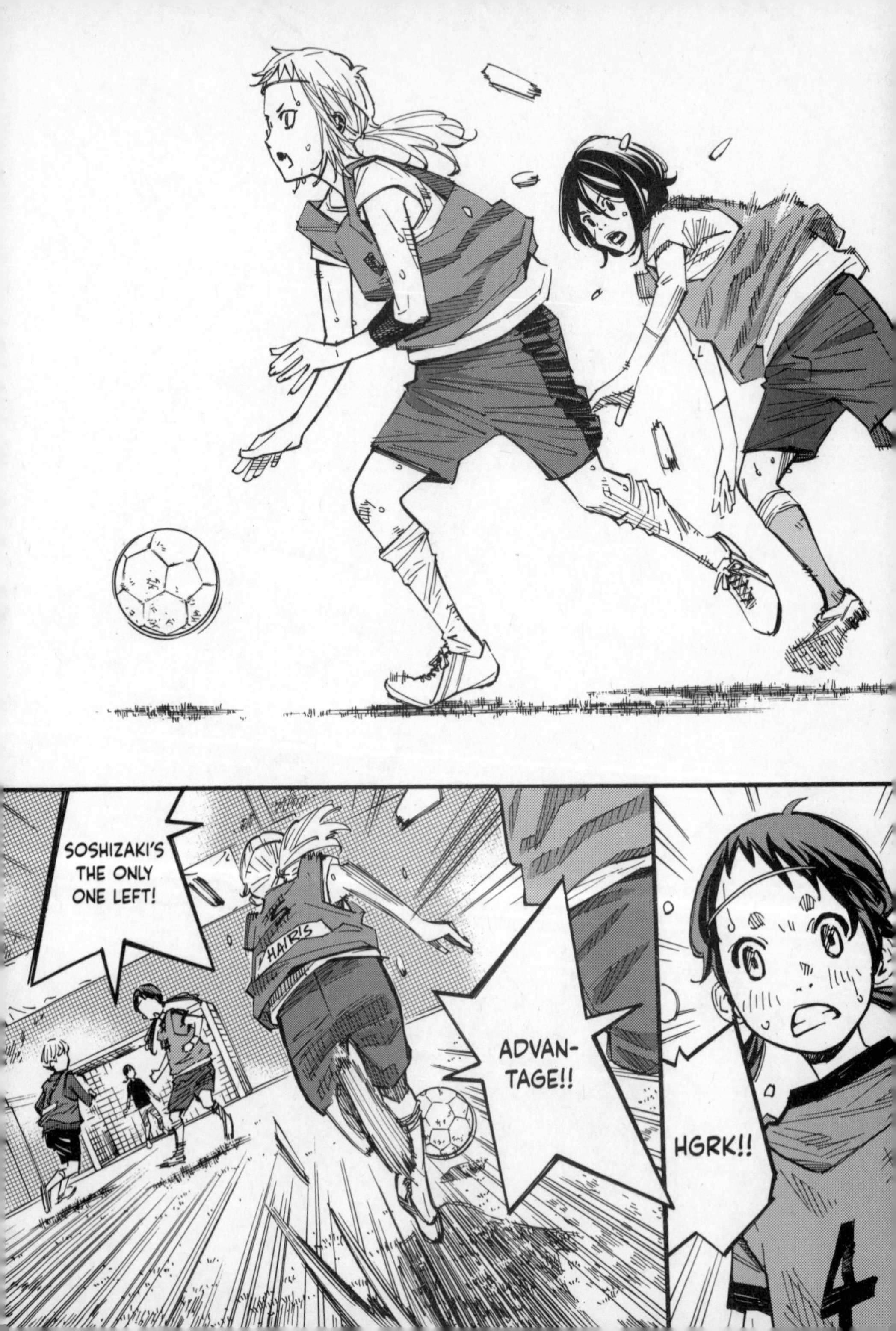
HGRK!!
SOSHIZAKI'S THE ONLY ONE LEFT!
ADVAN-TAGE!!
HAIRIS
4

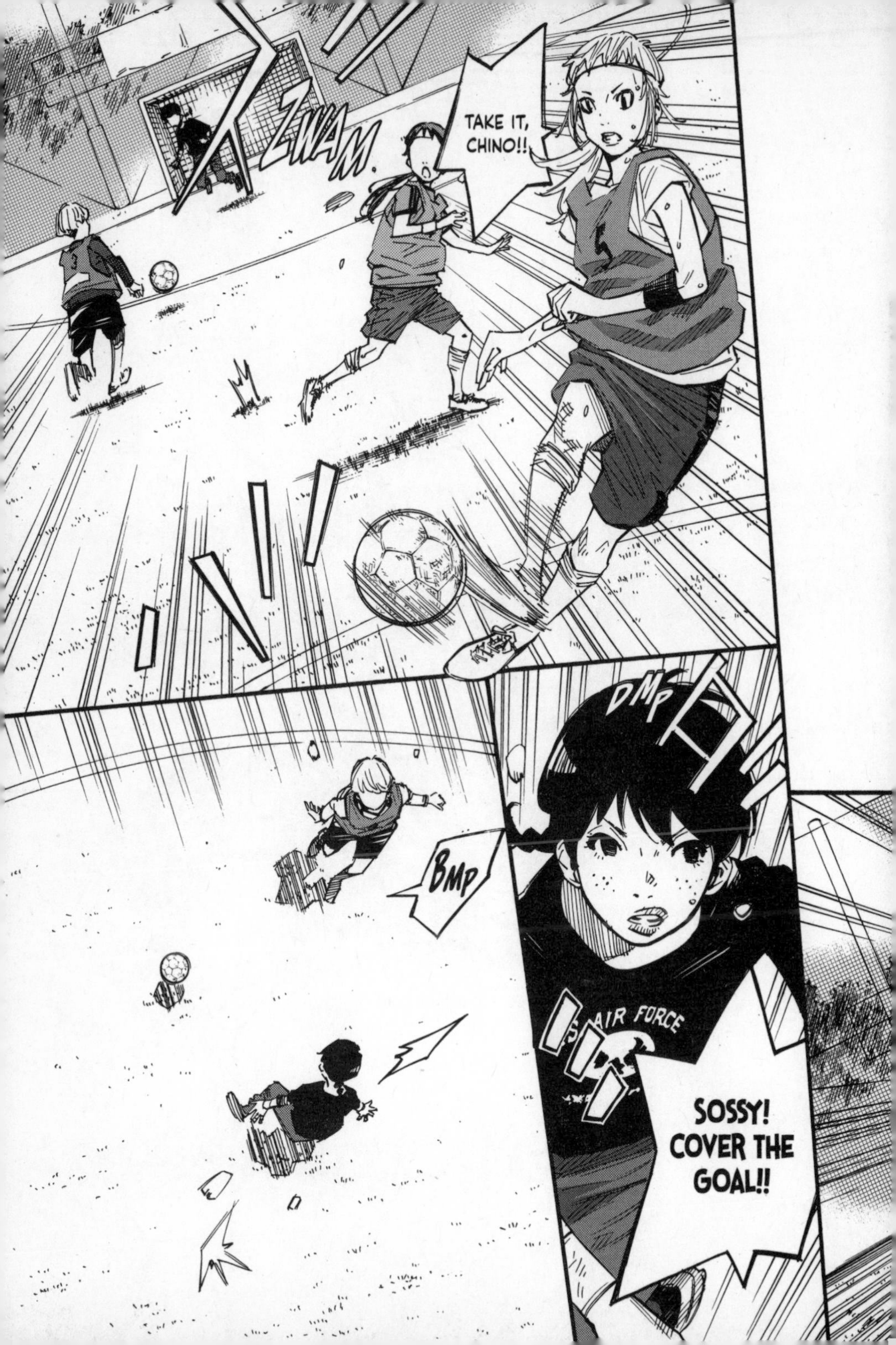
TAKE IT, CHINO!!
ZWAM
DMP
AIR FORCE
SOSSY! COVER THE GOAL!!
BMP

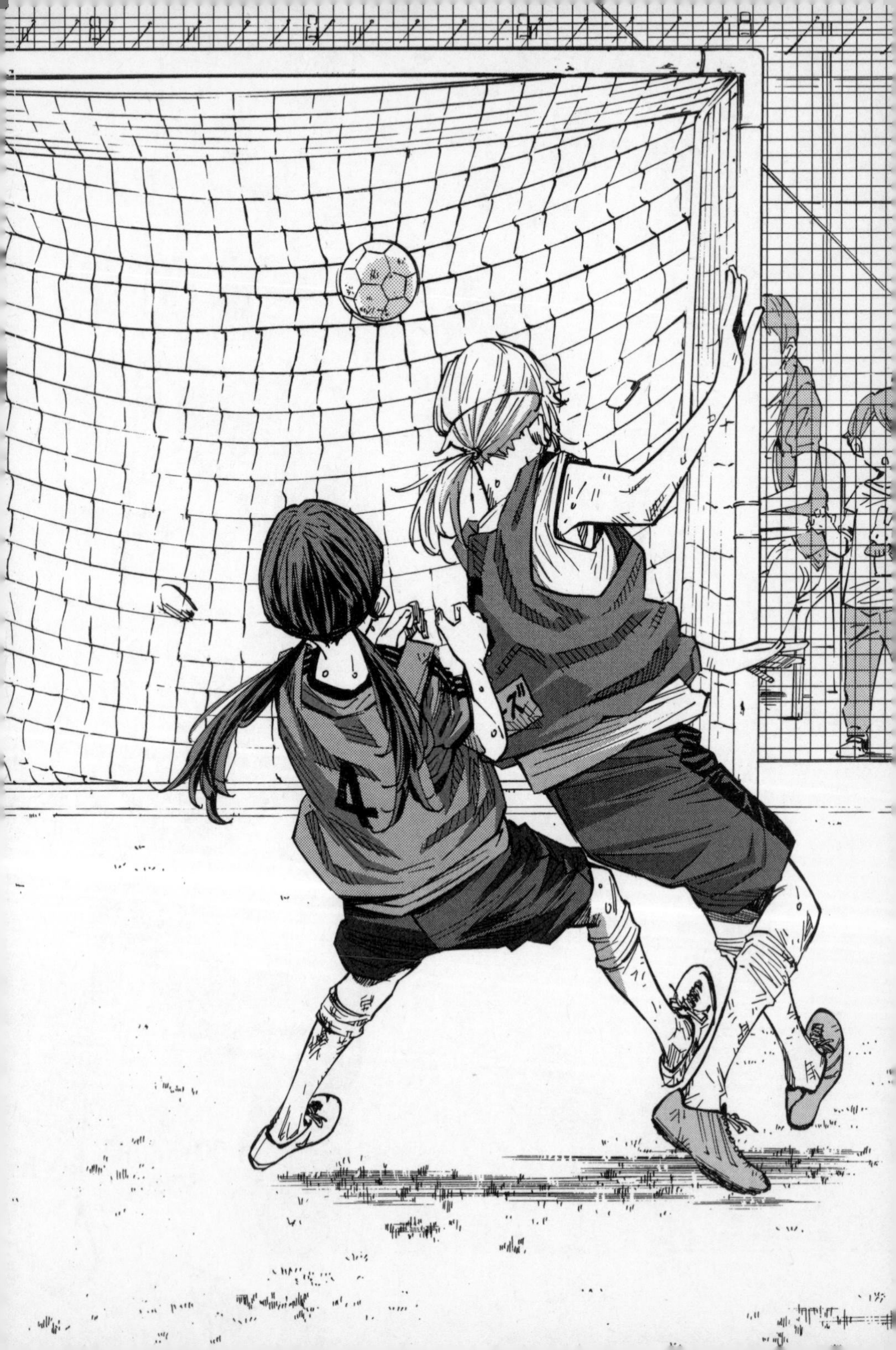

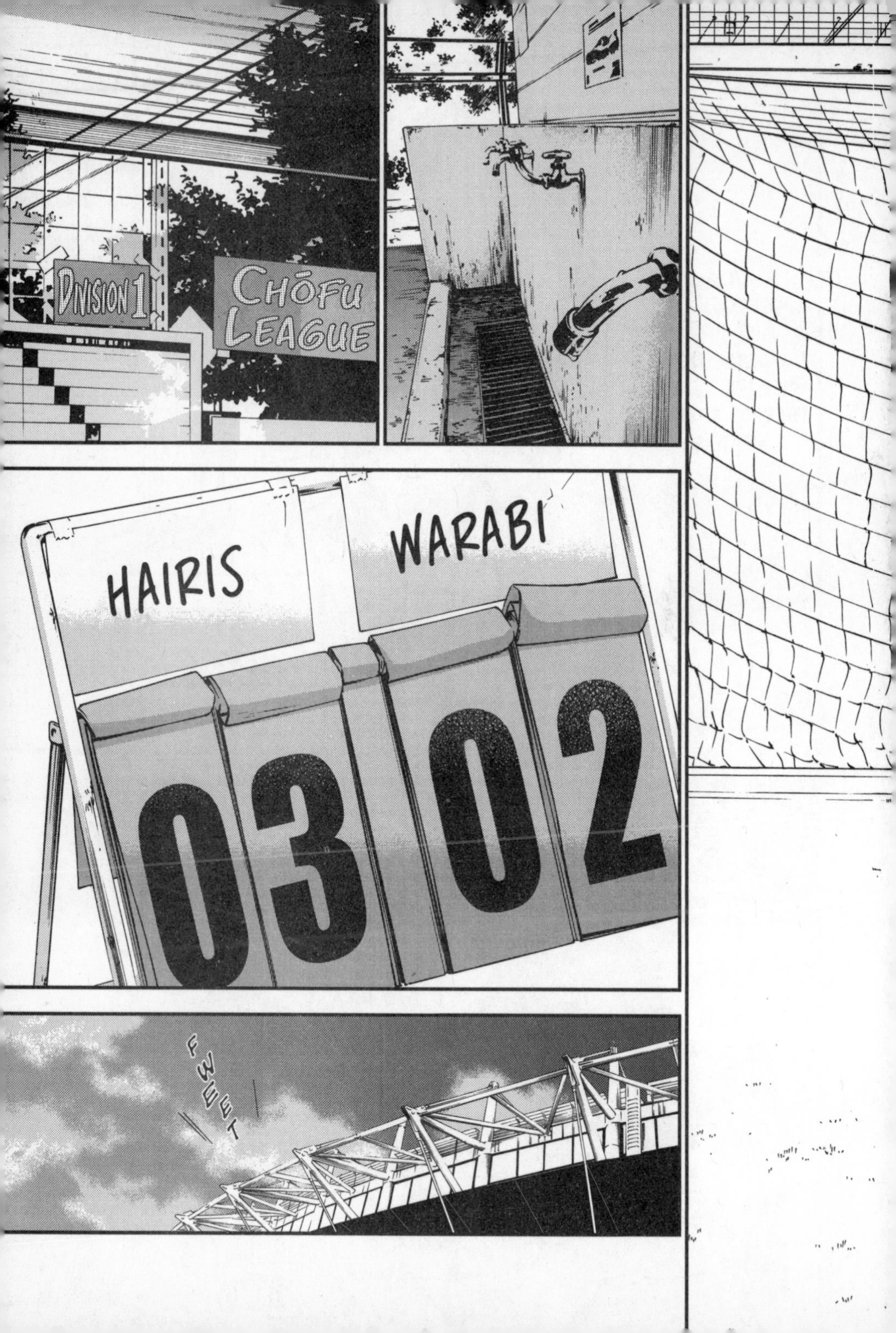
CHŌFU LEAGUE
DIVISION 1
HAIRIS
WARABI
03 02
FWEET

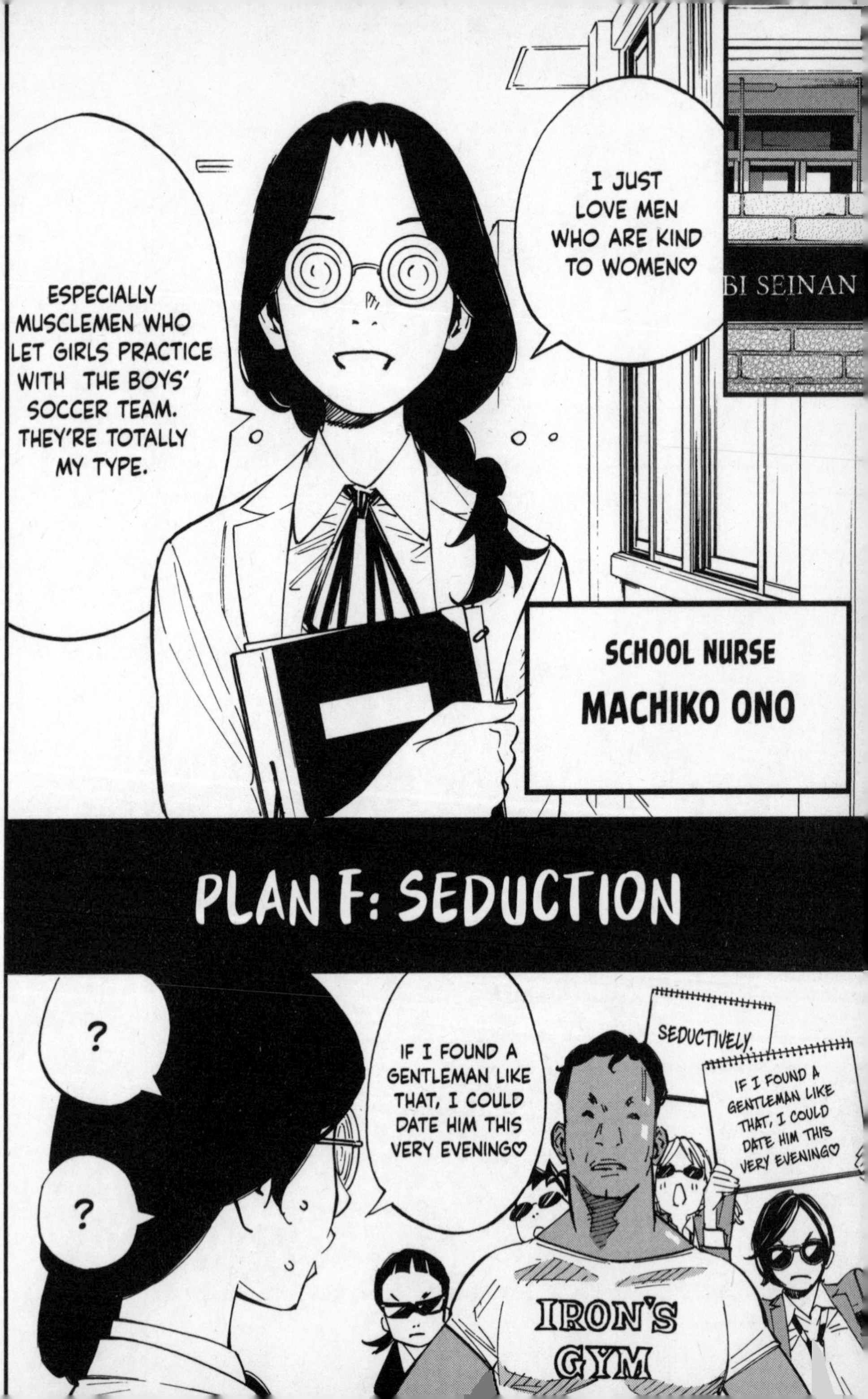
BI SEINAN
I JUST LOVE MEN WHO ARE KIND TO WOMEN♡
ESPECIALLY MUSCLEMEN WHO LET GIRLS PRACTICE WITH THE BOYS' SOCCER TEAM. THEY'RE TOTALLY MY TYPE.
SCHOOL NURSE
MACHIKO ONO
PLAN F: SEDUCTION
SEDUCTIVELY.
IF I FOUND A GENTLEMAN LIKE THAT, I COULD DATE HIM THIS VERY EVENING♡
IF I FOUND A GENTLEMAN LIKE THAT, I COULD DATE HIM THIS VERY EVENING♡
?
?
IRON'S GYM

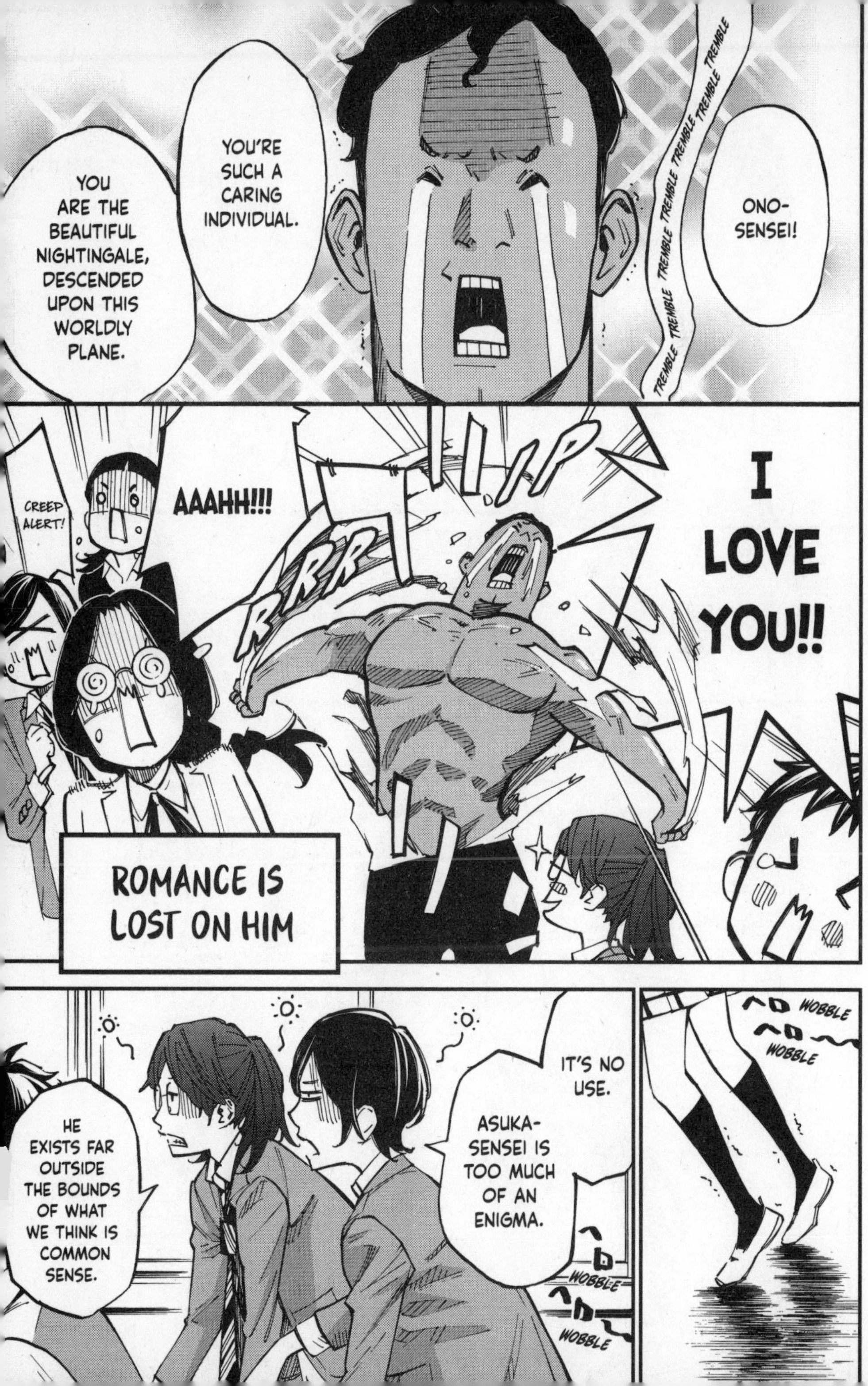
ONO-SENSEI!
TREMBLE TREMBLE TREMBLE TREMBLE TREMBLE TREMBLE TREMBLE
YOU'RE SUCH A CARING INDIVIDUAL.
YOU ARE THE BEAUTIFUL NIGHTINGALE, DESCENDED UPON THIS WORLDLY PLANE.
I LOVE YOU!!
AAAHH!!!
CREEP ALERT!
ROMANCE IS LOST ON HIM
WOBBLE
WOBBLE
IT'S NO USE.
ASUKA-SENSEI IS TOO MUCH OF AN ENIGMA.
WOBBLE
WOBBLE
HE EXISTS FAR OUTSIDE THE BOUNDS OF WHAT WE THINK IS COMMON SENSE.

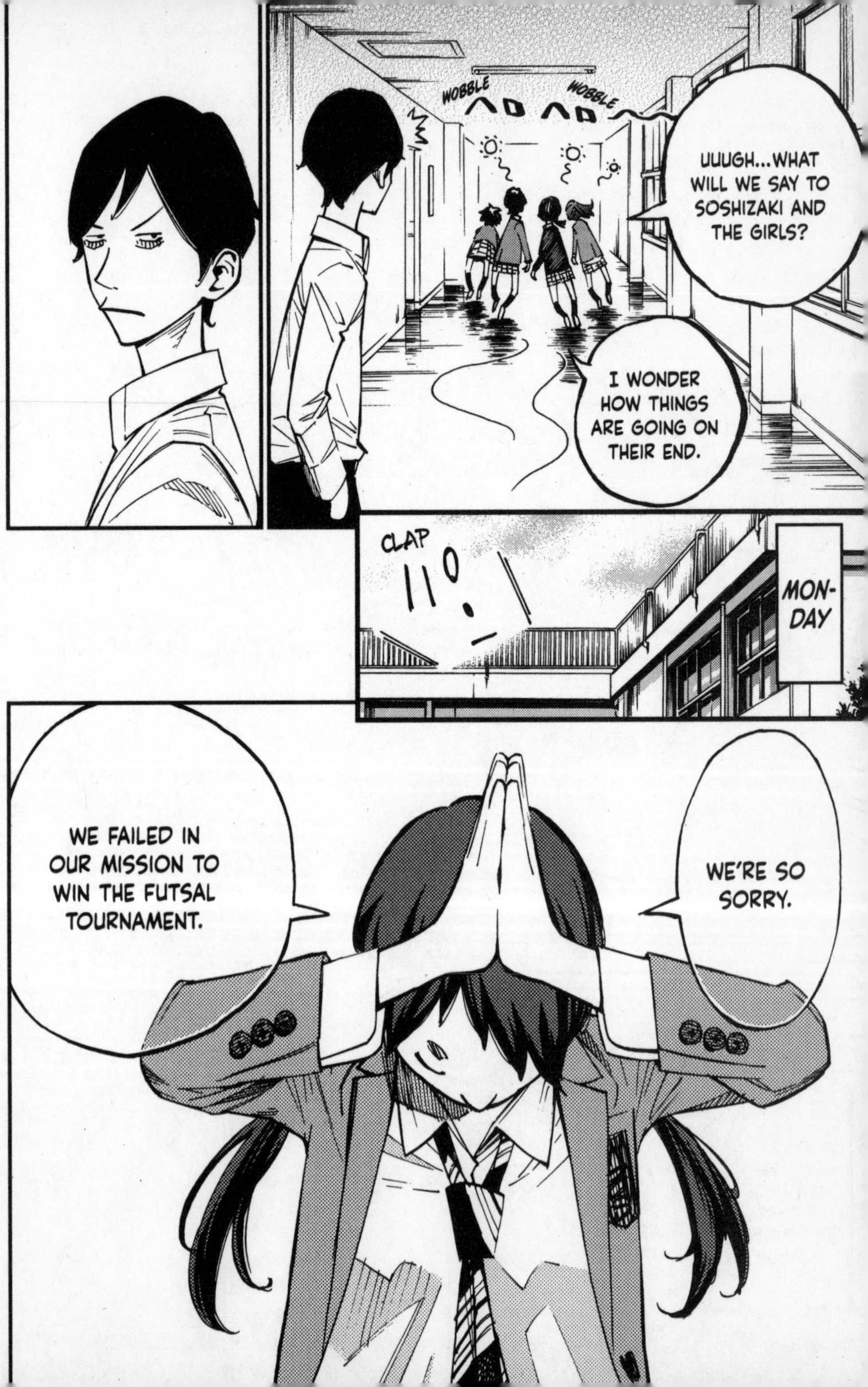
WOBBLE
WOBBLE
UUUGH...WHAT WILL WE SAY TO SOSHIZAKI AND THE GIRLS?
I WONDER HOW THINGS ARE GOING ON THEIR END.
MON-DAY
CLAP
WE'RE SO SORRY.
WE FAILED IN OUR MISSION TO WIN THE FUTSAL TOURNAMENT.

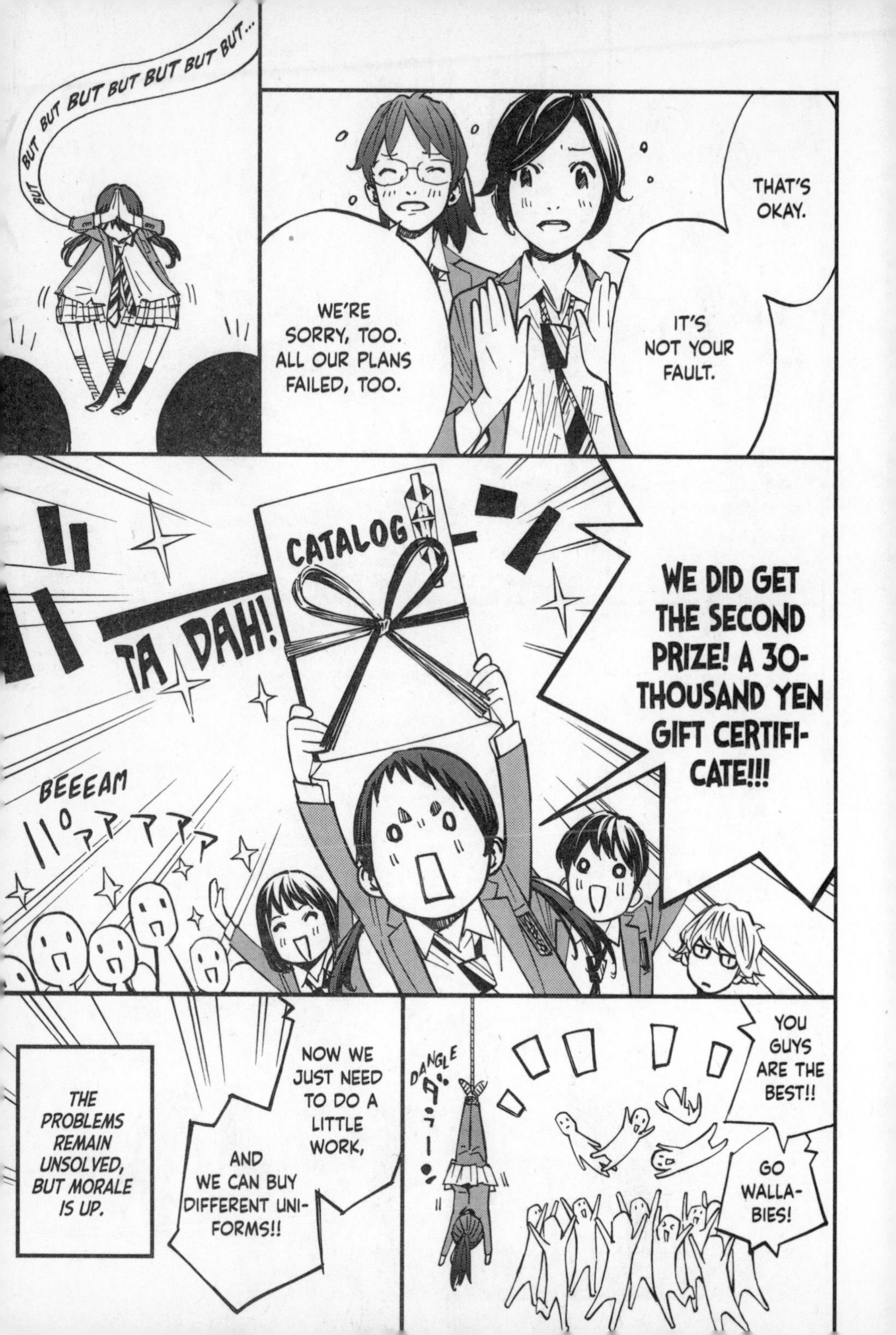
THAT'S OKAY.
IT'S NOT YOUR FAULT.
WE'RE SORRY, TOO. ALL OUR PLANS FAILED, TOO.
BUT BUT BUT BUT BUT BUT BUT...
WE DID GET THE SECOND PRIZE! A 30-THOUSAND YEN GIFT CERTIFICATE!!!
CATALOG
TA DAH!
BEEEAM
YOU GUYS ARE THE BEST!!
GO WALLABIES!
DANGLE
NOW WE JUST NEED TO DO A LITTLE WORK,
AND WE CAN BUY DIFFERENT UNIFORMS!!
THE PROBLEMS REMAIN UNSOLVED, BUT MORALE IS UP.

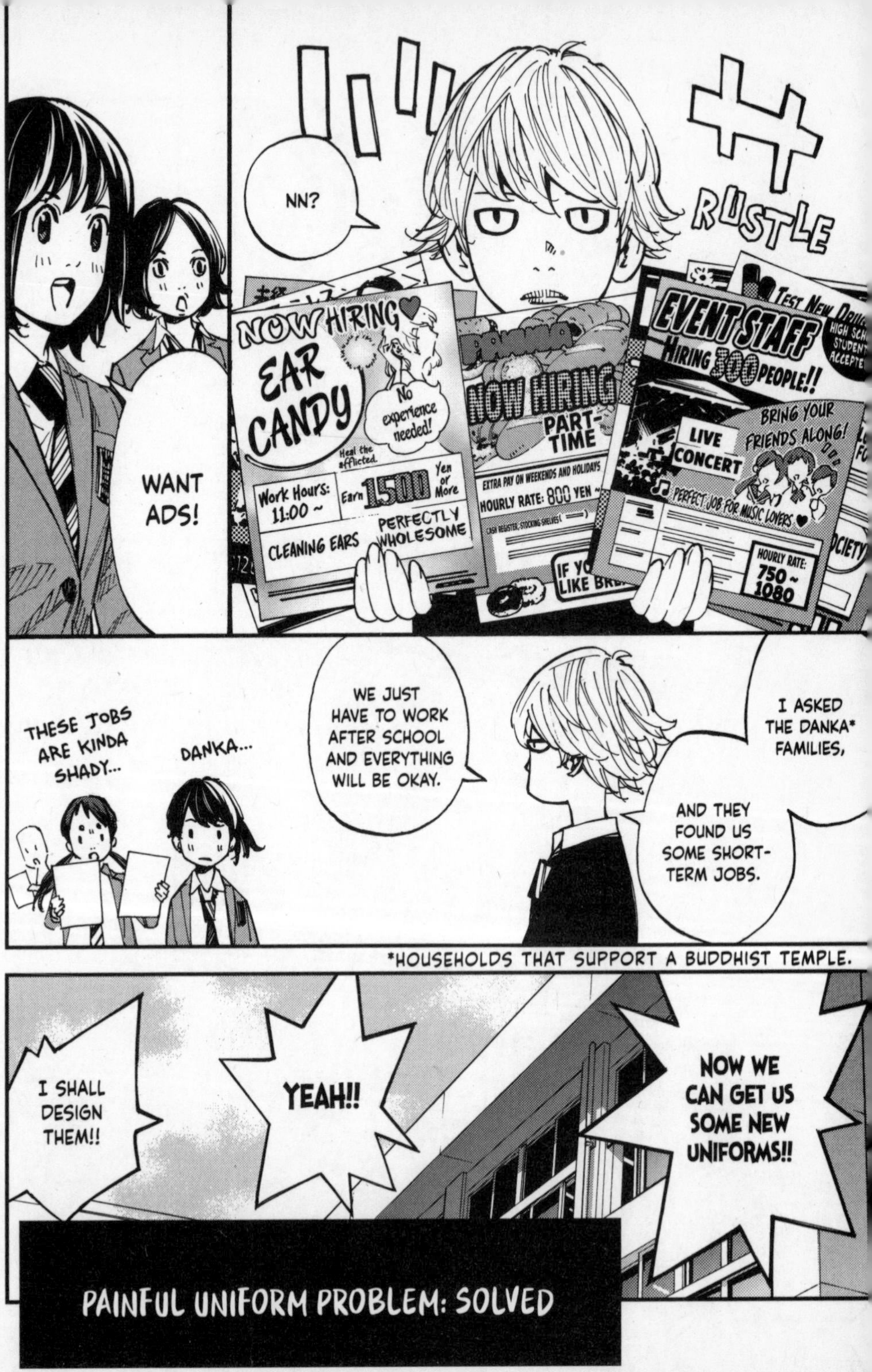
NN?
RUSTLE
TEST NEW DRUG
EVENT STAFF
HIRING 300 PEOPLE!!
BRING YOUR FRIENDS ALONG!
LIVE CONCERT
PERFECT JOB FOR MUSIC LOVERS
HOURLY RATE: 750 ~ 1080
NOW HIRING
PART-TIME
EXTRA PAY ON WEEKENDS AND HOLIDAYS
HOURLY RATE: 800 YEN ~
CASH REGISTER, STOCKING SHELVES
NOW HIRING
EAR CANDY
No experience needed!
Heal the afflicted.
Work Hours: 11:00 ~
Earn 1500 Yen or More
CLEANING EARS
PERFECTLY WHOLESOME
WANT ADS!
I ASKED THE DANKA* FAMILIES,
AND THEY FOUND US SOME SHORT-TERM JOBS.
WE JUST HAVE TO WORK AFTER SCHOOL AND EVERYTHING WILL BE OKAY.
DANKA...
THESE JOBS ARE KINDA SHADY...
*HOUSEHOLDS THAT SUPPORT A BUDDHIST TEMPLE.
NOW WE CAN GET US SOME NEW UNIFORMS!!
YEAH!!
I SHALL DESIGN THEM!!
PAINFUL UNIFORM PROBLEM: SOLVED

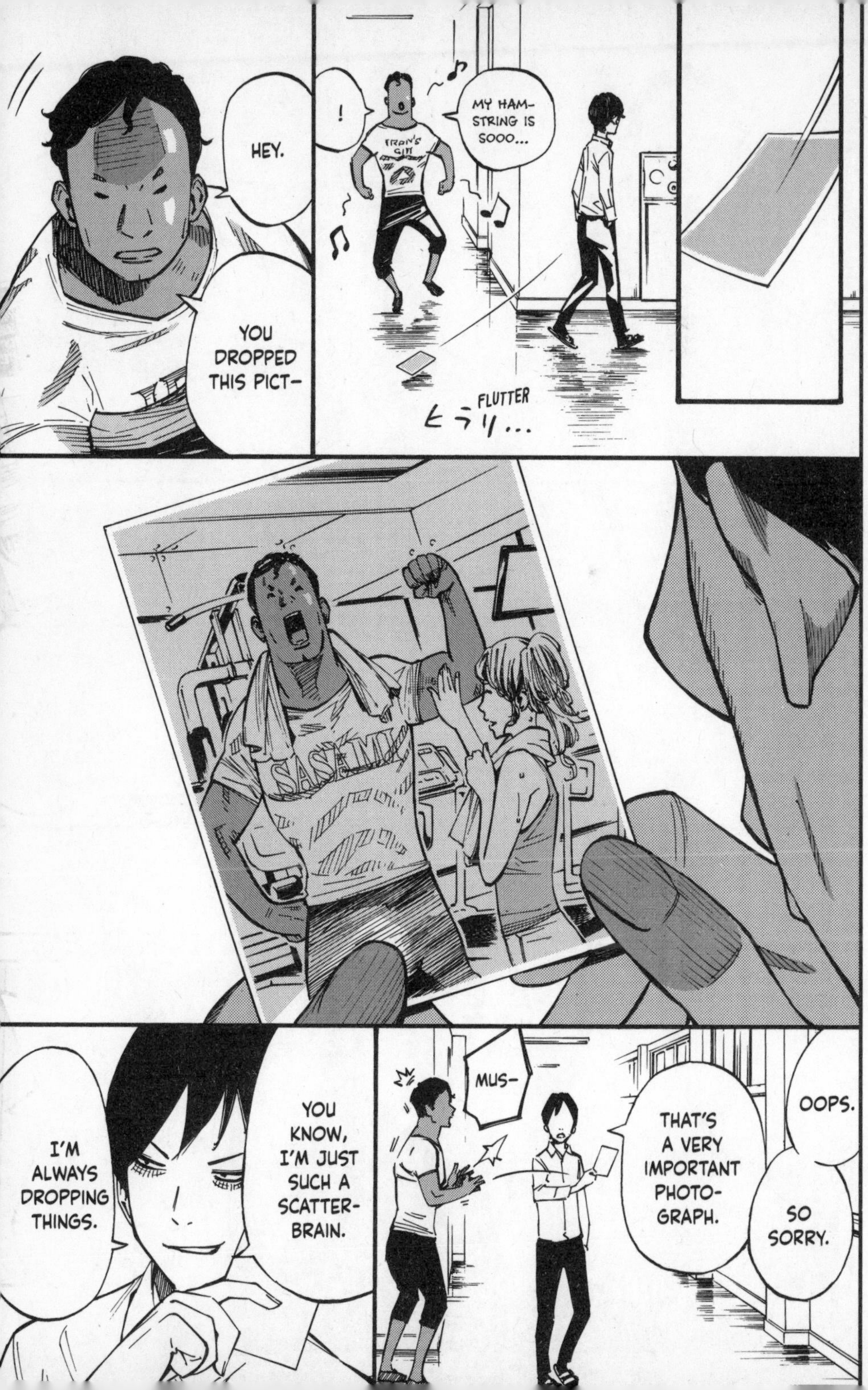
MY HAM-STRING IS SOOO...
!
FLUTTER
ヒラリ…
HEY.
YOU DROPPED THIS PICT-
OOPS.
SO SORRY.
THAT'S A VERY IMPORTANT PHOTO-GRAPH.
MUS-
YOU KNOW, I'M JUST SUCH A SCATTER-BRAIN.
I'M ALWAYS DROPPING THINGS.

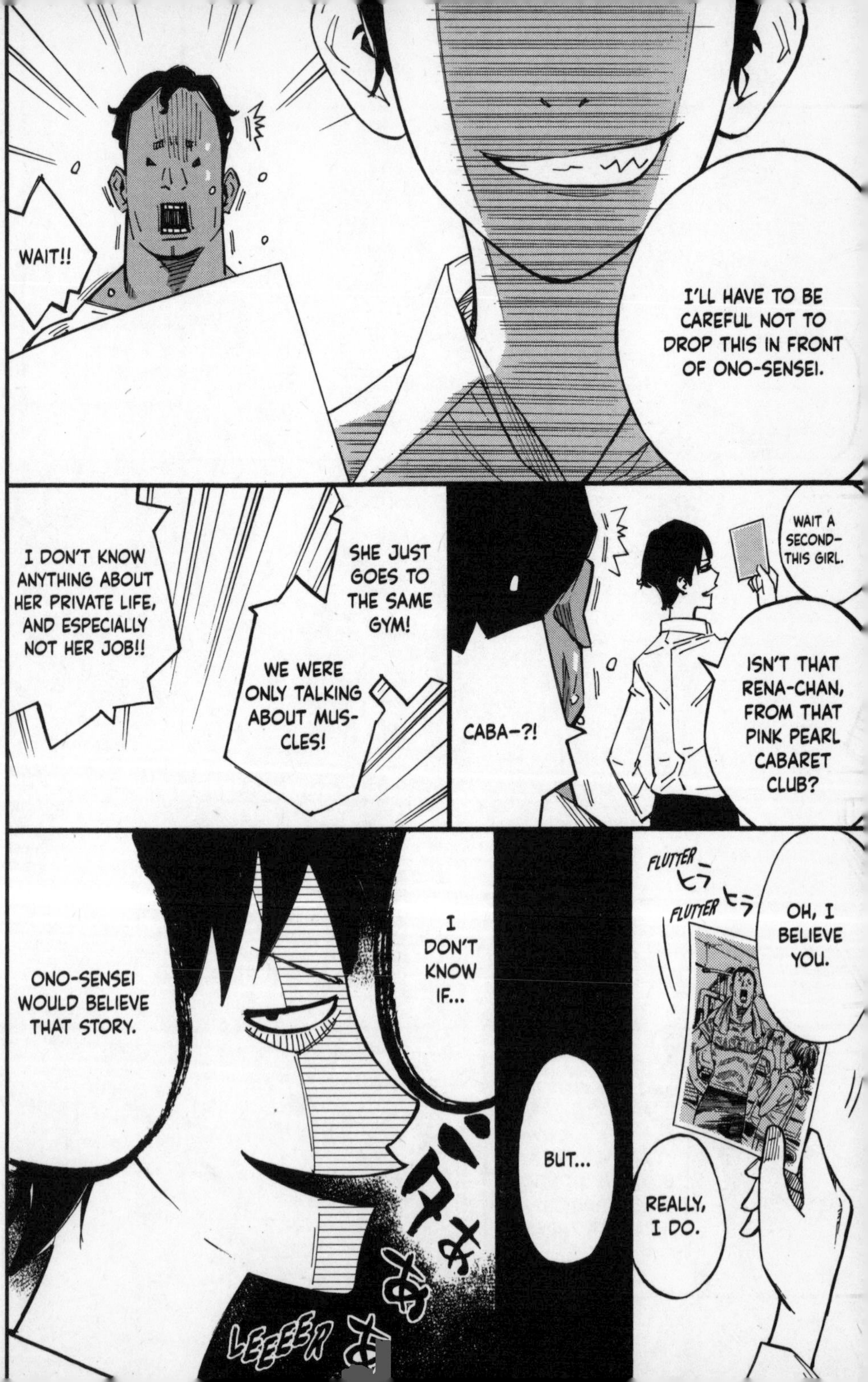
I'LL HAVE TO BE CAREFUL NOT TO DROP THIS IN FRONT OF ONO-SENSEI.
WAIT!!
WAIT A SECOND—THIS GIRL.
ISN'T THAT RENA-CHAN, FROM THAT PINK PEARL CABARET CLUB?
CABA—?!
SHE JUST GOES TO THE SAME GYM!
WE WERE ONLY TALKING ABOUT MUS-CLES!
I DON'T KNOW ANYTHING ABOUT HER PRIVATE LIFE, AND ESPECIALLY NOT HER JOB!!
FLUTTER
FLUTTER
OH, I BELIEVE YOU.
REALLY, I DO.
BUT...
I DON'T KNOW IF...
ONO-SENSEI WOULD BELIEVE THAT STORY.
LEEEER

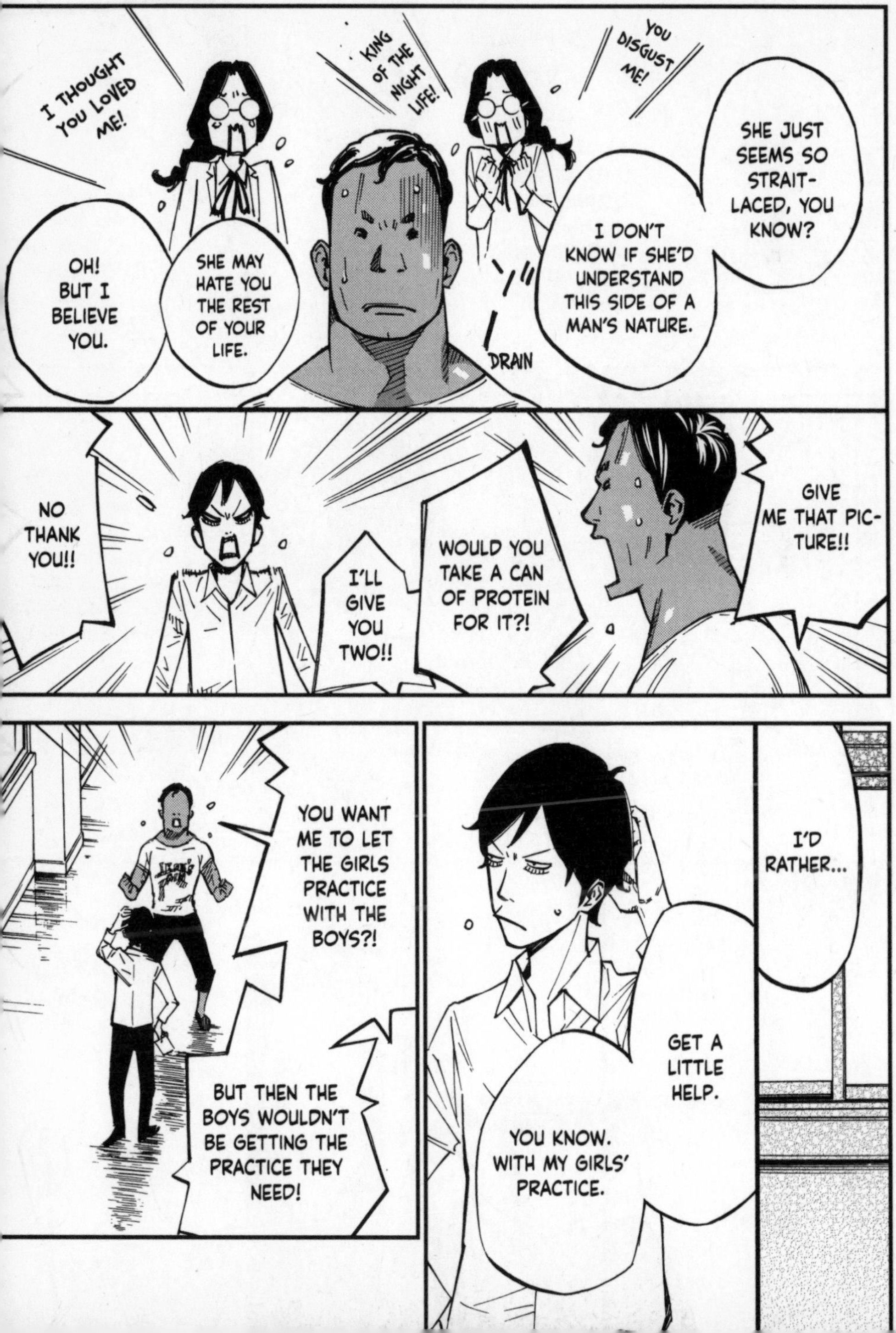
SHE JUST SEEMS SO STRAIT-LACED, YOU KNOW?
I DON'T KNOW IF SHE'D UNDERSTAND THIS SIDE OF A MAN'S NATURE.
YOU DISGUST ME!
DRAIN
KING OF THE NIGHT LIFE!
I THOUGHT YOU LOVED ME!
SHE MAY HATE YOU THE REST OF YOUR LIFE.
OH! BUT I BELIEVE YOU.
GIVE ME THAT PICTURE!!
WOULD YOU TAKE A CAN OF PROTEIN FOR IT?!
I'LL GIVE YOU TWO!!
NO THANK YOU!!
I'D RATHER...
GET A LITTLE HELP.
YOU KNOW. WITH MY GIRLS' PRACTICE.
YOU WANT ME TO LET THE GIRLS PRACTICE WITH THE BOYS?!
BUT THEN THE BOYS WOULDN'T BE GETTING THE PRACTICE THEY NEED!

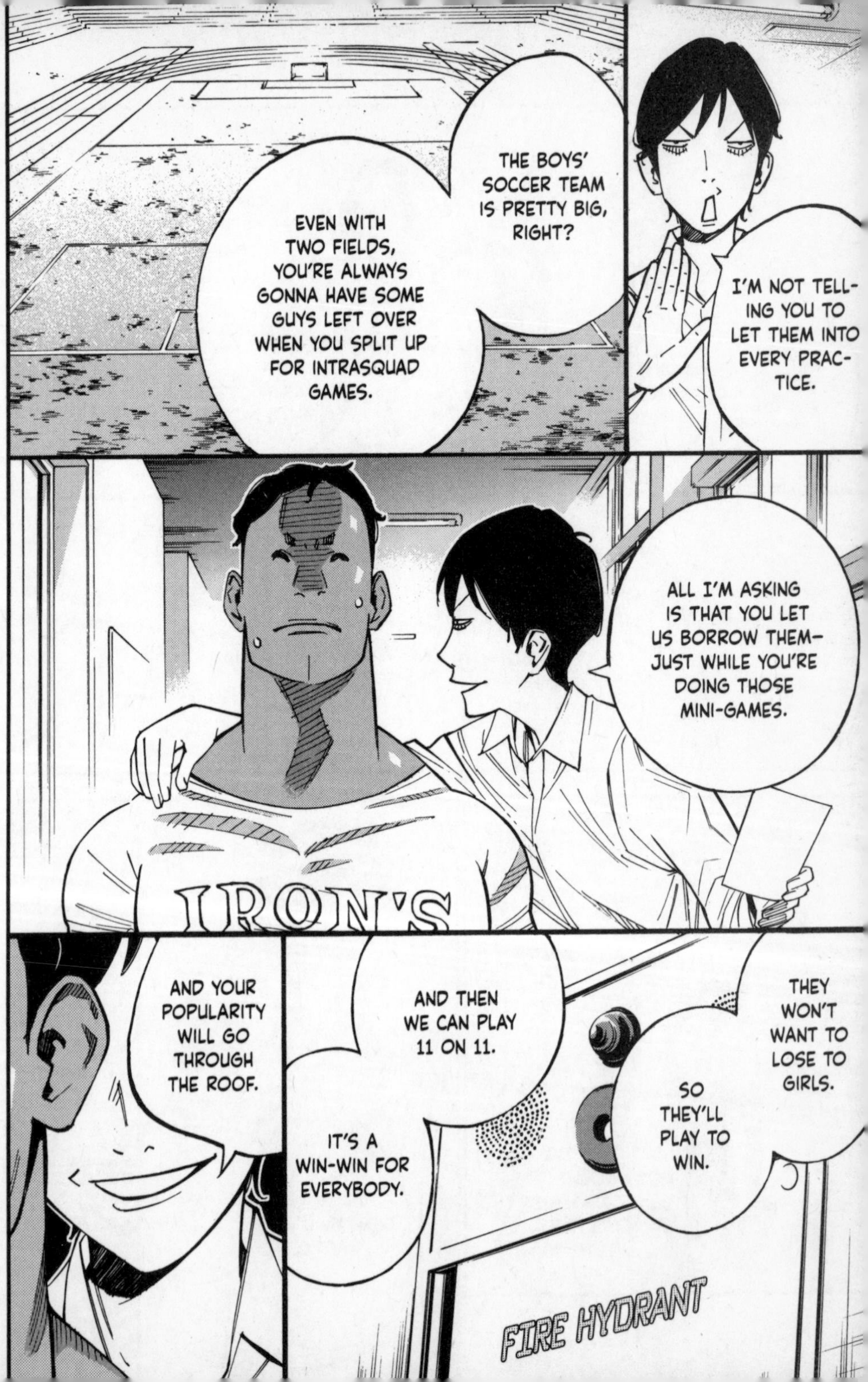
I'M NOT TELLING YOU TO LET THEM INTO EVERY PRACTICE.
THE BOYS' SOCCER TEAM IS PRETTY BIG, RIGHT?
EVEN WITH TWO FIELDS, YOU'RE ALWAYS GONNA HAVE SOME GUYS LEFT OVER WHEN YOU SPLIT UP FOR INTRASQUAD GAMES.
ALL I'M ASKING IS THAT YOU LET US BORROW THEM—JUST WHILE YOU'RE DOING THOSE MINI-GAMES.
IRON'S
THEY WON'T WANT TO LOSE TO GIRLS.
SO THEY'LL PLAY TO WIN.
AND THEN WE CAN PLAY 11 ON 11.
IT'S A WIN-WIN FOR EVERYBODY.
FIRE HYDRANT
AND YOUR POPULARITY WILL GO THROUGH THE ROOF.

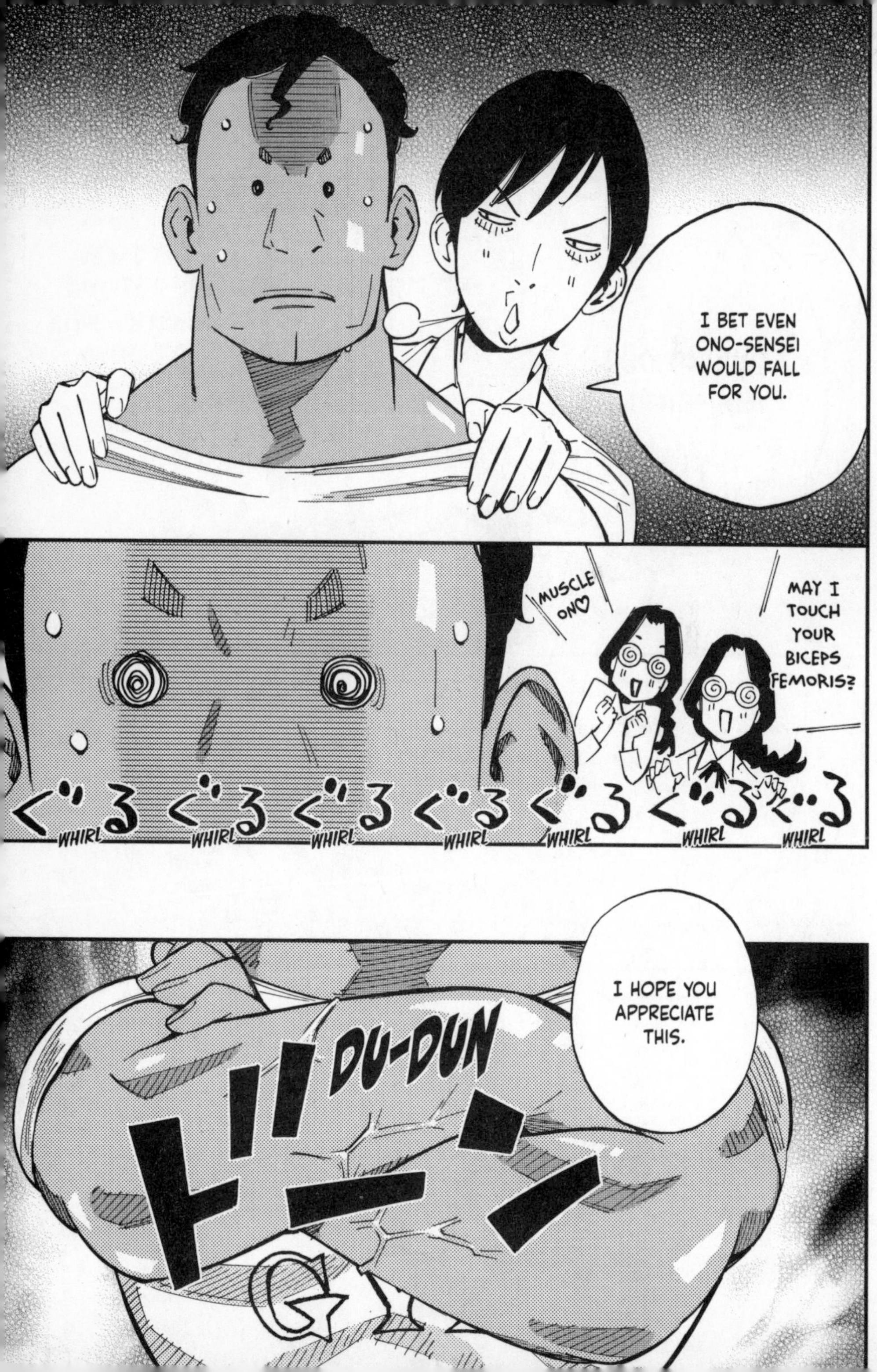
I BET EVEN ONO-SENSEI WOULD FALL FOR YOU.
MAY I TOUCH YOUR BICEPS FEMORIS?
MUSCLE ON♡
ぐるぐるぐるぐるぐるぐるぐるぐるぐるぐるぐるぐるぐるぐる
WHIRL WHIRL WHIRL WHIRL WHIRL WHIRL WHIRL
I HOPE YOU APPRECIATE THIS.
ドーン
DU-DUN

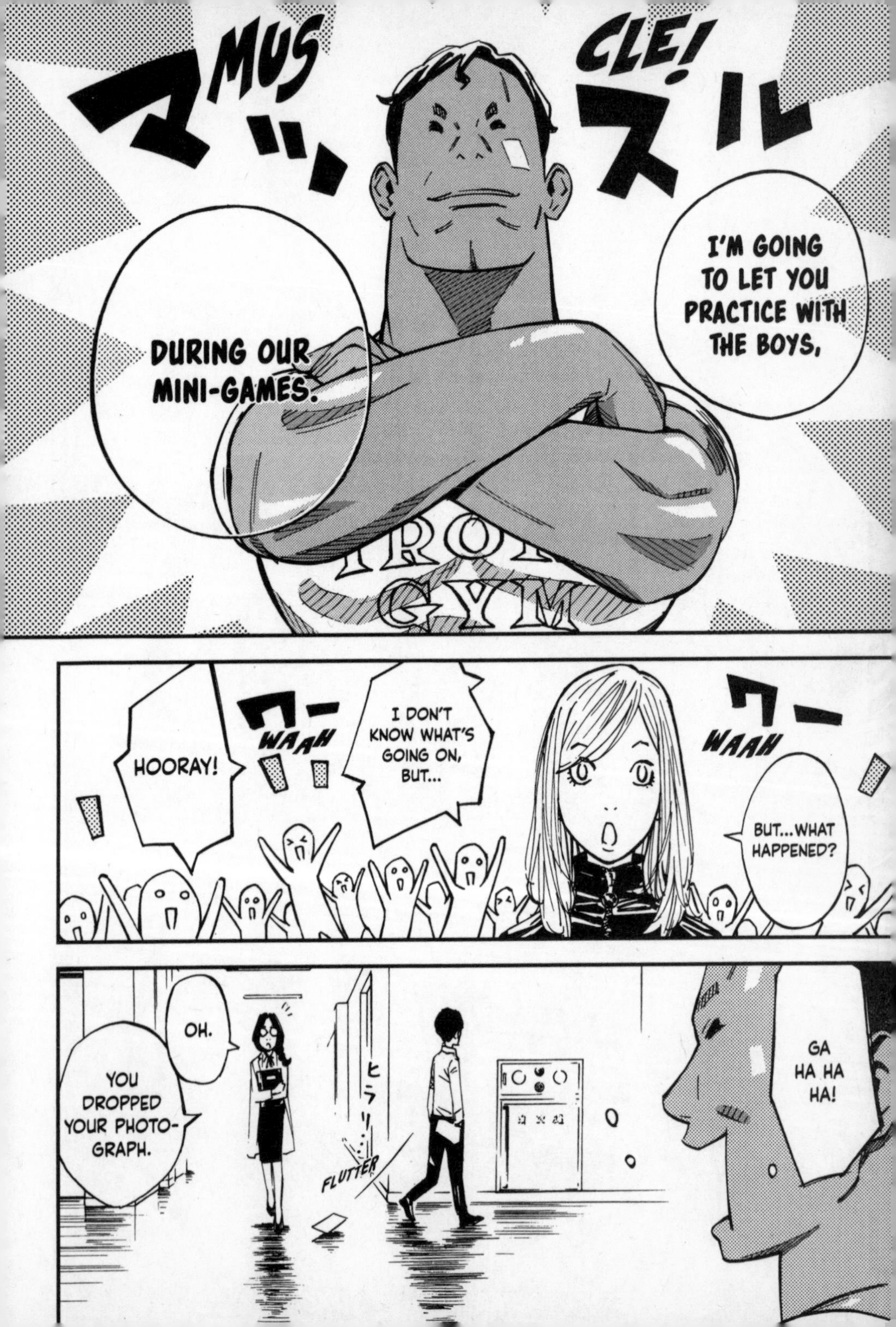
マッスル
MUSCLE!
I'M GOING TO LET YOU PRACTICE WITH THE BOYS,
DURING OUR MINI-GAMES.
ワー
WAAH
BUT...WHAT HAPPENED?
I DON'T KNOW WHAT'S GOING ON, BUT...
ワー
WAAH
HOORAY!
GA HA HA HA!
ヒラリ
FLUTTER
OH.
YOU DROPPED YOUR PHOTO-GRAPH.

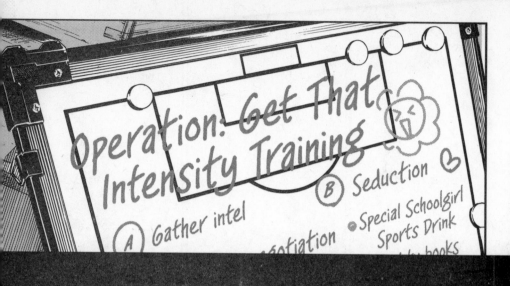

Operation: Get That Intensity Training

(A) Gather intel

(B) Seduction ♡

...gotiation ● Special Schoolgirl Sports Drink
...ly books

ACCOMPLISHED.

50
THIS POINT

THIS POINT

東京都
Tokyo Met.

板橋区
Itabashi Ward.

WARABI

HUP!

HUP-TWO!!

HUP-TWO!!

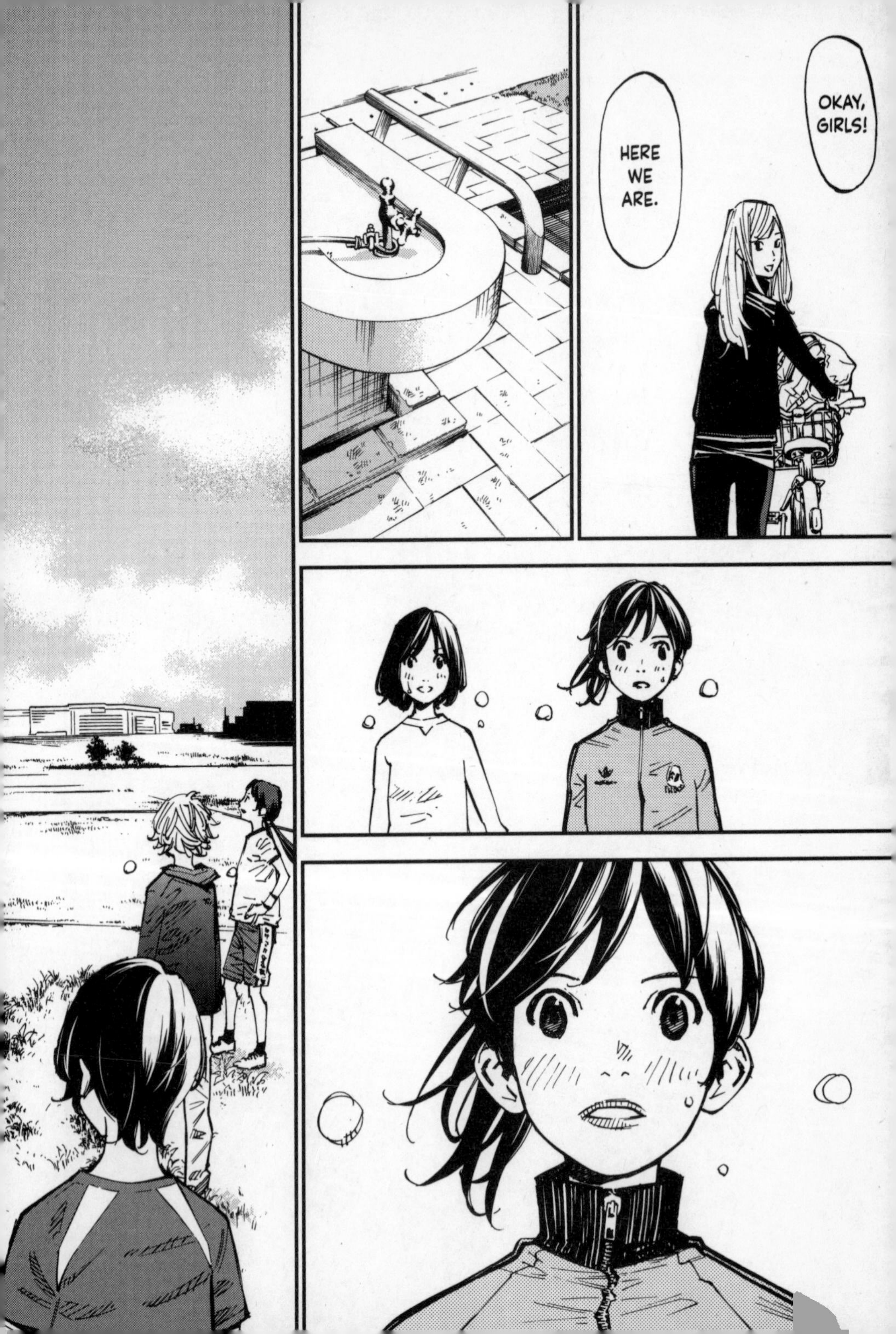
OKAY, GIRLS!
HERE WE ARE.

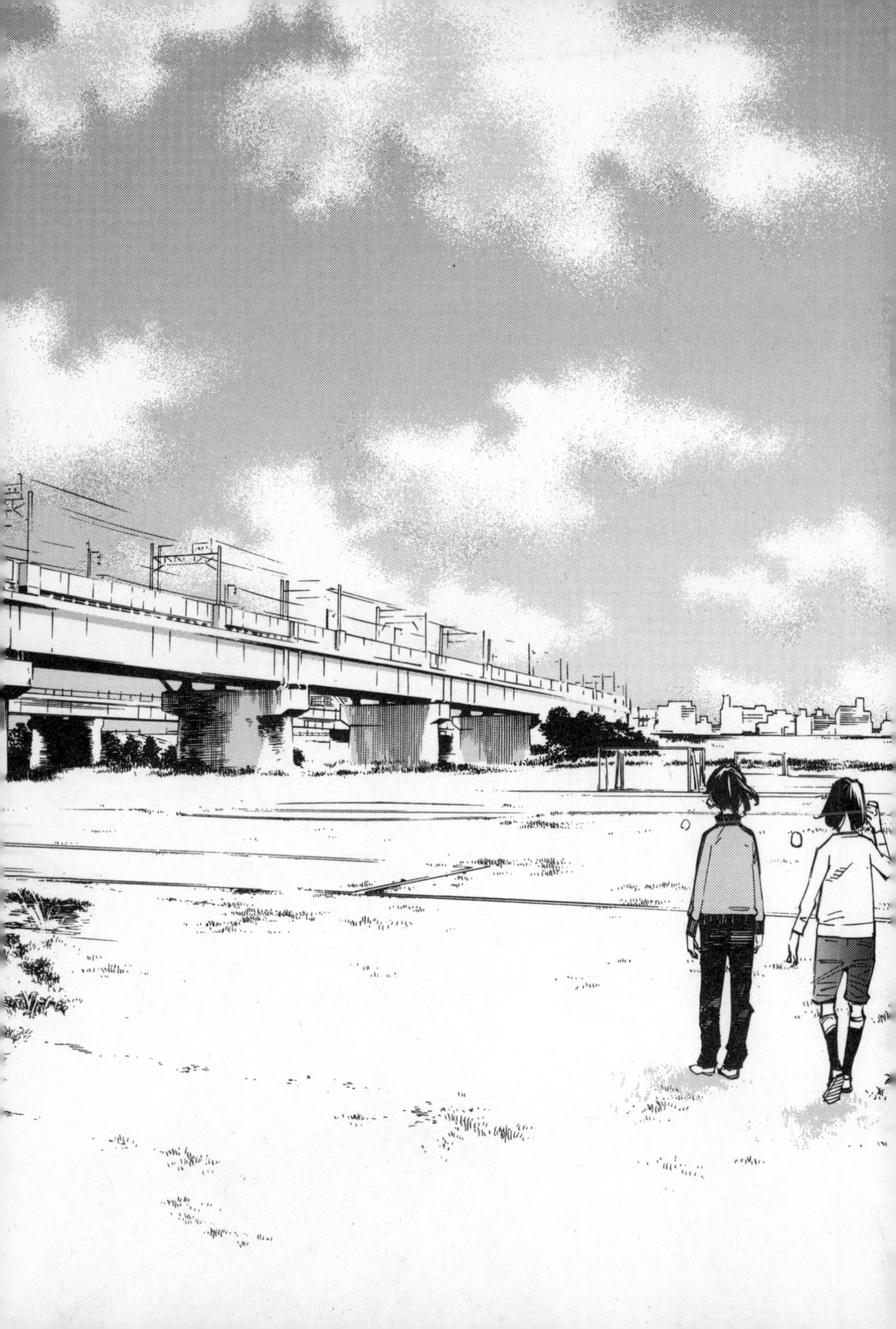

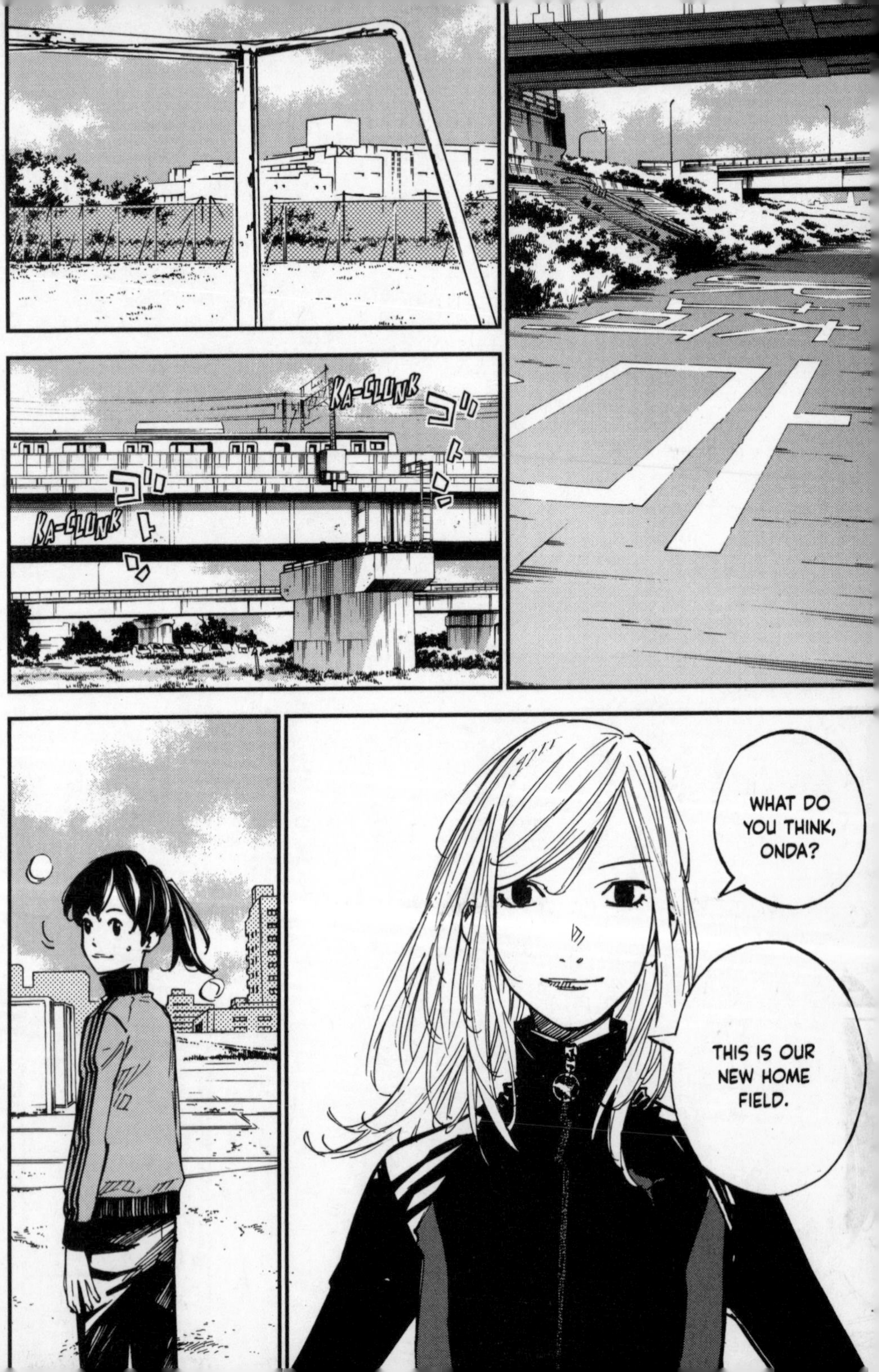
KA-CLUNK
ゴットン
KA-CLUNK
ゴットン
WHAT DO YOU THINK, ONDA?
THIS IS OUR NEW HOME FIELD.

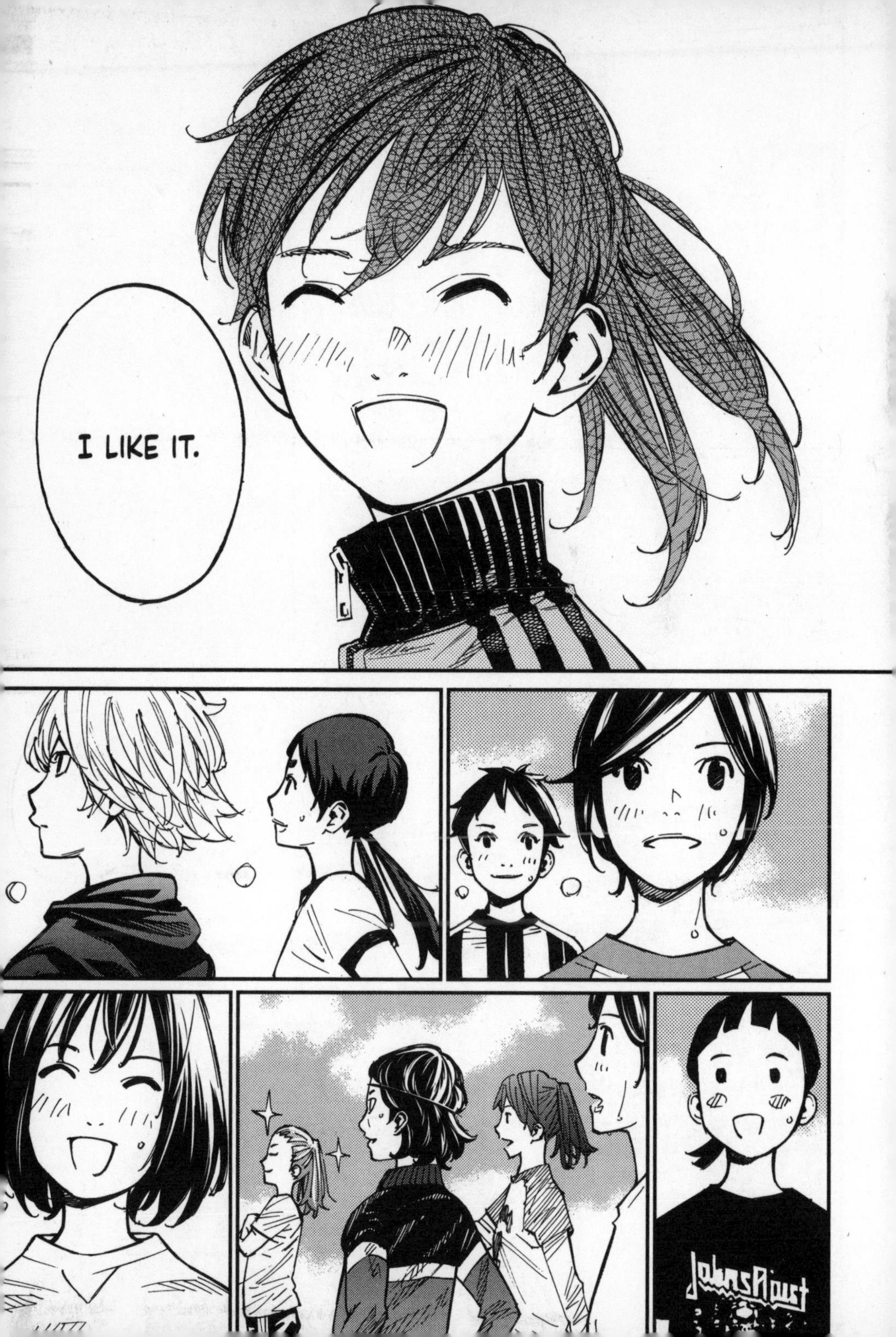
I LIKE IT.
JohnsAoust

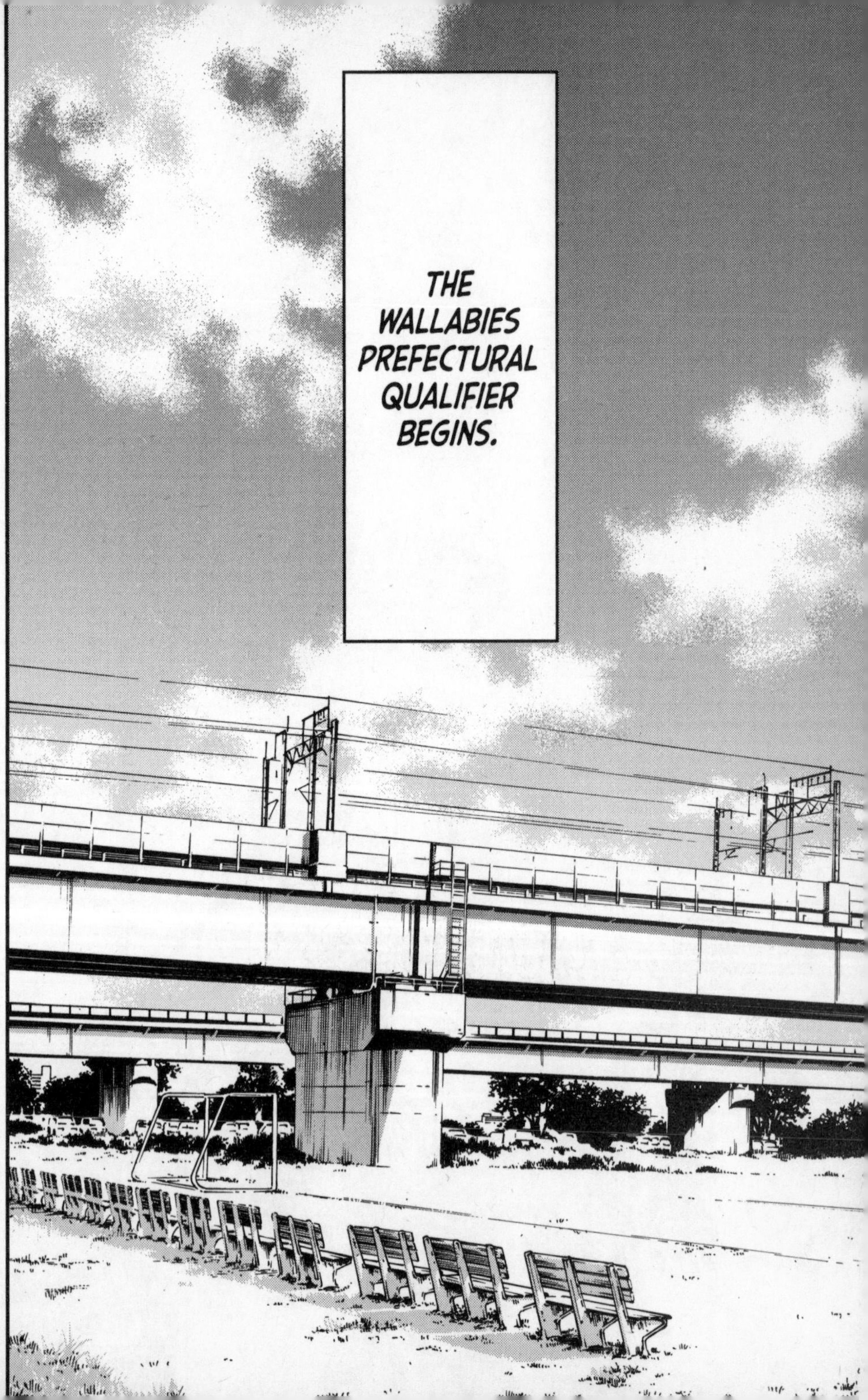
THE WALLABIES PREFECTURAL QUALIFIER BEGINS.

Farewell, My Dear Cramer

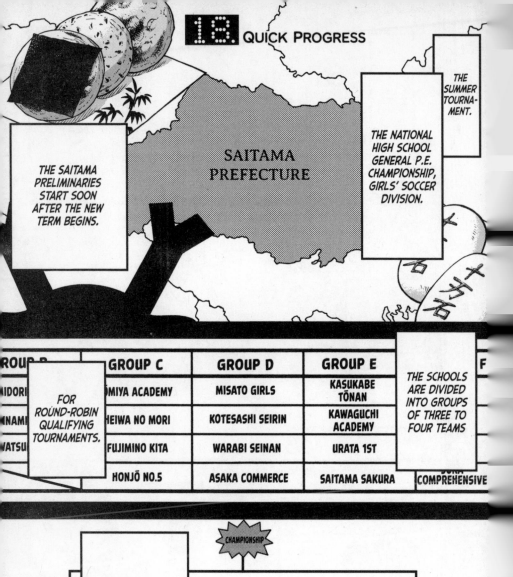

18. QUICK PROGRESS

SAITAMA PREFECTURE

THE SAITAMA PRELIMINARIES START SOON AFTER THE NEW TERM BEGINS.

THE NATIONAL HIGH SCHOOL GENERAL P.E. CHAMPIONSHIP, GIRLS' SOCCER DIVISION.

THE SUMMER TOURNAMENT.

ROUP B		GROUP C	GROUP D	GROUP E		F
MIDORI	FOR ROUND-ROBIN QUALIFYING TOURNAMENTS.	ŌMIYA ACADEMY	MISATO GIRLS	KASUKABE TŌNAN	THE SCHOOLS ARE DIVIDED INTO GROUPS OF THREE TO FOUR TEAMS	
NAMI		HEIWA NO MORI	KOTESASHI SEIRIN	KAWAGUCHI ACADEMY		
ATSU		FUJIMINO KITA	WARABI SEINAN	URATA 1ST		
		HONJŌ NO.5	ASAKA COMMERCE	SAITAMA SAKURA		COMPREHENSIVE

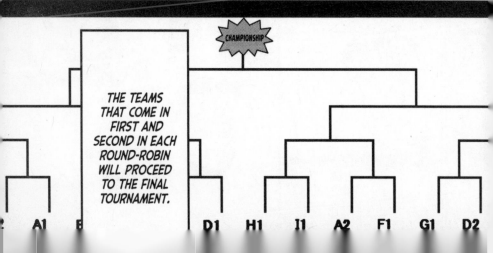

CHAMPIONSHIP

THE TEAMS THAT COME IN FIRST AND SECOND IN EACH ROUND-ROBIN WILL PROCEED TO THE FINAL TOURNAMENT.

A1 D1 H1 I1 A2 F1 G1 D2

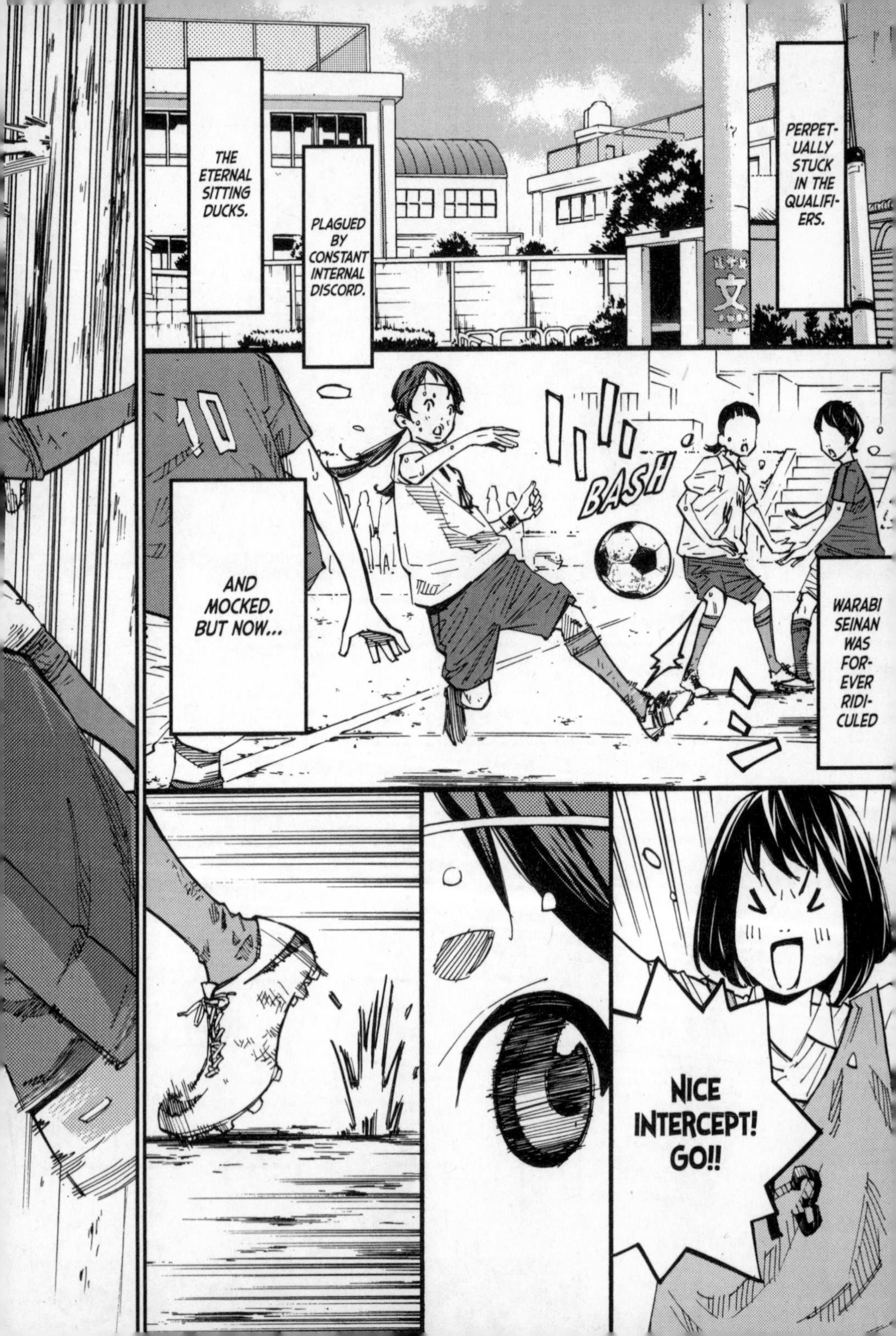
PERPETUALLY STUCK IN THE QUALIFIERS.
PLAGUED BY CONSTANT INTERNAL DISCORD.
THE ETERNAL SITTING DUCKS.
WARABI SEINAN WAS FOREVER RIDICULED
BASH
AND MOCKED. BUT NOW...
NICE INTERCEPT! GO!!

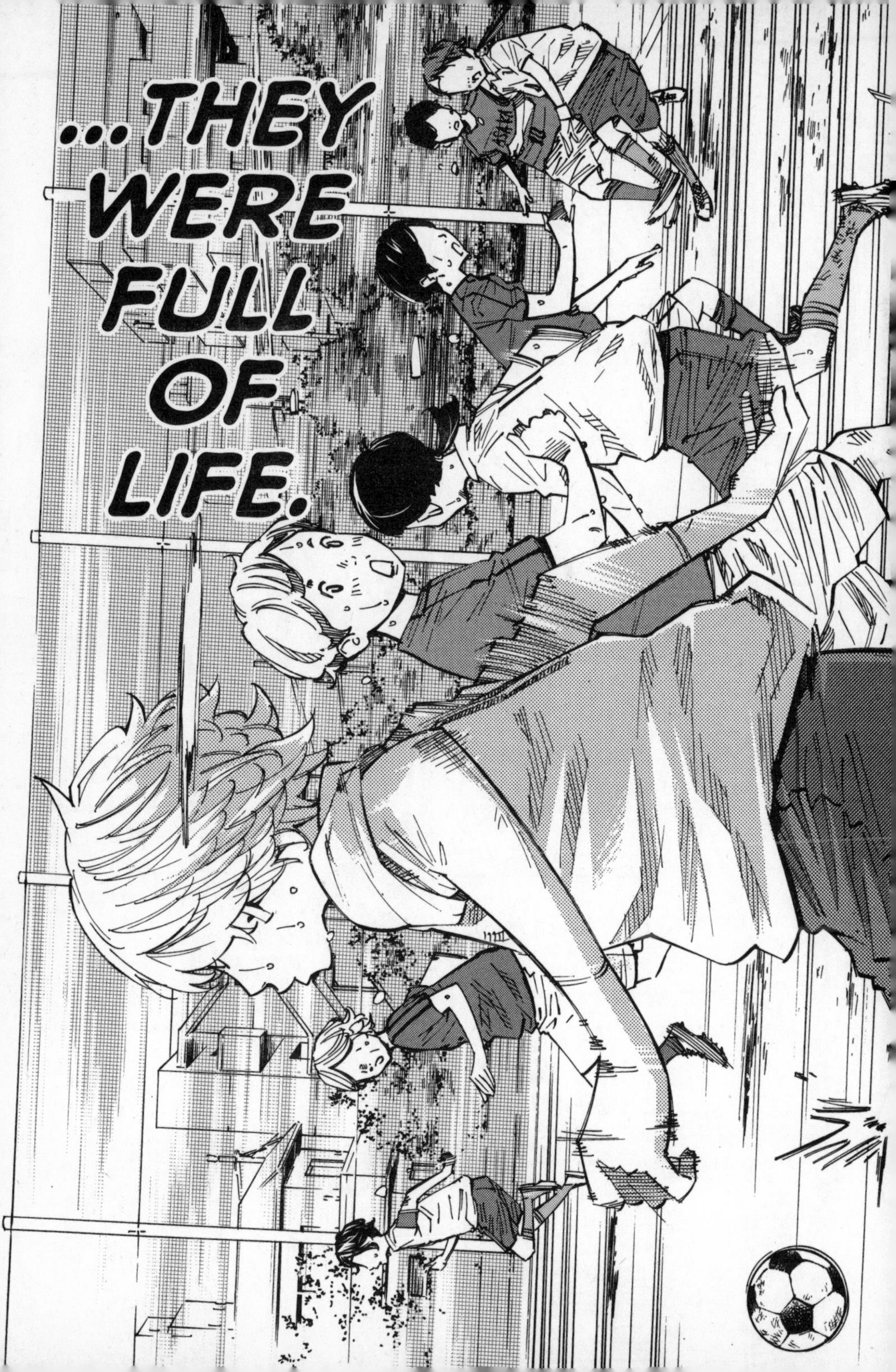
...THEY WERE FULL OF LIFE.

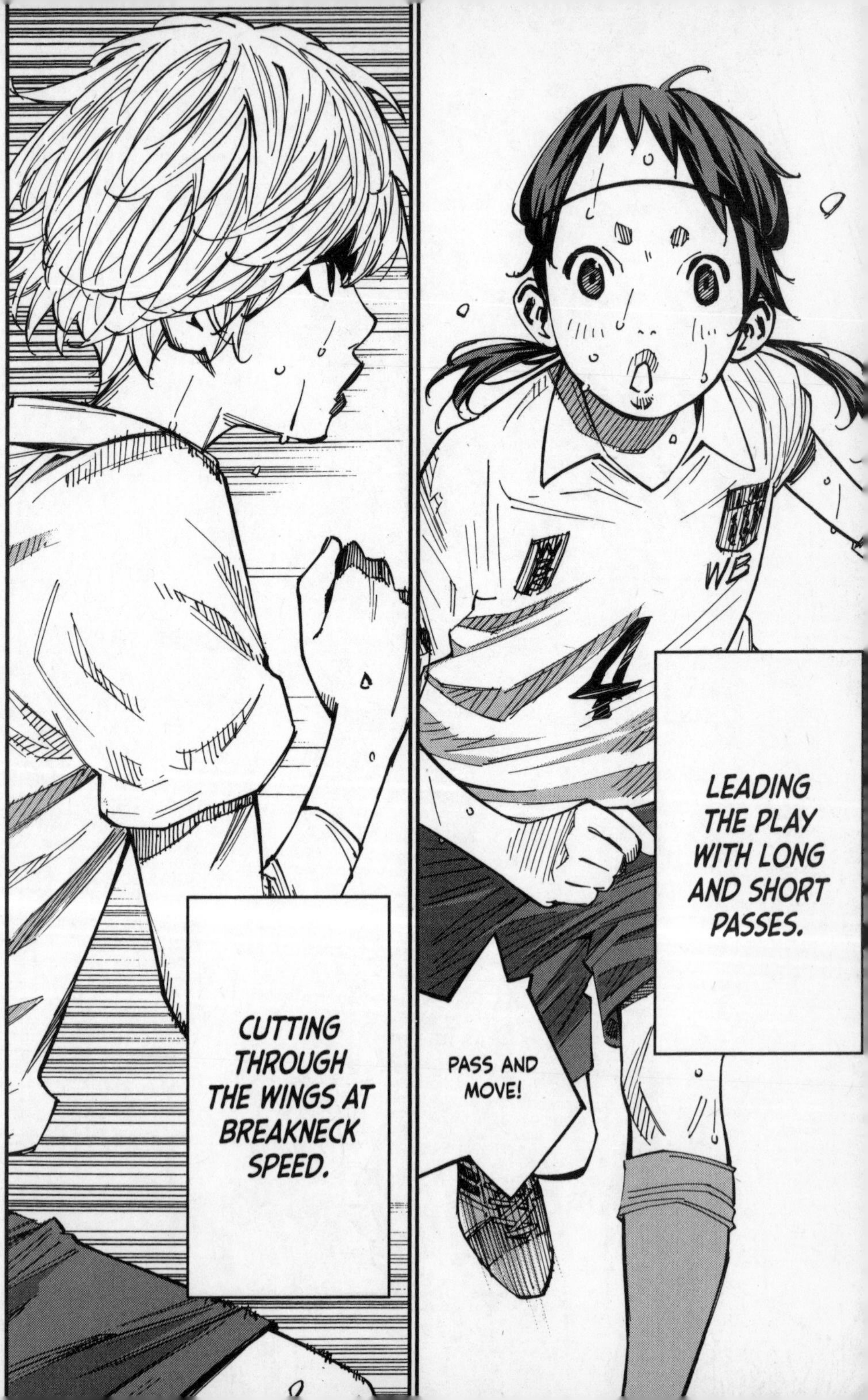
LEADING THE PLAY WITH LONG AND SHORT PASSES.
PASS AND MOVE!
CUTTING THROUGH THE WINGS AT BREAKNECK SPEED.

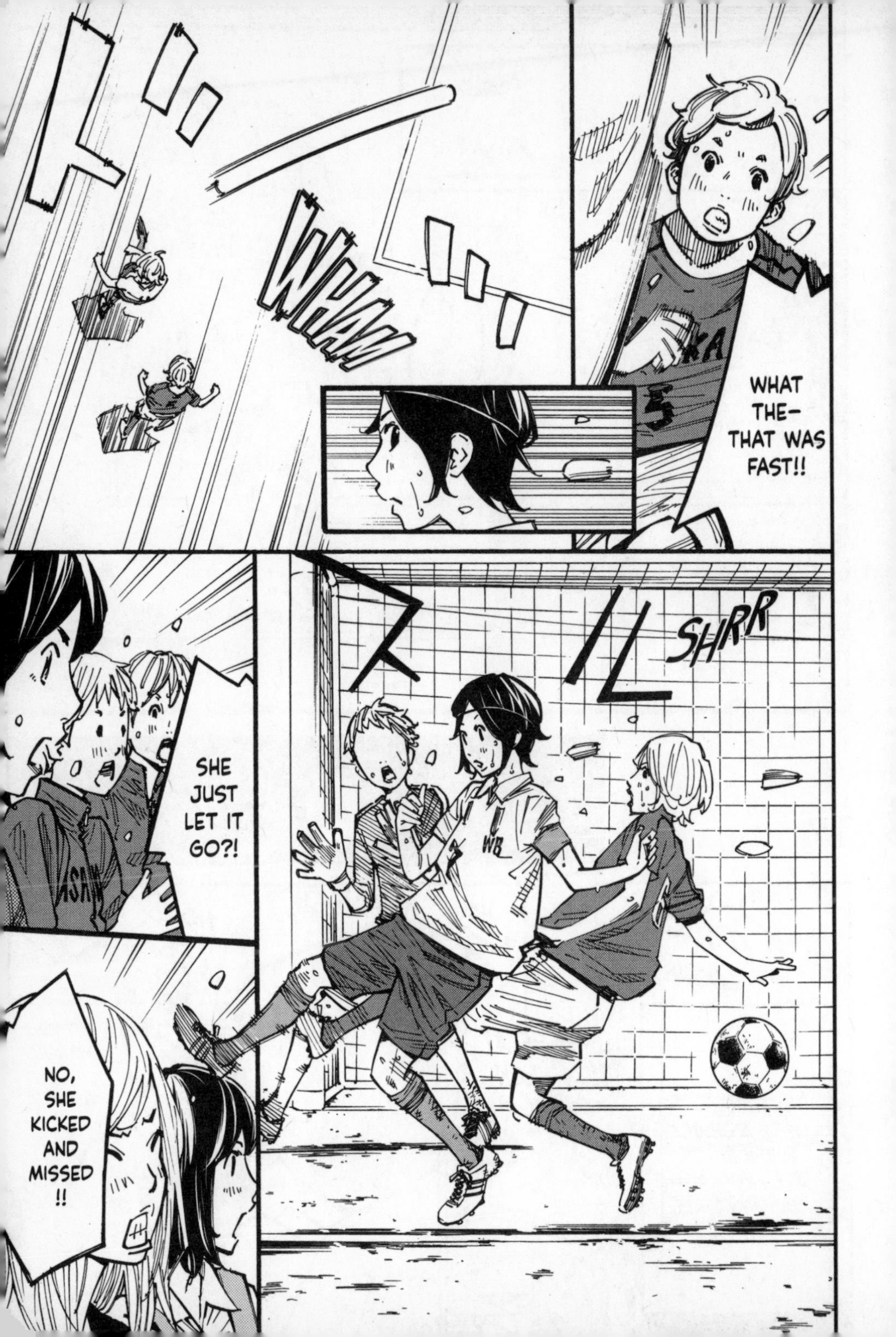
WHAT THE-
THAT WAS FAST!!
WHAM
SHRR
SHE JUST LET IT GO?!
NO, SHE KICKED AND MISSED!!

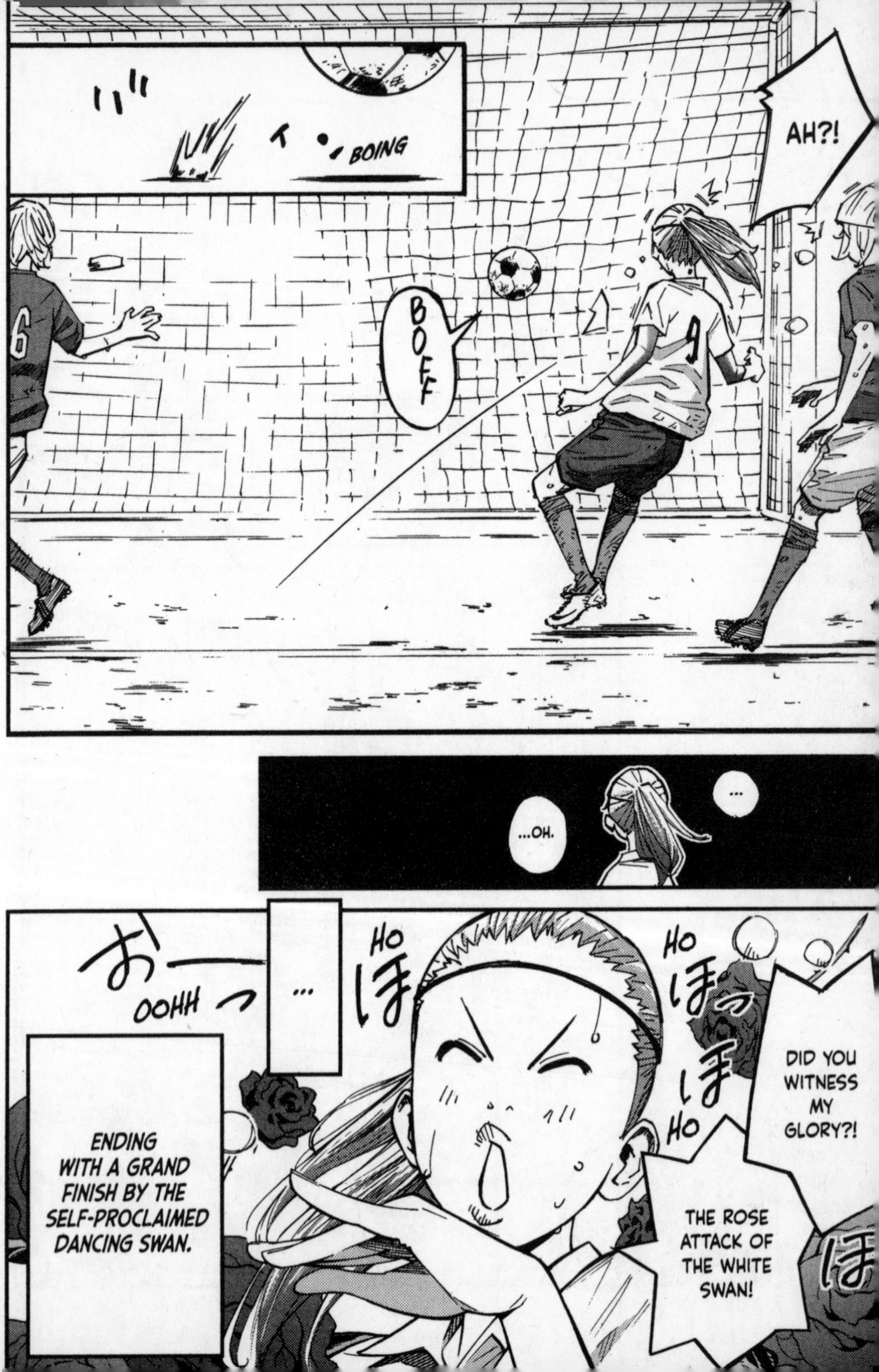
AH?!
BOING
BOFF
...
...OH.
DID YOU WITNESS MY GLORY?!
THE ROSE ATTACK OF THE WHITE SWAN!
HO HO HO HO
...
OOHH
ENDING WITH A GRAND FINISH BY THE SELF-PROCLAIMED DANCING SWAN.

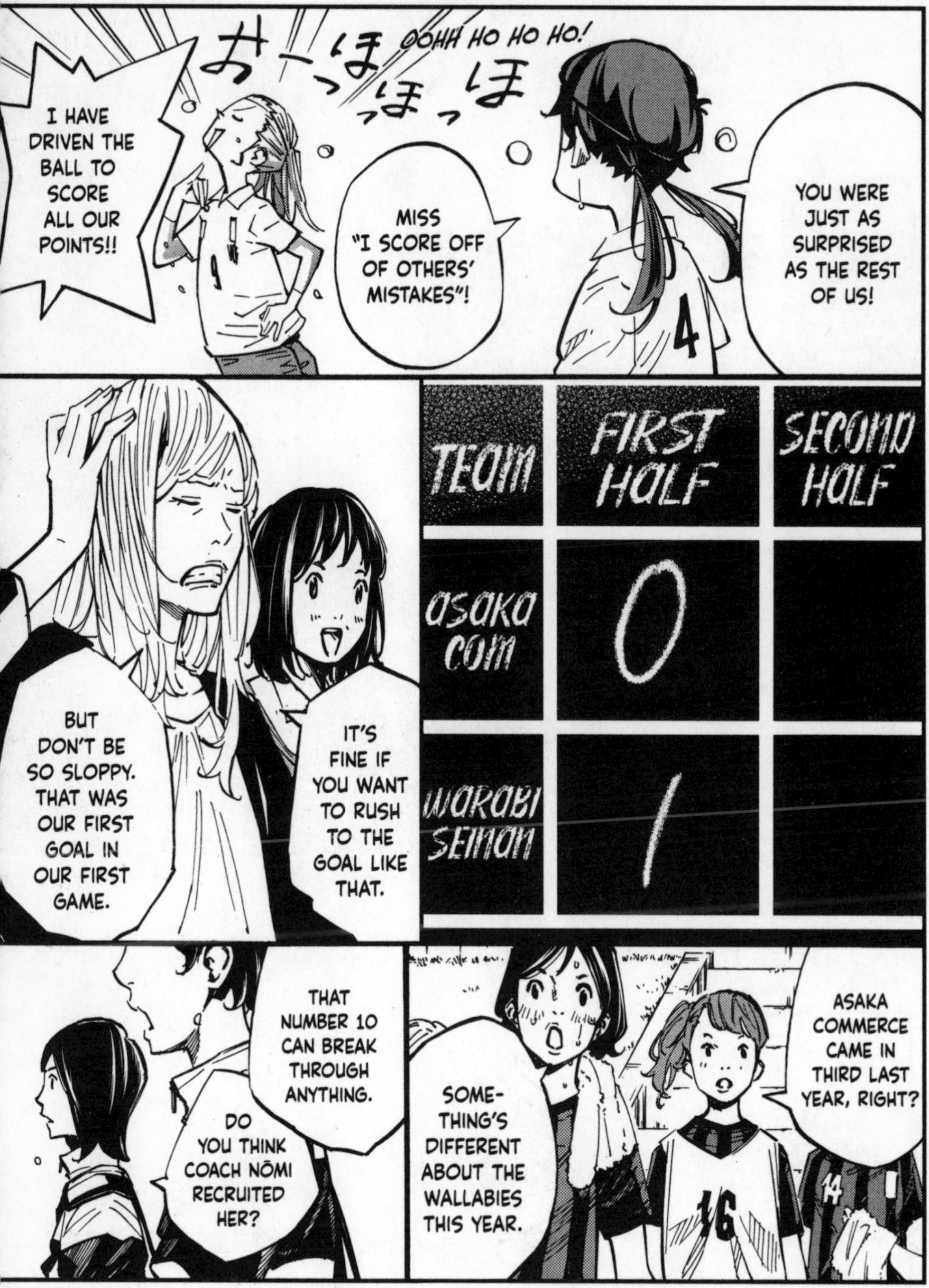
YOU WERE JUST AS SURPRISED AS THE REST OF US!
おーっほっほっほ
OOHH HO HO HO!
MISS "I SCORE OFF OF OTHERS' MISTAKES"!
I HAVE DRIVEN THE BALL TO SCORE ALL OUR POINTS!!
TEAM
FIRST HALF
SECOND HALF
ASAKA COM
0
WARABI SEINAN
1
IT'S FINE IF YOU WANT TO RUSH TO THE GOAL LIKE THAT.
BUT DON'T BE SO SLOPPY. THAT WAS OUR FIRST GOAL IN OUR FIRST GAME.
ASAKA COMMERCE CAME IN THIRD LAST YEAR, RIGHT?
SOME-THING'S DIFFERENT ABOUT THE WALLABIES THIS YEAR.
THAT NUMBER 10 CAN BREAK THROUGH ANYTHING.
DO YOU THINK COACH NŌMI RECRUITED HER?

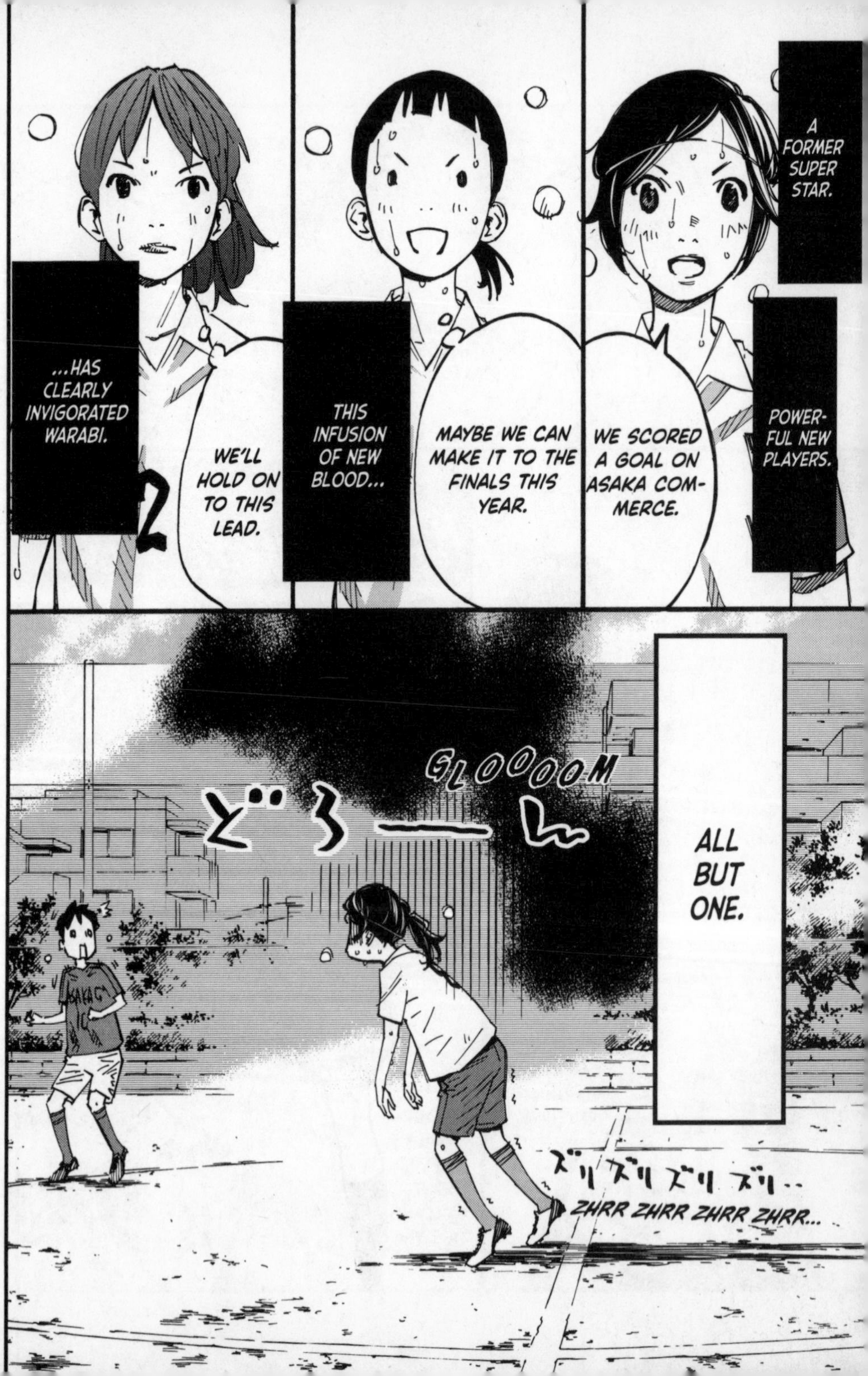
A FORMER SUPER STAR.
POWER-FUL NEW PLAYERS.
WE SCORED A GOAL ON ASAKA COM-MERCE.
THIS INFUSION OF NEW BLOOD...
MAYBE WE CAN MAKE IT TO THE FINALS THIS YEAR.
...HAS CLEARLY INVIGORATED WARABI.
WE'LL HOLD ON TO THIS LEAD.
ALL BUT ONE.
どろーーん
GLOOOOM
ズリズリズリズリ..
ZHRR ZHRR ZHRR ZHRR...

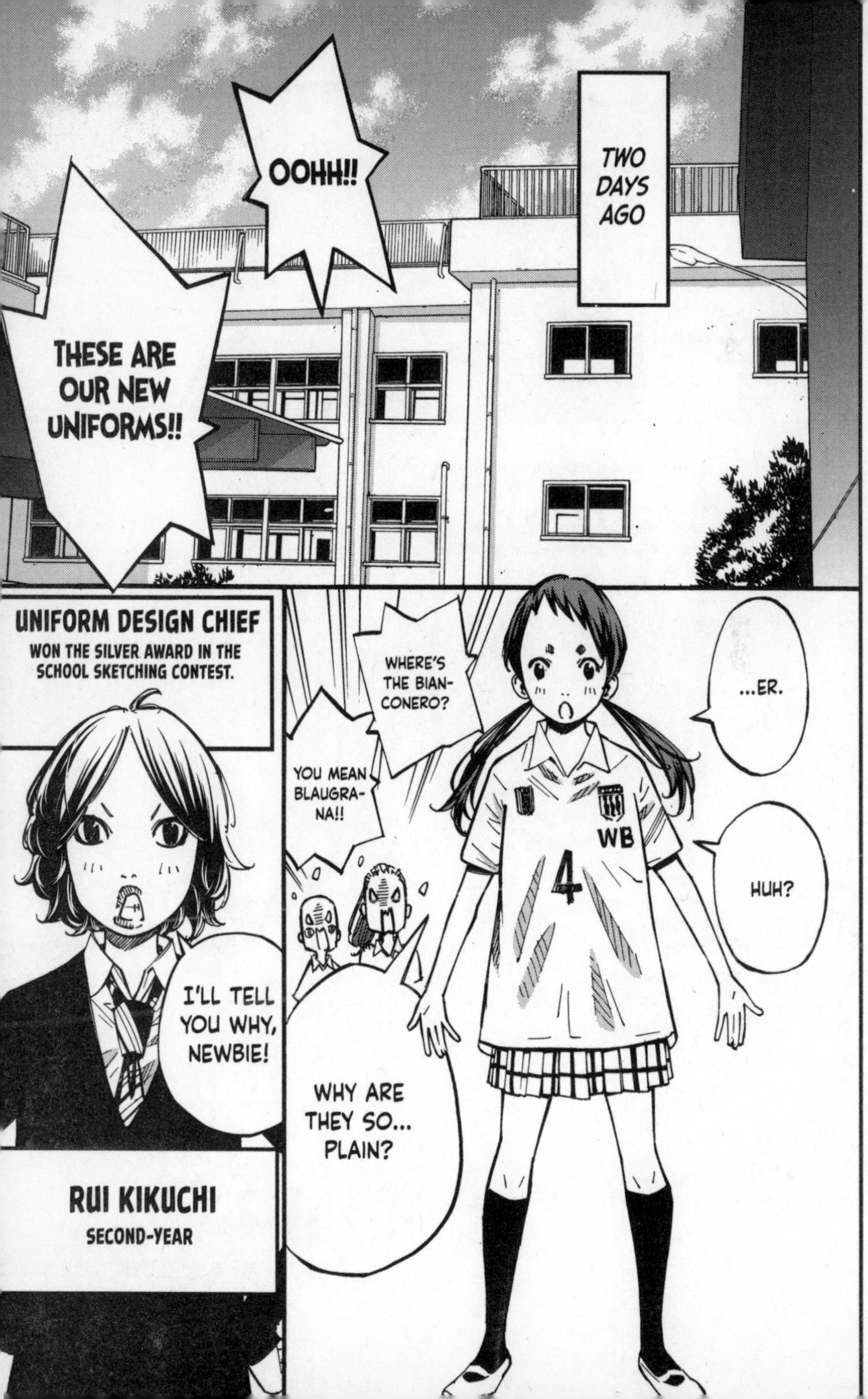
TWO DAYS AGO
OOHH!!
THESE ARE OUR NEW UNIFORMS!!
...ER.
WHERE'S THE BIAN-CONERO?
HUH?
YOU MEAN BLAUGRA-NA!!
WB
4
WHY ARE THEY SO... PLAIN?
UNIFORM DESIGN CHIEF
WON THE SILVER AWARD IN THE SCHOOL SKETCHING CONTEST.
I'LL TELL YOU WHY, NEWBIE!
RUI KIKUCHI
SECOND-YEAR

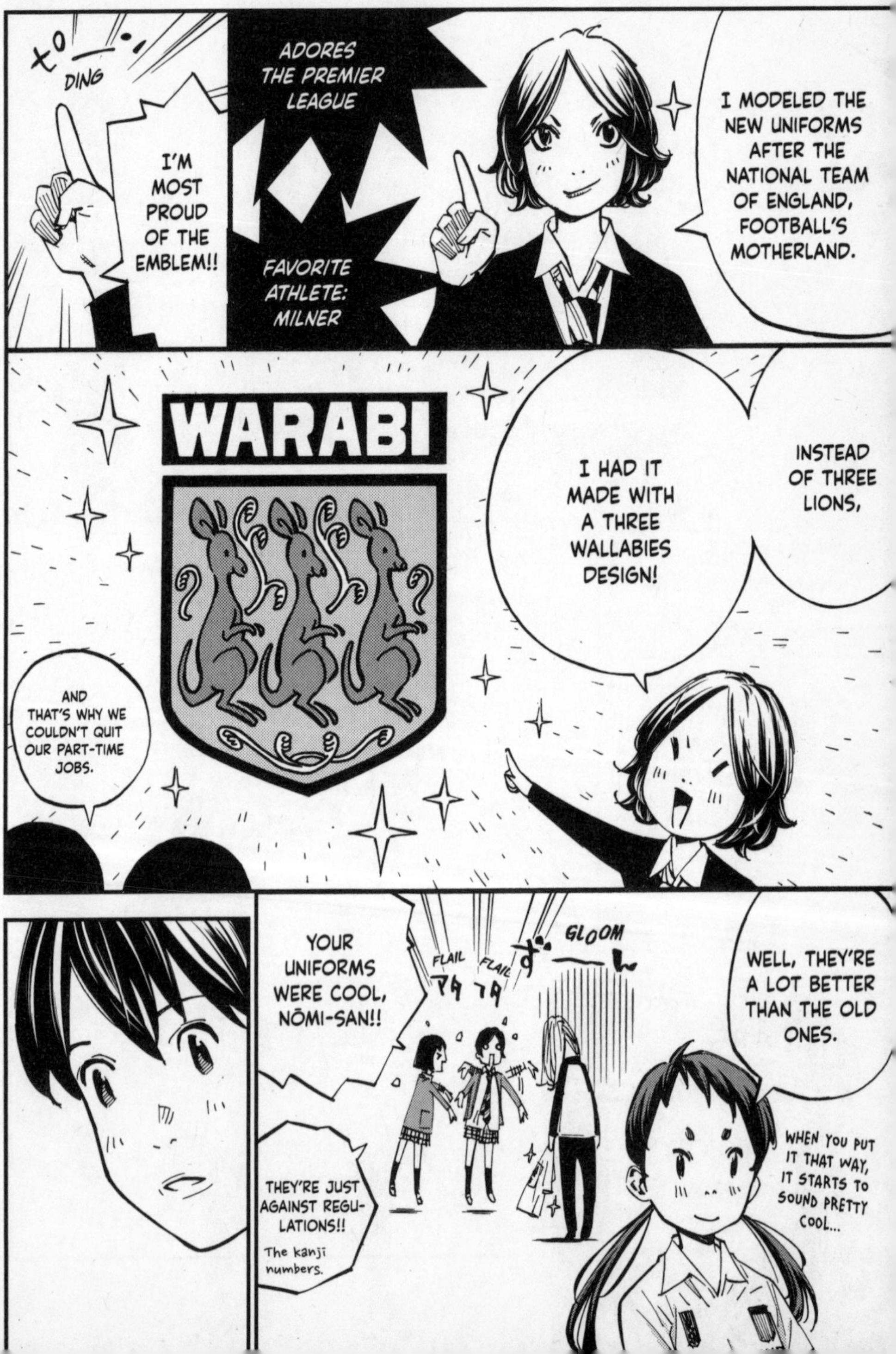
I MODELED THE NEW UNIFORMS AFTER THE NATIONAL TEAM OF ENGLAND, FOOTBALL'S MOTHERLAND.
ADORES THE PREMIER LEAGUE
FAVORITE ATHLETE: MILNER
DING
I'M MOST PROUD OF THE EMBLEM!!
INSTEAD OF THREE LIONS,
I HAD IT MADE WITH A THREE WALLABIES DESIGN!
WARABI
AND THAT'S WHY WE COULDN'T QUIT OUR PART-TIME JOBS.
WELL, THEY'RE A LOT BETTER THAN THE OLD ONES.
WHEN YOU PUT IT THAT WAY, IT STARTS TO SOUND PRETTY COOL...
GLOOM
FLAIL FLAIL
YOUR UNIFORMS WERE COOL, NŌMI-SAN!!
THEY'RE JUST AGAINST REGULATIONS!!
The kanji numbers.

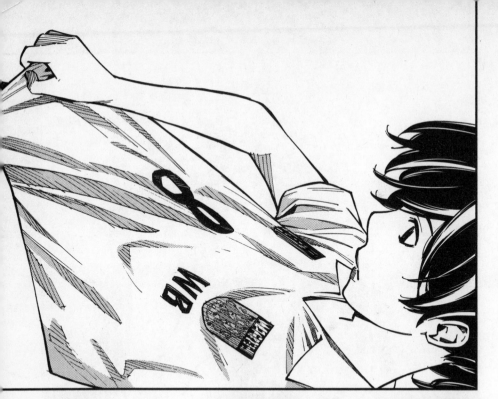

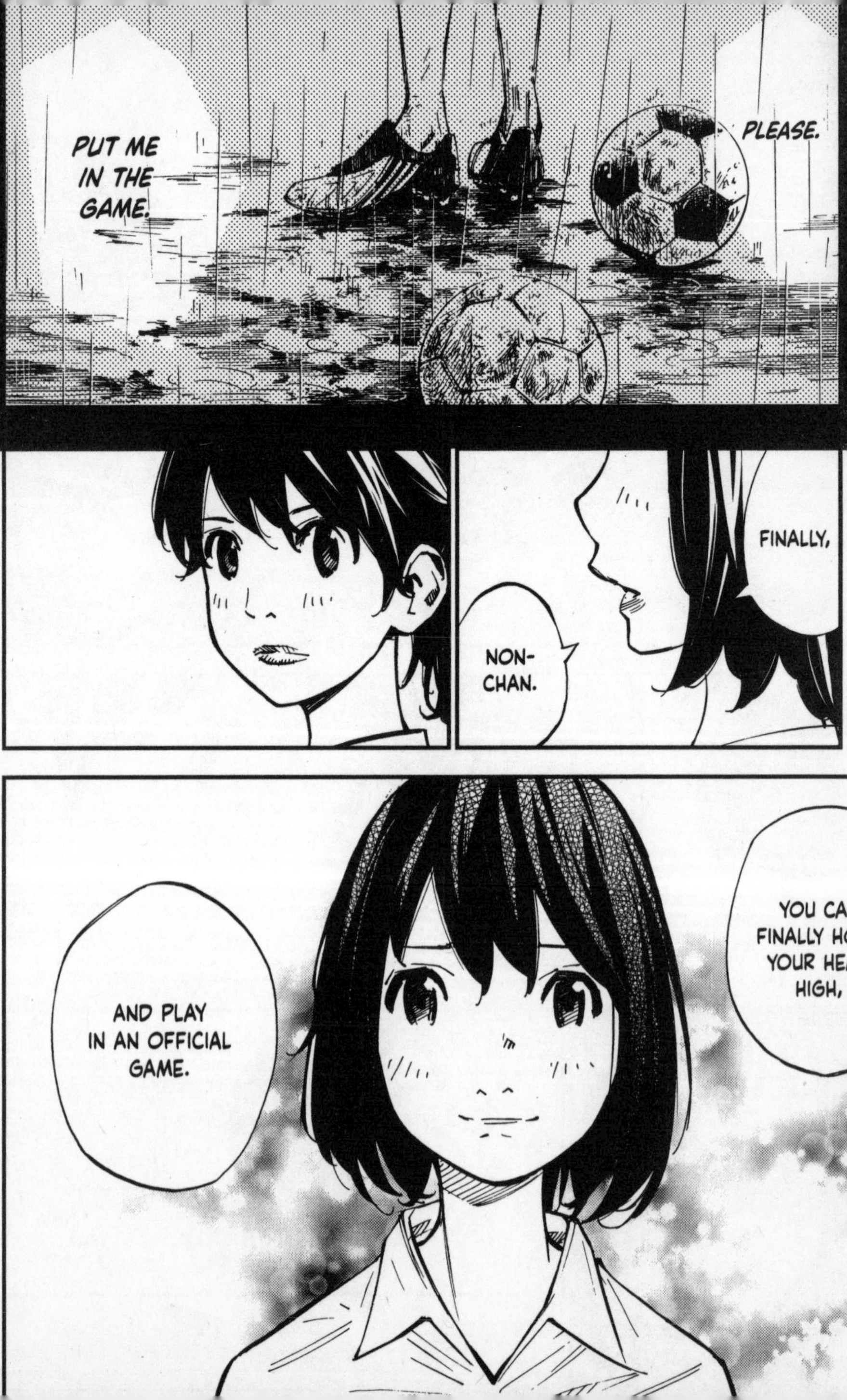
PLEASE.
PUT ME IN THE GAME.
FINALLY,
NON-CHAN.
YOU CAN FINALLY HOLD YOUR HEAD HIGH,
AND PLAY IN AN OFFICIAL GAME.

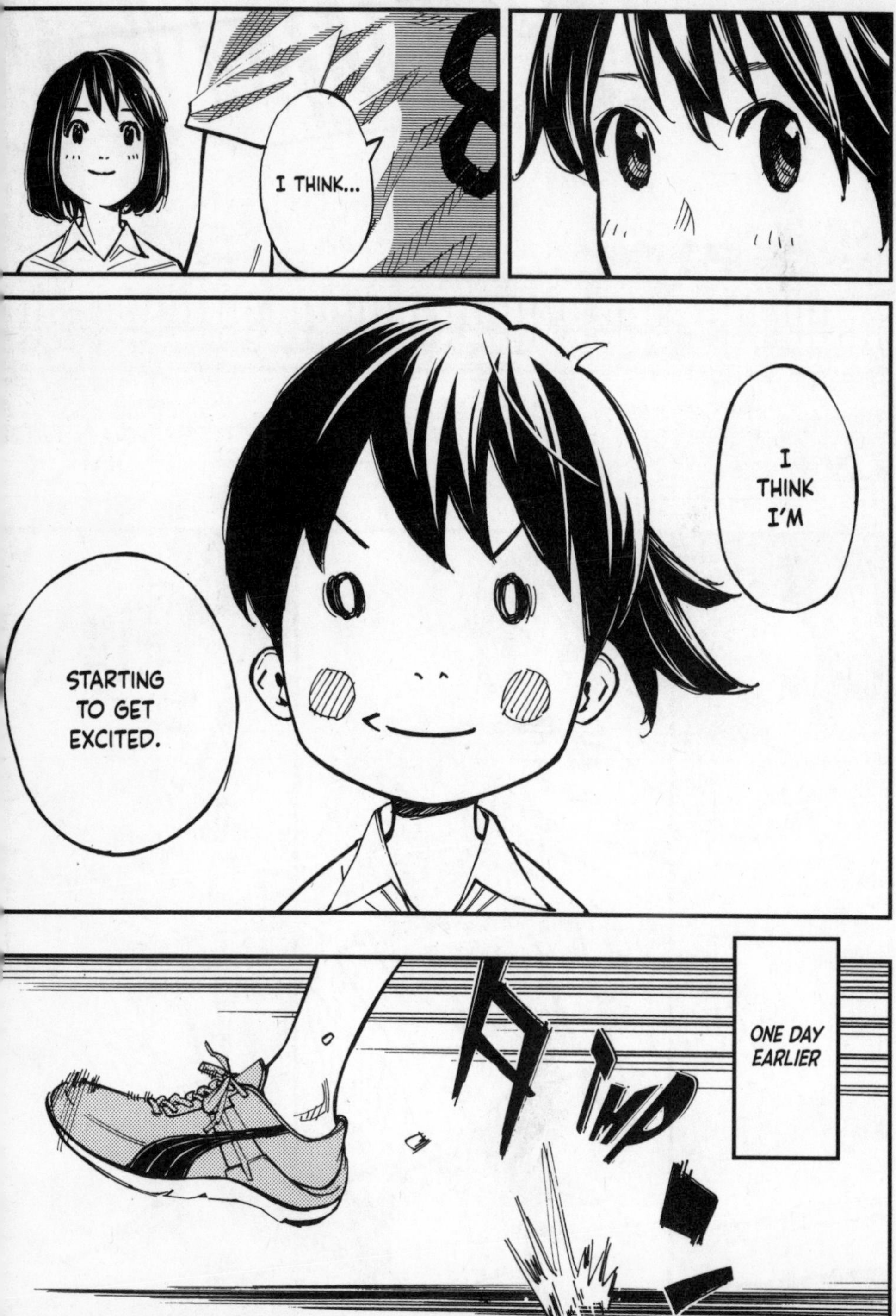
I THINK...
I THINK I'M
STARTING TO GET EXCITED.
ONE DAY EARLIER

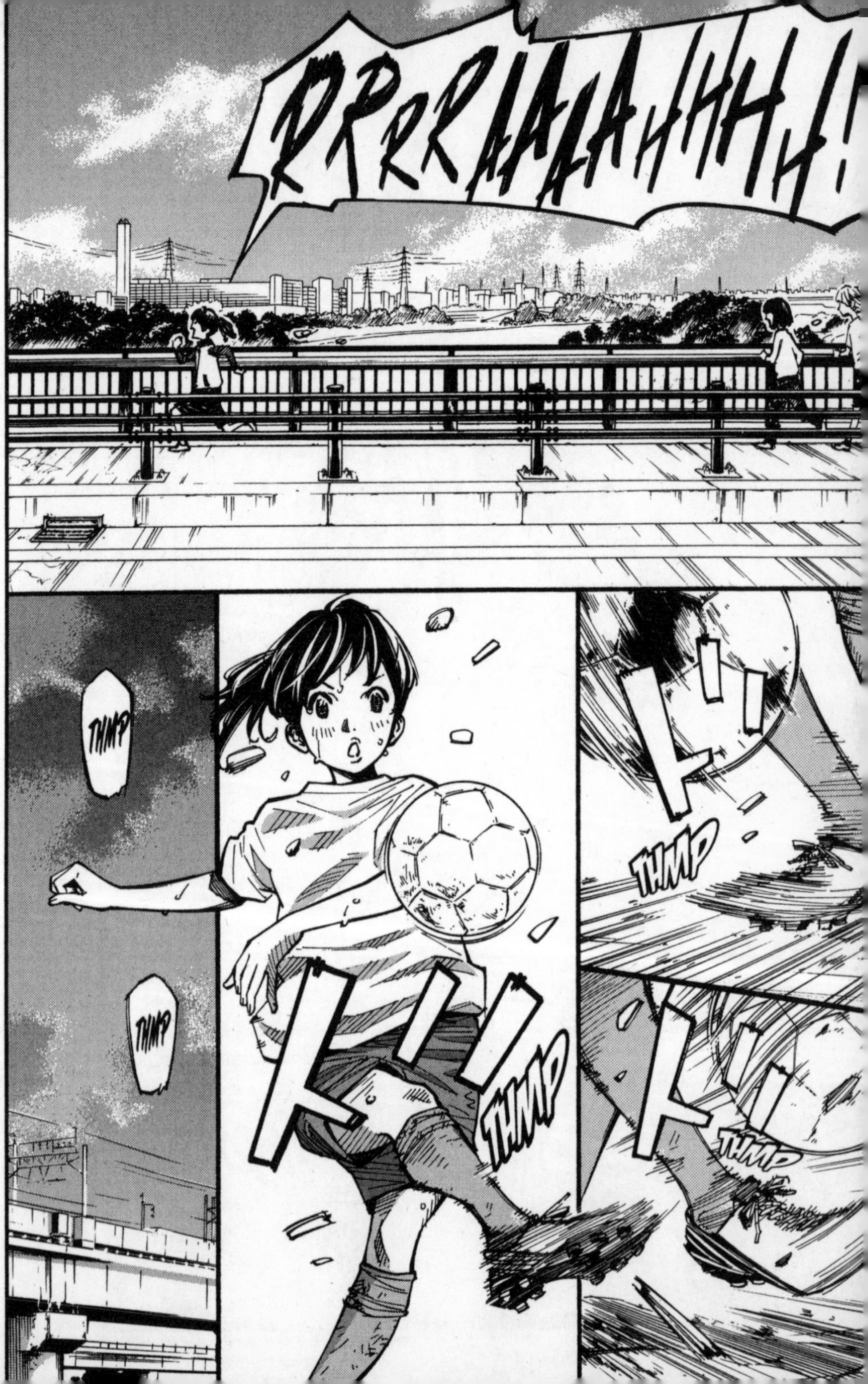
RRRRAAAAHHHH!
THMP
THMP
THMP
THMP
THMP

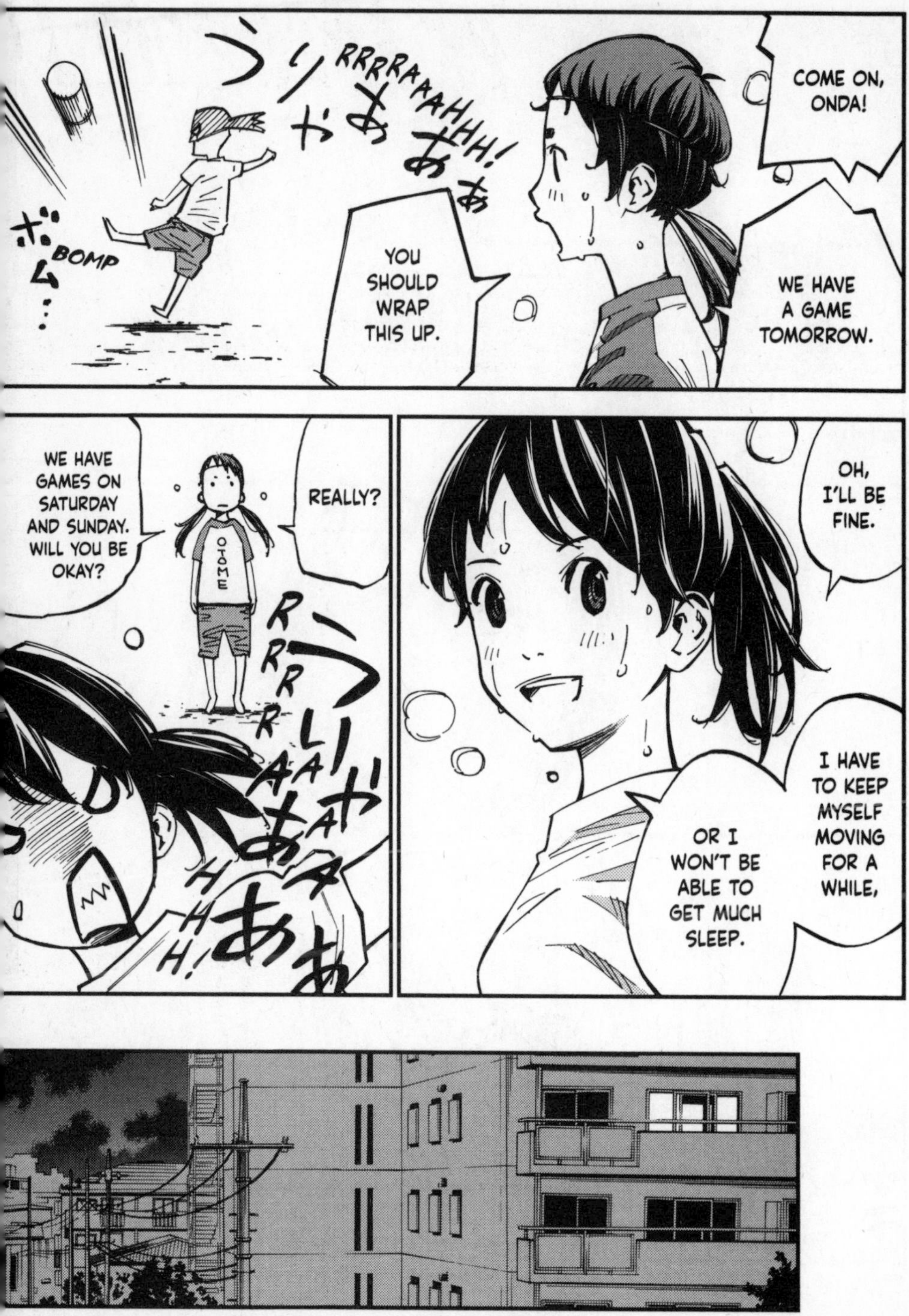
COME ON, ONDA!
WE HAVE A GAME TOMORROW.
YOU SHOULD WRAP THIS UP.
うりゃあああ
RRRRAAAHHH!
ボム…
BOMP
OH, I'LL BE FINE.
I HAVE TO KEEP MYSELF MOVING FOR A WHILE,
OR I WON'T BE ABLE TO GET MUCH SLEEP.
REALLY?
WE HAVE GAMES ON SATURDAY AND SUNDAY. WILL YOU BE OKAY?
うりゃあああ
RRRRAAAAHHH!

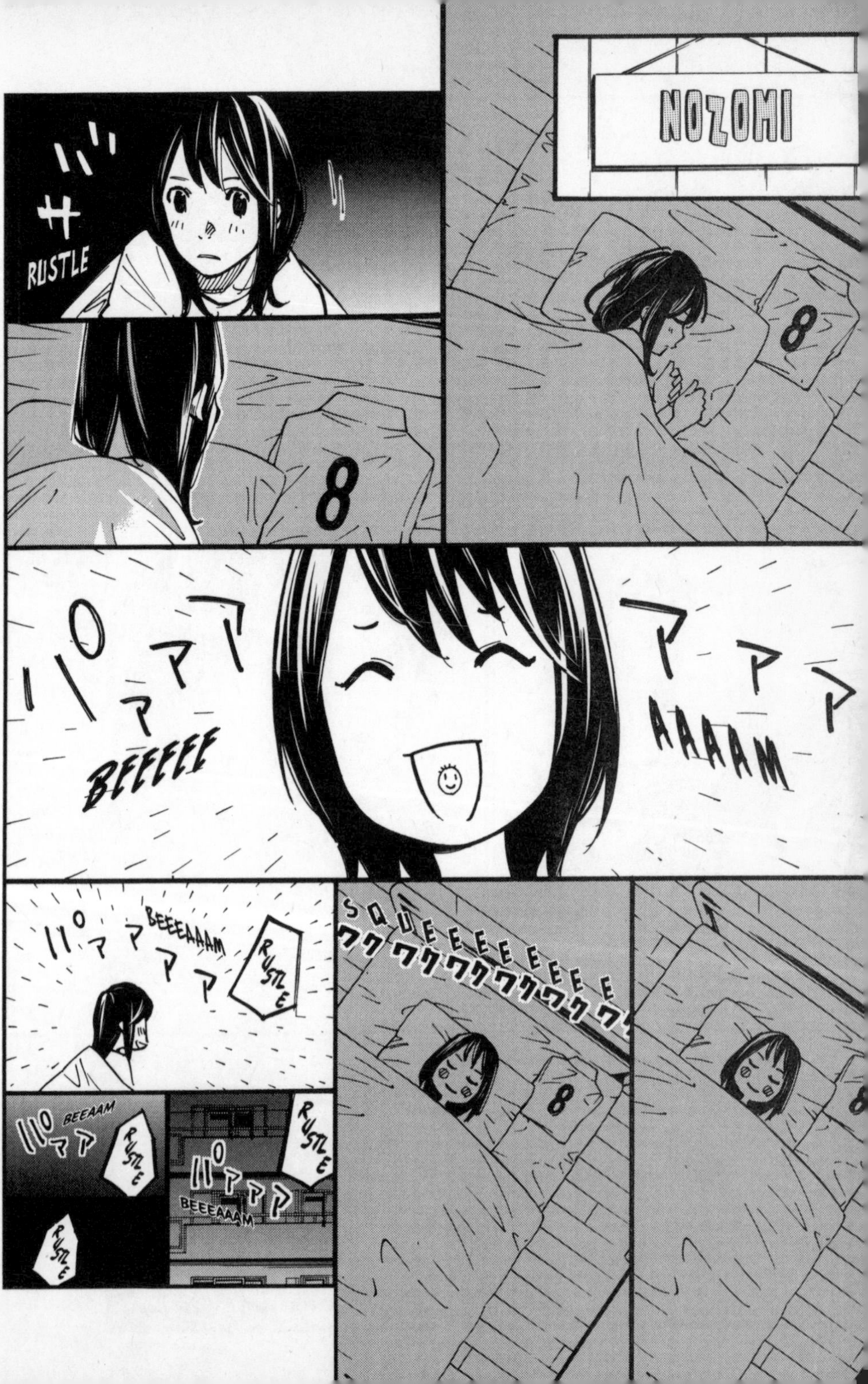
NOZOMI
RUSTLE
8
8
BEEEEE
AAAAAM
SQUEEEEEEEE
BEEEAAAM
RUSTLE
8
RUSTLE
BEEEAAAM
RUSTLE
BEEAAM
RUSTLE
RUSTLE

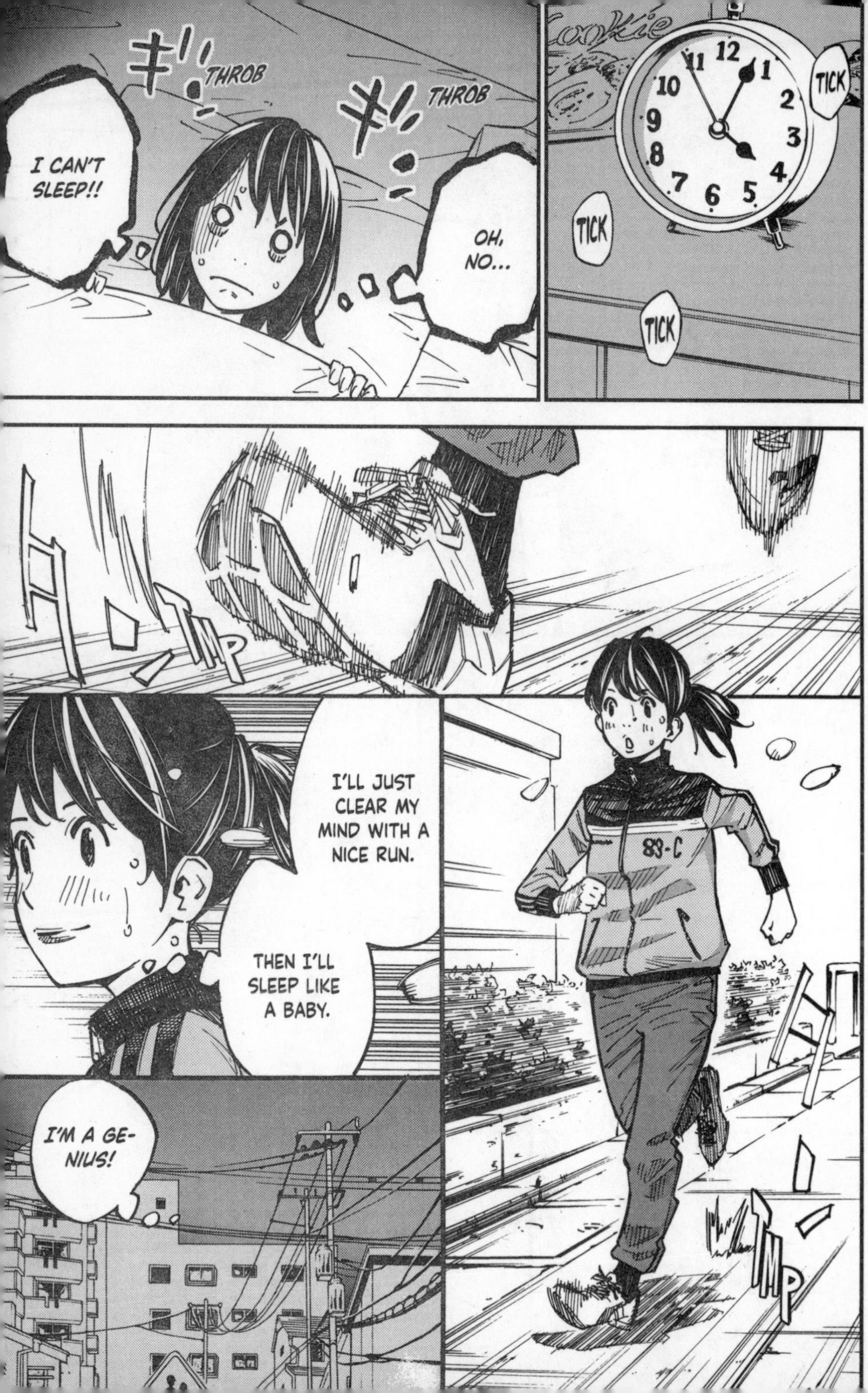
TICK
TICK
TICK
THROB
THROB
OH, NO...
I CAN'T SLEEP!!
TMP
83-C
TMP
I'LL JUST CLEAR MY MIND WITH A NICE RUN.
THEN I'LL SLEEP LIKE A BABY.
I'M A GE-NIUS!

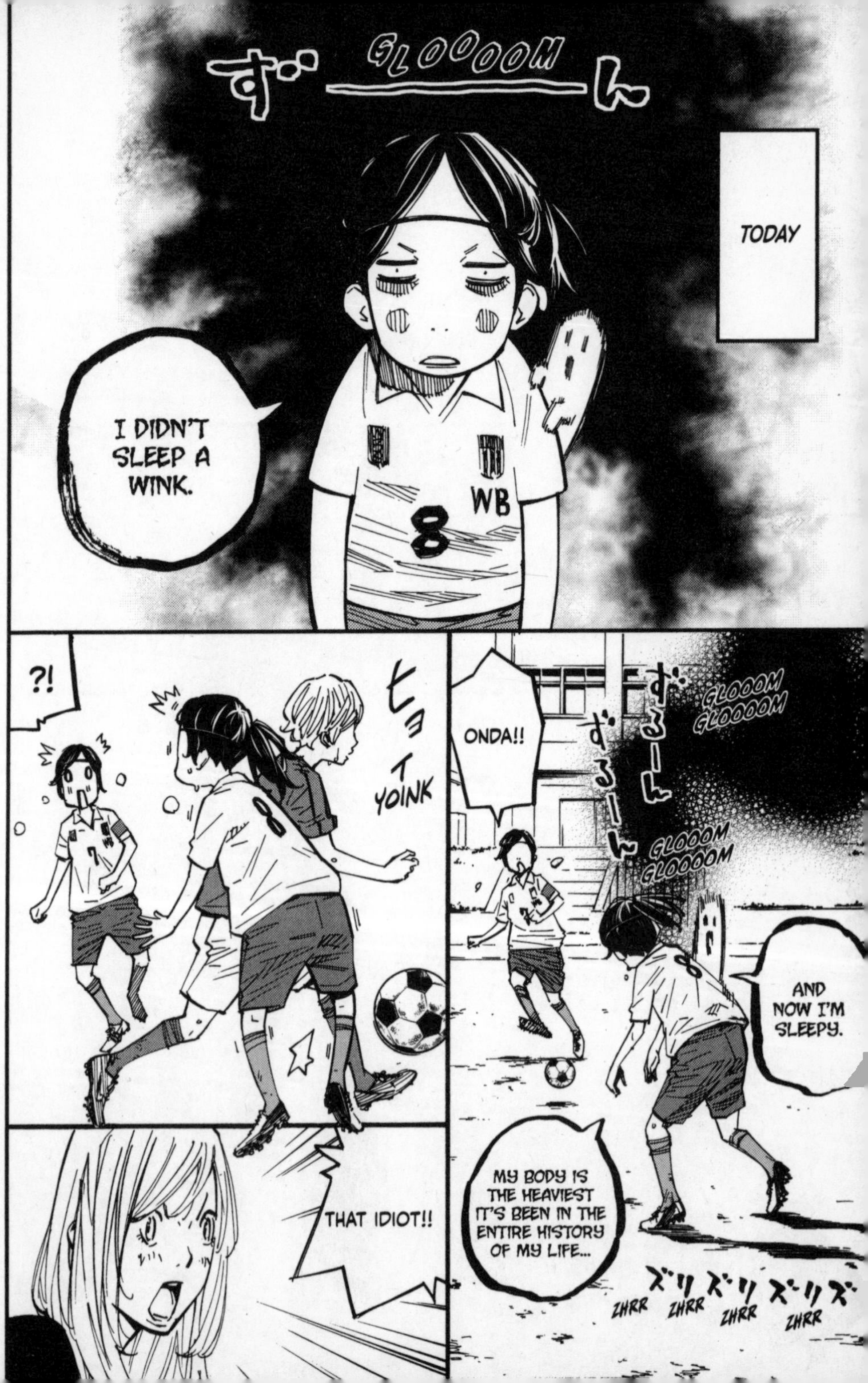
GLOOOOM
TODAY
I DIDN'T SLEEP A WINK.
ONDA!!
GLOOOM GLOOOOM
GLOOOM GLOOOOM
AND NOW I'M SLEEPY.
MY BODY IS THE HEAVIEST IT'S BEEN IN THE ENTIRE HISTORY OF MY LIFE...
ZHRR ZHRR ZHRR ZHRR
?!
YOINK
THAT IDIOT!!

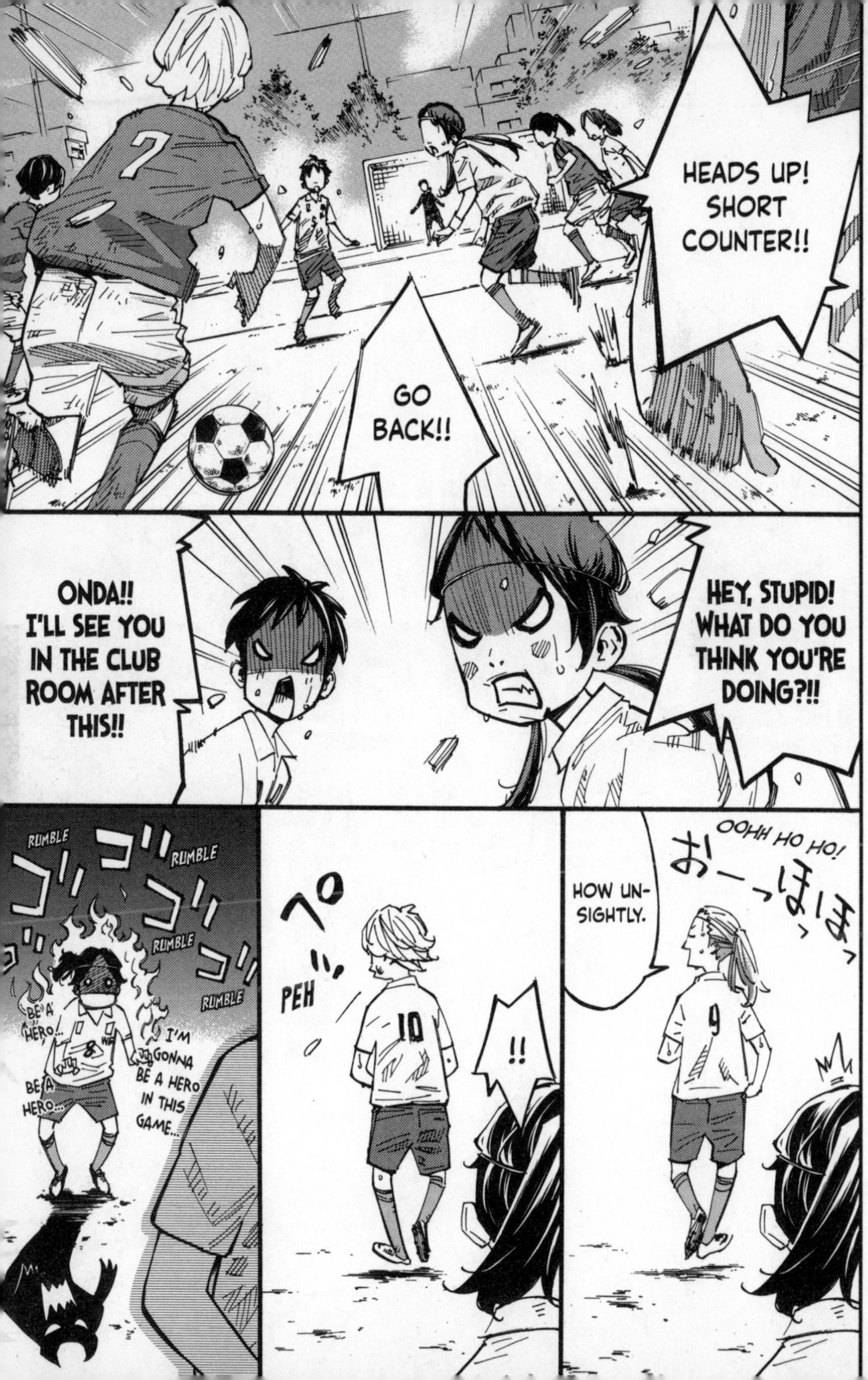
HEADS UP! SHORT COUNTER!!
GO BACK!!
HEY, STUPID! WHAT DO YOU THINK YOU'RE DOING?!!
ONDA!! I'LL SEE YOU IN THE CLUB ROOM AFTER THIS!!
OOHH HO HO!
おーっほほっ
HOW UN-SIGHTLY.
!!
ペ
PEH
RUMBLE
RUMBLE
RUMBLE
RUMBLE
I'M GONNA BE A HERO IN THIS GAME...
BE A HERO...
BE A HERO...

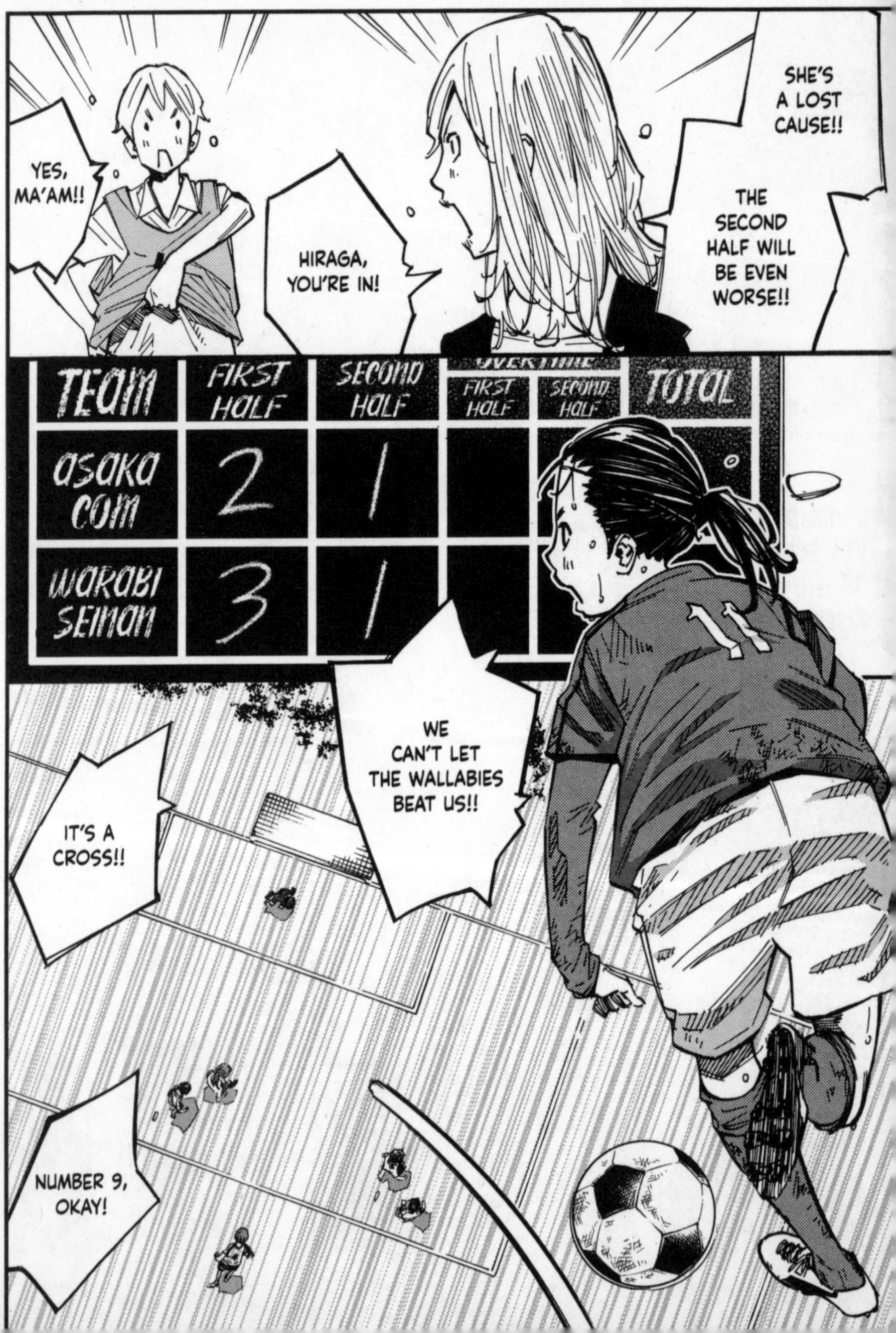
SHE'S A LOST CAUSE!!
THE SECOND HALF WILL BE EVEN WORSE!!
HIRAGA, YOU'RE IN!
YES, MA'AM!!
TEAM
FIRST HALF
SECOND HALF
FIRST HALF
SECOND HALF
TOTAL
asaka com
2
1
warabi seinan
3
1
WE CAN'T LET THE WALLABIES BEAT US!!
IT'S A CROSS!!
NUMBER 9, OKAY!

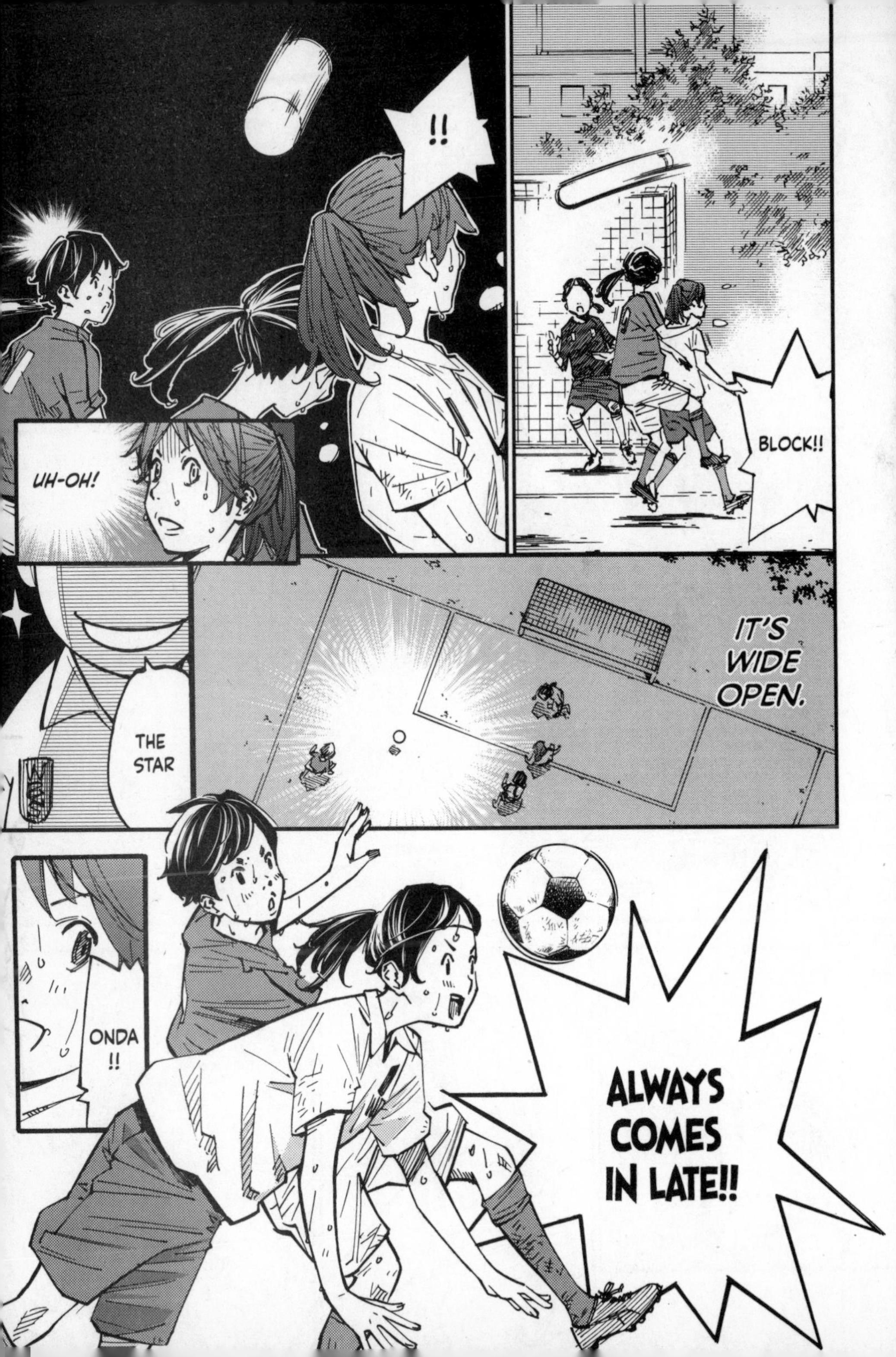
BLOCK!!
!!
UH-OH!
IT'S WIDE OPEN.
THE STAR
ALWAYS COMES IN LATE!!
ONDA !!

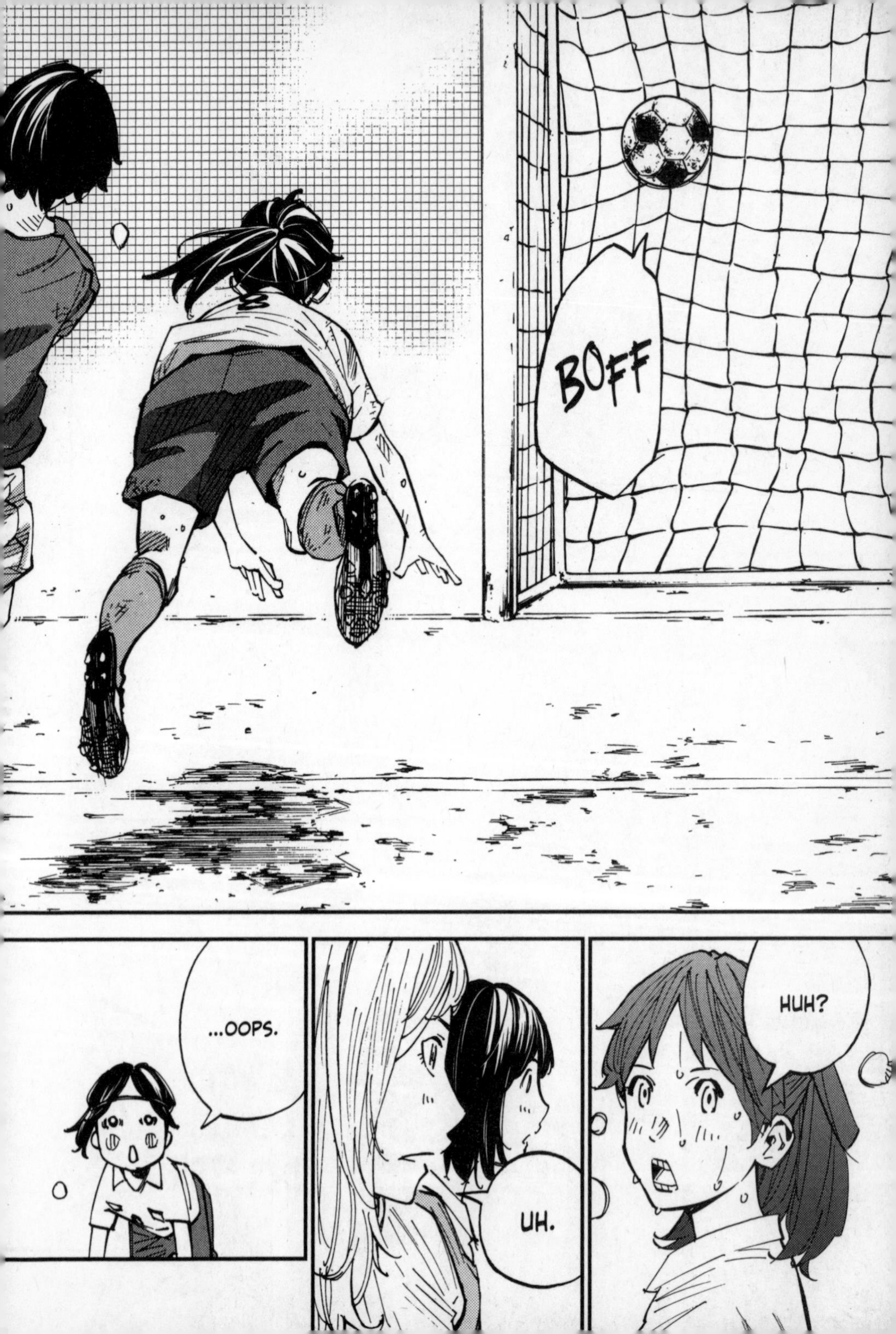
BOFF
HUH?
UH.
...OOPS.

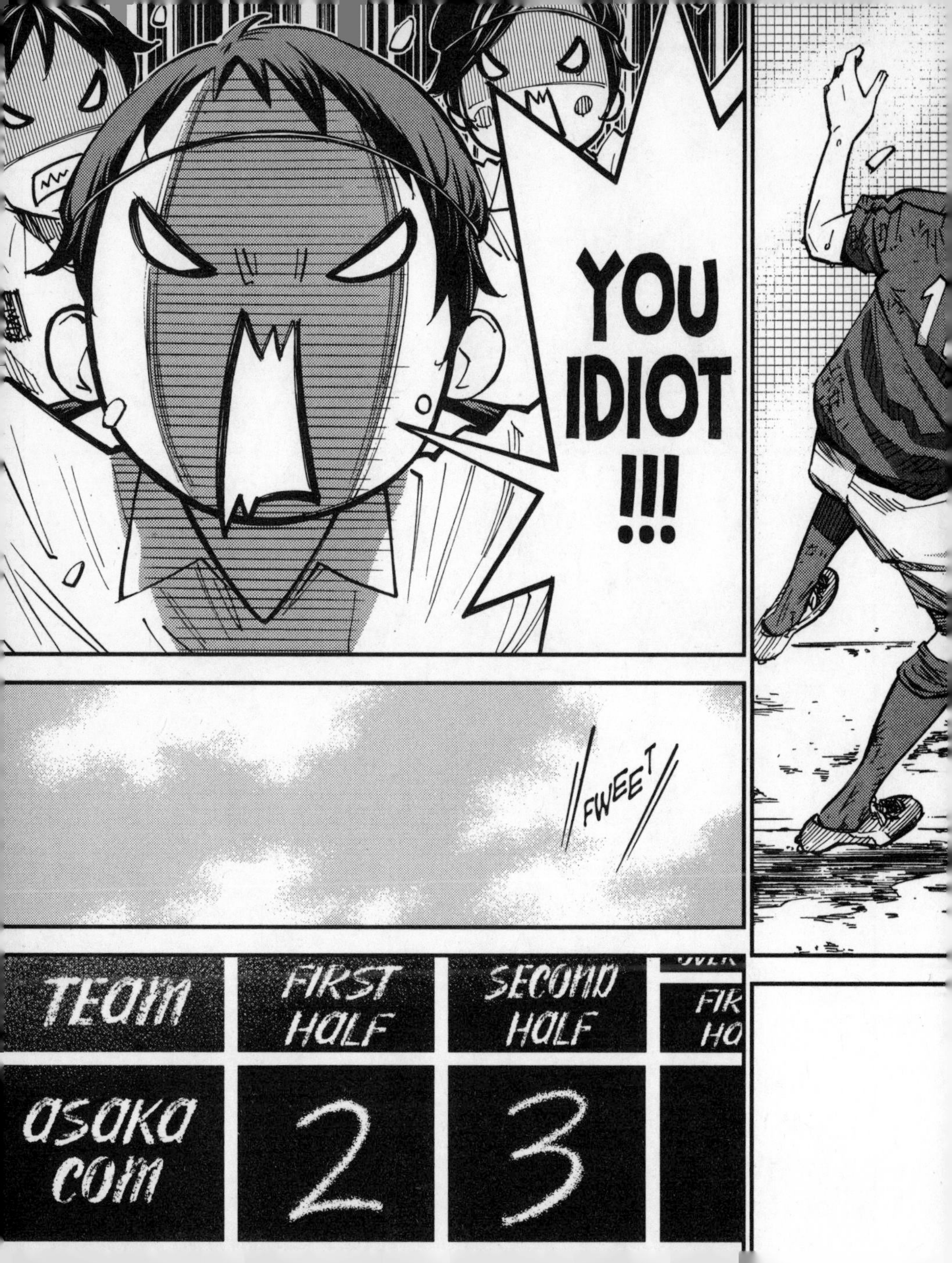
YOU IDIOT !!!
FWEET
TEAM
FIRST HALF
SECOND HALF
asaka com
2
3

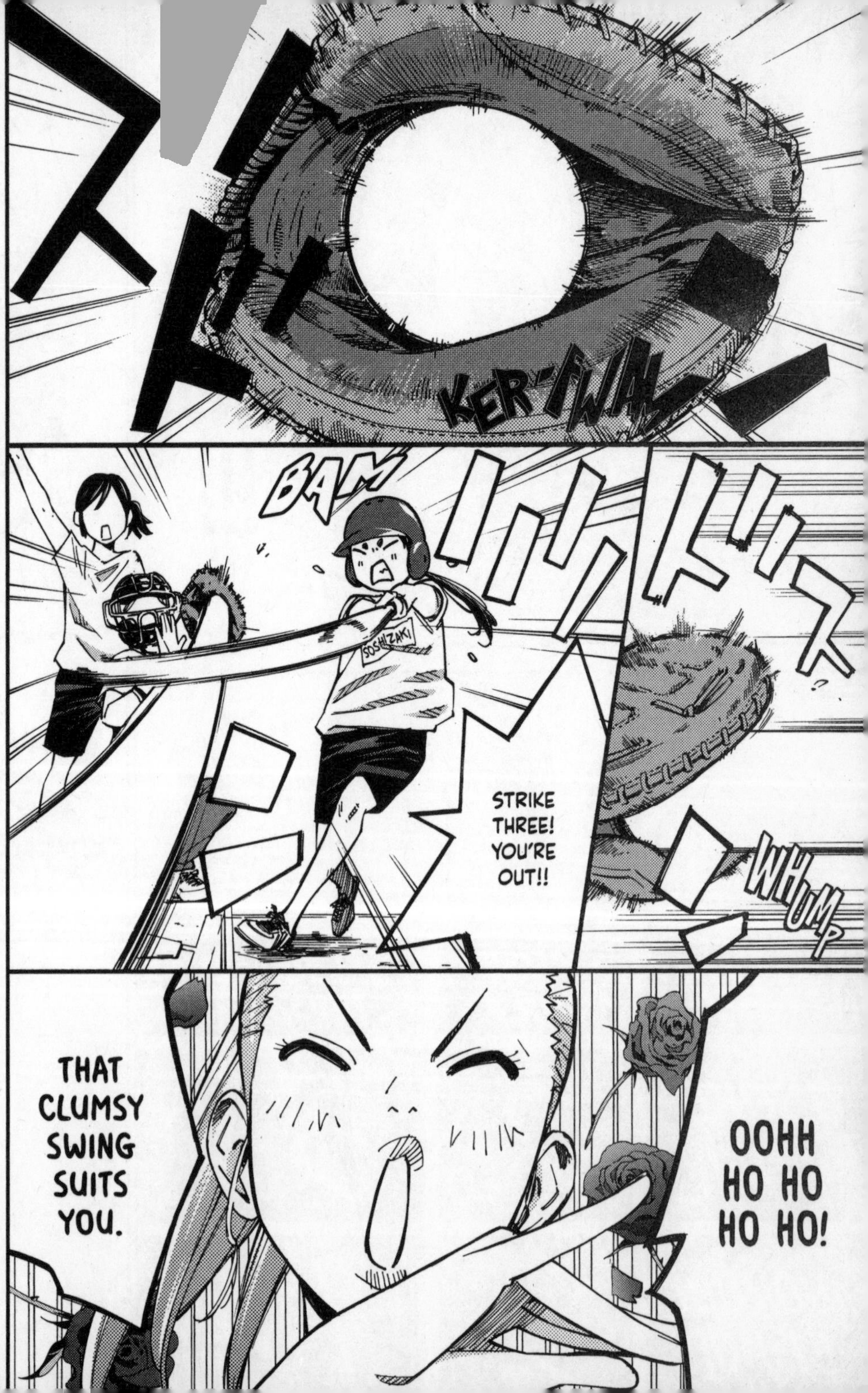
KER-TWAK
WHUMP
STRIKE THREE! YOU'RE OUT!!
BAM
SOSHIZAKI
OOHH HO HO HO HO!
THAT CLUMSY SWING SUITS YOU.

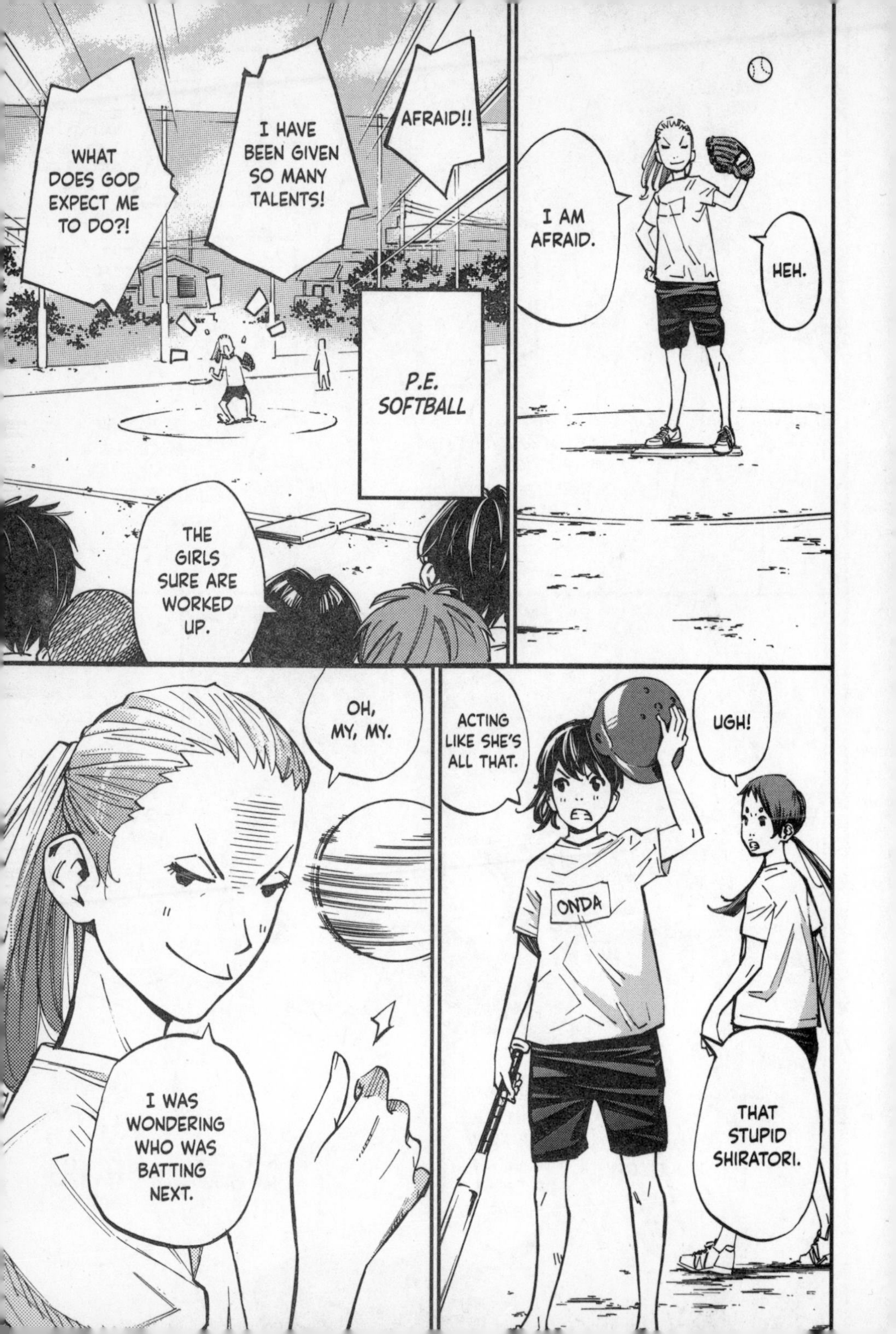
HEH.
I AM AFRAID.
AFRAID!!
I HAVE BEEN GIVEN SO MANY TALENTS!
WHAT DOES GOD EXPECT ME TO DO?!
P.E. SOFTBALL
THE GIRLS SURE ARE WORKED UP.
UGH!
ACTING LIKE SHE'S ALL THAT.
ONDA
THAT STUPID SHIRATORI.
OH, MY, MY.
I WAS WONDERING WHO WAS BATTING NEXT.

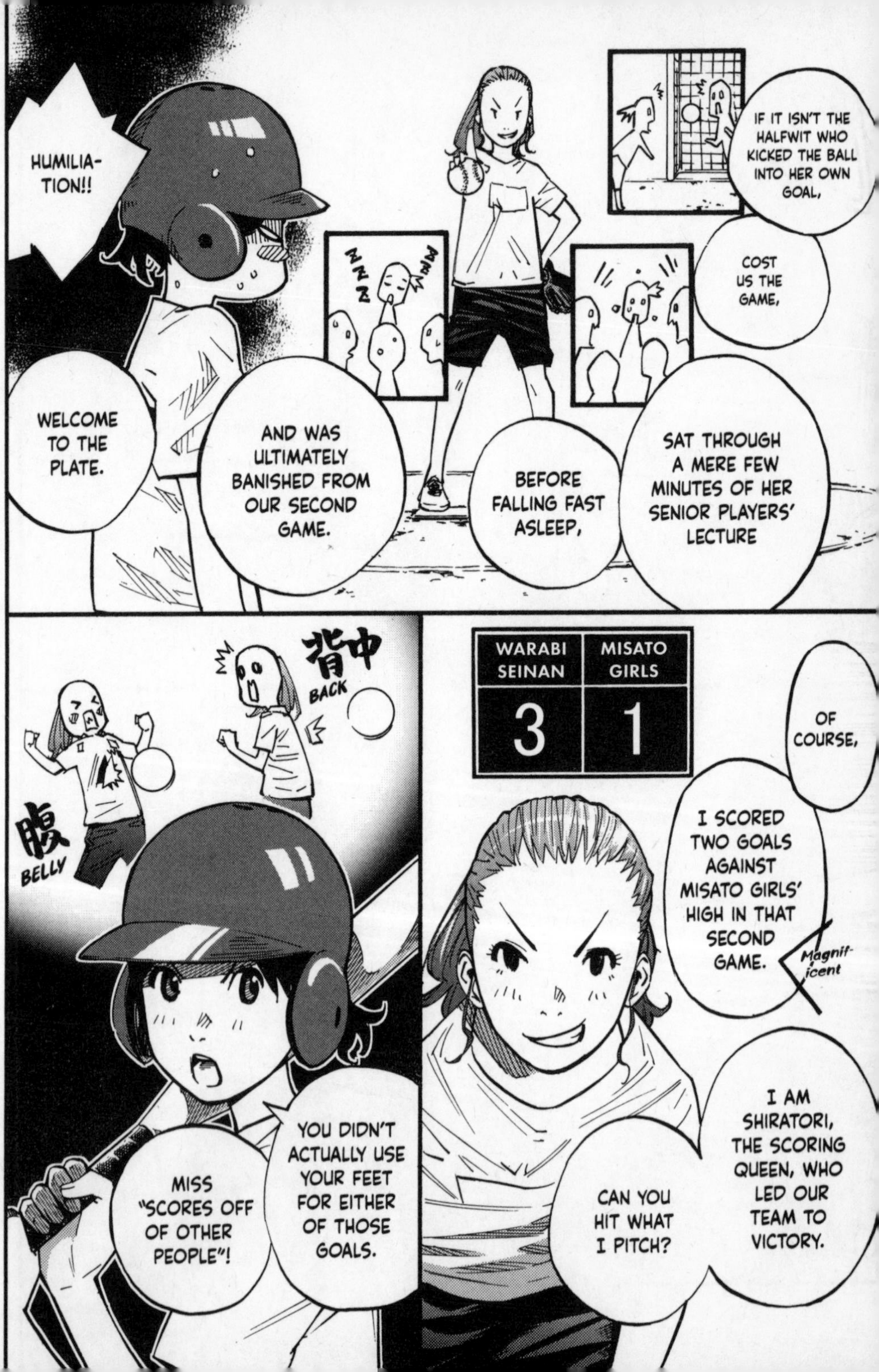
IF IT ISN'T THE HALFWIT WHO KICKED THE BALL INTO HER OWN GOAL,
COST US THE GAME,
SAT THROUGH A MERE FEW MINUTES OF HER SENIOR PLAYERS' LECTURE
BEFORE FALLING FAST ASLEEP,
AND WAS ULTIMATELY BANISHED FROM OUR SECOND GAME.
WELCOME TO THE PLATE.
HUMILIA-TION!!
WARABI SEINAN 3
MISATO GIRLS 1
OF COURSE,
I SCORED TWO GOALS AGAINST MISATO GIRLS' HIGH IN THAT SECOND GAME.
Magnif-icent
I AM SHIRATORI, THE SCORING QUEEN, WHO LED OUR TEAM TO VICTORY.
CAN YOU HIT WHAT I PITCH?
背中 BACK
腹 BELLY
YOU DIDN'T ACTUALLY USE YOUR FEET FOR EITHER OF THOSE GOALS.
MISS "SCORES OFF OF OTHER PEOPLE"!

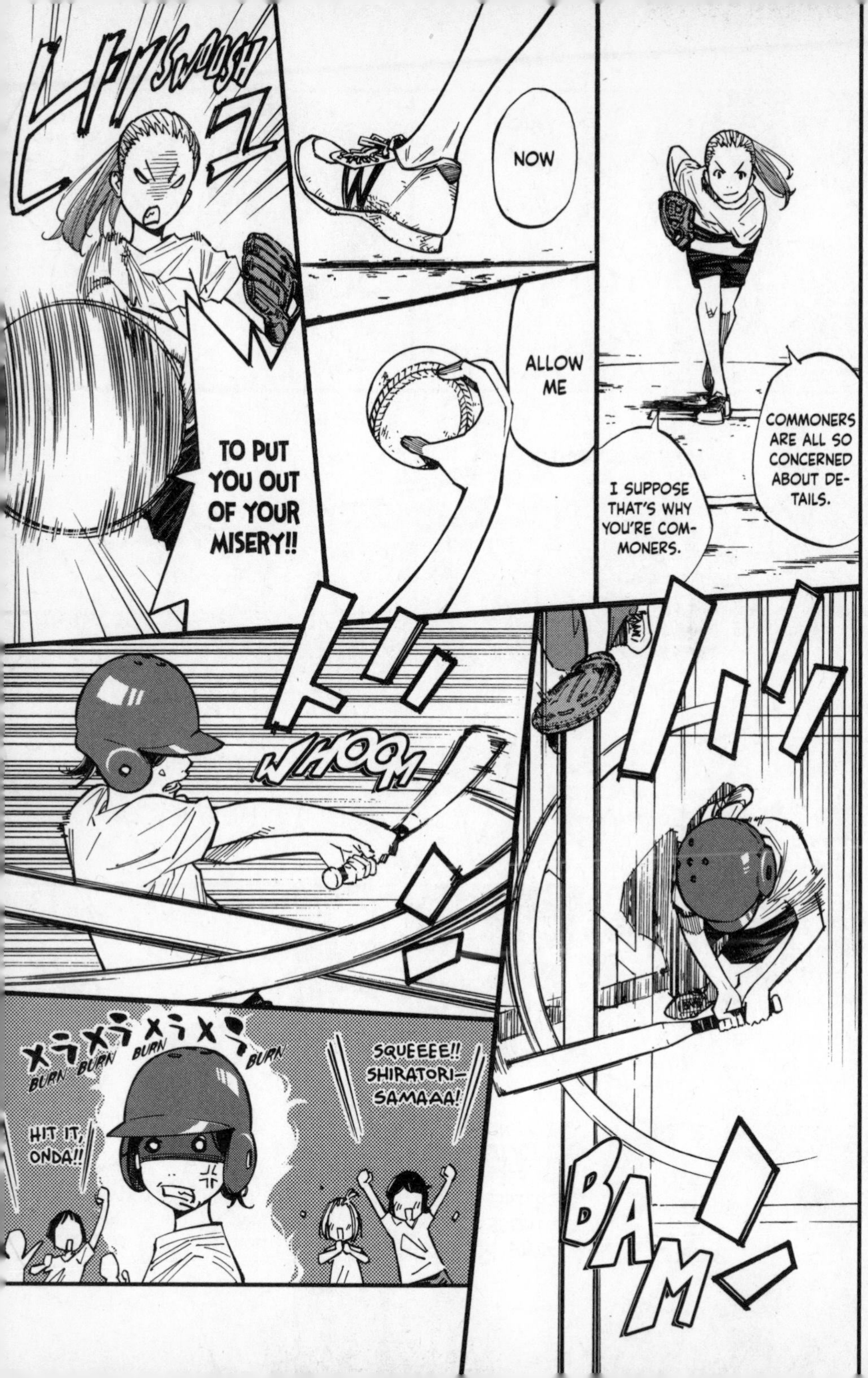
COMMONERS ARE ALL SO CONCERNED ABOUT DETAILS.
I SUPPOSE THAT'S WHY YOU'RE COMMONERS.
NOW
ALLOW ME
SWOOSH
TO PUT YOU OUT OF YOUR MISERY!!
BAM
WHOOM
BURN BURN BURN BURN
HIT IT, ONDA!!
SQUEEEE!! SHIRATORI-SAMAAA!

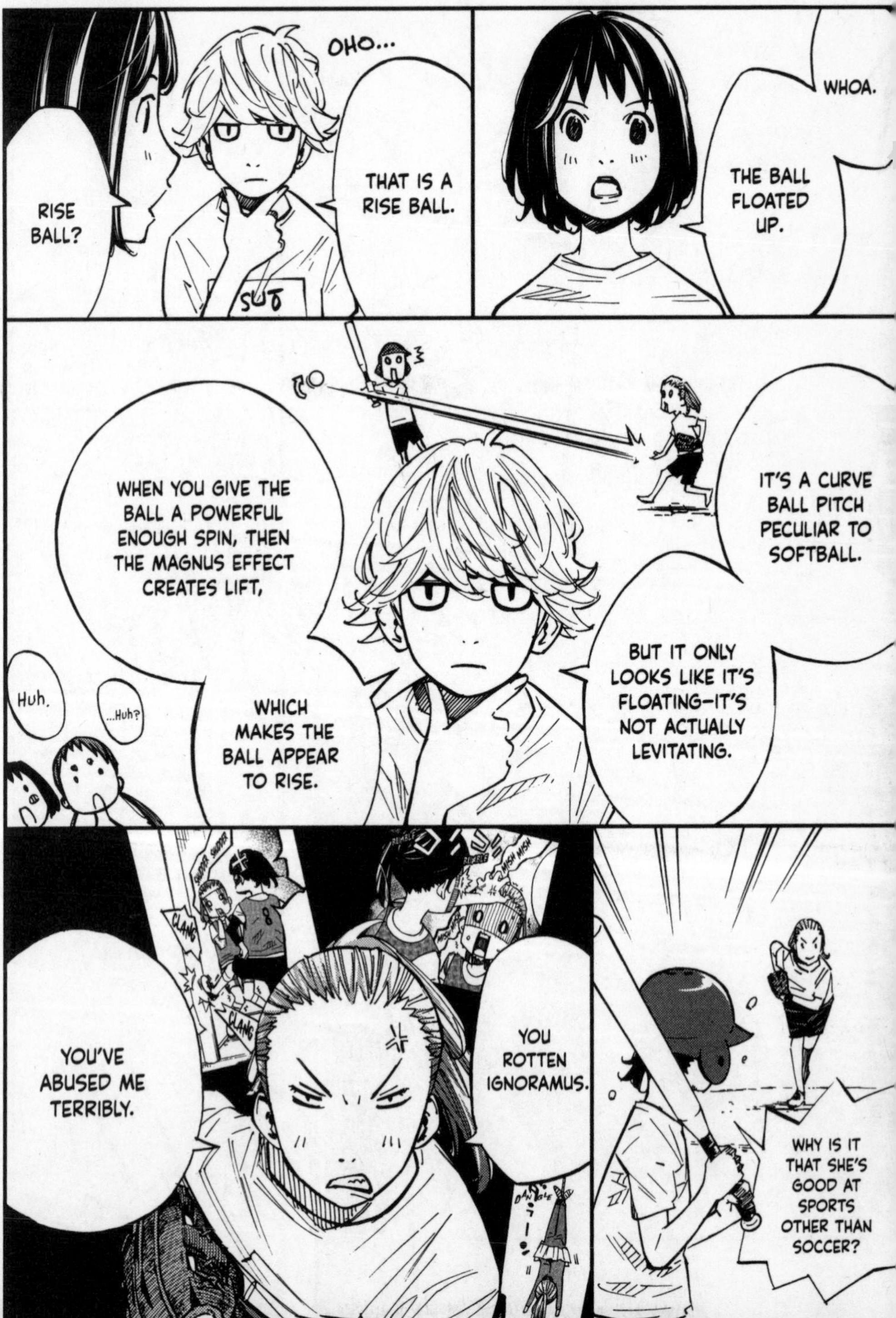
WHOA.
THE BALL FLOATED UP.
OHO...
THAT IS A RISE BALL.
RISE BALL?
IT'S A CURVE BALL PITCH PECULIAR TO SOFTBALL.
BUT IT ONLY LOOKS LIKE IT'S FLOATING—IT'S NOT ACTUALLY LEVITATING.
WHEN YOU GIVE THE BALL A POWERFUL ENOUGH SPIN, THEN THE MAGNUS EFFECT CREATES LIFT,
WHICH MAKES THE BALL APPEAR TO RISE.
...Huh?
Huh.
WHY IS IT THAT SHE'S GOOD AT SPORTS OTHER THAN SOCCER?
YOU ROTTEN IGNORAMUS.
YOU'VE ABUSED ME TERRIBLY.
CLANG
CLANG

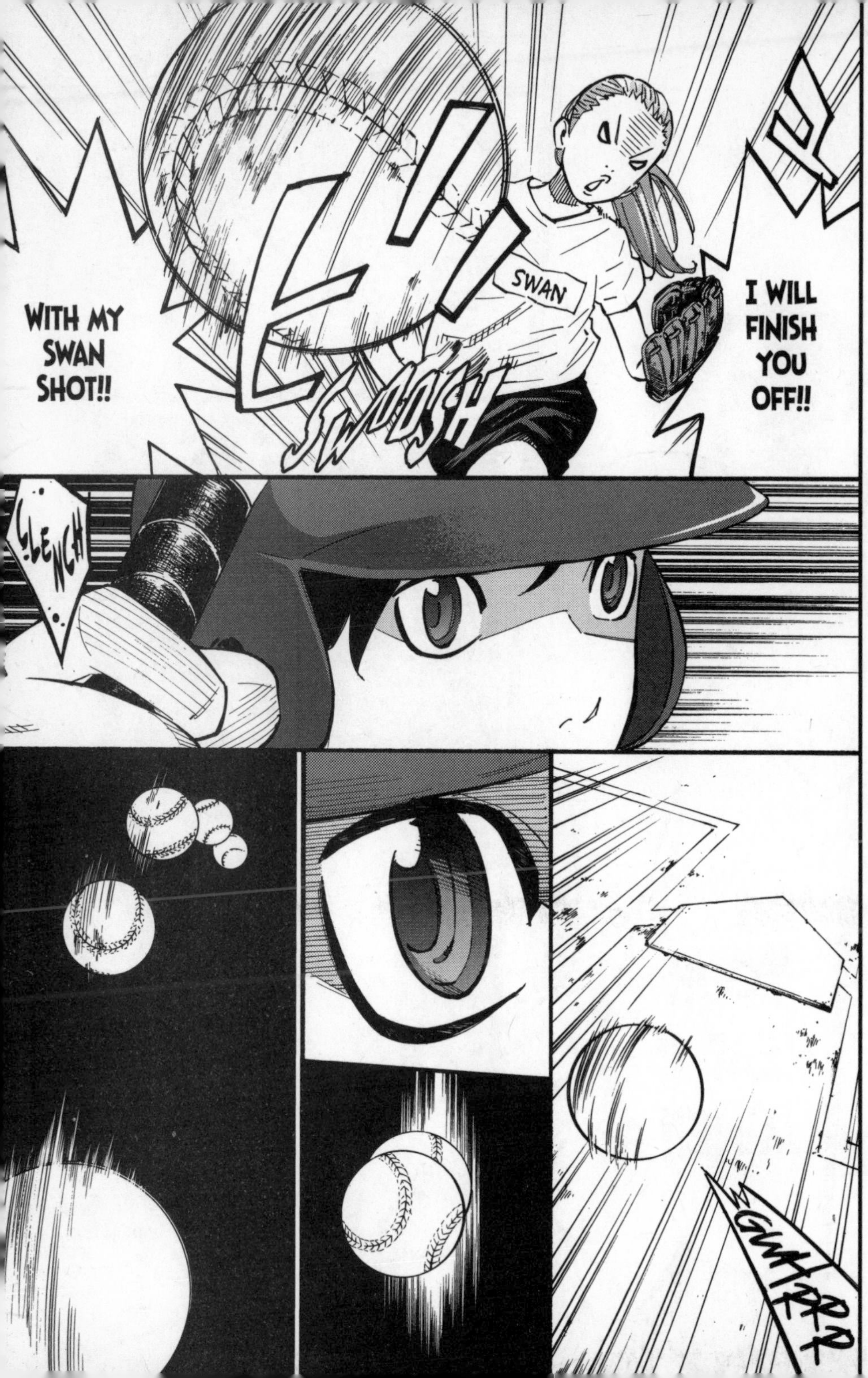
I WILL FINISH YOU OFF!!
SWAN
WITH MY SWAN SHOT!!
SWOOSH
CLENCH
GWHRRR

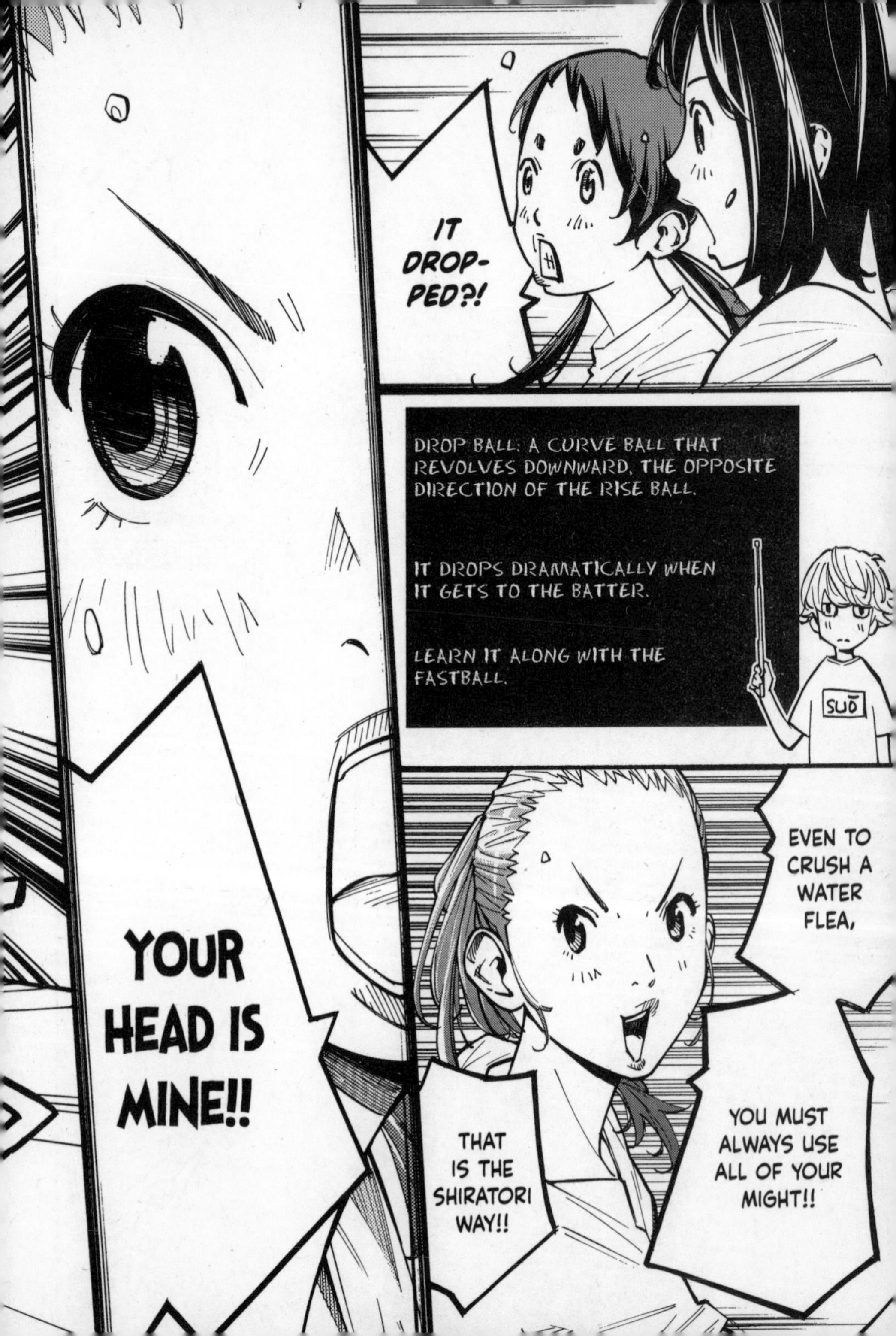
IT DROPPED?!
DROP BALL: A CURVE BALL THAT REVOLVES DOWNWARD, THE OPPOSITE DIRECTION OF THE RISE BALL.
IT DROPS DRAMATICALLY WHEN IT GETS TO THE BATTER.
LEARN IT ALONG WITH THE FASTBALL.
SUŌ
EVEN TO CRUSH A WATER FLEA,
YOU MUST ALWAYS USE ALL OF YOUR MIGHT!!
THAT IS THE SHIRATORI WAY!!
YOUR HEAD IS MINE!!

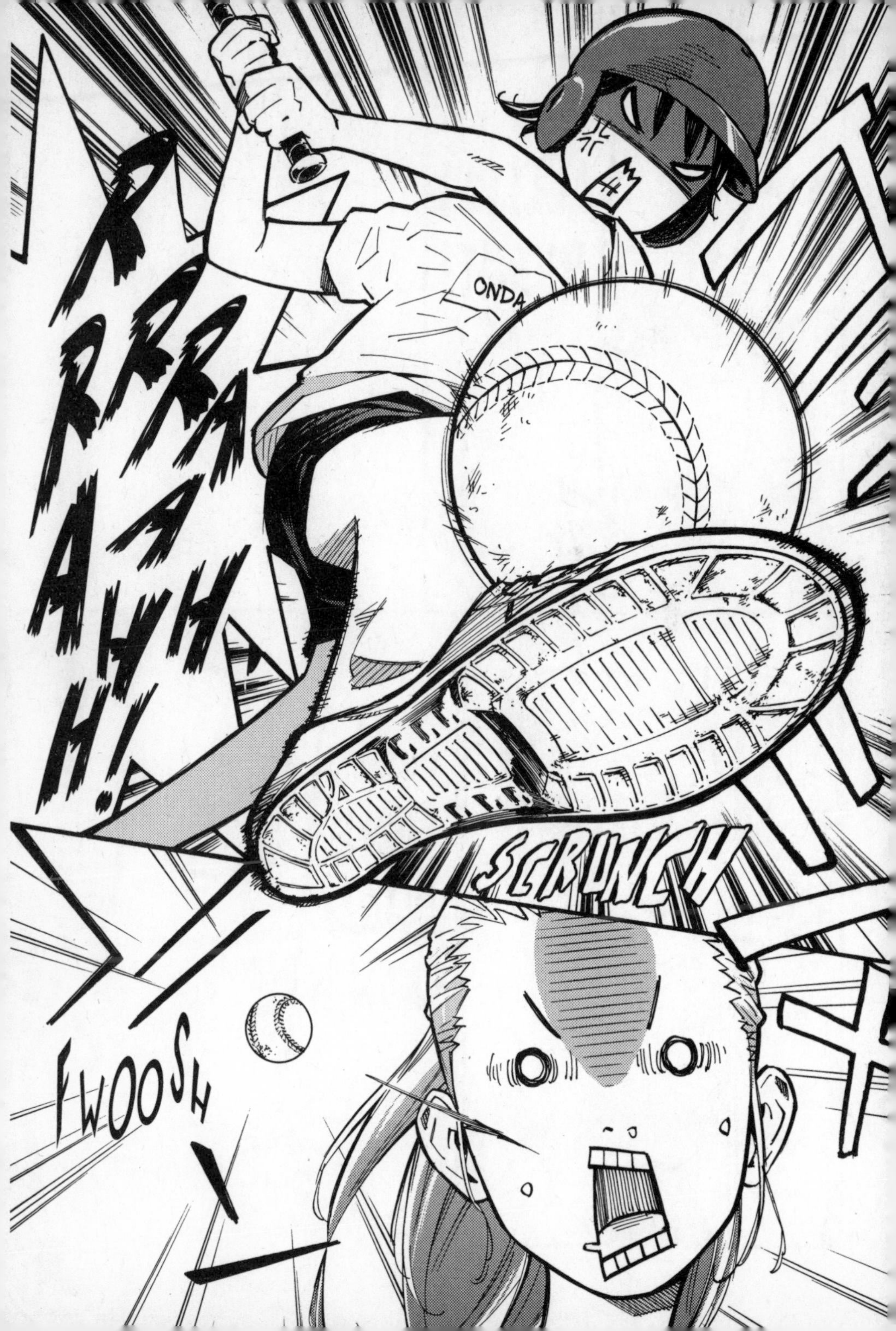

RRRRAAAHHH!!
ONDA
SCRUNCH
FWOOSH

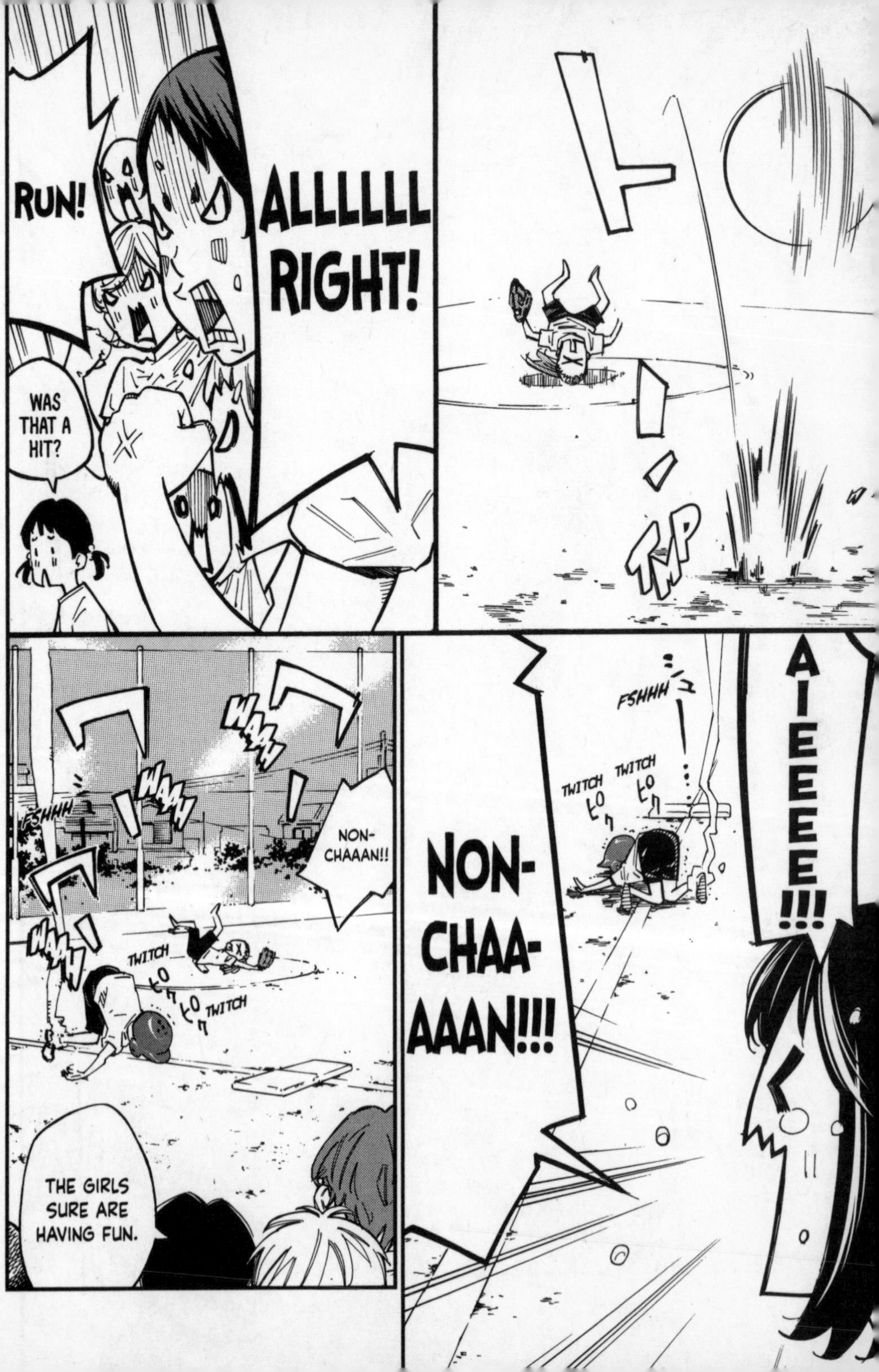
TMP
ALLLLLL RIGHT!
RUN!
WAS THAT A HIT?
AIEEEE!!!
FSHHH
TWITCH
TWITCH
NON-CHAA-AAAN!!!
WAAH
NON-CHAAAN!!
WAAH
FSHHH
WAAH
TWITCH
TWITCH
THE GIRLS SURE ARE HAVING FUN.

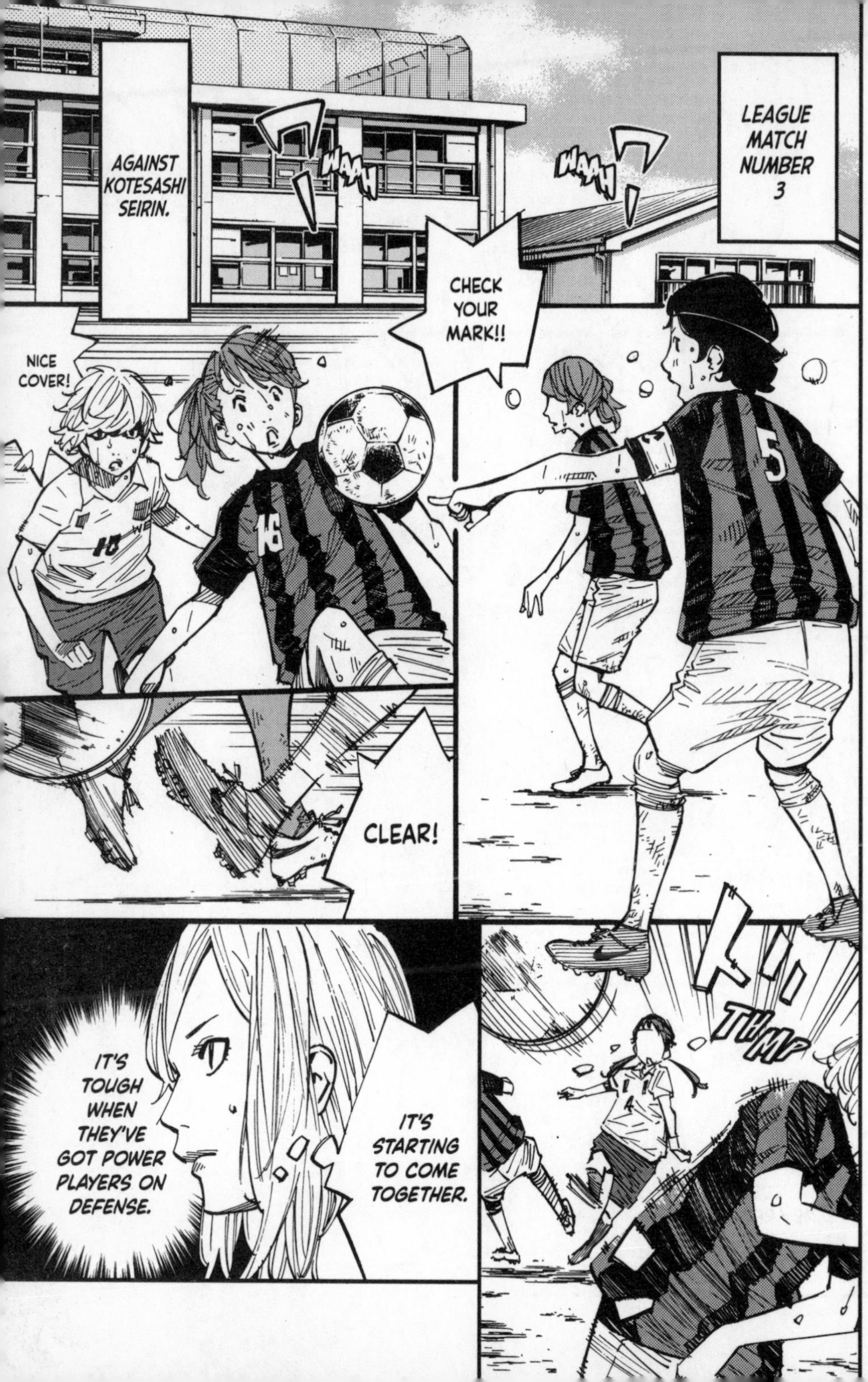
LEAGUE MATCH NUMBER 3
WAAH
WAAH
AGAINST KOTESASHI SEIRIN.
CHECK YOUR MARK!!
NICE COVER!
CLEAR!
THMP
IT'S STARTING TO COME TOGETHER.
IT'S TOUGH WHEN THEY'VE GOT POWER PLAYERS ON DEFENSE.

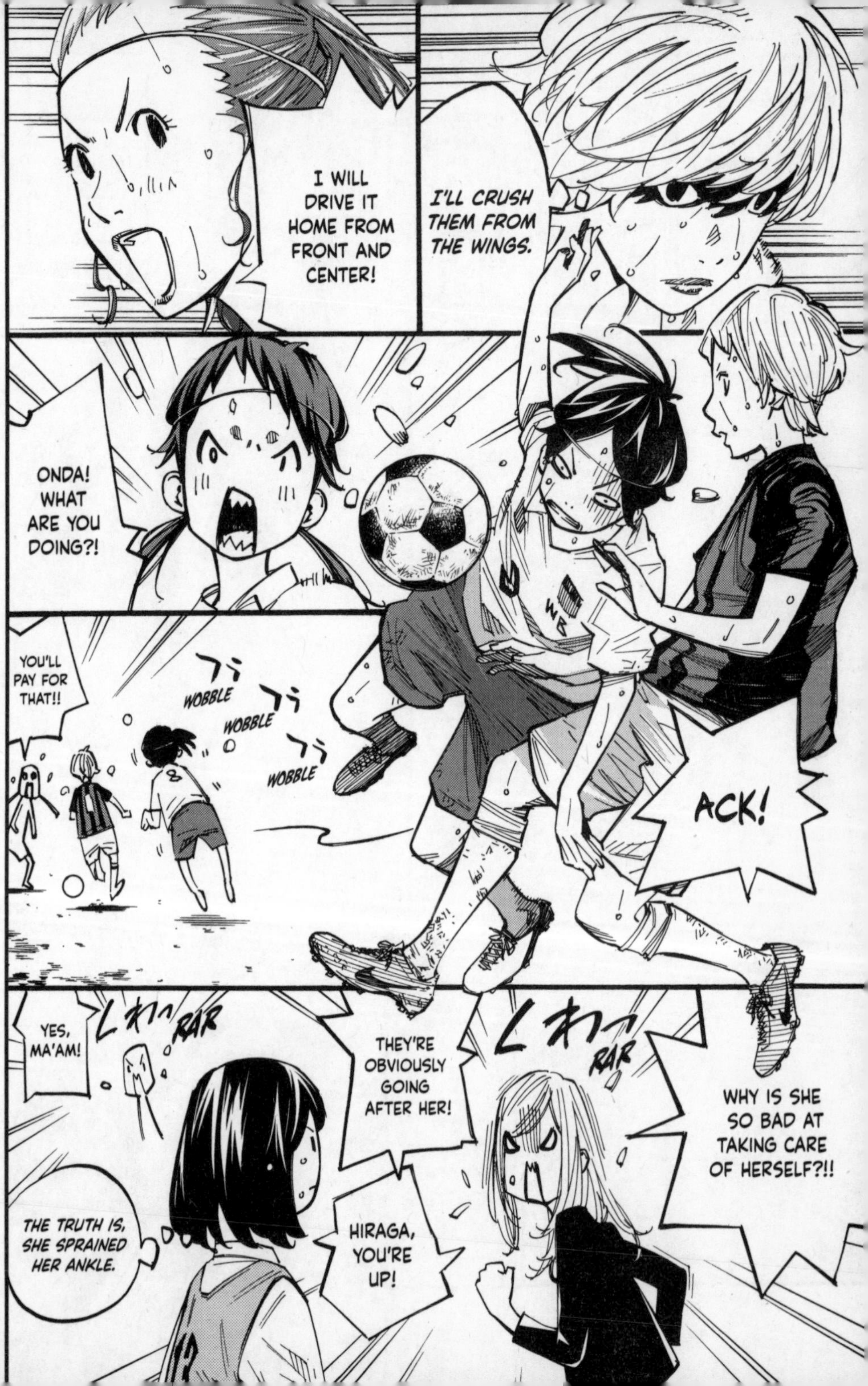
I'LL CRUSH THEM FROM THE WINGS.
I WILL DRIVE IT HOME FROM FRONT AND CENTER!
ACK!
ONDA! WHAT ARE YOU DOING?!
YOU'LL PAY FOR THAT!!
WOBBLE
WOBBLE
WOBBLE
WHY IS SHE SO BAD AT TAKING CARE OF HERSELF?!!
RAR
THEY'RE OBVIOUSLY GOING AFTER HER!
HIRAGA, YOU'RE UP!
RAR
YES, MA'AM!
THE TRUTH IS, SHE SPRAINED HER ANKLE.

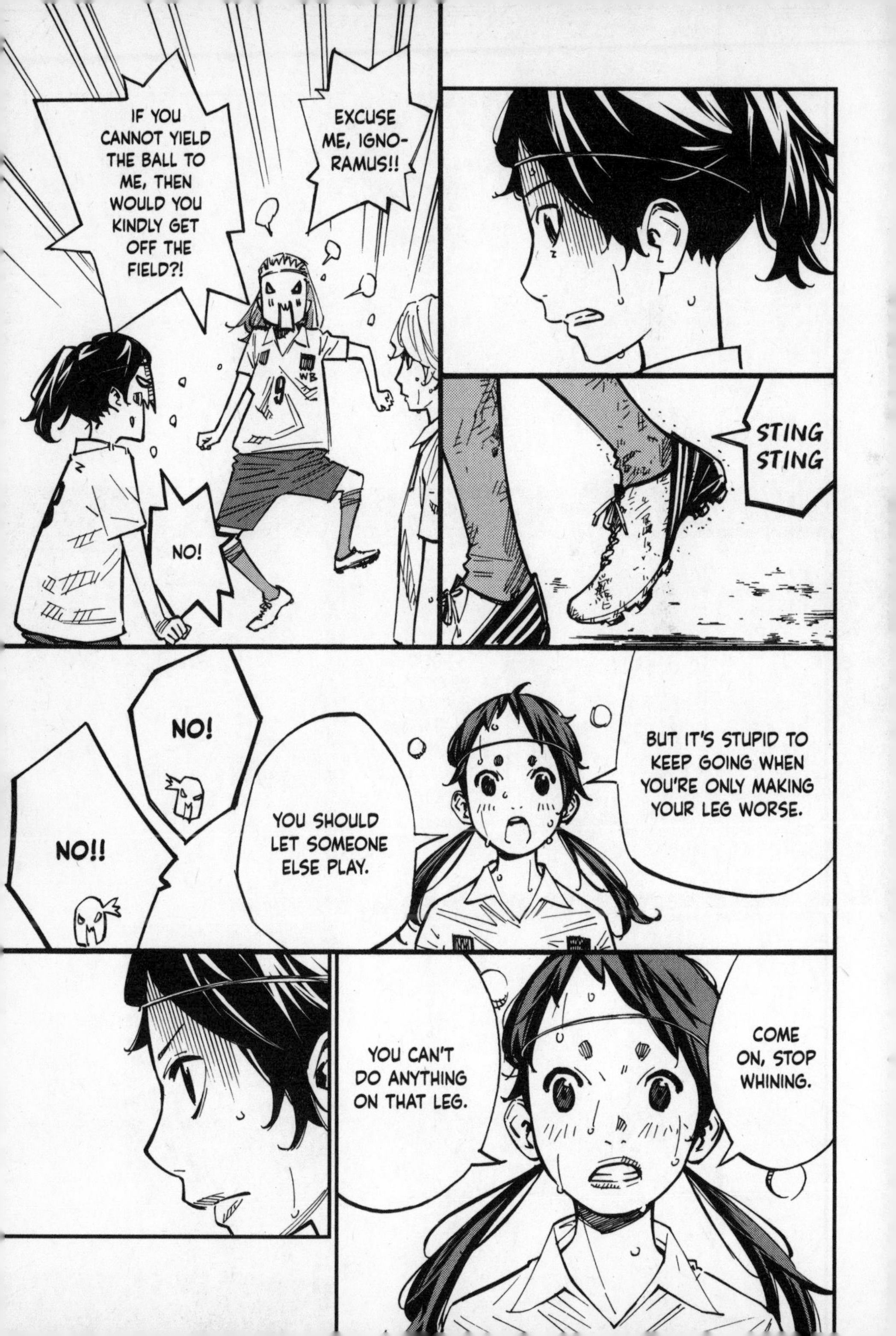
STING STING
EXCUSE ME, IGNORAMUS!!
IF YOU CANNOT YIELD THE BALL TO ME, THEN WOULD YOU KINDLY GET OFF THE FIELD?!
NO!
BUT IT'S STUPID TO KEEP GOING WHEN YOU'RE ONLY MAKING YOUR LEG WORSE.
YOU SHOULD LET SOMEONE ELSE PLAY.
NO!
NO!!
COME ON, STOP WHINING.
YOU CAN'T DO ANYTHING ON THAT LEG.

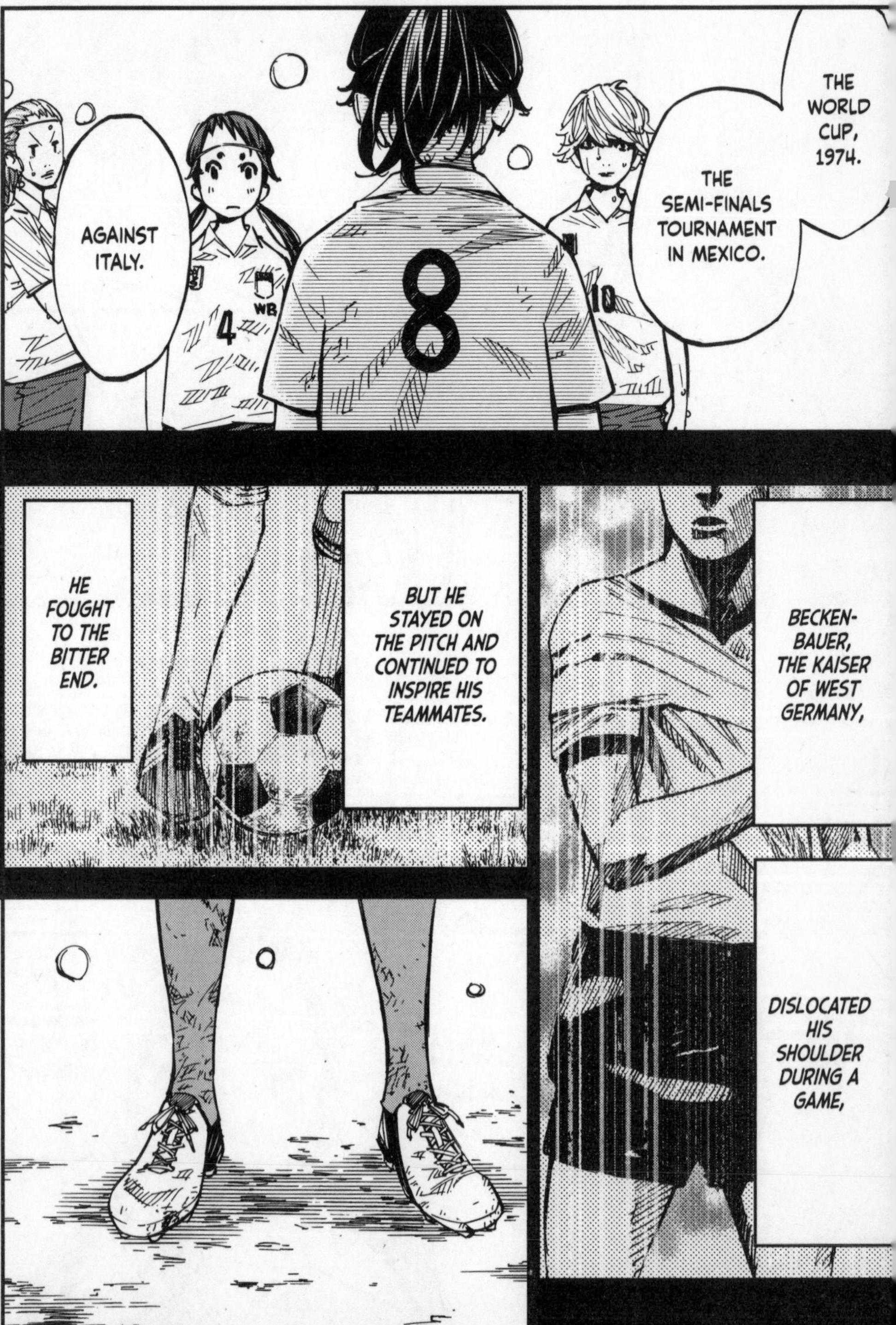

THE WORLD CUP, 1974.
THE SEMI-FINALS TOURNAMENT IN MEXICO.
AGAINST ITALY.
BECKEN-BAUER, THE KAISER OF WEST GERMANY,
DISLOCATED HIS SHOULDER DURING A GAME,
BUT HE STAYED ON THE PITCH AND CONTINUED TO INSPIRE HIS TEAMMATES.
HE FOUGHT TO THE BITTER END.

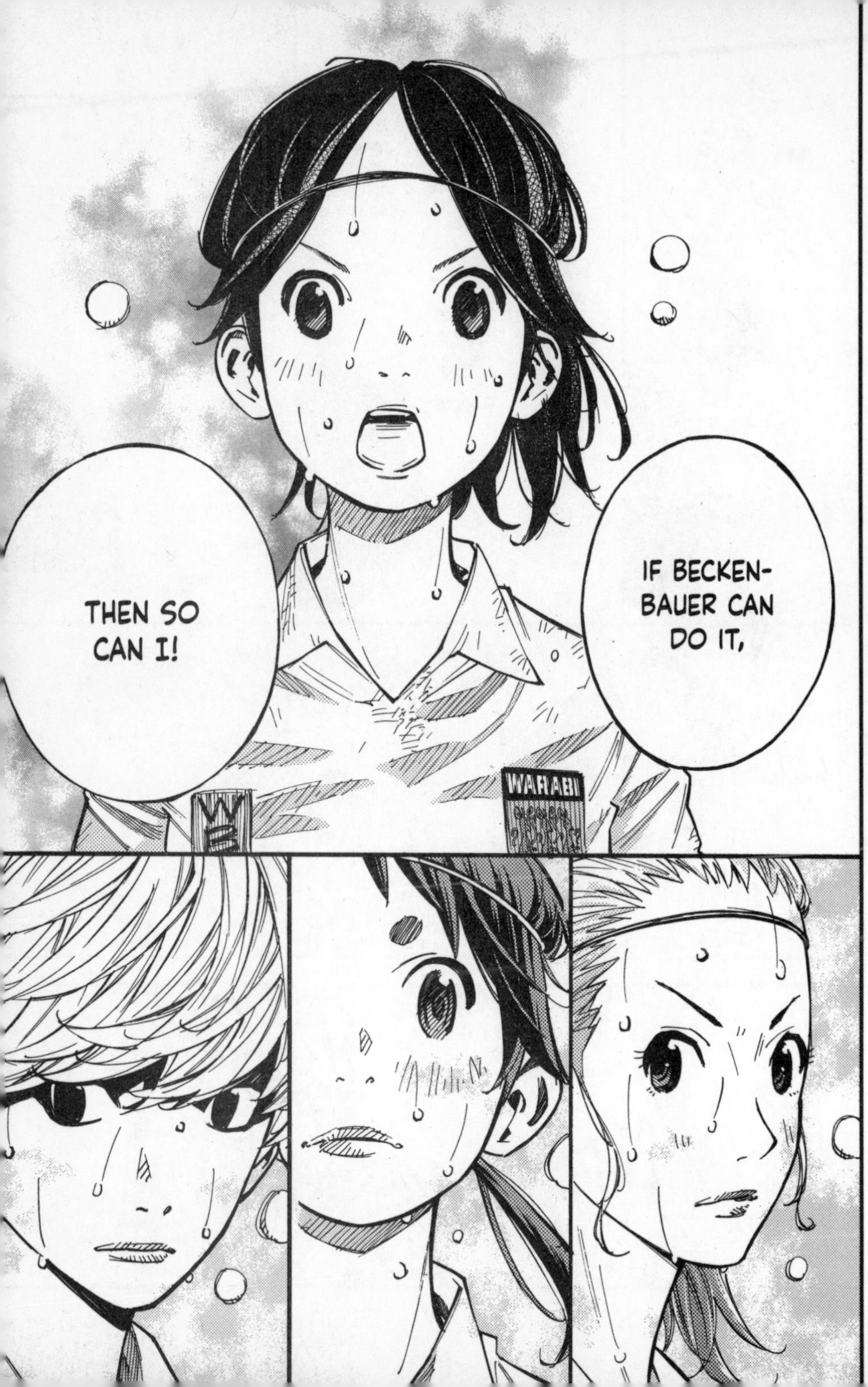
IF BECKEN-BAUER CAN DO IT,
THEN SO CAN I!
WARABI

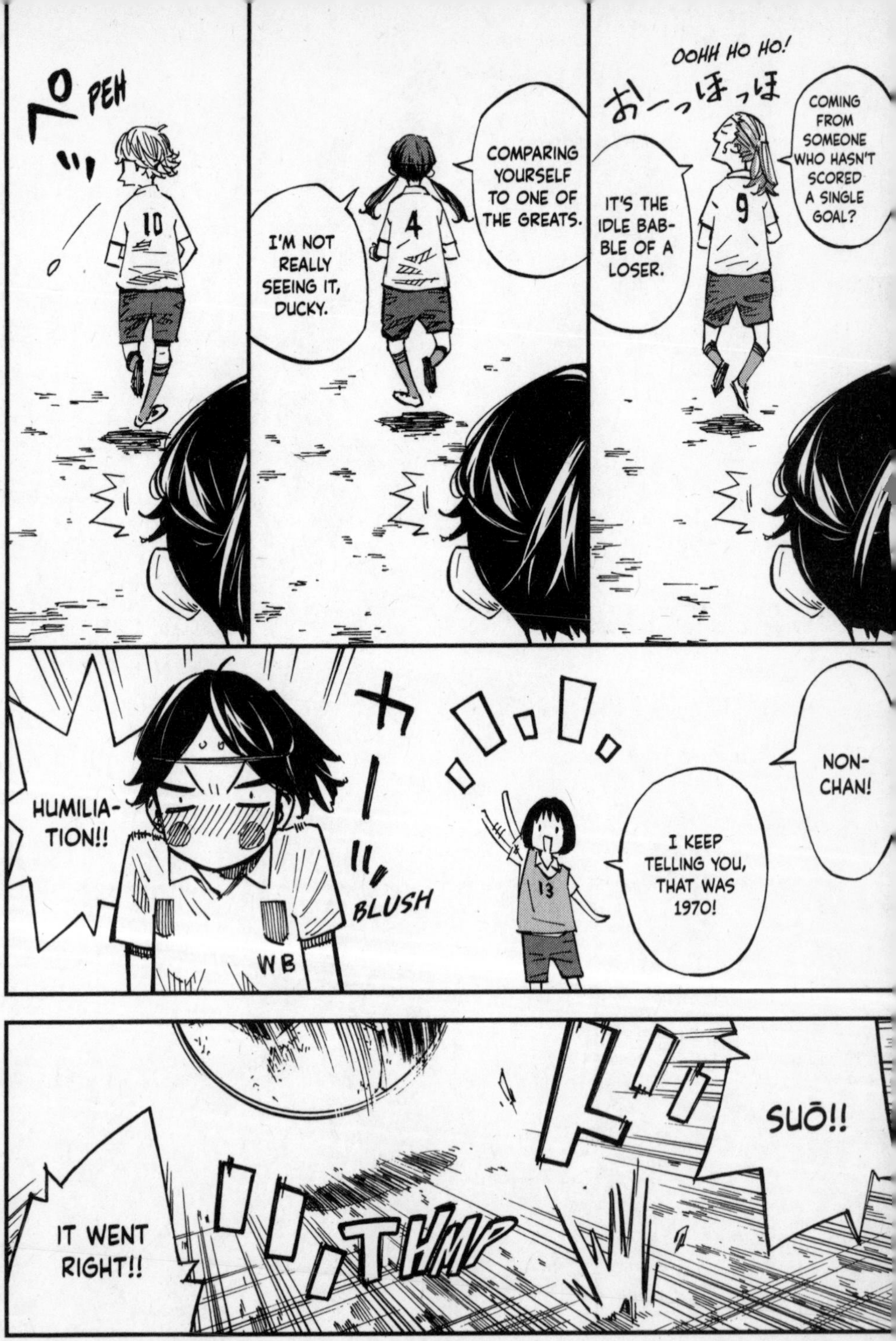
おーっほっほ
OOHH HO HO!
COMING FROM SOMEONE WHO HASN'T SCORED A SINGLE GOAL?
IT'S THE IDLE BAB-BLE OF A LOSER.
COMPARING YOURSELF TO ONE OF THE GREATS.
I'M NOT REALLY SEEING IT, DUCKY.
ぺっ
PEH
NON-CHAN!
I KEEP TELLING YOU, THAT WAS 1970!
カーッ
BLUSH
HUMILIA-TION!!
WB
SUŌ!!
ドッ
THMP
IT WENT RIGHT!!

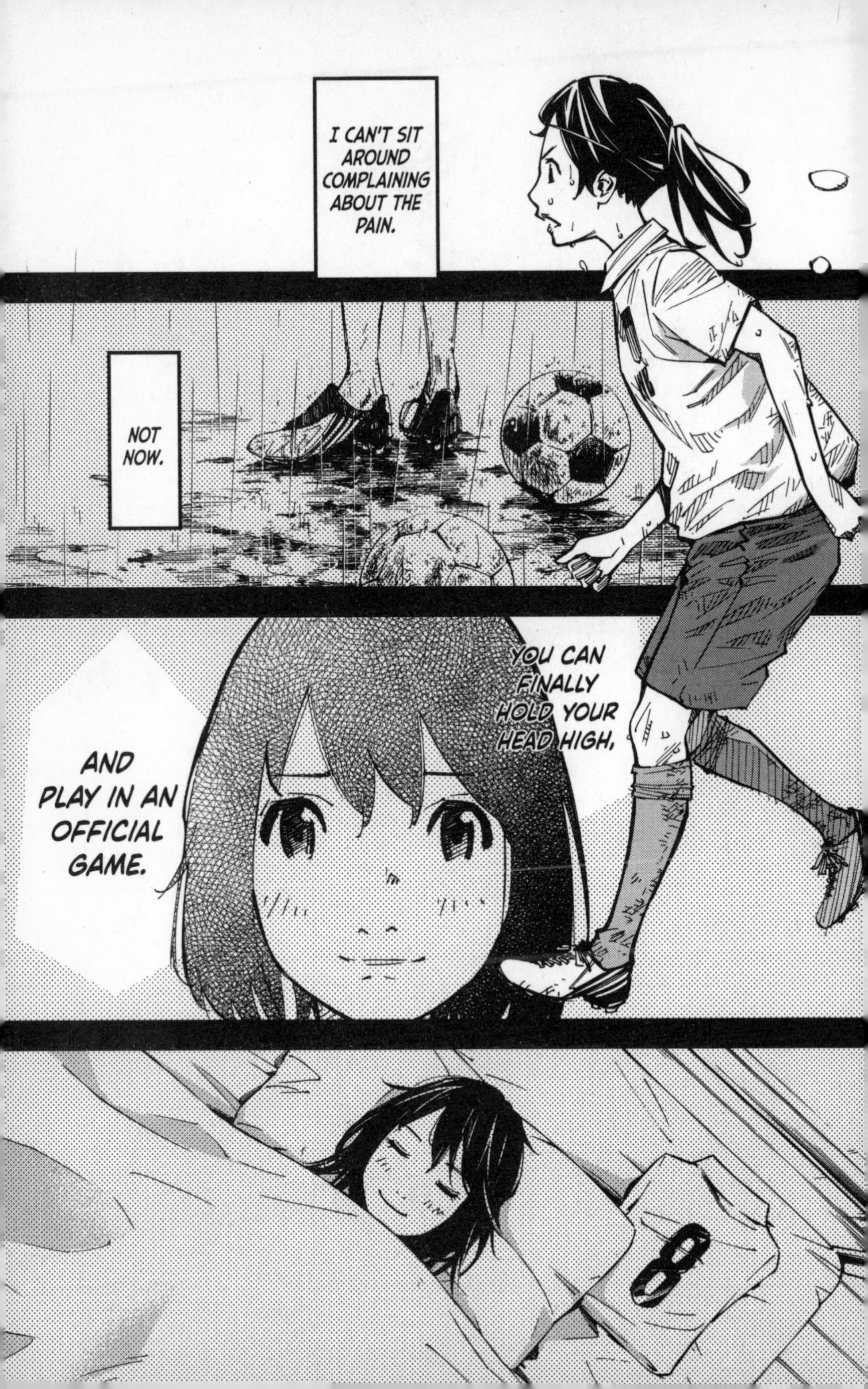
I CAN'T SIT AROUND COMPLAINING ABOUT THE PAIN.
NOT NOW.
YOU CAN FINALLY HOLD YOUR HEAD HIGH,
AND PLAY IN AN OFFICIAL GAME.

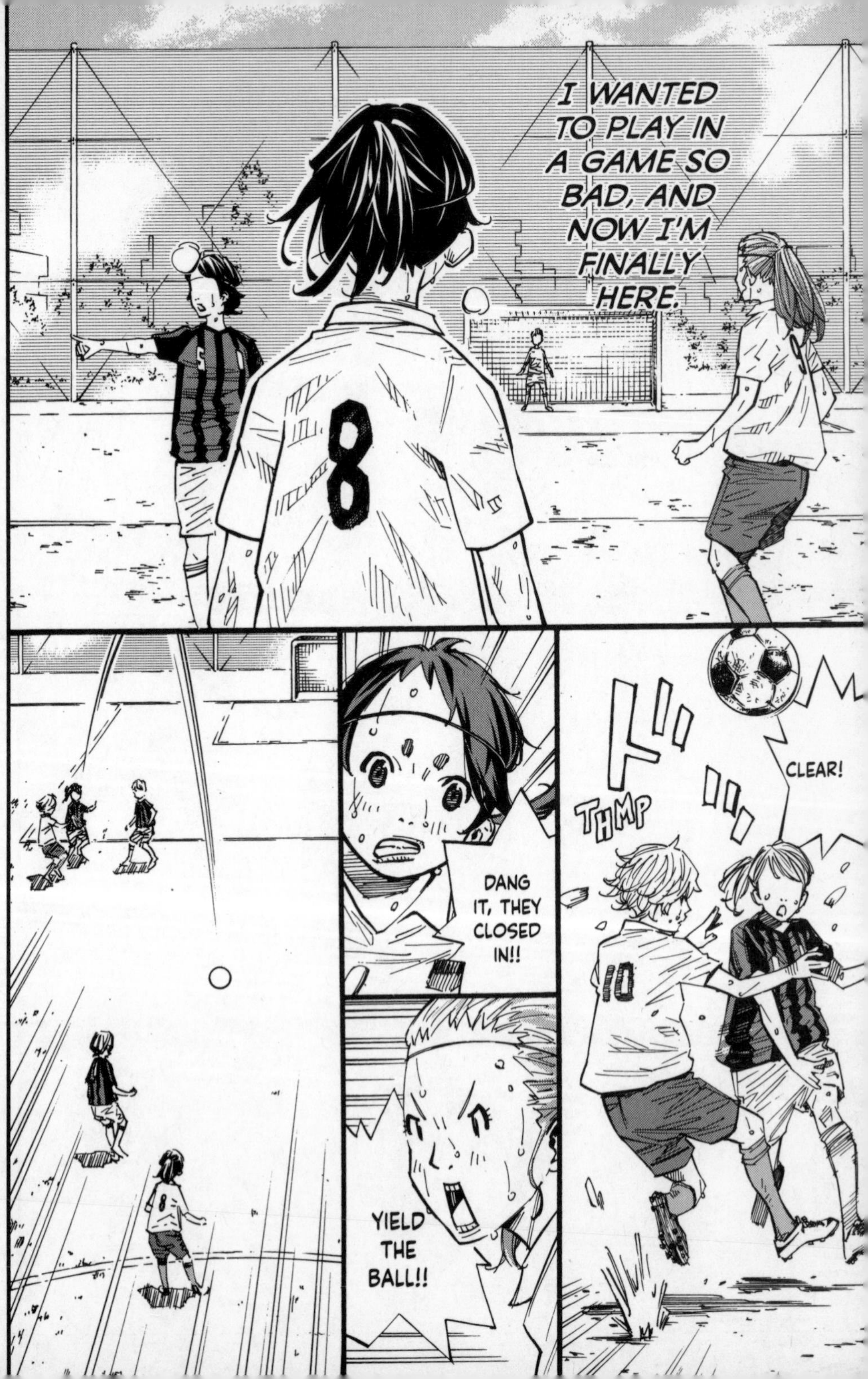
I WANTED TO PLAY IN A GAME SO BAD, AND NOW I'M FINALLY HERE.
THMP
CLEAR!
DANG IT, THEY CLOSED IN!!
YIELD THE BALL!!

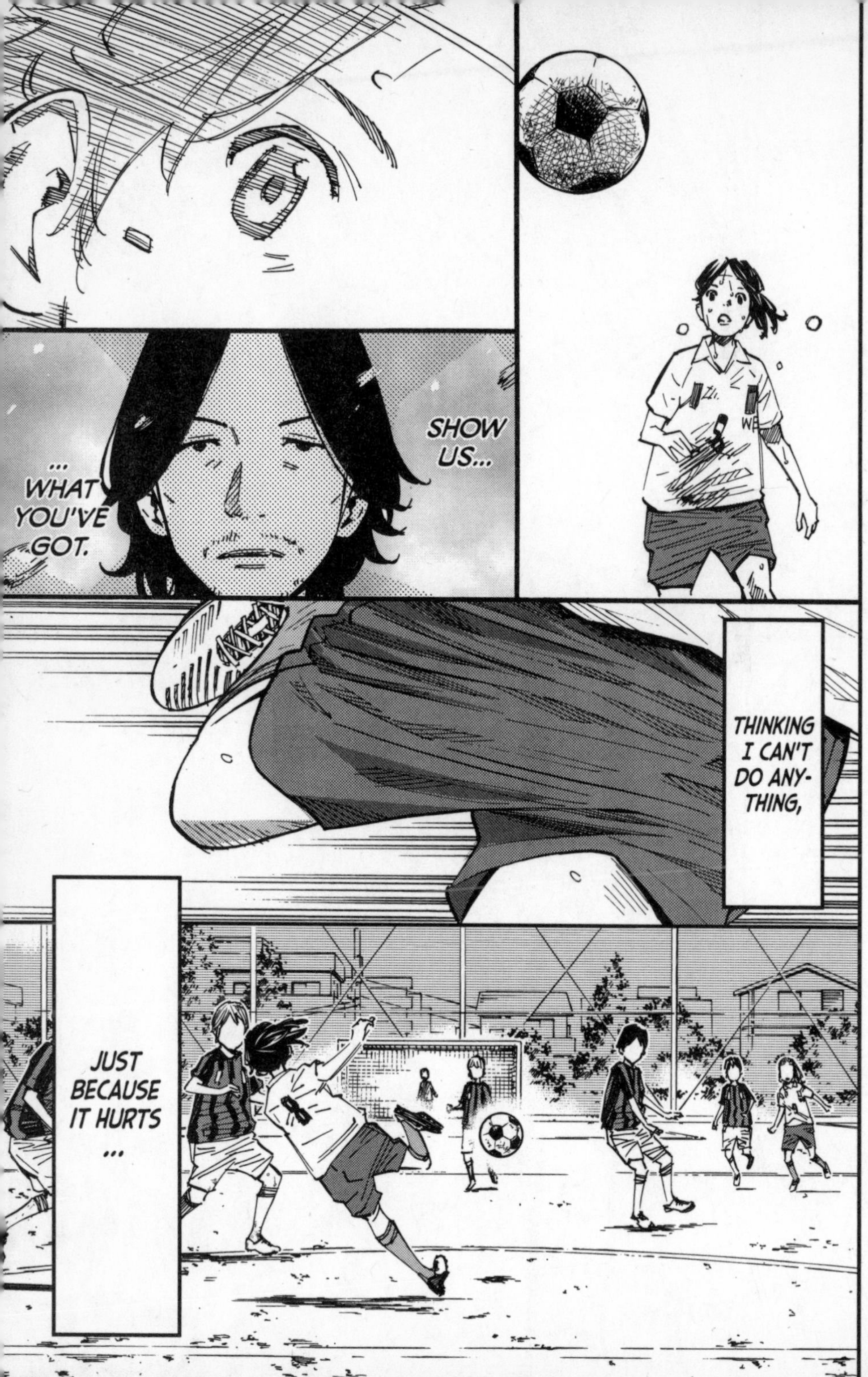
SHOW US...
... WHAT YOU'VE GOT.
THINKING I CAN'T DO ANY-THING,
JUST BECAUSE IT HURTS ...

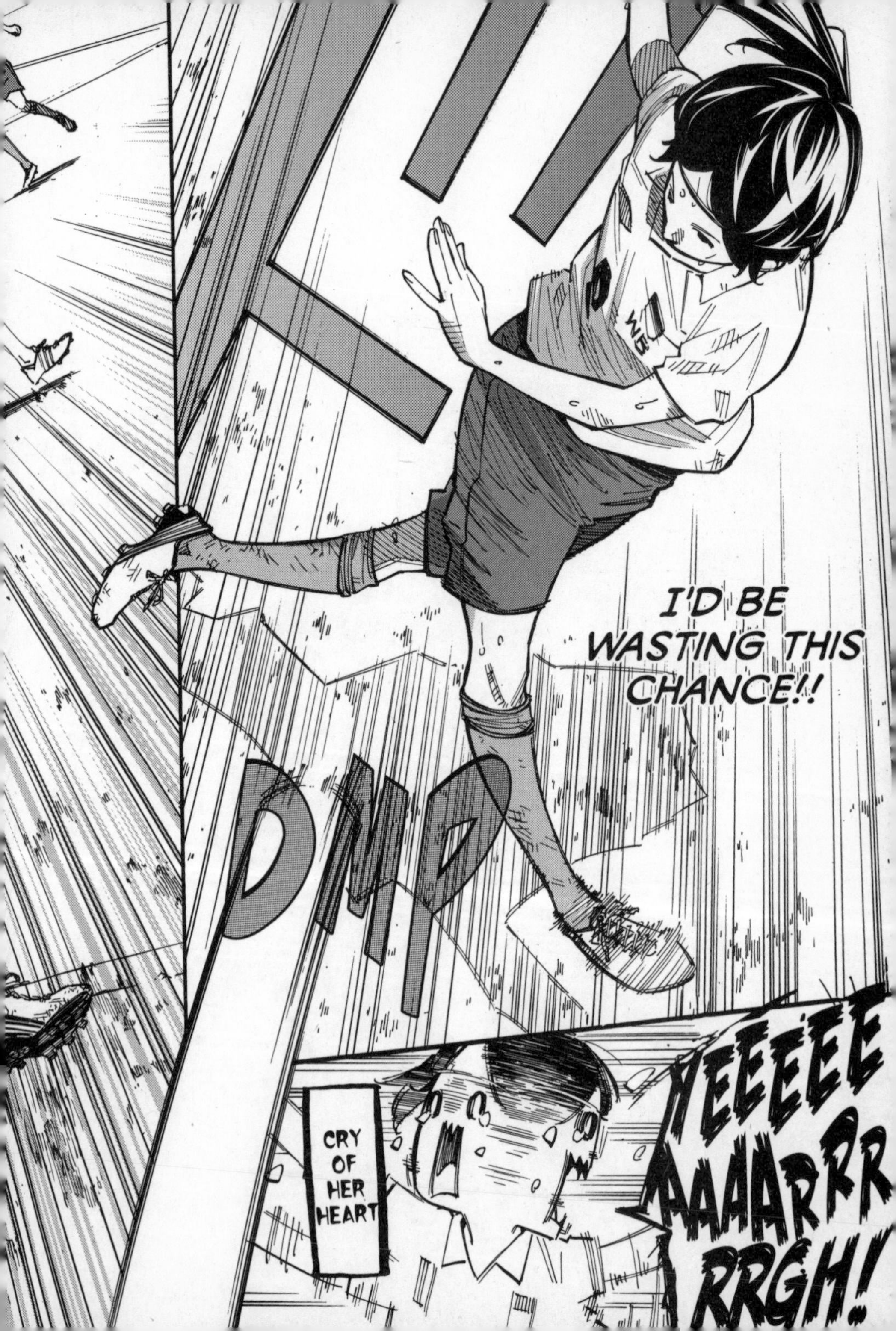
I'D BE WASTING THIS CHANCE!!
DMP
YEEEEE AAAARRR RRGH!
CRY OF HER HEART

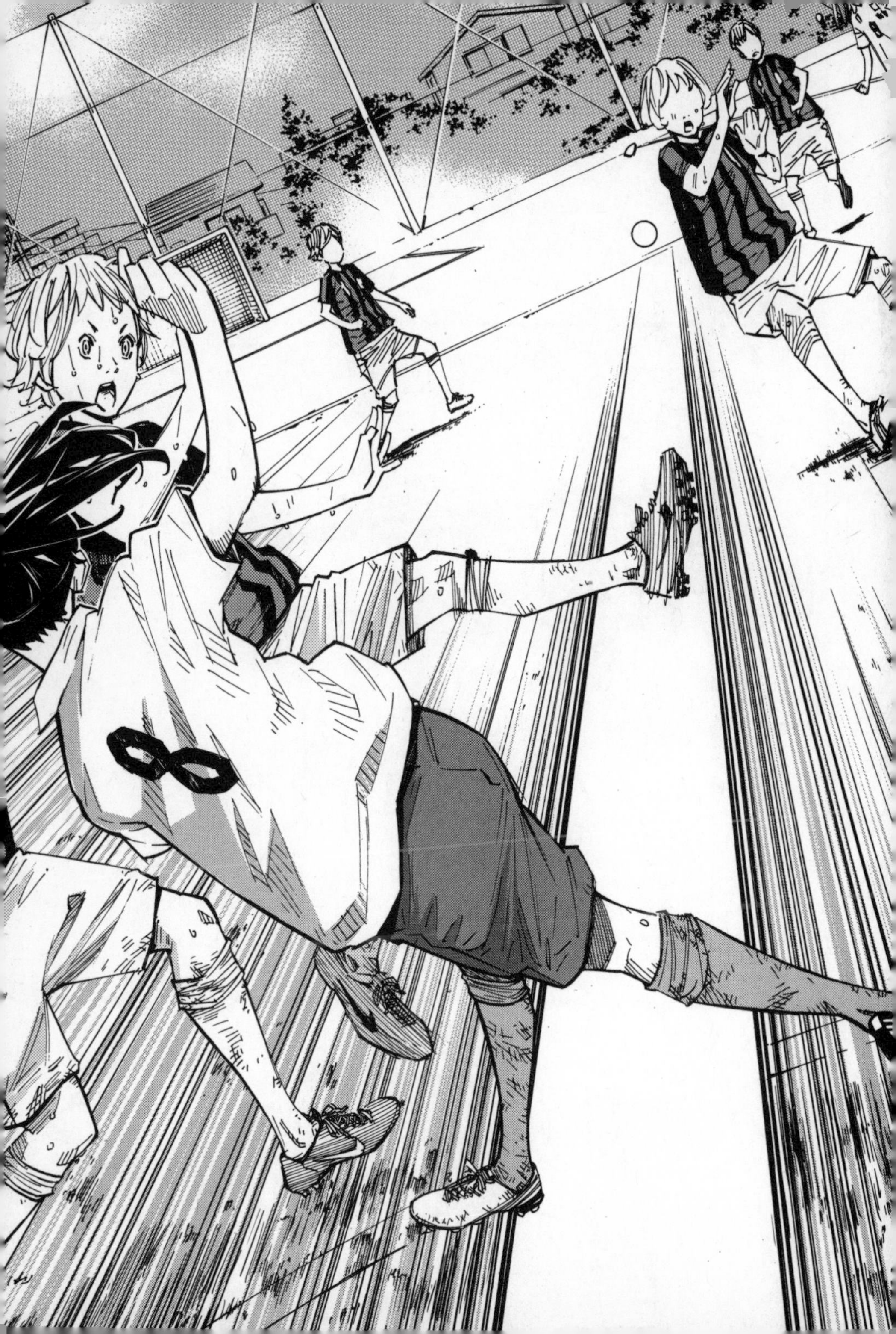

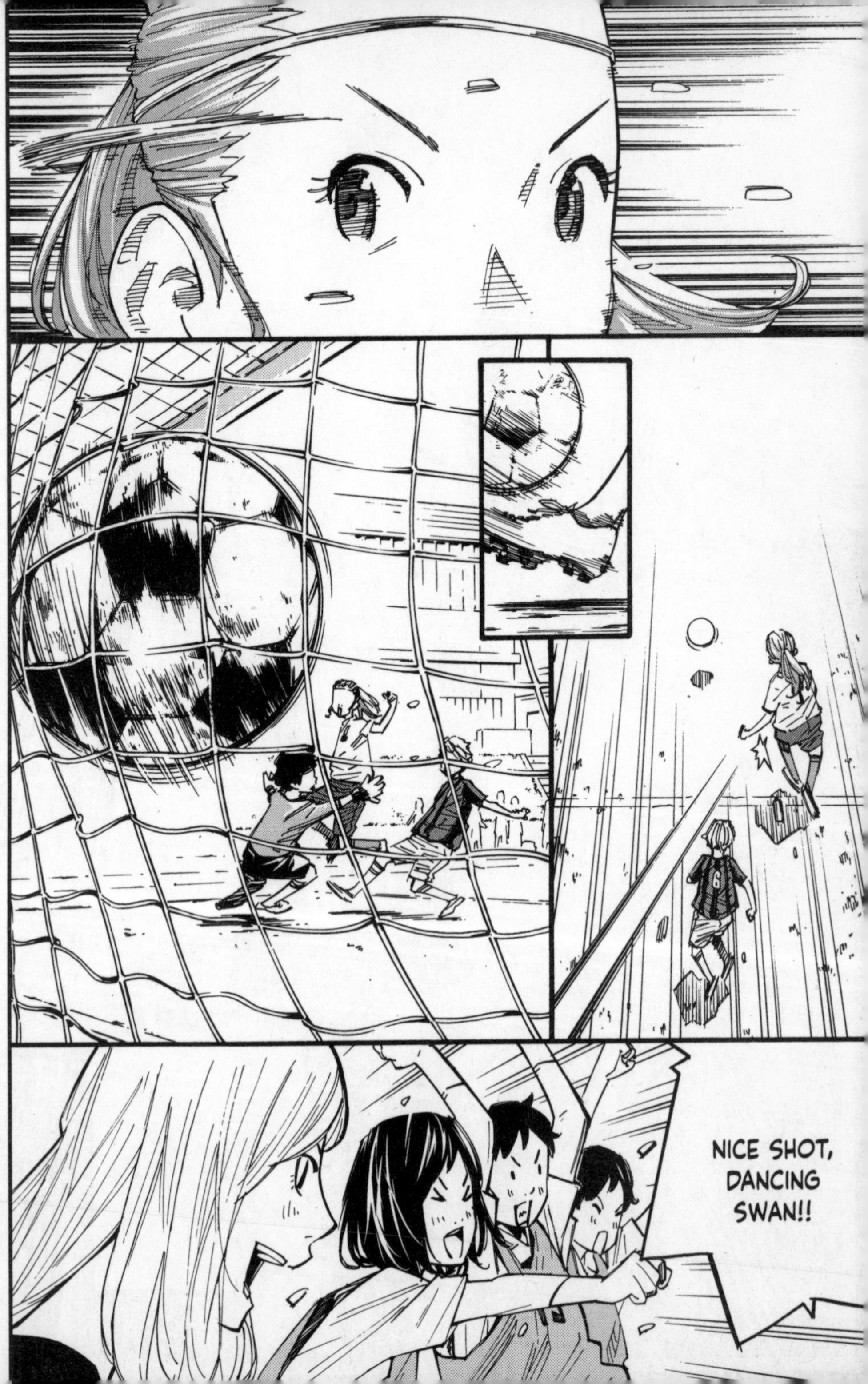
NICE SHOT, DANCING SWAN!!

A DIRECT THROUGH PASS, WITH AN INJURED LEG.

SHE'S CRAZY.

THEN SO CAN I, EH?

I CAN'T GO ON...

STING

STING

IF BECKENBAUER CAN DO IT,

TEAM	FIRST HALF	SECOND HALF	OVERTIME		
			WARABI SEINAN		
			FIRST HALF		SEC HO
asaka com	3	2		RANKED SECOND IN GROUP D.	
warabi seinan	3	1			

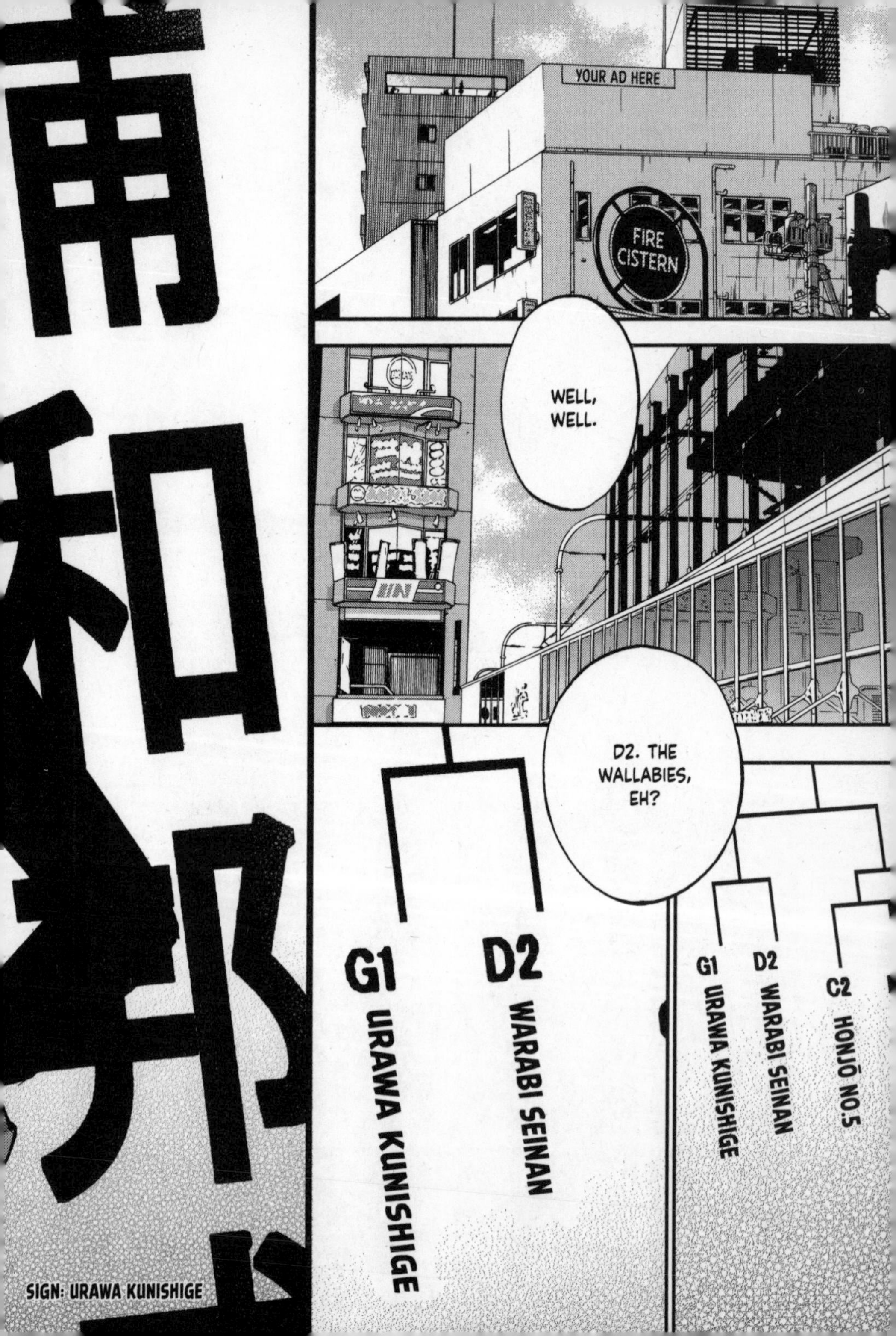
YOUR AD HERE
FIRE CISTERN
WELL, WELL.
D2. THE WALLABIES, EH?
C2 HONJŌ NO.5
D2 WARABI SEINAN
G1 URAWA KUNISHIGE
D2 WARABI SEINAN
G1 URAWA KUNISHIGE
SIGN: URAWA KUNISHIGE

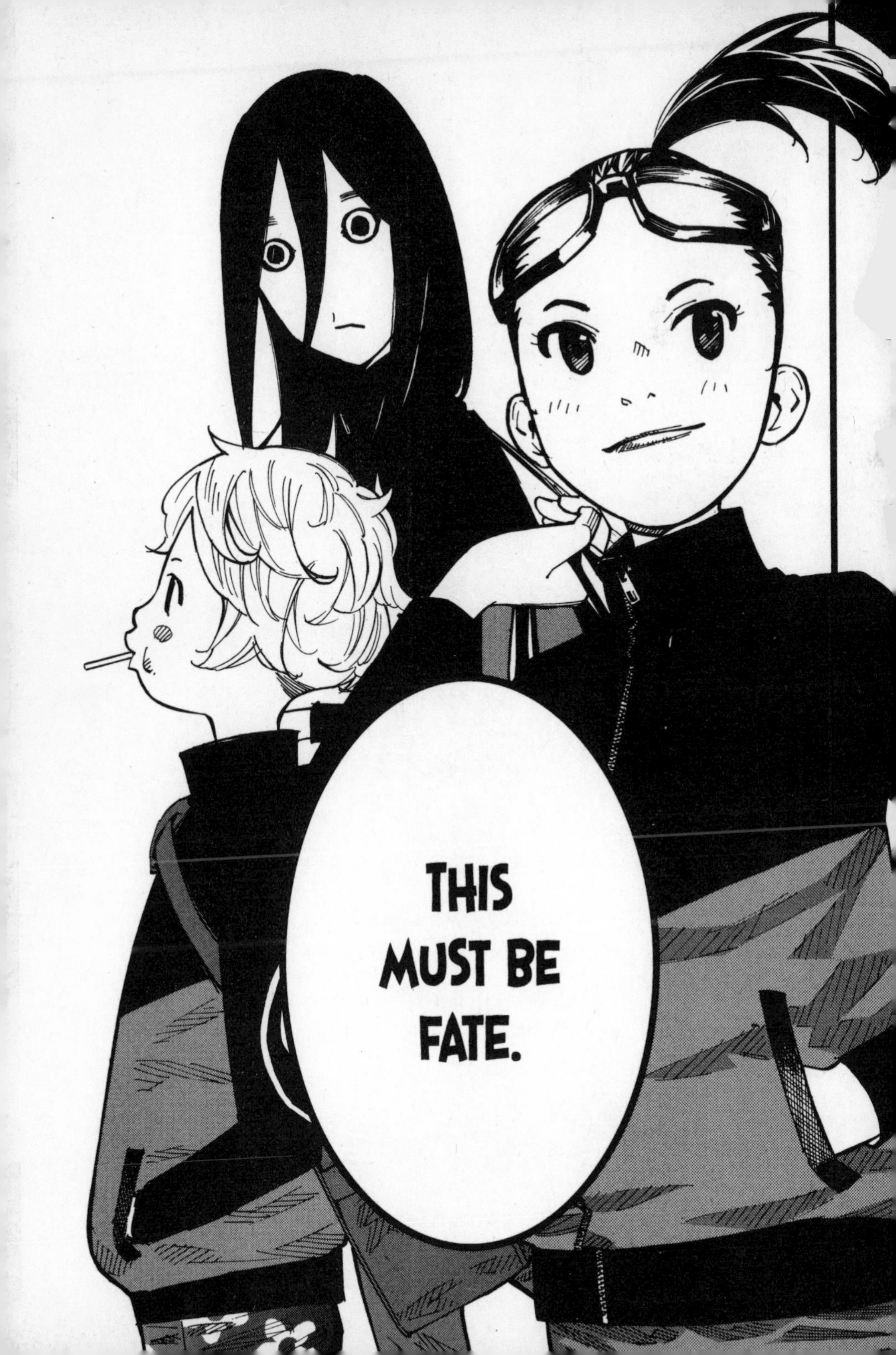
THIS MUST BE FATE.

Farewell, My Dear Cramer

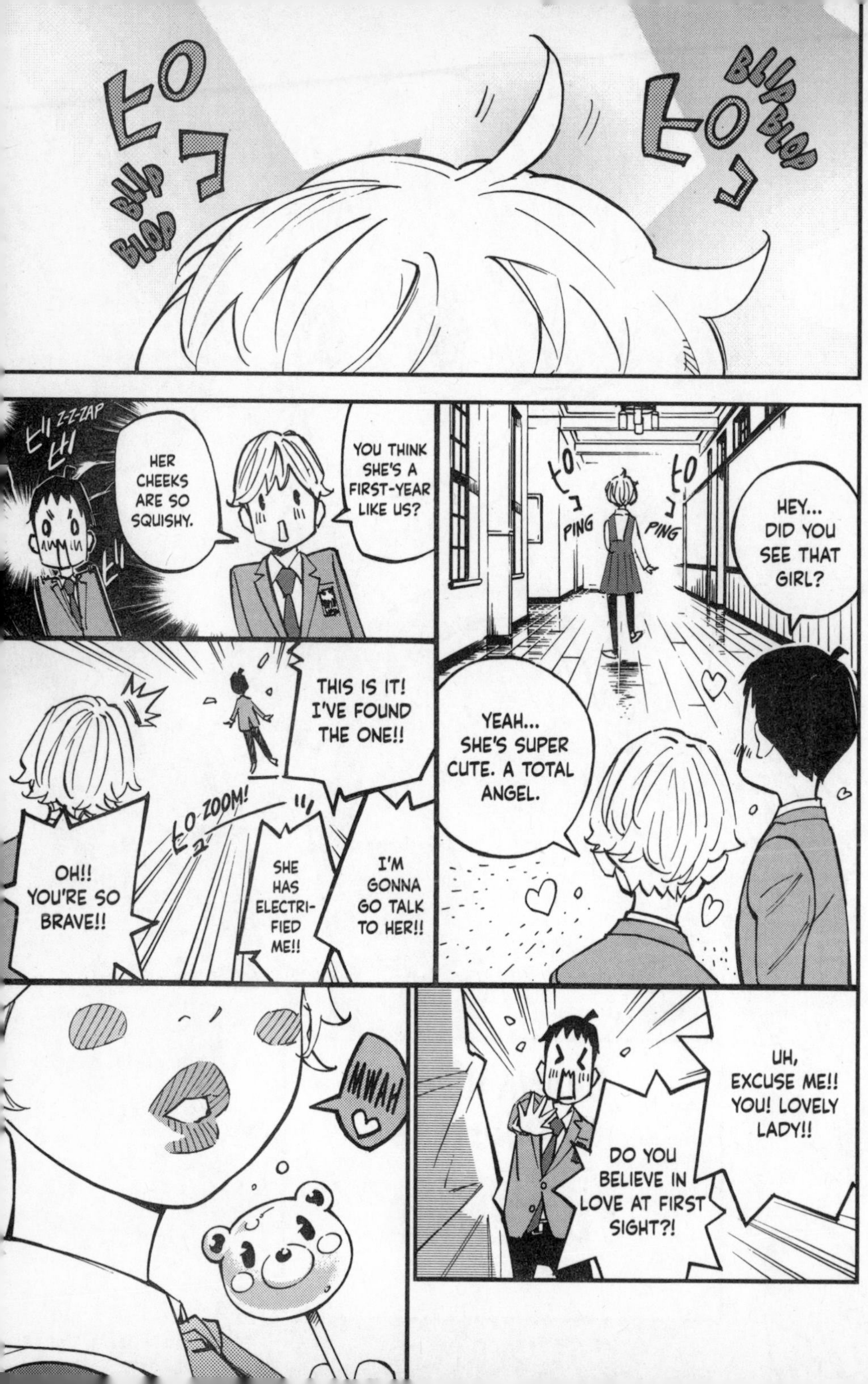
BLIP BLOP
BLIP BLOP
PING
PING
HEY... DID YOU SEE THAT GIRL?
YEAH... SHE'S SUPER CUTE. A TOTAL ANGEL.
YOU THINK SHE'S A FIRST-YEAR LIKE US?
HER CHEEKS ARE SO SQUISHY.
Z-Z-ZAP
THIS IS IT! I'VE FOUND THE ONE!!
ZOOM!
I'M GONNA GO TALK TO HER!!
SHE HAS ELECTRIFIED ME!!
OH!! YOU'RE SO BRAVE!!
UH, EXCUSE ME!! YOU! LOVELY LADY!!
DO YOU BELIEVE IN LOVE AT FIRST SIGHT?!
MWAH

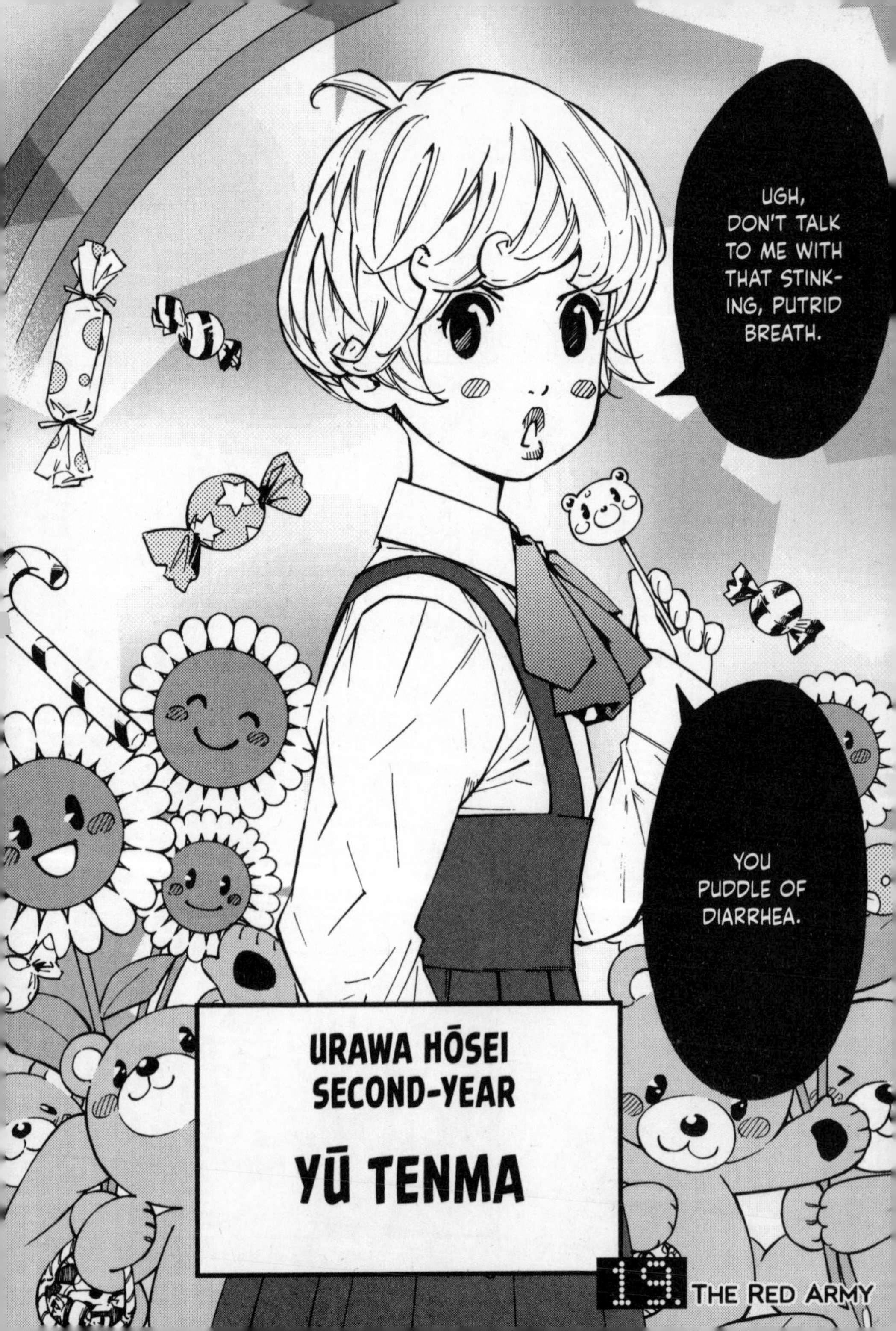

UGH, DON'T TALK TO ME WITH THAT STINK-ING, PUTRID BREATH.
YOU PUDDLE OF DIARRHEA.
URAWA HŌSEI SECOND-YEAR
YŪ TENMA
19. THE RED ARMY

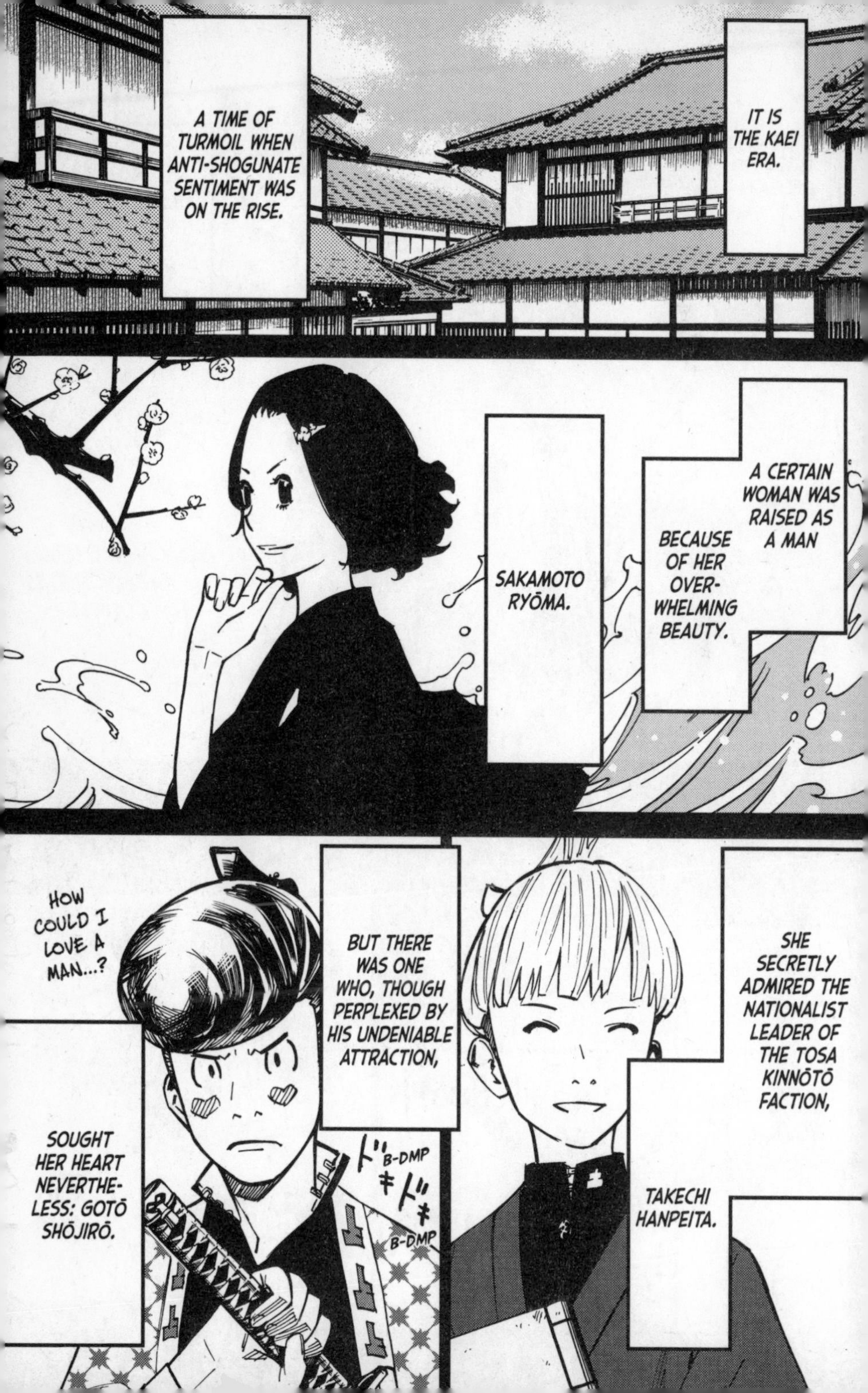
IT IS THE KAEI ERA.
A TIME OF TURMOIL WHEN ANTI-SHOGUNATE SENTIMENT WAS ON THE RISE.
A CERTAIN WOMAN WAS RAISED AS A MAN
BECAUSE OF HER OVER-WHELMING BEAUTY.
SAKAMOTO RYŌMA.
SHE SECRETLY ADMIRED THE NATIONALIST LEADER OF THE TOSA KINNŌTŌ FACTION,
TAKECHI HANPEITA.
BUT THERE WAS ONE WHO, THOUGH PERPLEXED BY HIS UNDENIABLE ATTRACTION,
HOW COULD I LOVE A MAN...?
ドキ B-DMP
ドキ B-DMP
SOUGHT HER HEART NEVERTHE-LESS: GOTŌ SHŌJIRŌ.

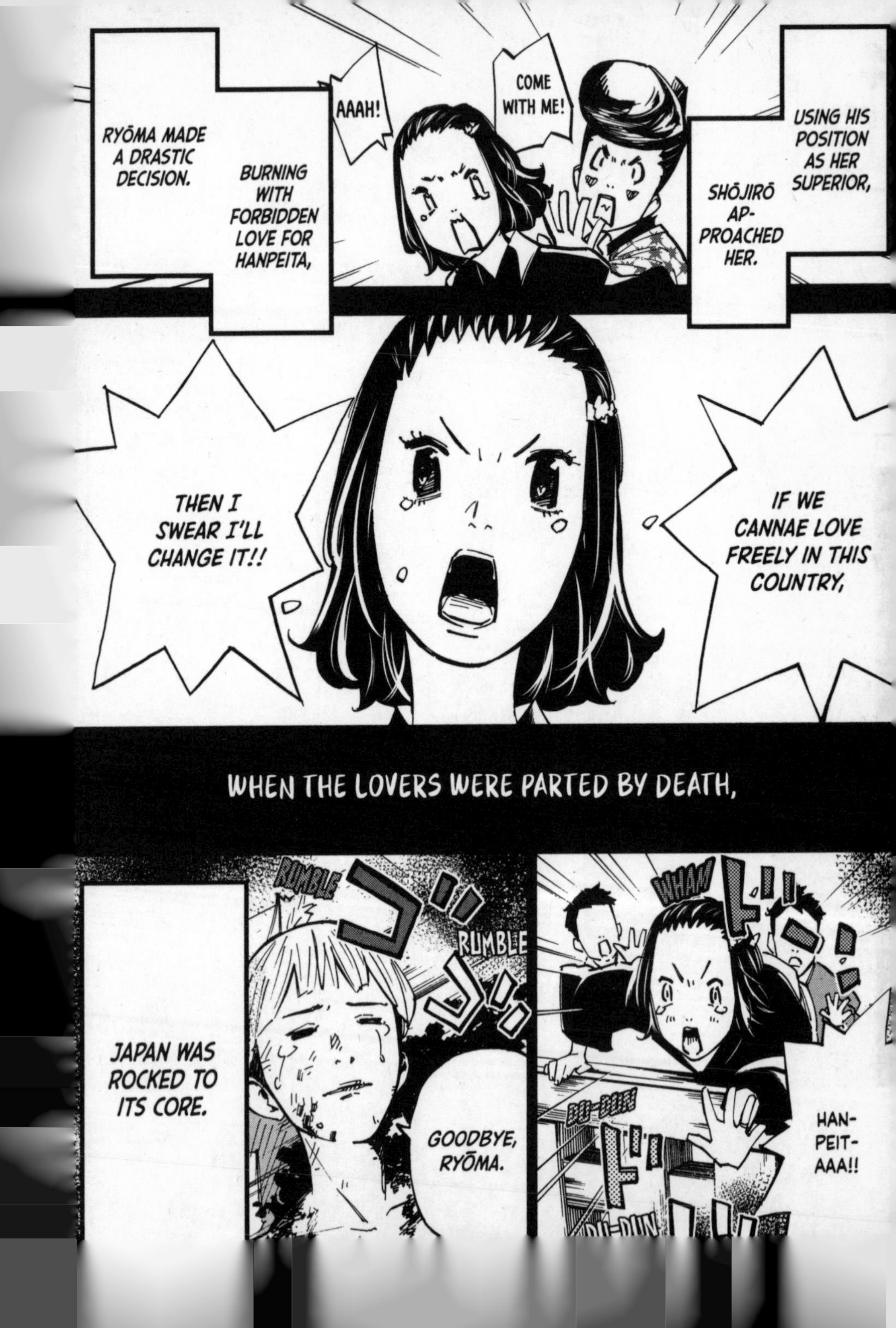
USING HIS POSITION AS HER SUPERIOR,
SHŌJIRŌ AP-PROACHED HER.
COME WITH ME!
AAAH!
BURNING WITH FORBIDDEN LOVE FOR HANPEITA,
RYŌMA MADE A DRASTIC DECISION.
IF WE CANNAE LOVE FREELY IN THIS COUNTRY,
THEN I SWEAR I'LL CHANGE IT!!
WHEN THE LOVERS WERE PARTED BY DEATH,
WHAM
HAN-PEIT-AAA!!
DO-DUN
DO-DUN
RUMBLE
RUMBLE
GOODBYE, RYŌMA.
JAPAN WAS ROCKED TO ITS CORE.

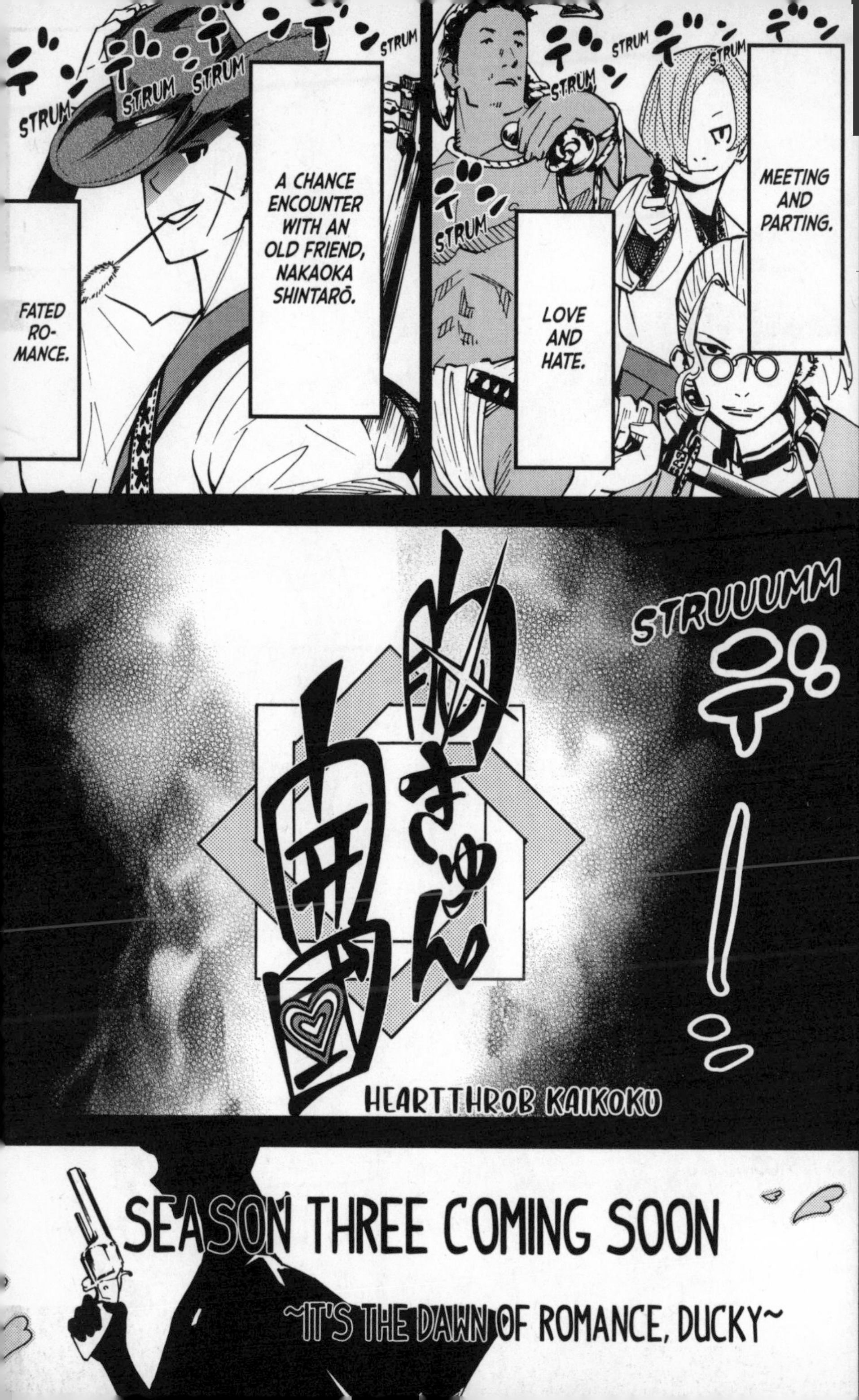
STRUM
STRUM
STRUM
MEETING AND PARTING.
STRUM
LOVE AND HATE.
STRUM
STRUM STRUM
STRUM
A CHANCE ENCOUNTER WITH AN OLD FRIEND, NAKAOKA SHINTARŌ.
FATED RO-MANCE.
STRUUUMM
HEARTTHROB KAIKOKU
SEASON THREE COMING SOON
~IT'S THE DAWN OF ROMANCE, DUCKY~

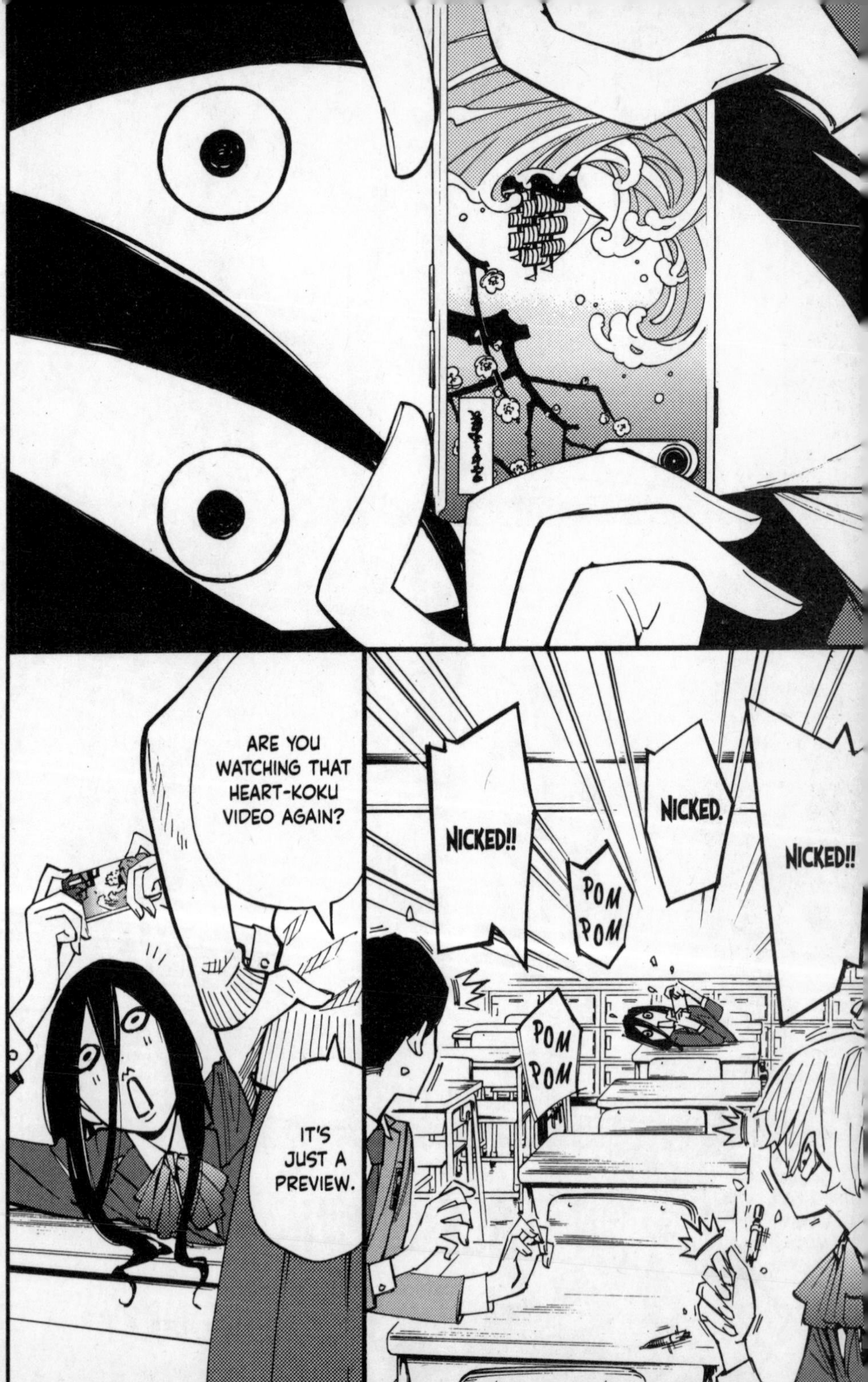
NICKED!!
NICKED.
NICKED!!
POM POM
POM POM
ARE YOU WATCHING THAT HEART-KOKU VIDEO AGAIN?
IT'S JUST A PREVIEW.

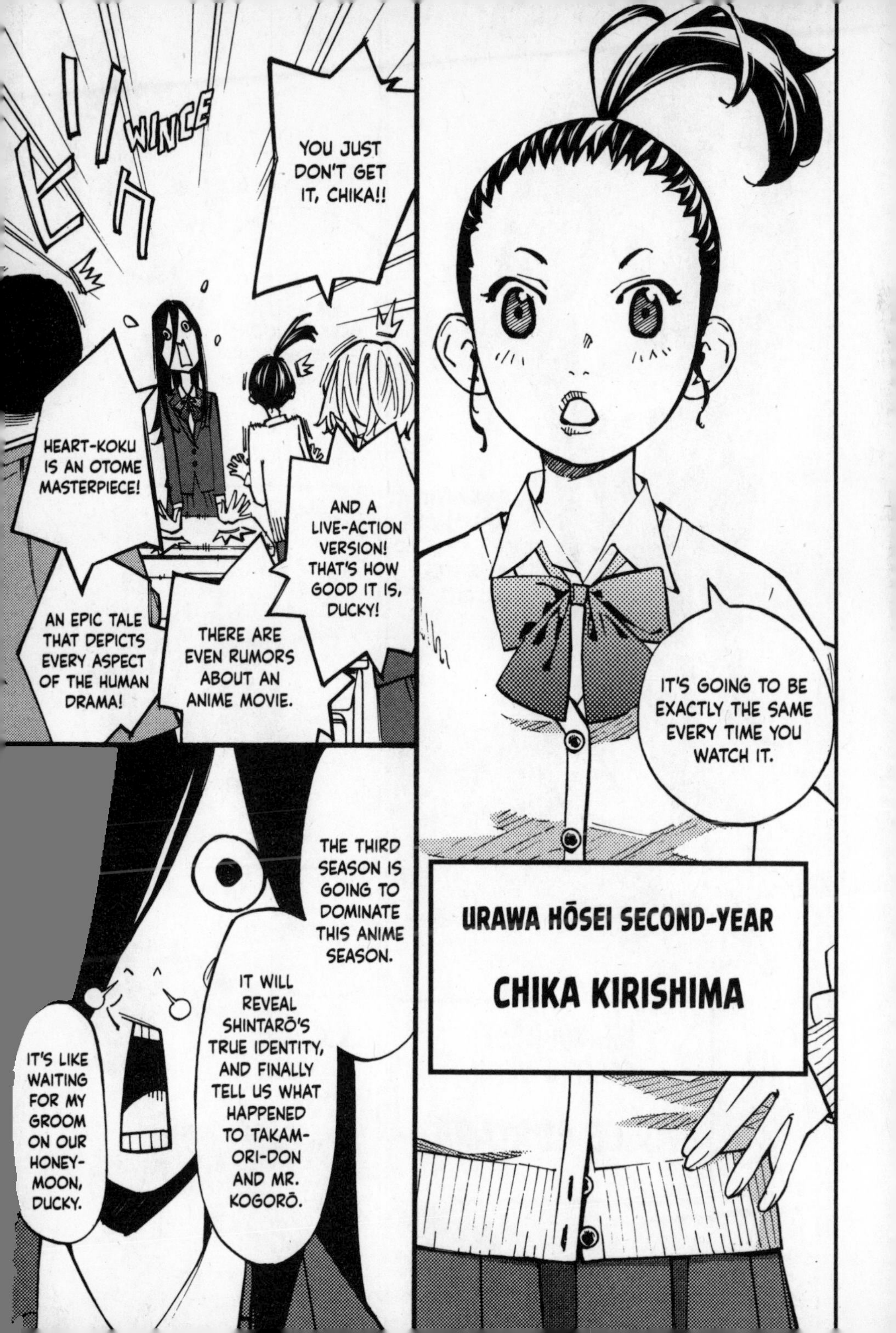
IT'S GOING TO BE EXACTLY THE SAME EVERY TIME YOU WATCH IT.
URAWA HŌSEI SECOND-YEAR
CHIKA KIRISHIMA
YOU JUST DON'T GET IT, CHIKA!!
WINCE
HEART-KOKU IS AN OTOME MASTERPIECE!
AN EPIC TALE THAT DEPICTS EVERY ASPECT OF THE HUMAN DRAMA!
THERE ARE EVEN RUMORS ABOUT AN ANIME MOVIE.
AND A LIVE-ACTION VERSION! THAT'S HOW GOOD IT IS, DUCKY!
THE THIRD SEASON IS GOING TO DOMINATE THIS ANIME SEASON.
IT WILL REVEAL SHINTARŌ'S TRUE IDENTITY, AND FINALLY TELL US WHAT HAPPENED TO TAKAMORI-DON AND MR. KOGORŌ.
IT'S LIKE WAITING FOR MY GROOM ON OUR HONEYMOON, DUCKY.

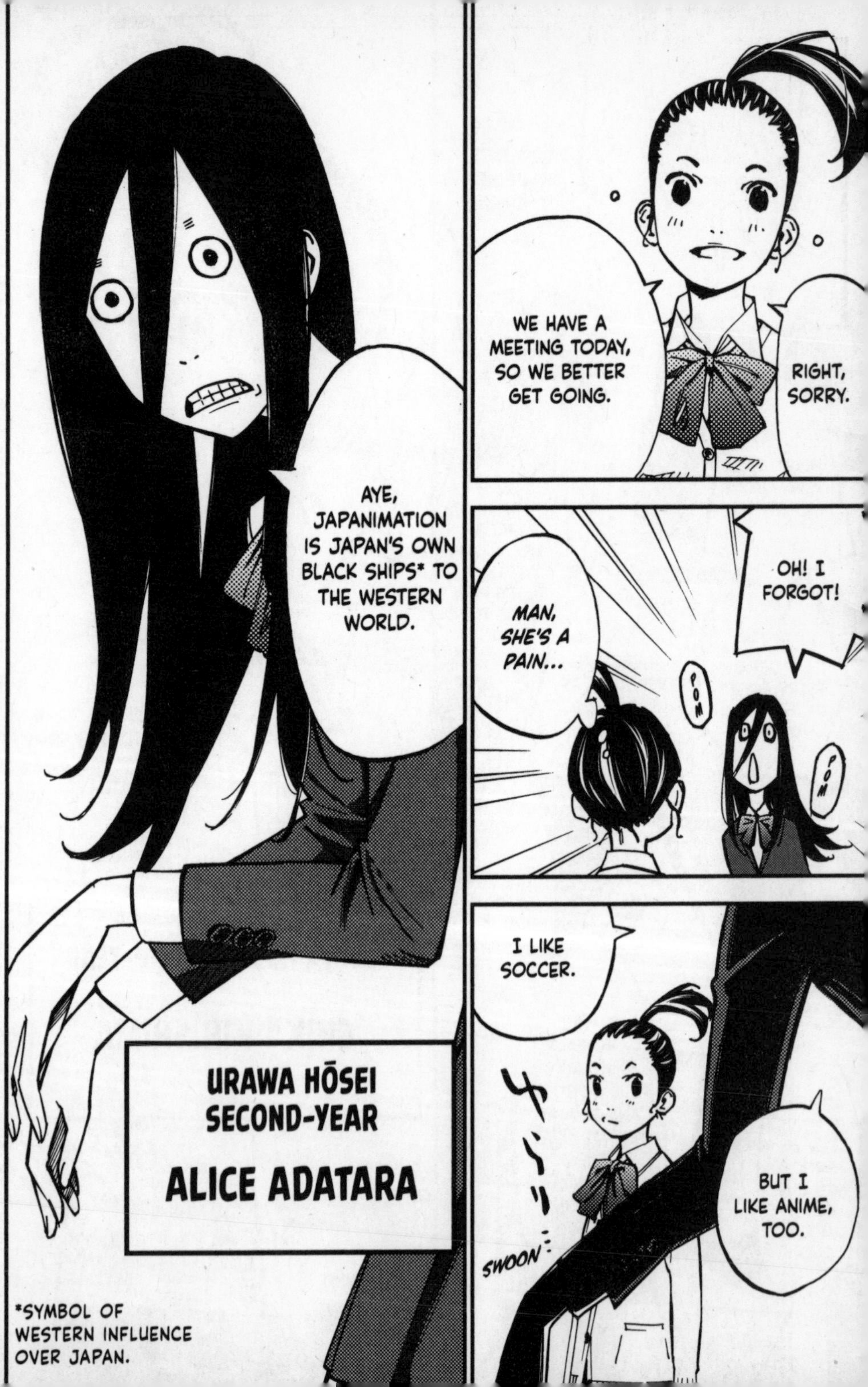
RIGHT, SORRY.
WE HAVE A MEETING TODAY, SO WE BETTER GET GOING.
OH! I FORGOT!
MAN, SHE'S A PAIN...
POM
POM
I LIKE SOCCER.
SWOON
BUT I LIKE ANIME, TOO.
AYE, JAPANIMATION IS JAPAN'S OWN BLACK SHIPS* TO THE WESTERN WORLD.
URAWA HŌSEI SECOND-YEAR
ALICE ADATARA

*SYMBOL OF WESTERN INFLUENCE OVER JAPAN.

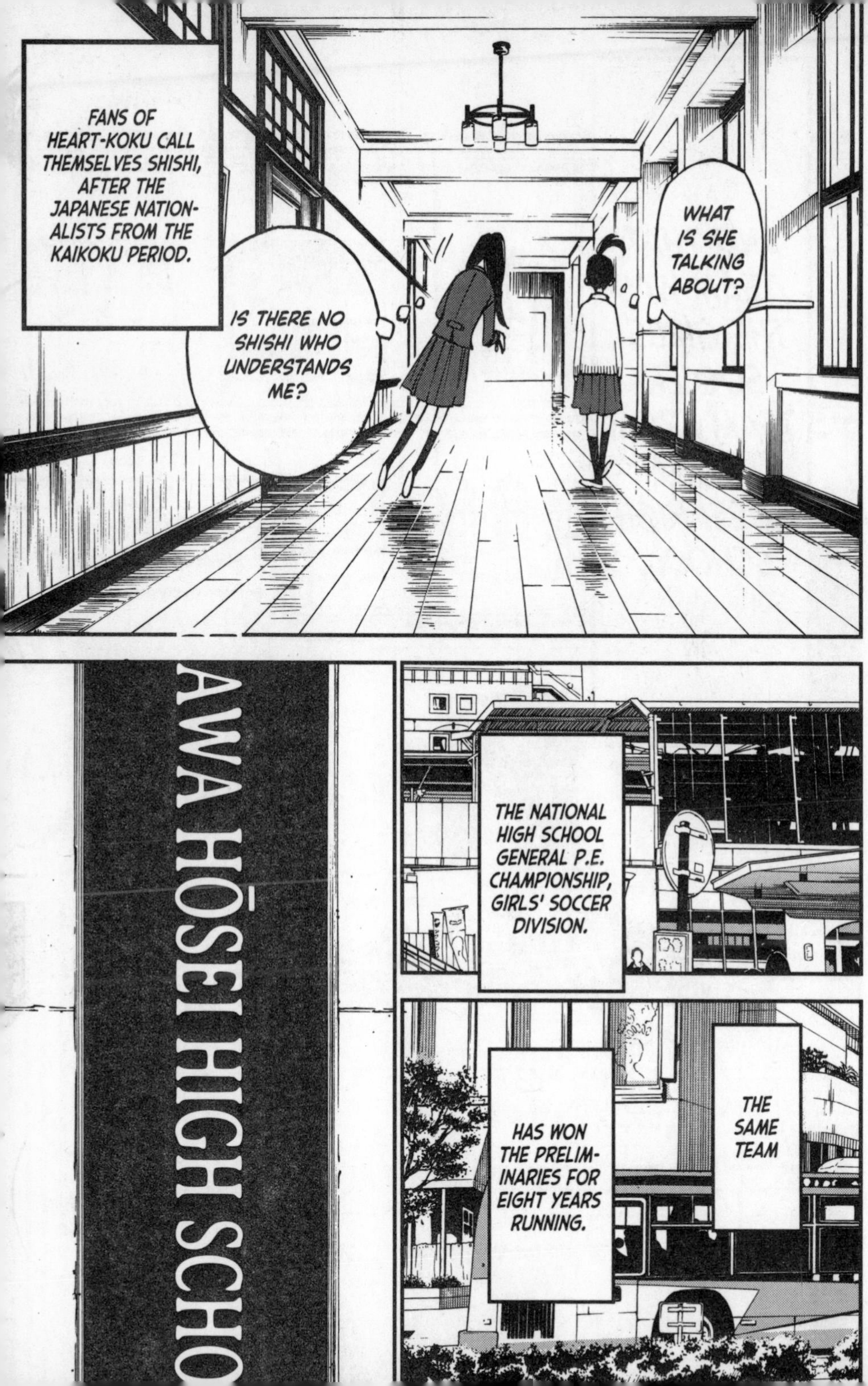
WHAT IS SHE TALKING ABOUT?
FANS OF HEART-KOKU CALL THEMSELVES SHISHI, AFTER THE JAPANESE NATION-ALISTS FROM THE KAIKOKU PERIOD.
IS THERE NO SHISHI WHO UNDERSTANDS ME?
THE NATIONAL HIGH SCHOOL GENERAL P.E. CHAMPIONSHIP, GIRLS' SOCCER DIVISION.
THE SAME TEAM
HAS WON THE PRELIM-INARIES FOR EIGHT YEARS RUNNING.
AWA HŌSEI HIGH SCHO

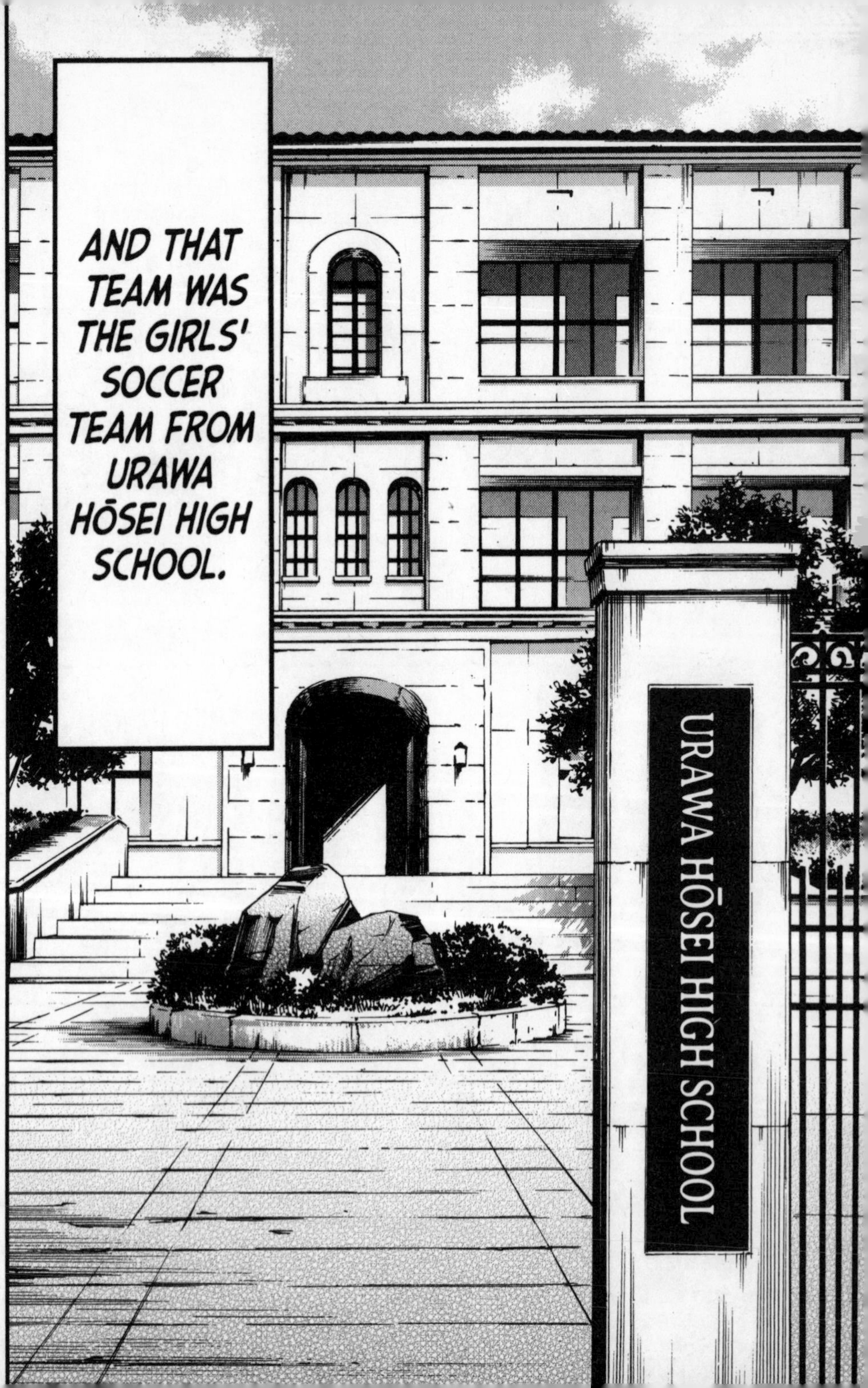
AND THAT TEAM WAS THE GIRLS' SOCCER TEAM FROM URAWA HŌSEI HIGH SCHOOL.
URAWA HŌSEI HIGH SCHOOL

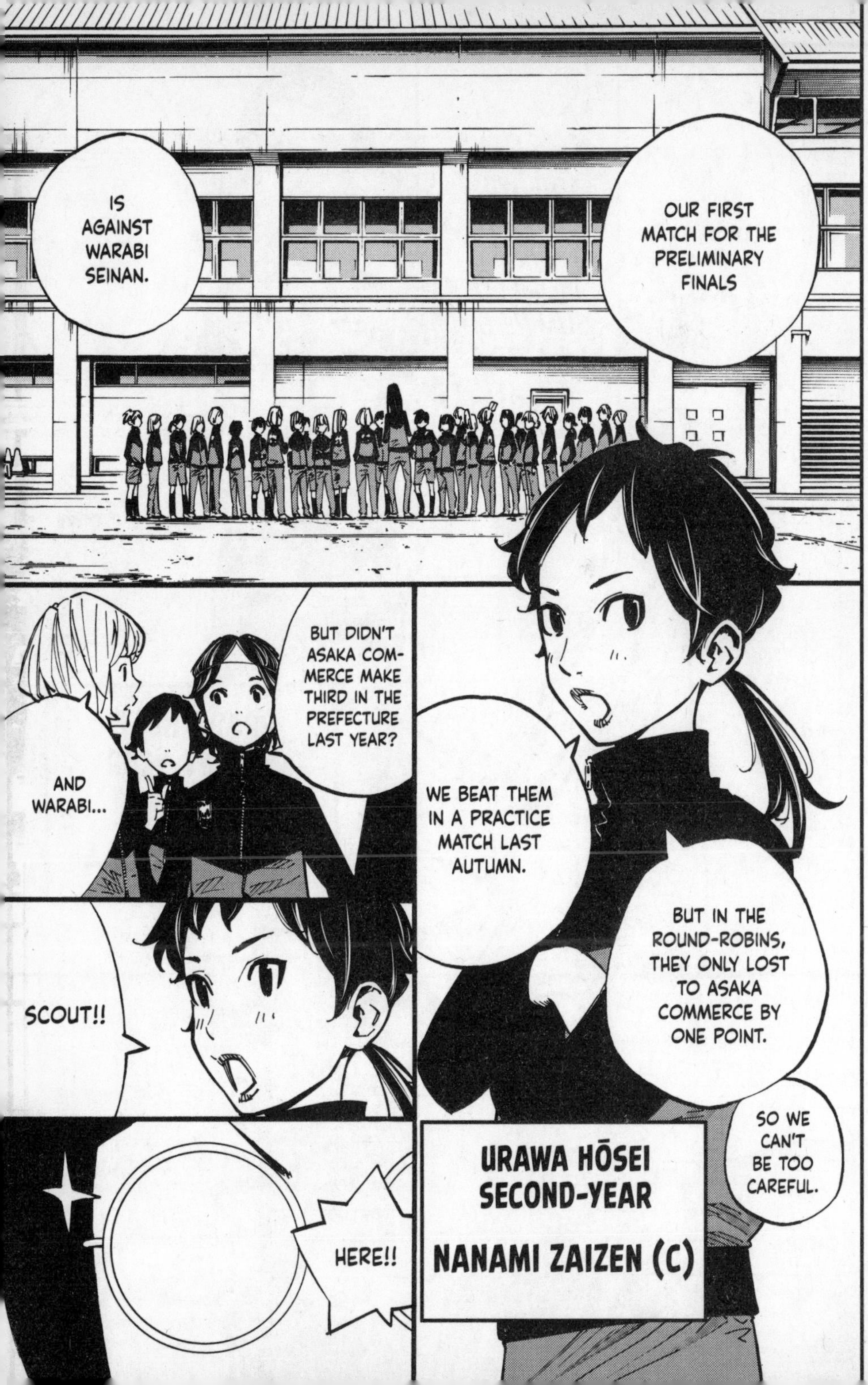
OUR FIRST MATCH FOR THE PRELIMINARY FINALS
IS AGAINST WARABI SEINAN.
WE BEAT THEM IN A PRACTICE MATCH LAST AUTUMN.
BUT IN THE ROUND-ROBINS, THEY ONLY LOST TO ASAKA COMMERCE BY ONE POINT.
SO WE CAN'T BE TOO CAREFUL.
URAWA HŌSEI SECOND-YEAR
NANAMI ZAIZEN (C)
BUT DIDN'T ASAKA COMMERCE MAKE THIRD IN THE PREFECTURE LAST YEAR?
AND WARABI...
SCOUT!!
HERE!!

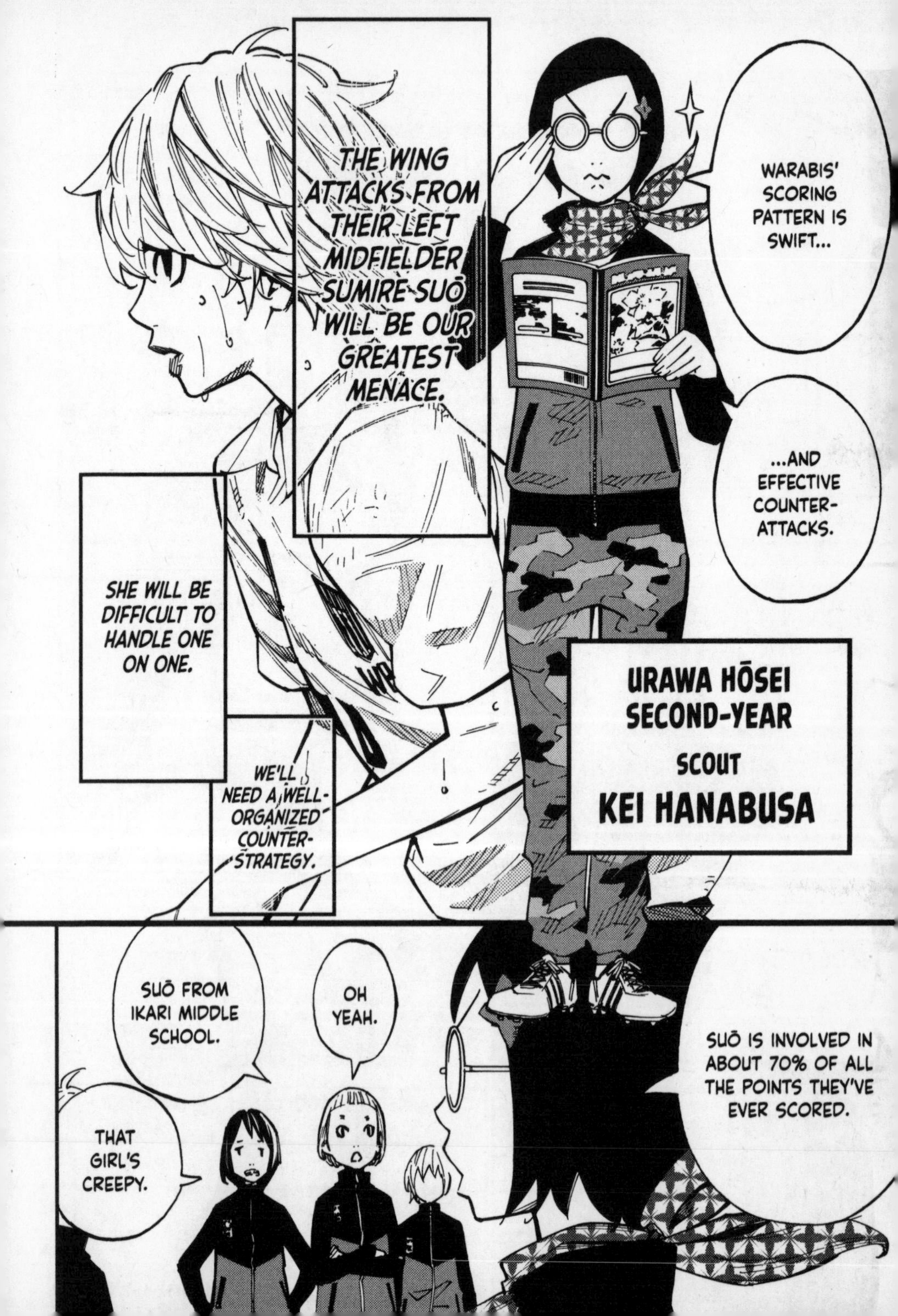
WARABIS' SCORING PATTERN IS SWIFT...
...AND EFFECTIVE COUNTER-ATTACKS.
THE WING ATTACKS FROM THEIR LEFT MIDFIELDER SUMIRE SUŌ WILL BE OUR GREATEST MENACE.
URAWA HŌSEI SECOND-YEAR SCOUT KEI HANABUSA
SHE WILL BE DIFFICULT TO HANDLE ONE ON ONE.
WE'LL NEED A WELL-ORGANIZED COUNTER-STRATEGY.
SUŌ IS INVOLVED IN ABOUT 70% OF ALL THE POINTS THEY'VE EVER SCORED.
OH YEAH.
SUŌ FROM IKARI MIDDLE SCHOOL.
THAT GIRL'S CREEPY.

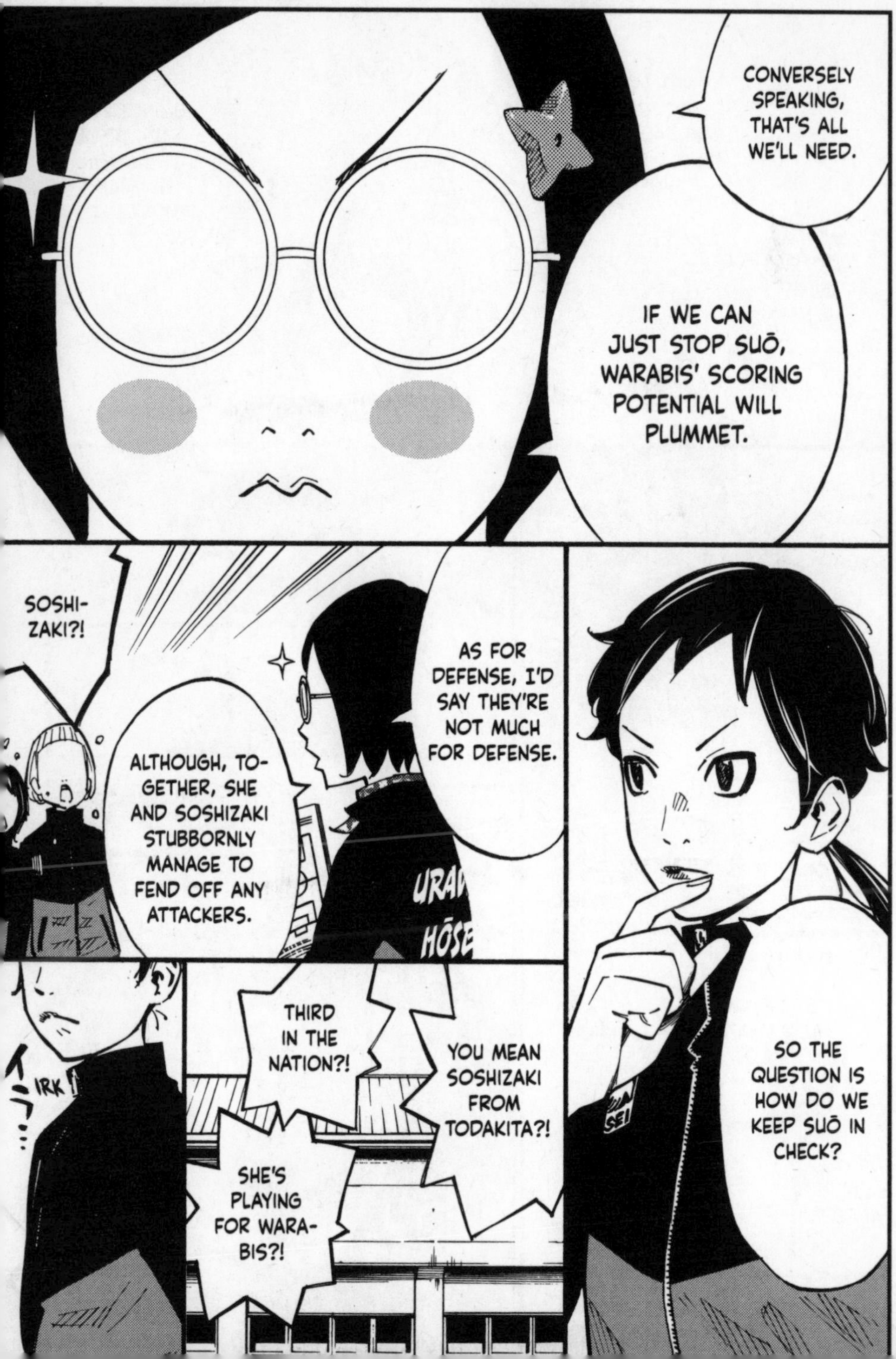
CONVERSELY SPEAKING, THAT'S ALL WE'LL NEED.
IF WE CAN JUST STOP SUŌ, WARABIS' SCORING POTENTIAL WILL PLUMMET.
SO THE QUESTION IS HOW DO WE KEEP SUŌ IN CHECK?
AS FOR DEFENSE, I'D SAY THEY'RE NOT MUCH FOR DEFENSE.
ALTHOUGH, TO-GETHER, SHE AND SOSHIZAKI STUBBORNLY MANAGE TO FEND OFF ANY ATTACKERS.
SOSHI-ZAKI?!
URAWA HŌSEI
YOU MEAN SOSHIZAKI FROM TODAKITA?!
THIRD IN THE NATION?!
SHE'S PLAYING FOR WARA-BIS?!
IRK

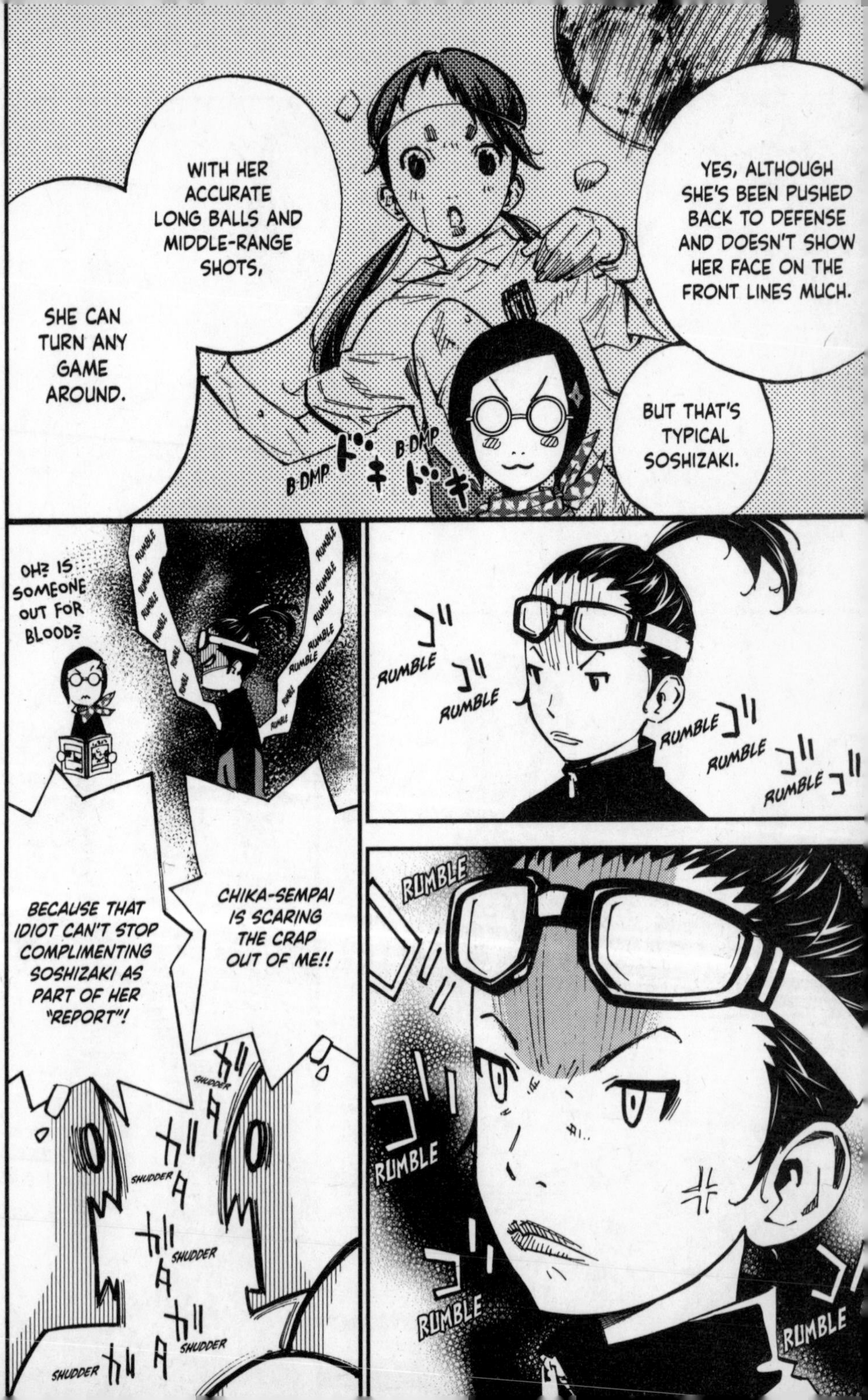
YES, ALTHOUGH SHE'S BEEN PUSHED BACK TO DEFENSE AND DOESN'T SHOW HER FACE ON THE FRONT LINES MUCH.
BUT THAT'S TYPICAL SOSHIZAKI.
WITH HER ACCURATE LONG BALLS AND MIDDLE-RANGE SHOTS,
SHE CAN TURN ANY GAME AROUND.
B-DMP
B-DMP
RUMBLE
RUMBLE
RUMBLE
RUMBLE
RUMBLE
RUMBLE
OH? IS SOMEONE OUT FOR BLOOD?
RUMBLE
RUMBLE
RUMBLE
RUMBLE
CHIKA-SEMPAI IS SCARING THE CRAP OUT OF ME!!
BECAUSE THAT IDIOT CAN'T STOP COMPLIMENTING SOSHIZAKI AS PART OF HER "REPORT"!
SHUDDER
SHUDDER
SHUDDER
SHUDDER
SHUDDER

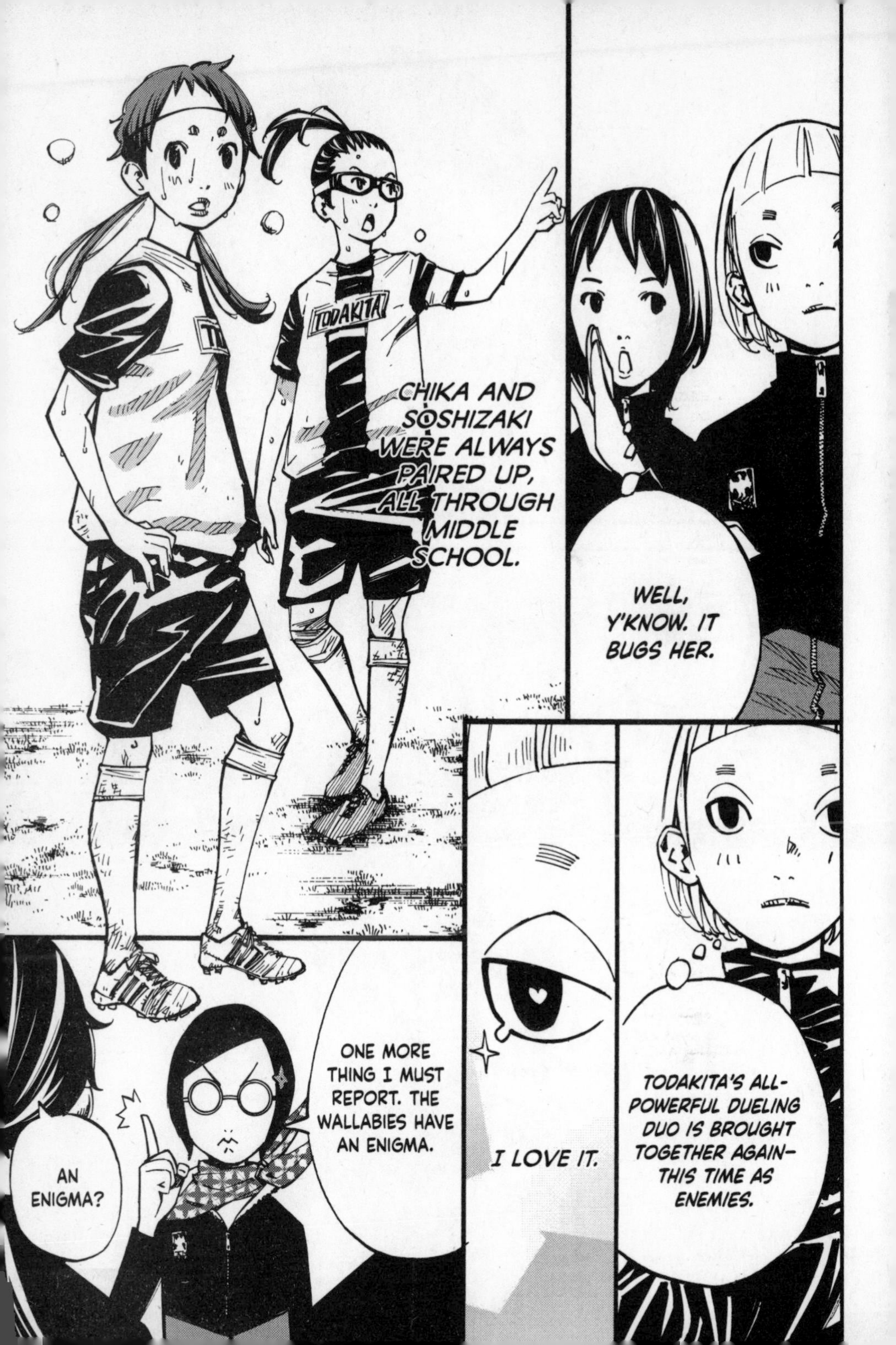
WELL, Y'KNOW. IT BUGS HER.
CHIKA AND SOSHIZAKI WERE ALWAYS PAIRED UP, ALL THROUGH MIDDLE SCHOOL.
TODAKITA'S ALL-POWERFUL DUELING DUO IS BROUGHT TOGETHER AGAIN—THIS TIME AS ENEMIES.
I LOVE IT.
ONE MORE THING I MUST REPORT. THE WALLABIES HAVE AN ENIGMA.
AN ENIGMA?

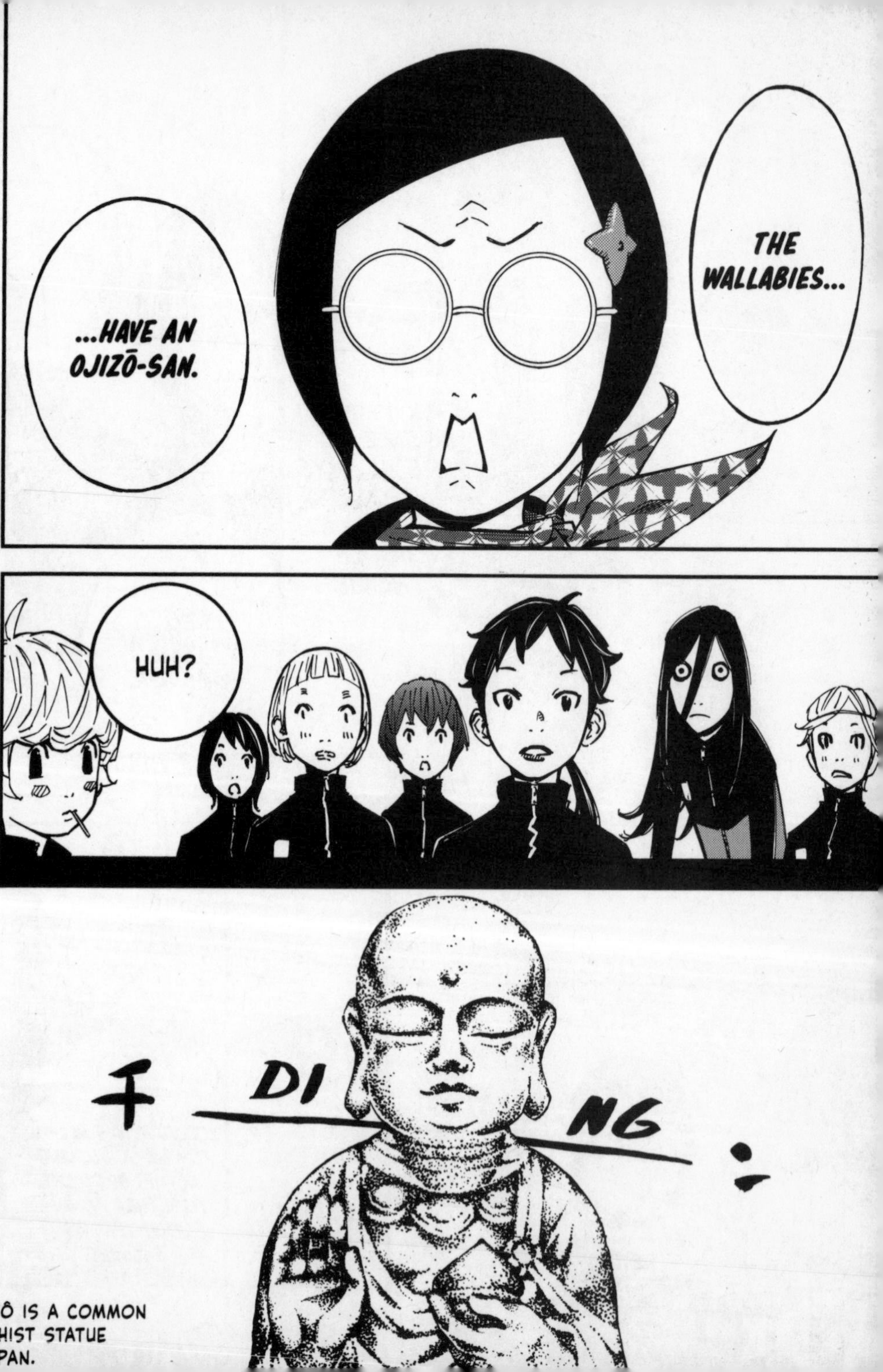
THE WALLABIES...
...HAVE AN OJIZŌ-SAN.
HUH?
DING
*OJIZÔ IS A COMMON BUDDHIST STATUE IN JAPAN.

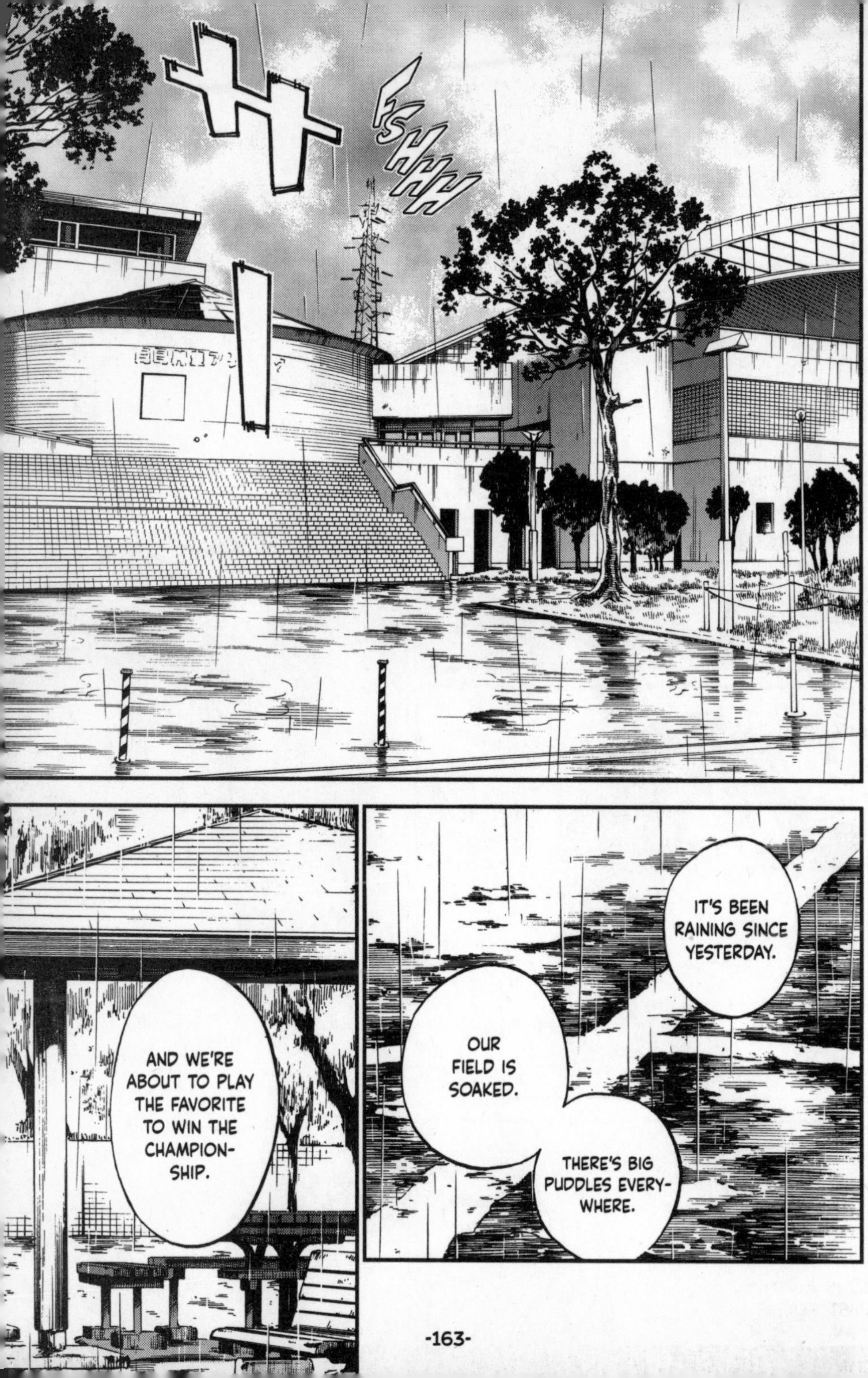
FSHHH
IT'S BEEN RAINING SINCE YESTERDAY.
OUR FIELD IS SOAKED.
THERE'S BIG PUDDLES EVERY-WHERE.
AND WE'RE ABOUT TO PLAY THE FAVORITE TO WIN THE CHAMPION-SHIP.

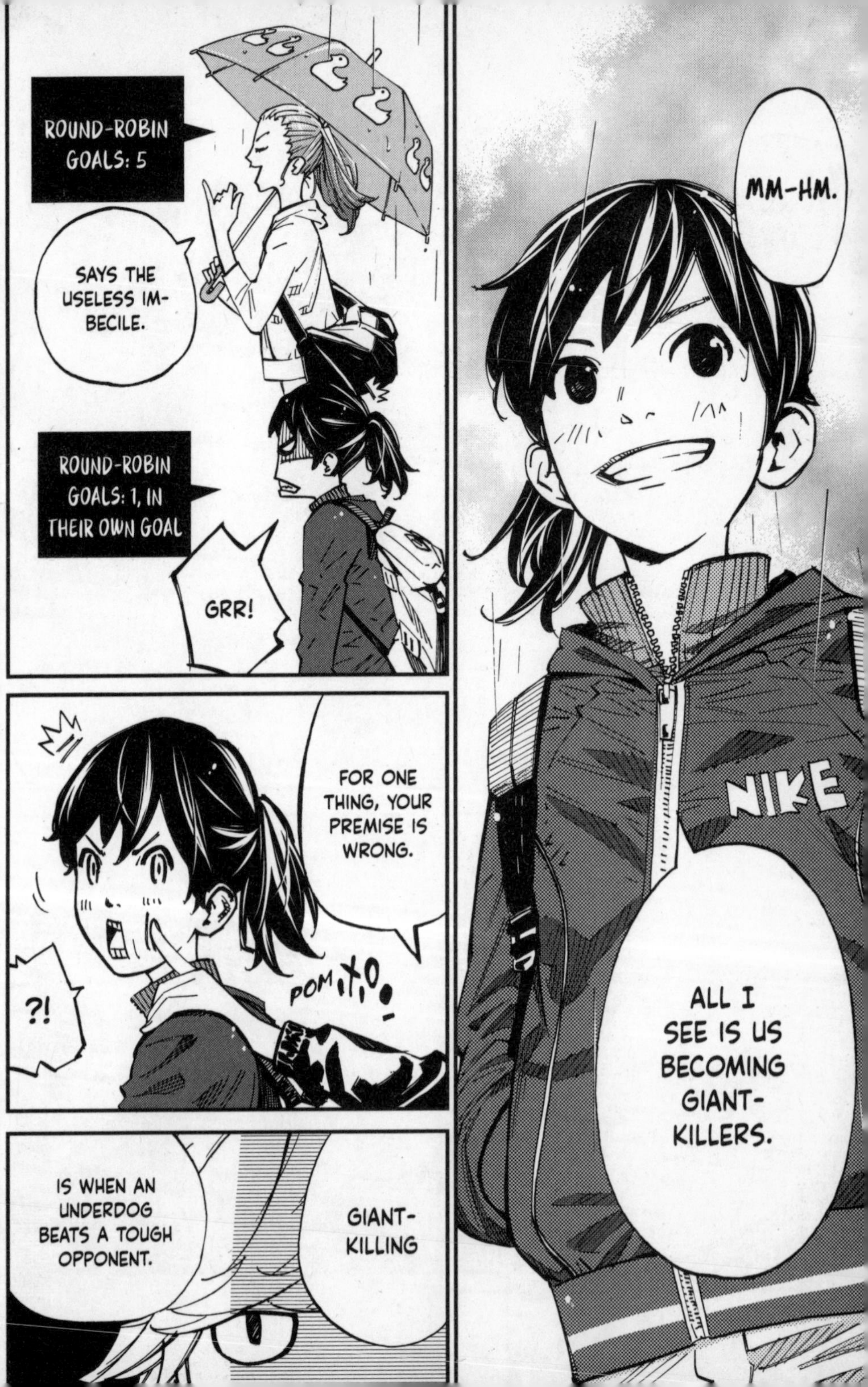
MM-HM.
ALL I SEE IS US BECOMING GIANT-KILLERS.
ROUND-ROBIN GOALS: 5
SAYS THE USELESS IM-BECILE.
ROUND-ROBIN GOALS: 1, IN THEIR OWN GOAL
GRR!
FOR ONE THING, YOUR PREMISE IS WRONG.
POM
?!
GIANT-KILLING
IS WHEN AN UNDERDOG BEATS A TOUGH OPPONENT.

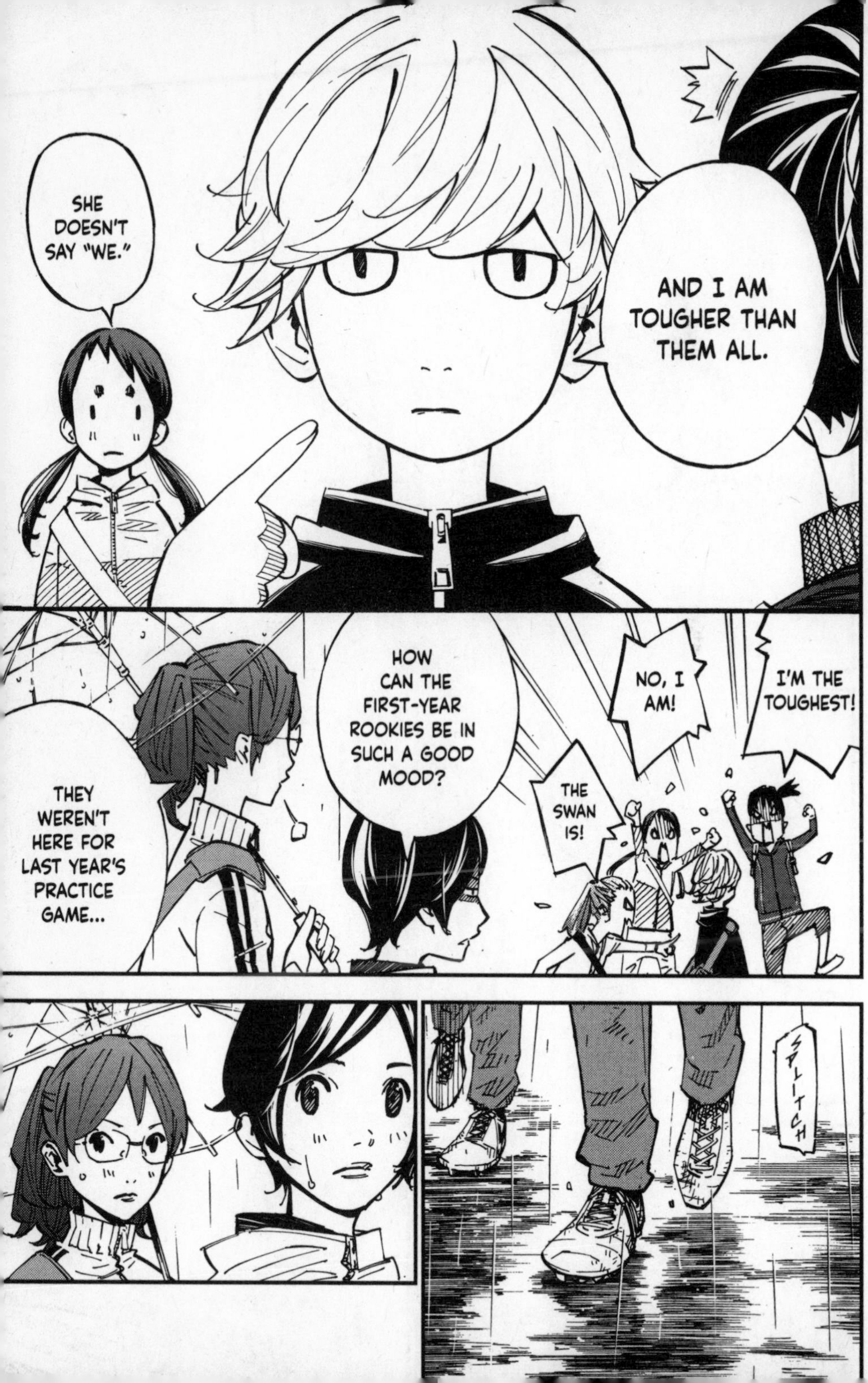
AND I AM TOUGHER THAN THEM ALL.
SHE DOESN'T SAY "WE."
I'M THE TOUGHEST!
NO, I AM!
THE SWAN IS!
HOW CAN THE FIRST-YEAR ROOKIES BE IN SUCH A GOOD MOOD?
THEY WEREN'T HERE FOR LAST YEAR'S PRACTICE GAME...
SPLITCH

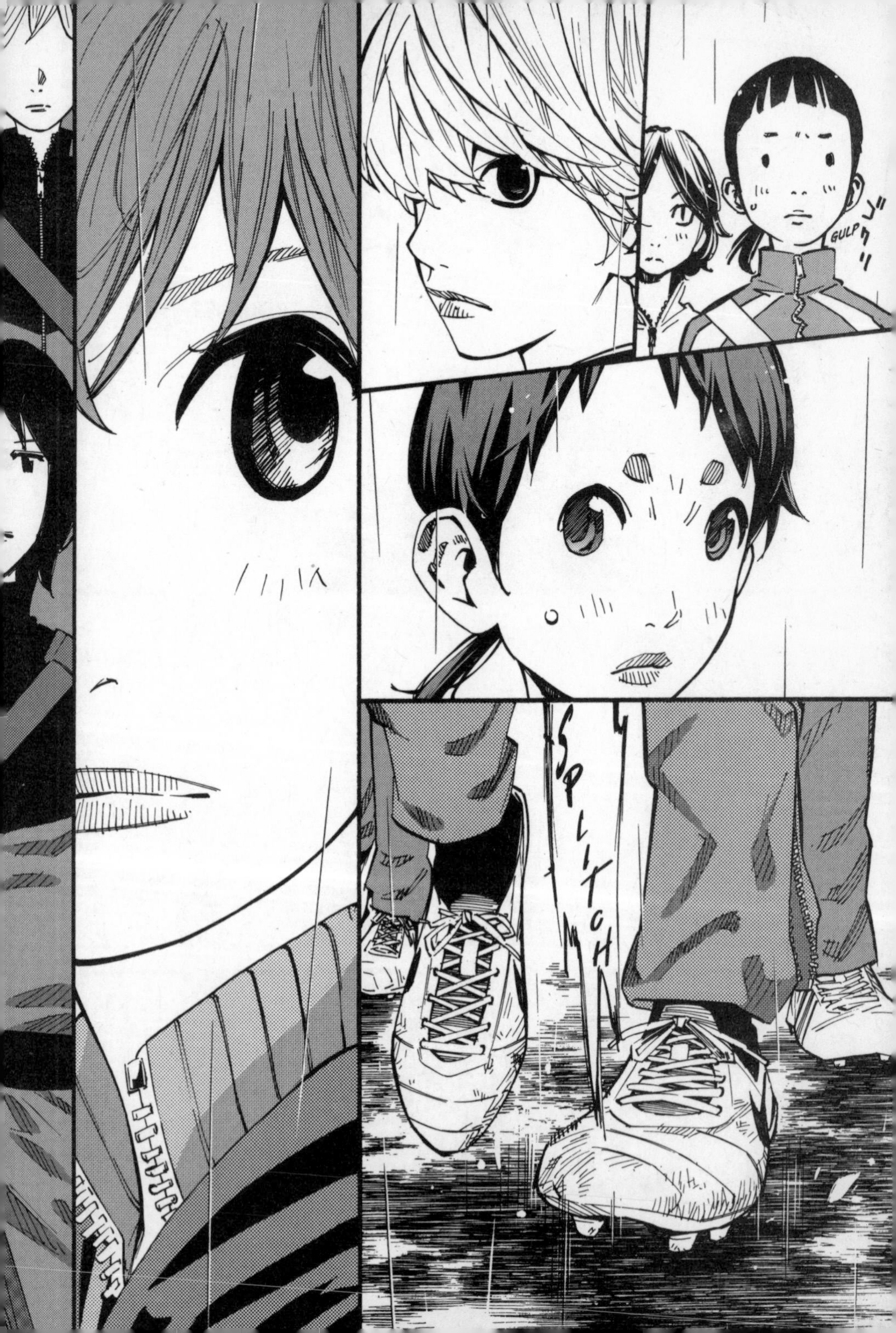
ゴクッ
GULP
SPLITCH

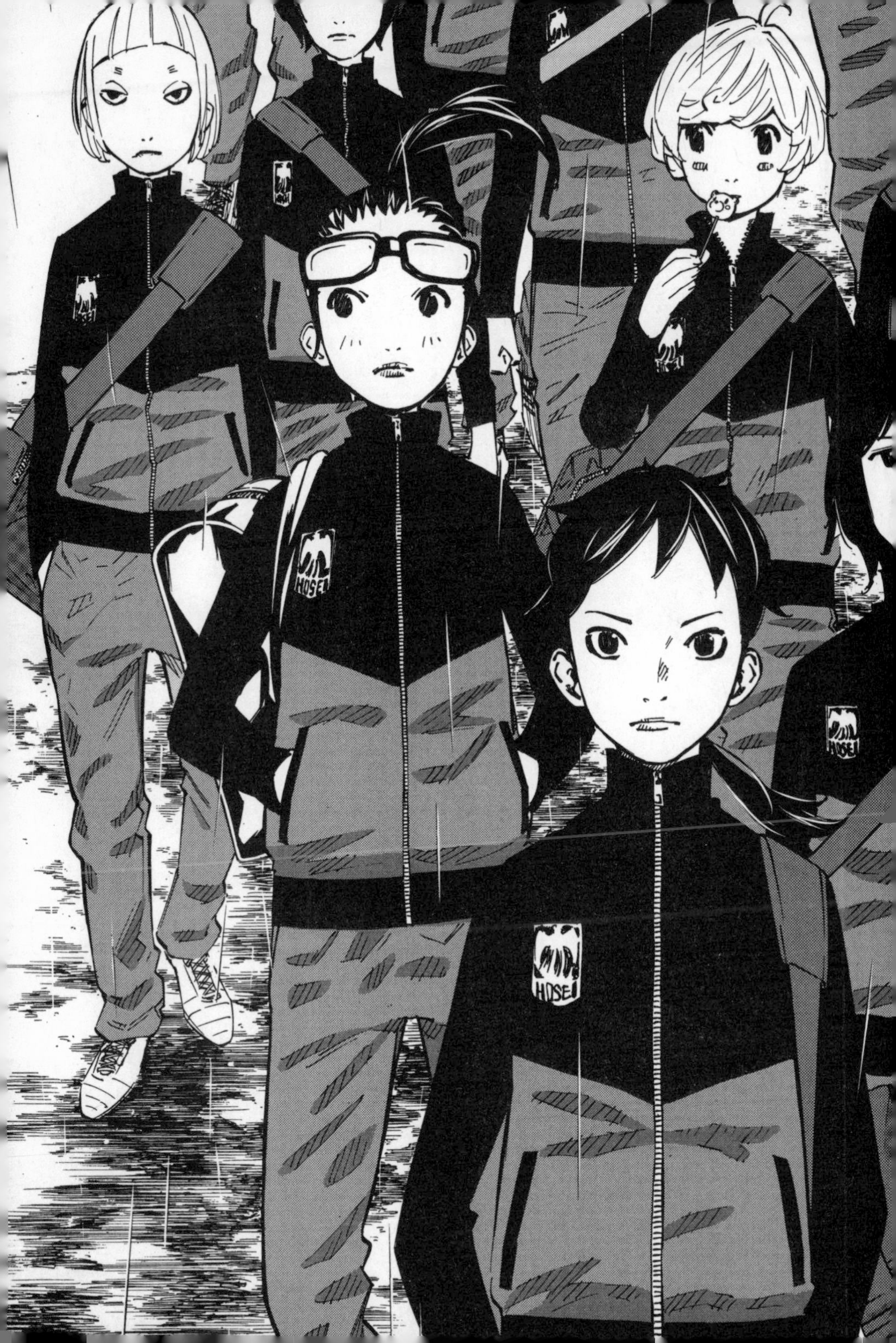
HOSEI
HOSEI
HOSEI

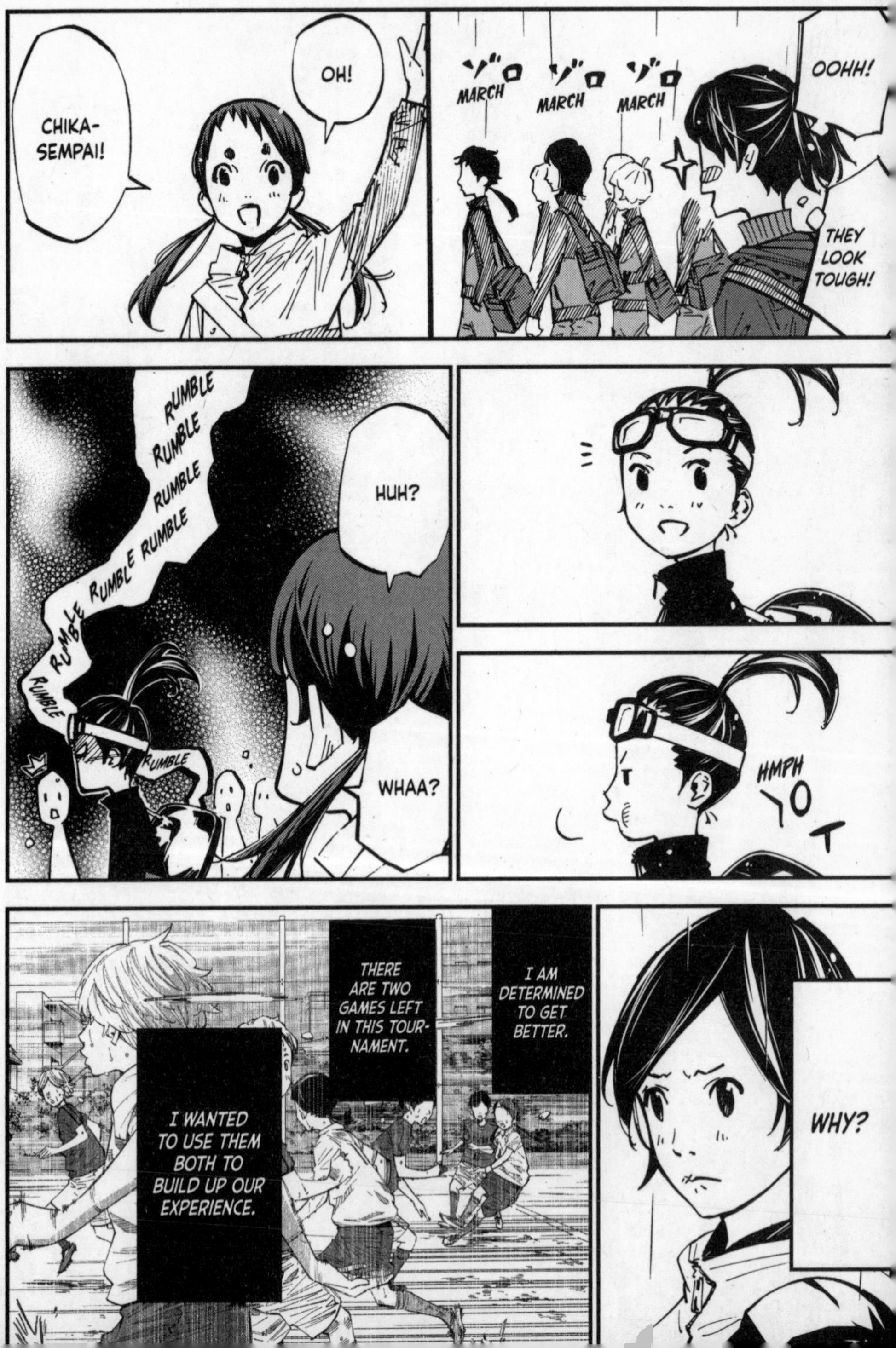
OOHH!
ゾロ MARCH
ゾロ MARCH
ゾロ MARCH
THEY LOOK TOUGH!
OH!
CHIKA-SEMPAI!
HMPH
HUH?
RUMBLE RUMBLE RUMBLE RUMBLE RUMBLE RUMBLE RUMBLE RUMBLE
RUMBLE
WHAA?
WHY?
I AM DETERMINED TO GET BETTER.
THERE ARE TWO GAMES LEFT IN THIS TOURNAMENT.
I WANTED TO USE THEM BOTH TO BUILD UP OUR EXPERIENCE.

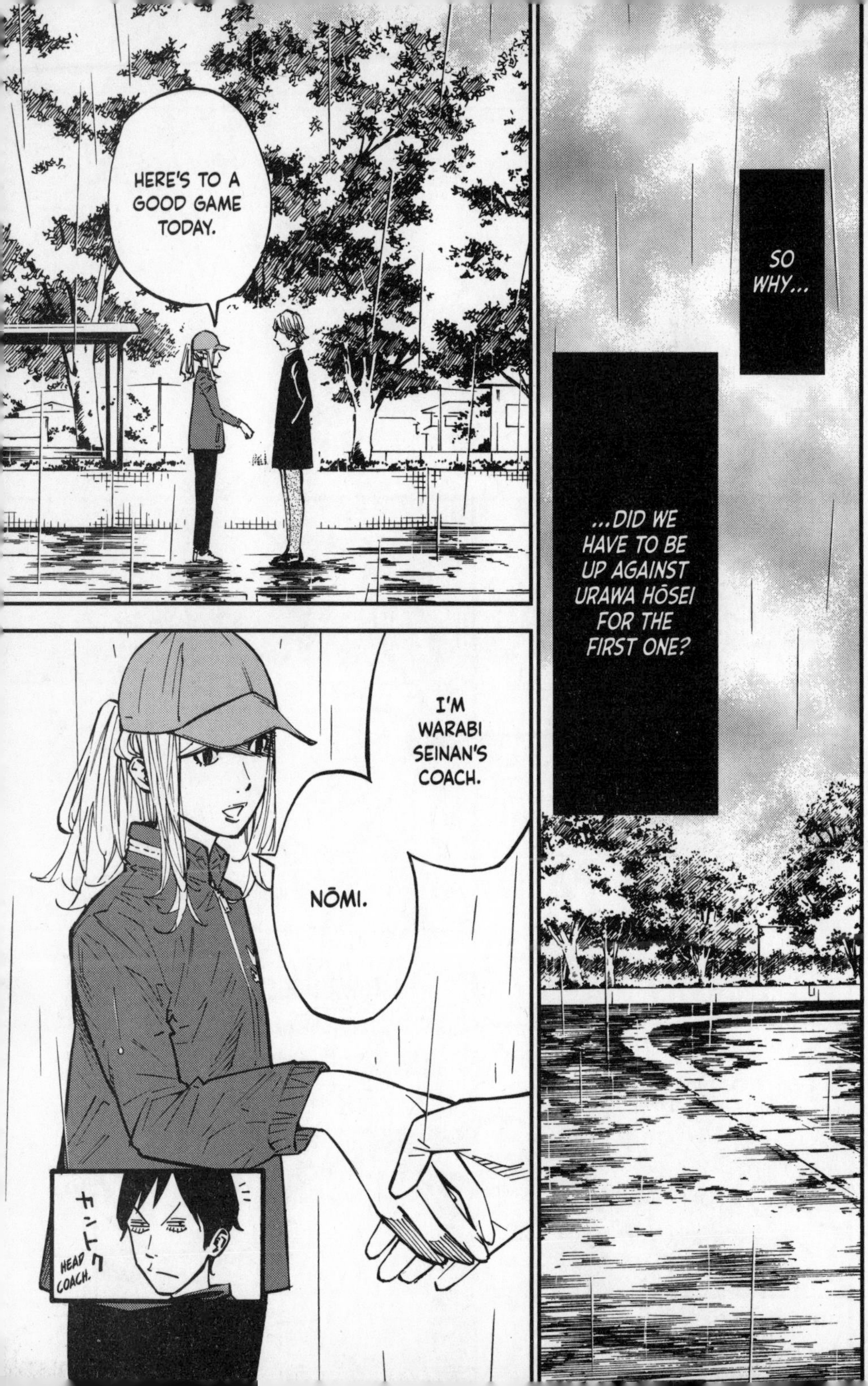
SO WHY...
...DID WE HAVE TO BE UP AGAINST URAWA HŌSEI FOR THE FIRST ONE?
HERE'S TO A GOOD GAME TODAY.
I'M WARABI SEINAN'S COACH.
NŌMI.
カントク
HEAD COACH.

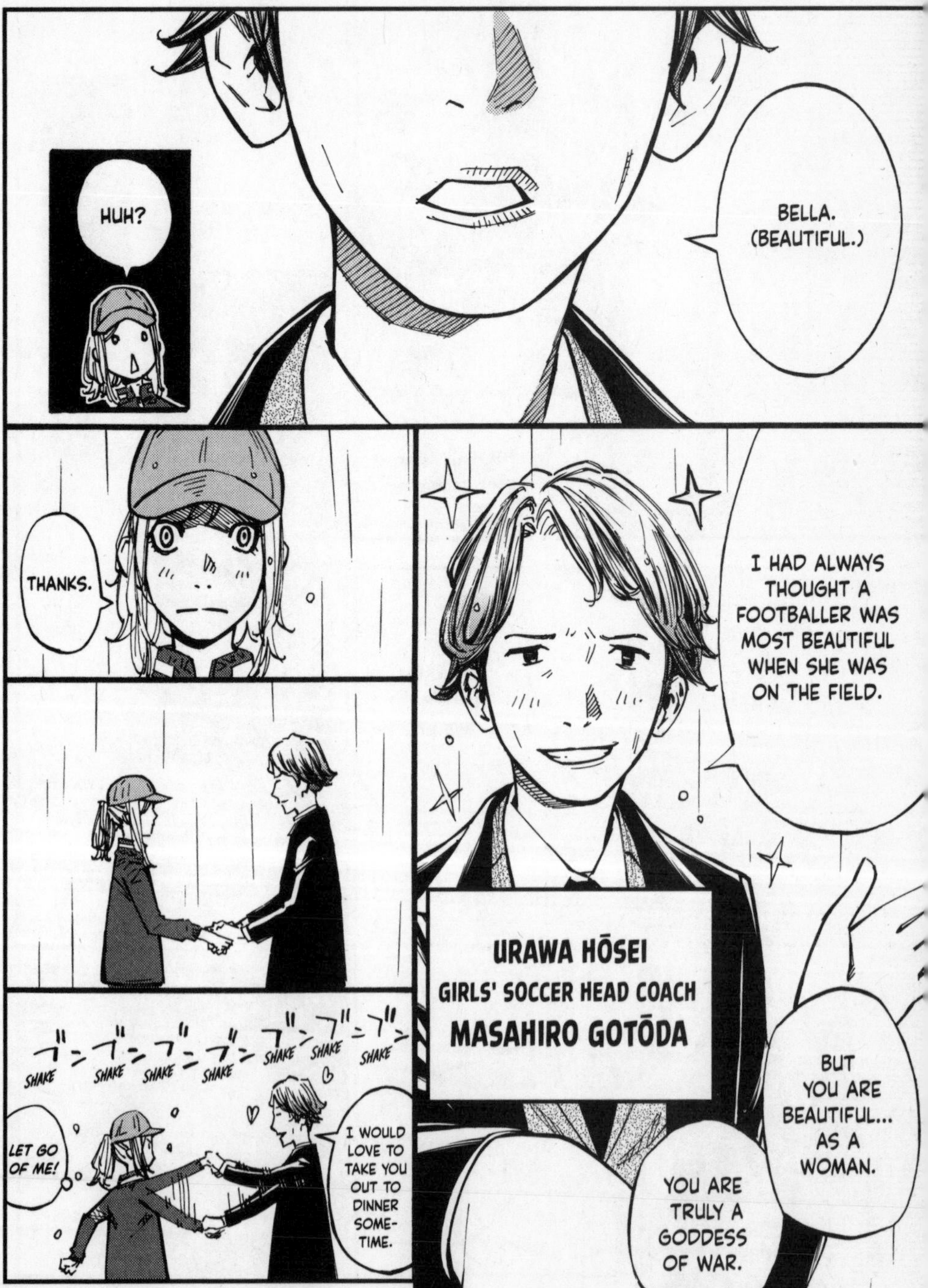
BELLA. (BEAUTIFUL.)
HUH?
I HAD ALWAYS THOUGHT A FOOTBALLER WAS MOST BEAUTIFUL WHEN SHE WAS ON THE FIELD.
URAWA HŌSEI GIRLS' SOCCER HEAD COACH MASAHIRO GOTŌDA
BUT YOU ARE BEAUTIFUL... AS A WOMAN.
YOU ARE TRULY A GODDESS OF WAR.
THANKS.
SHAKE SHAKE SHAKE SHAKE SHAKE SHAKE SHAKE
I WOULD LOVE TO TAKE YOU OUT TO DINNER SOME-TIME.
LET GO OF ME!

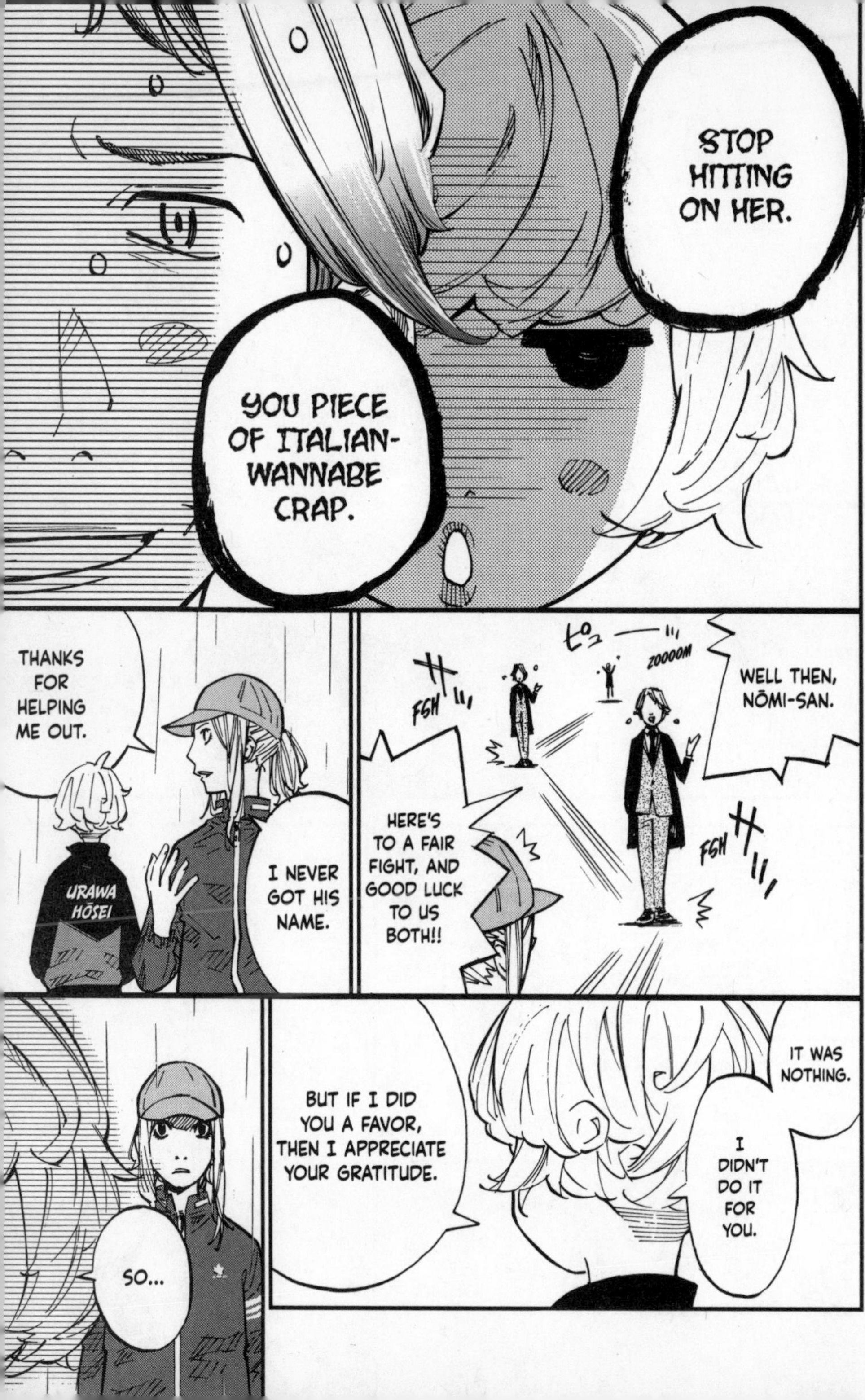
STOP HITTING ON HER.
YOU PIECE OF ITALIAN-WANNABE CRAP.
WELL THEN, NŌMI-SAN.
ZOOOOM
FSH
FSH
HERE'S TO A FAIR FIGHT, AND GOOD LUCK TO US BOTH!!
THANKS FOR HELPING ME OUT.
URAWA HŌSEI
I NEVER GOT HIS NAME.
IT WAS NOTHING.
I DIDN'T DO IT FOR YOU.
BUT IF I DID YOU A FAVOR, THEN I APPRECIATE YOUR GRATITUDE.
SO...

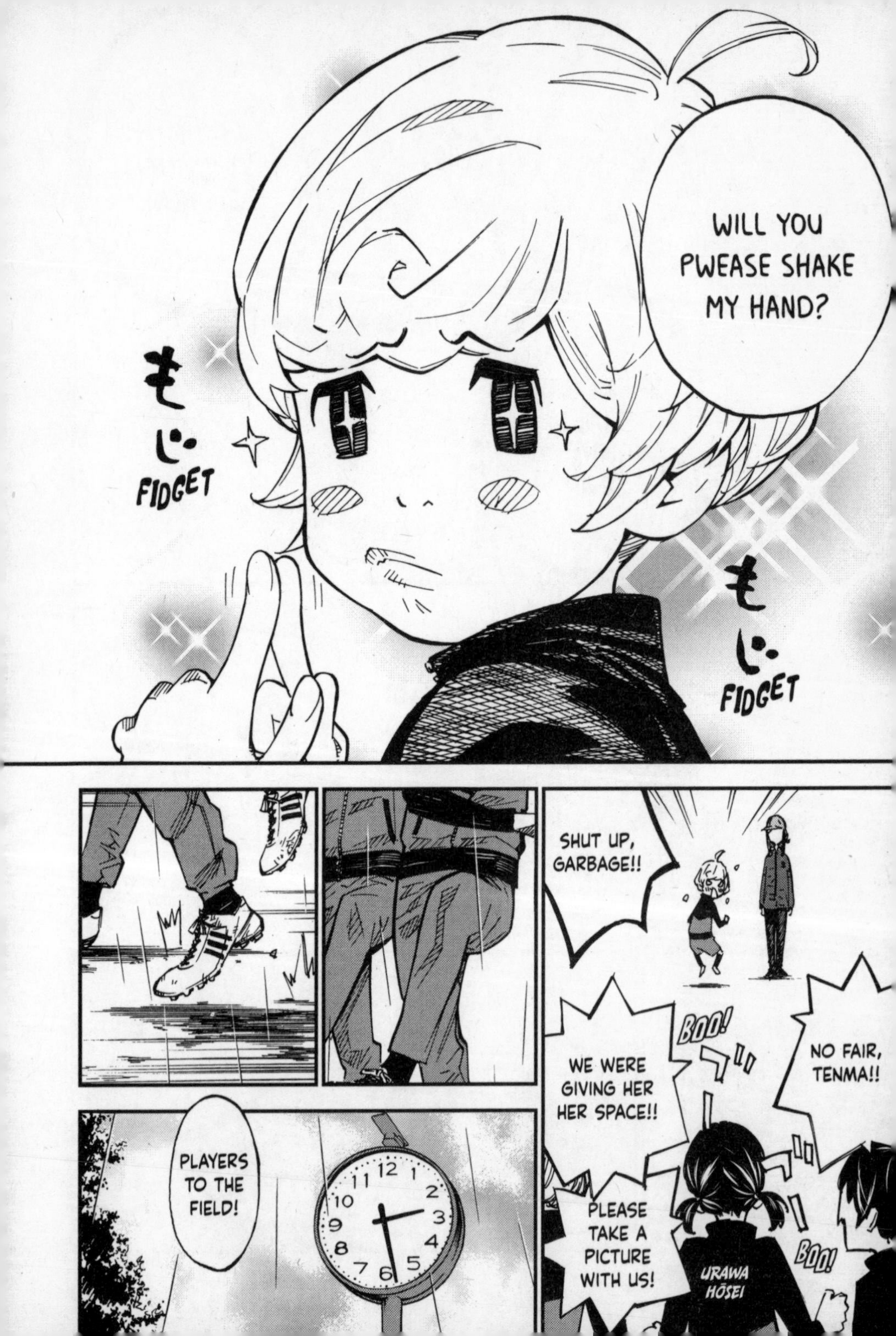
WILL YOU PWEASE SHAKE MY HAND?
もじ FIDGET
もじ FIDGET
SHUT UP, GARBAGE!!
NO FAIR, TENMA!!
BOO!
WE WERE GIVING HER HER SPACE!!
BOO!
PLEASE TAKE A PICTURE WITH US!
URAWA HŌSEI
PLAYERS TO THE FIELD!

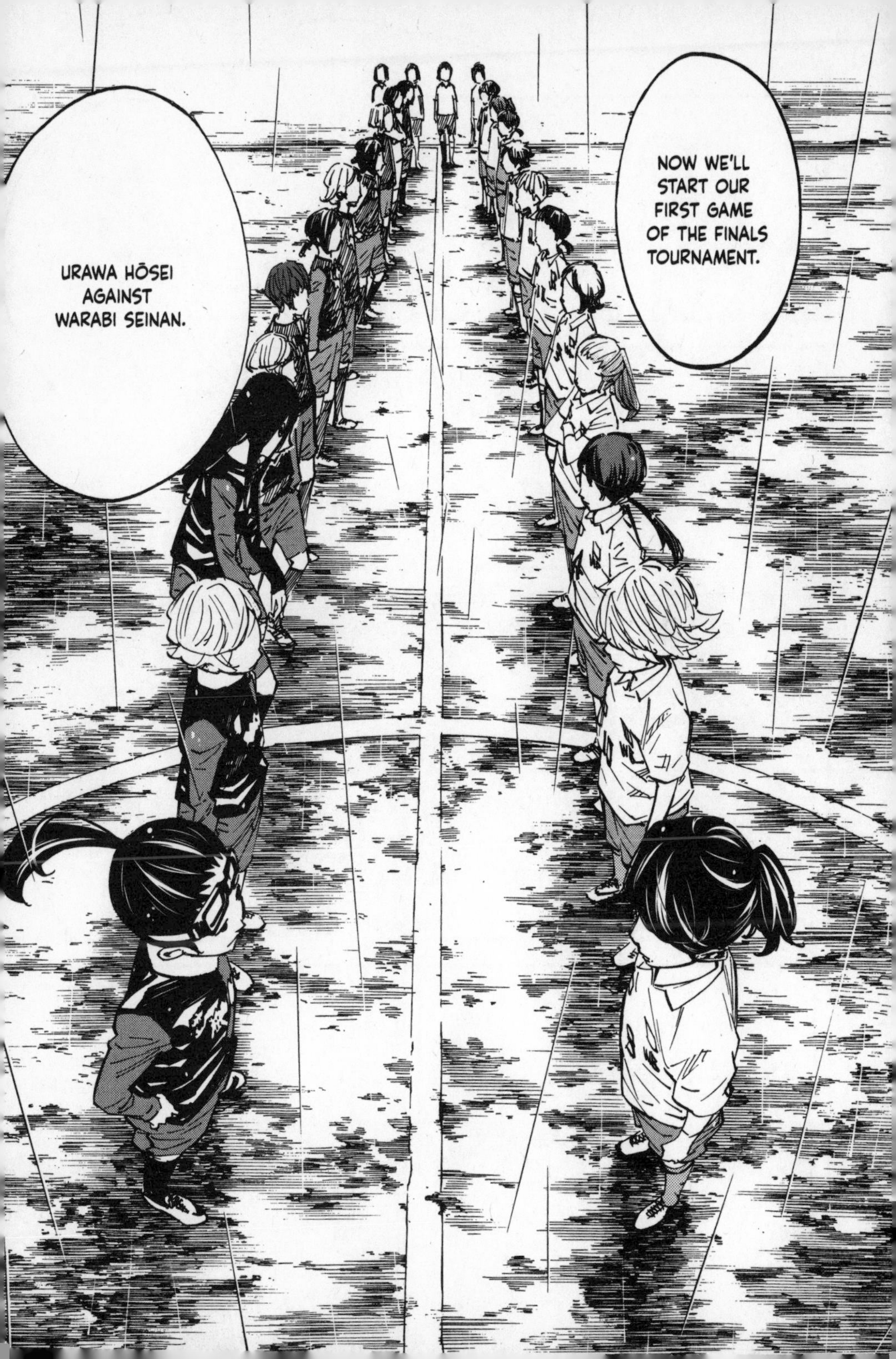
NOW WE'LL START OUR FIRST GAME OF THE FINALS TOURNAMENT.
URAWA HŌSEI AGAINST WARABI SEINAN.

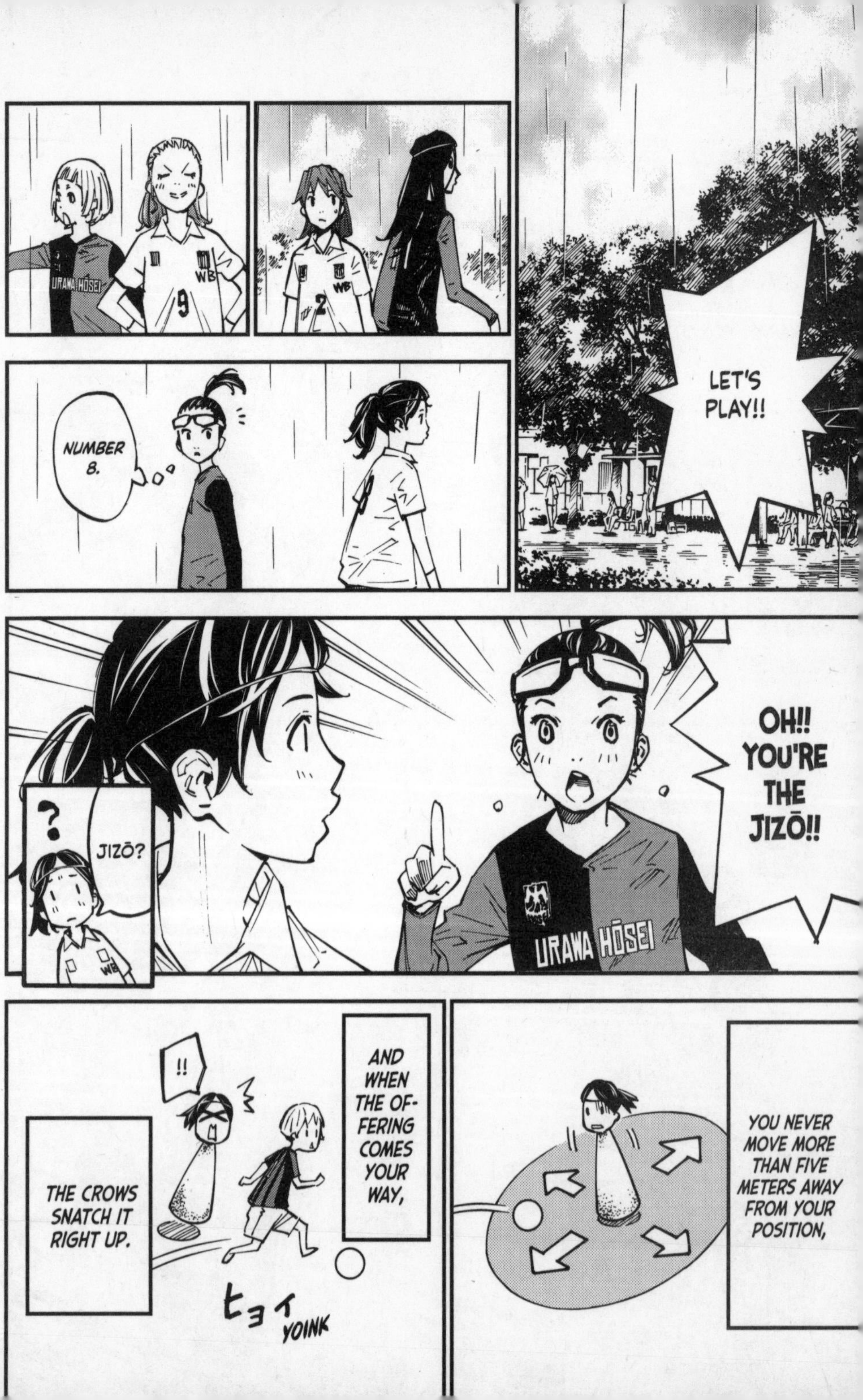

LET'S PLAY!!
NUMBER 8.
OH!! YOU'RE THE JIZŌ!!
?
JIZŌ?
YOU NEVER MOVE MORE THAN FIVE METERS AWAY FROM YOUR POSITION,
AND WHEN THE OF-FERING COMES YOUR WAY,
!!
THE CROWS SNATCH IT RIGHT UP.
ヒョイ
YOINK

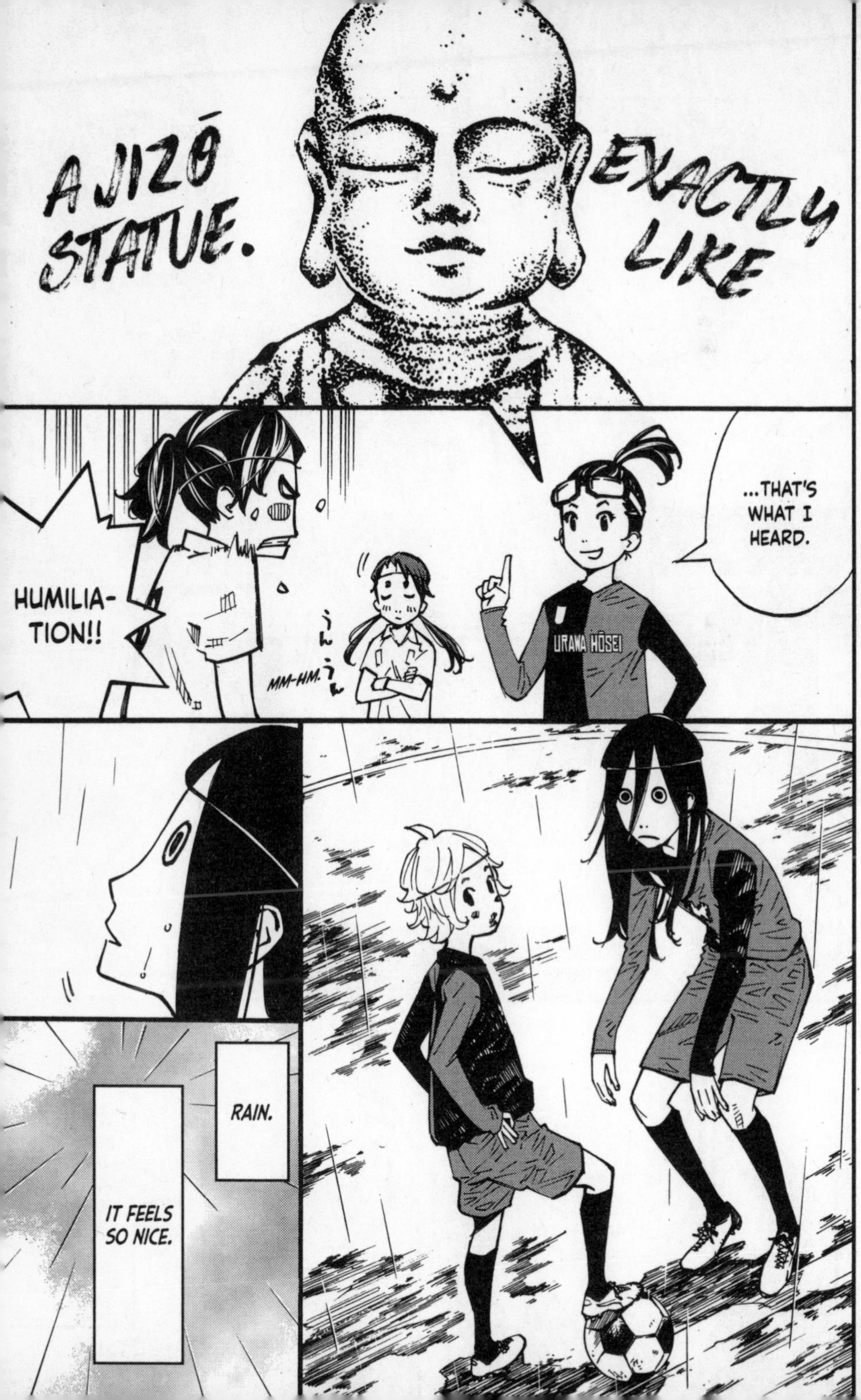
EXACTLY LIKE
A JIZŌ STATUE.
...THAT'S WHAT I HEARD.
MM-HM.
HUMILIA-TION!!
RAIN.
IT FEELS SO NICE.

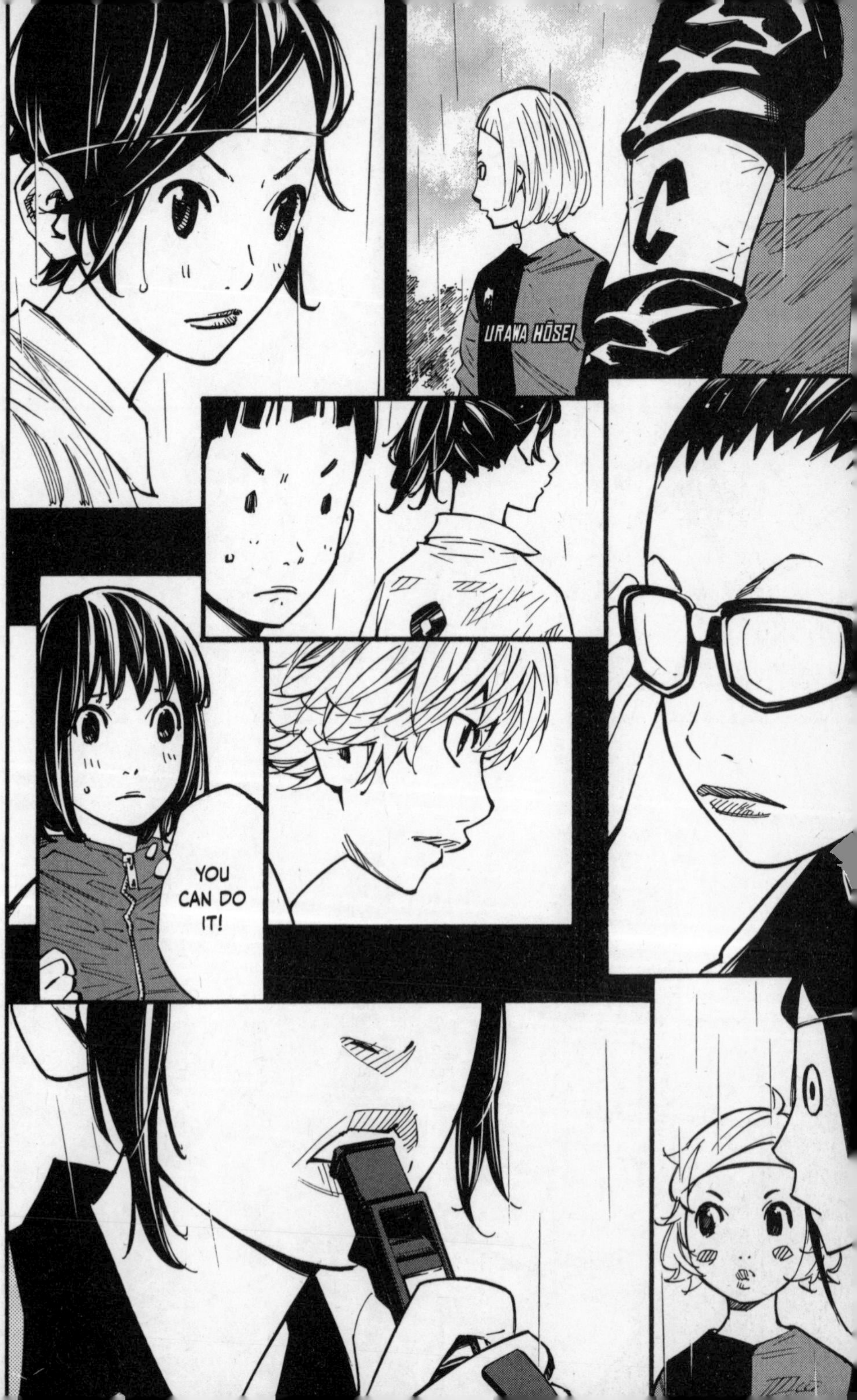
URAWA HŌSEI
YOU CAN DO IT!

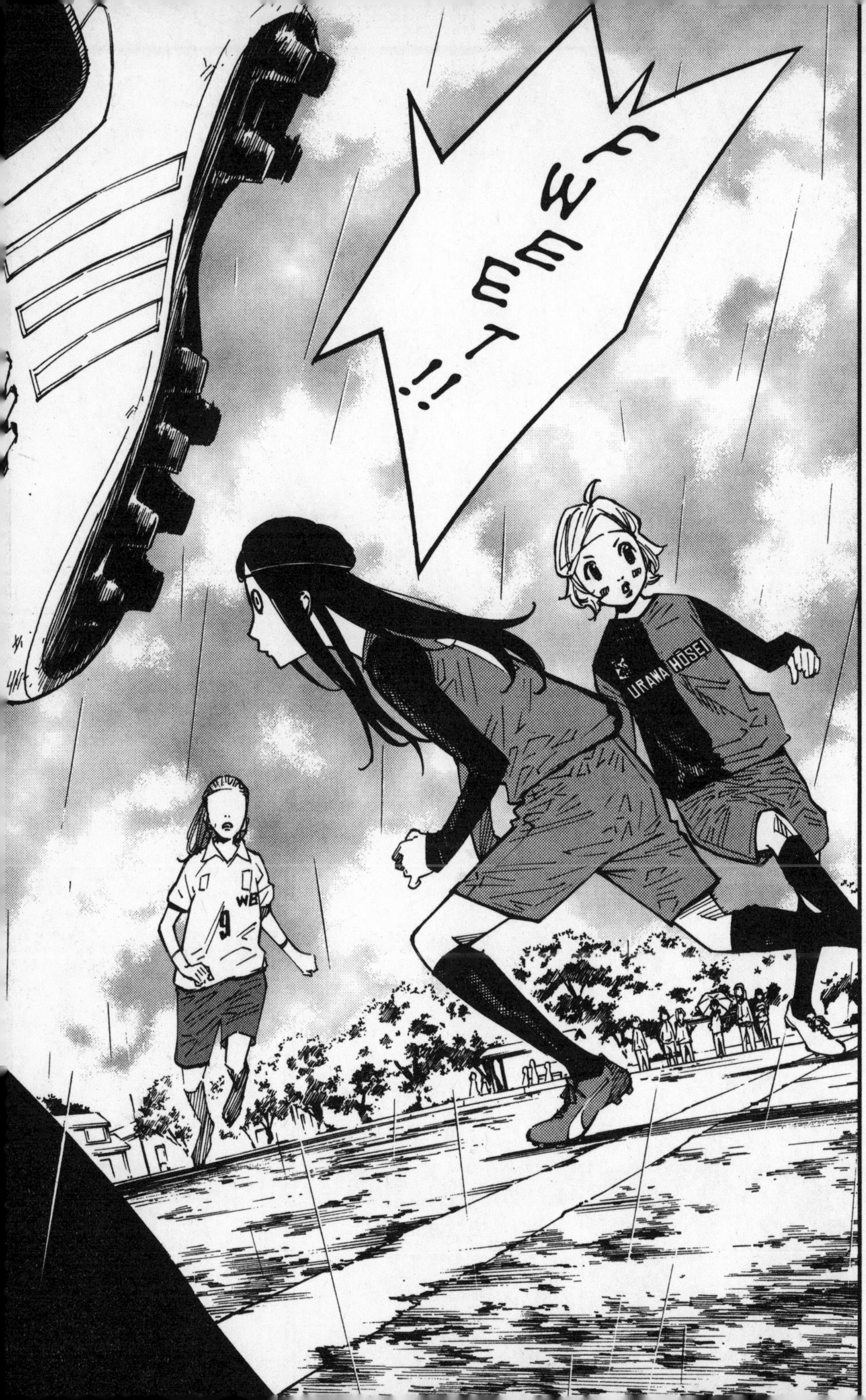
FWEET!!

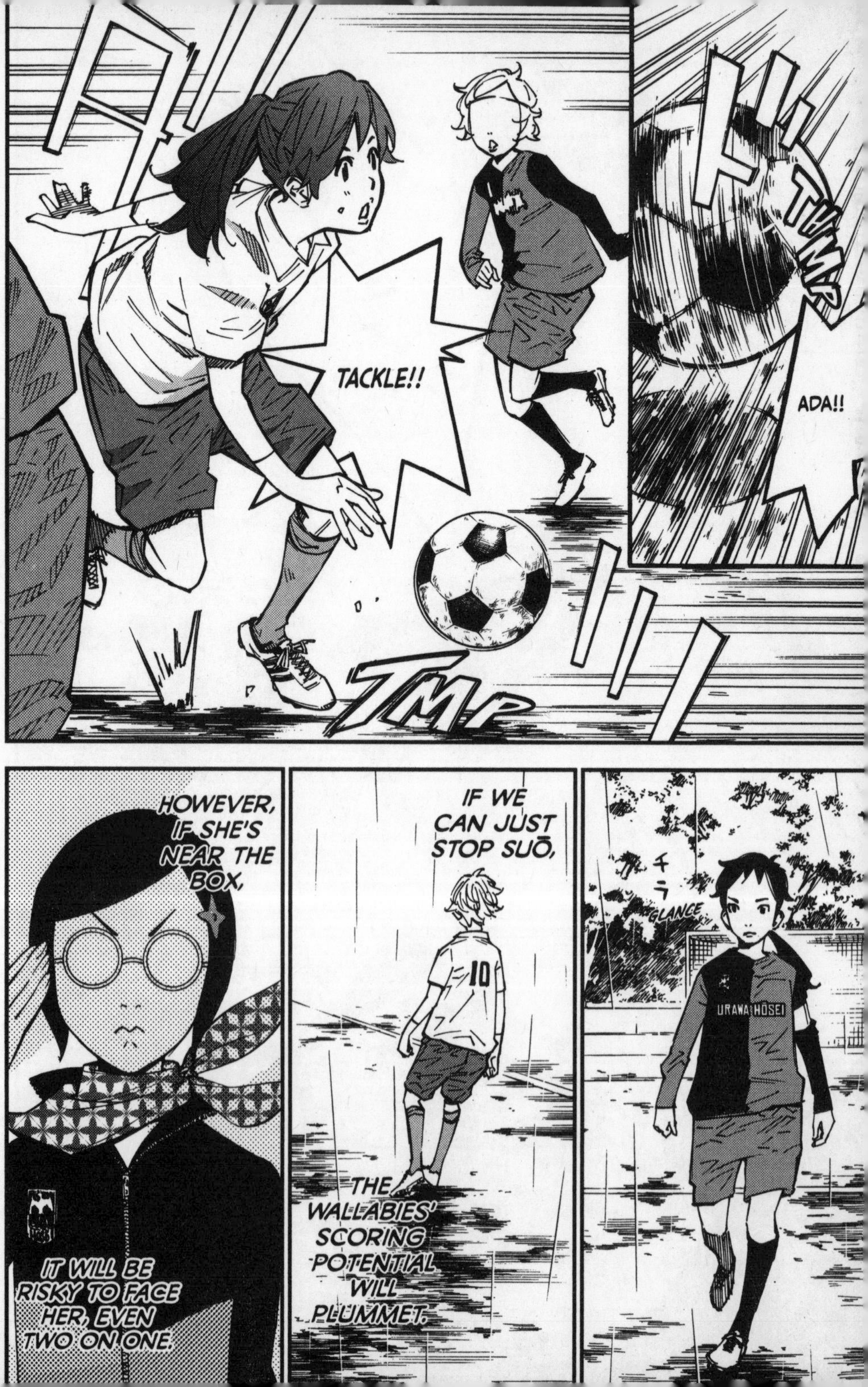
ド
THUMP
ADA!!
TACKLE!!
TMP
チラ
GLANCE
IF WE CAN JUST STOP SUŌ,
THE WALLABIES' SCORING POTENTIAL WILL PLUMMET.
HOWEVER, IF SHE'S NEAR THE BOX,
IT WILL BE RISKY TO FACE HER, EVEN TWO ON ONE.

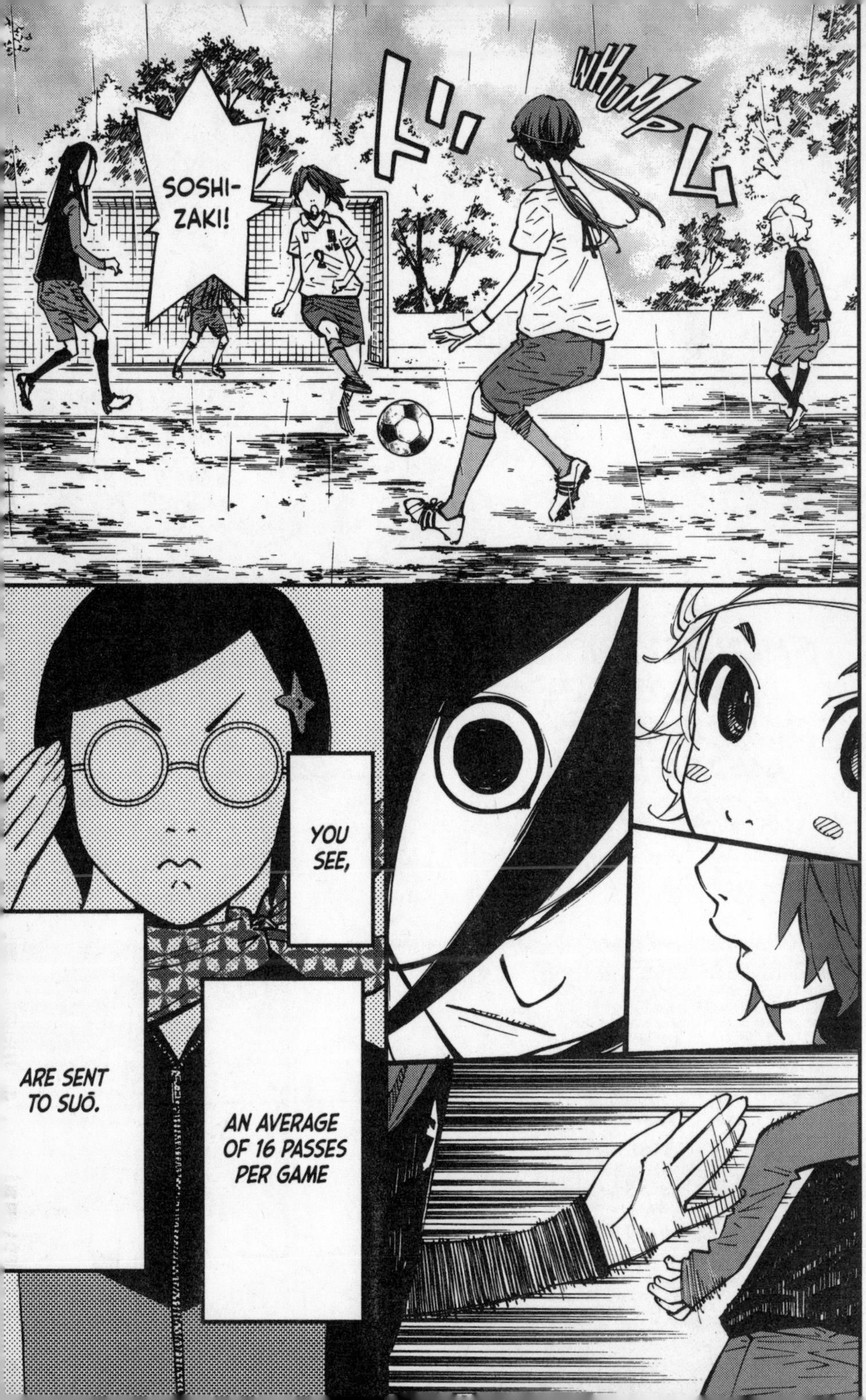
WHUMP
SOSHI-
ZAKI!
YOU SEE,
AN AVERAGE OF 16 PASSES PER GAME
ARE SENT TO SUŌ.

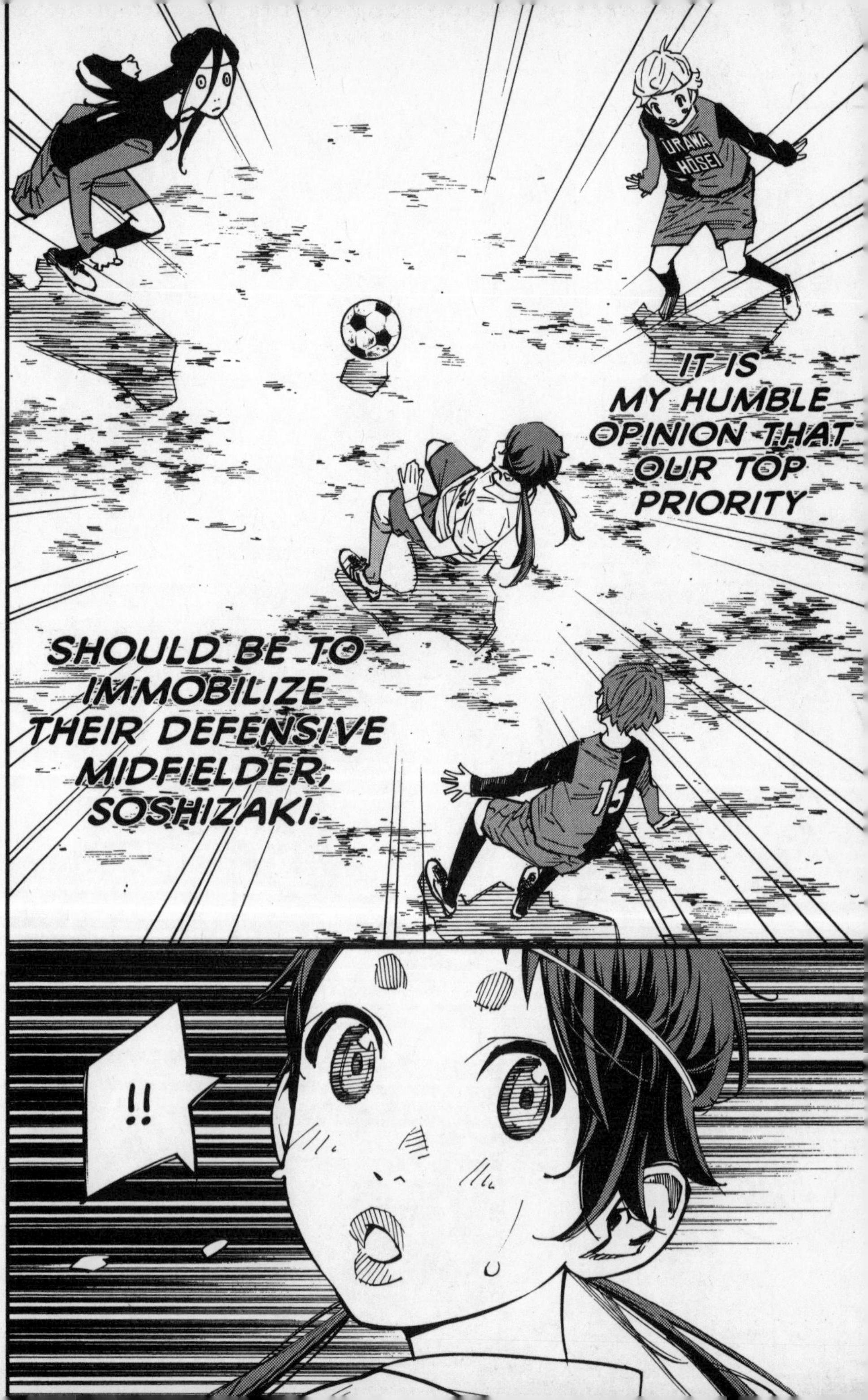
URAWA HOSEI
IT IS MY HUMBLE OPINION THAT OUR TOP PRIORITY
SHOULD BE TO IMMOBILIZE THEIR DEFENSIVE MIDFIELDER, SOSHIZAKI.
!!

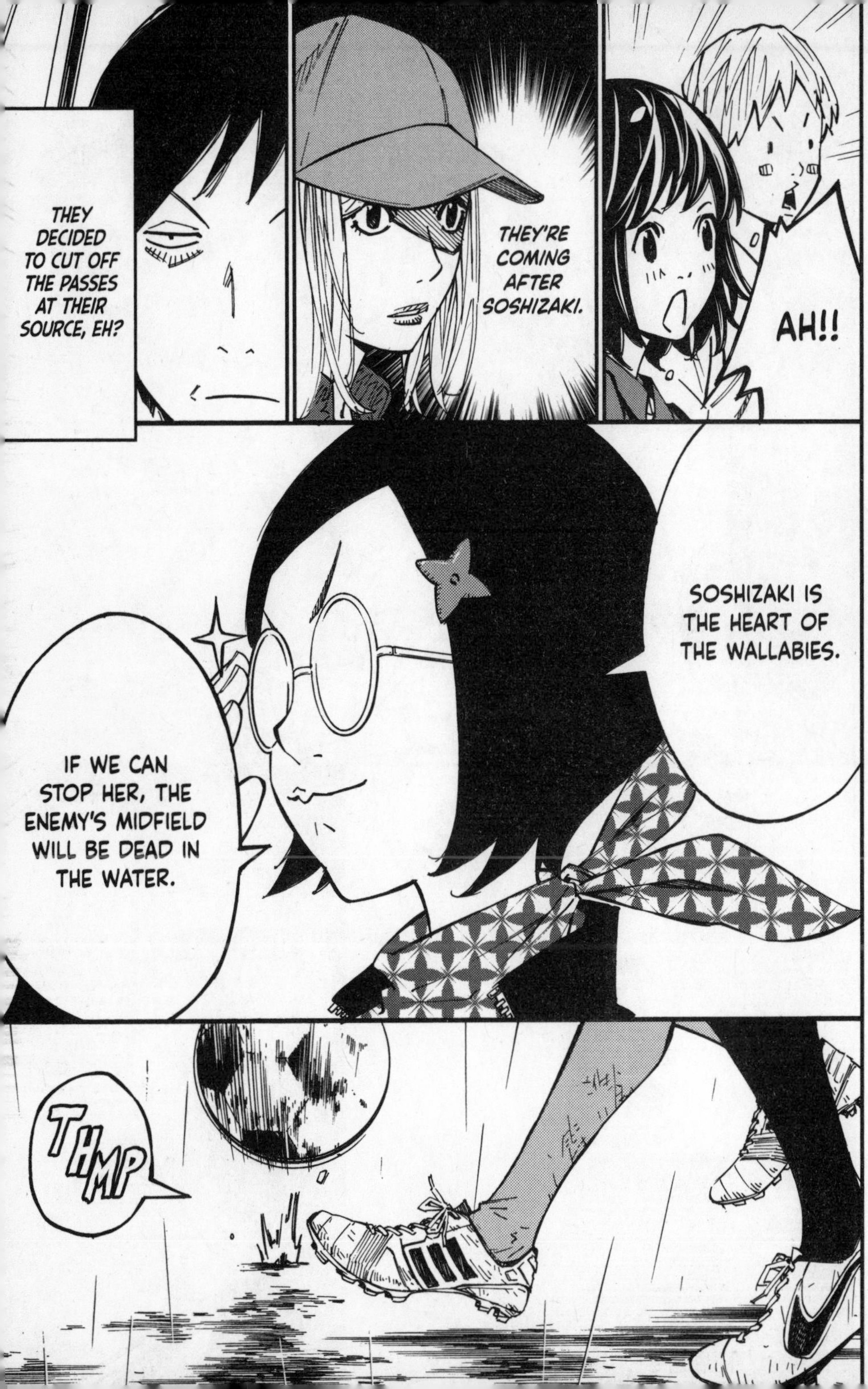
AH!!
THEY'RE COMING AFTER SOSHIZAKI.
THEY DECIDED TO CUT OFF THE PASSES AT THEIR SOURCE, EH?
SOSHIZAKI IS THE HEART OF THE WALLABIES.
IF WE CAN STOP HER, THE ENEMY'S MIDFIELD WILL BE DEAD IN THE WATER.
THMP

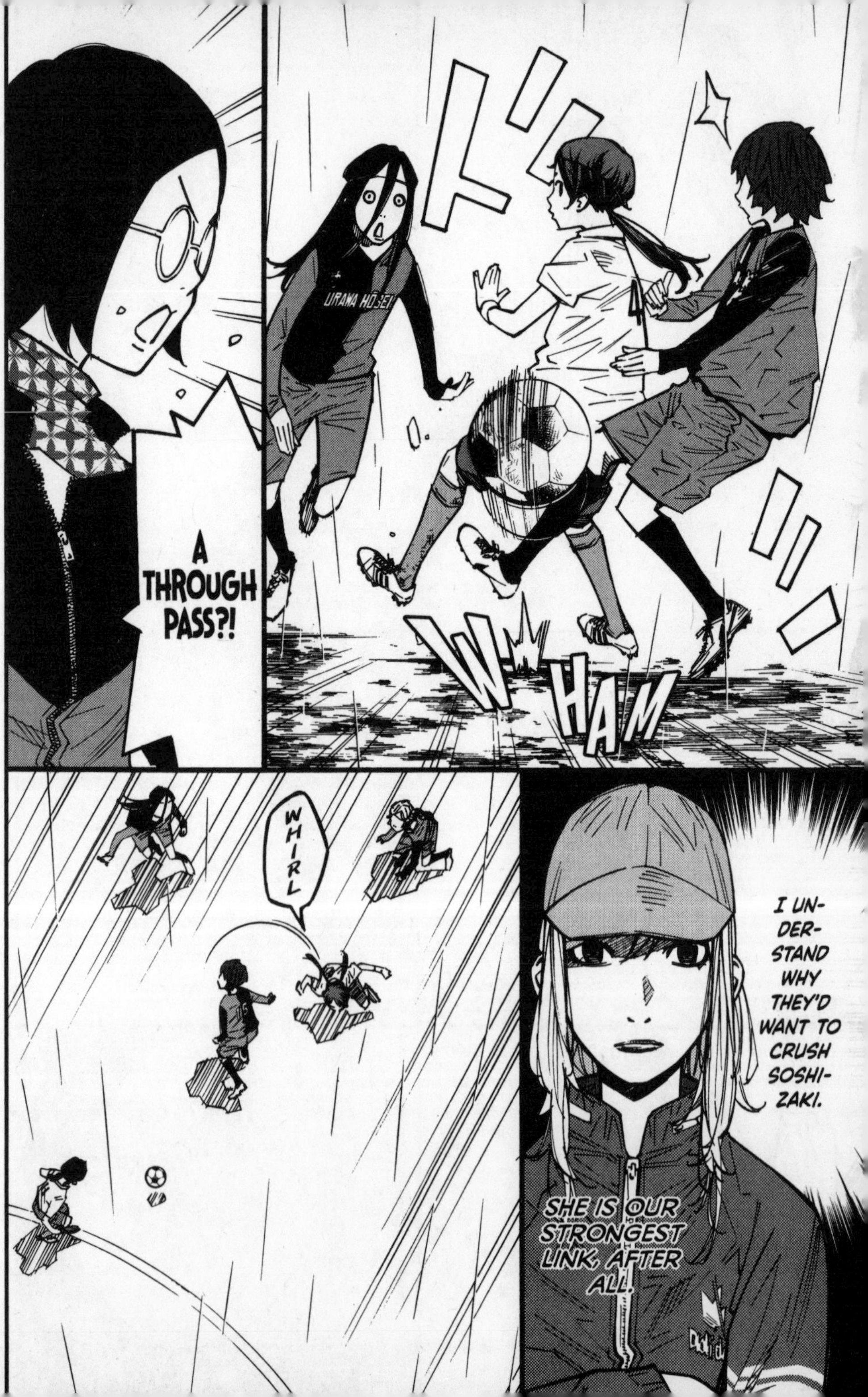
URAWA HŌSEI
WHAM
A THROUGH PASS?!
I UNDERSTAND WHY THEY'D WANT TO CRUSH SOSHIZAKI.
SHE IS OUR STRONGEST LINK, AFTER ALL.
WHIRL

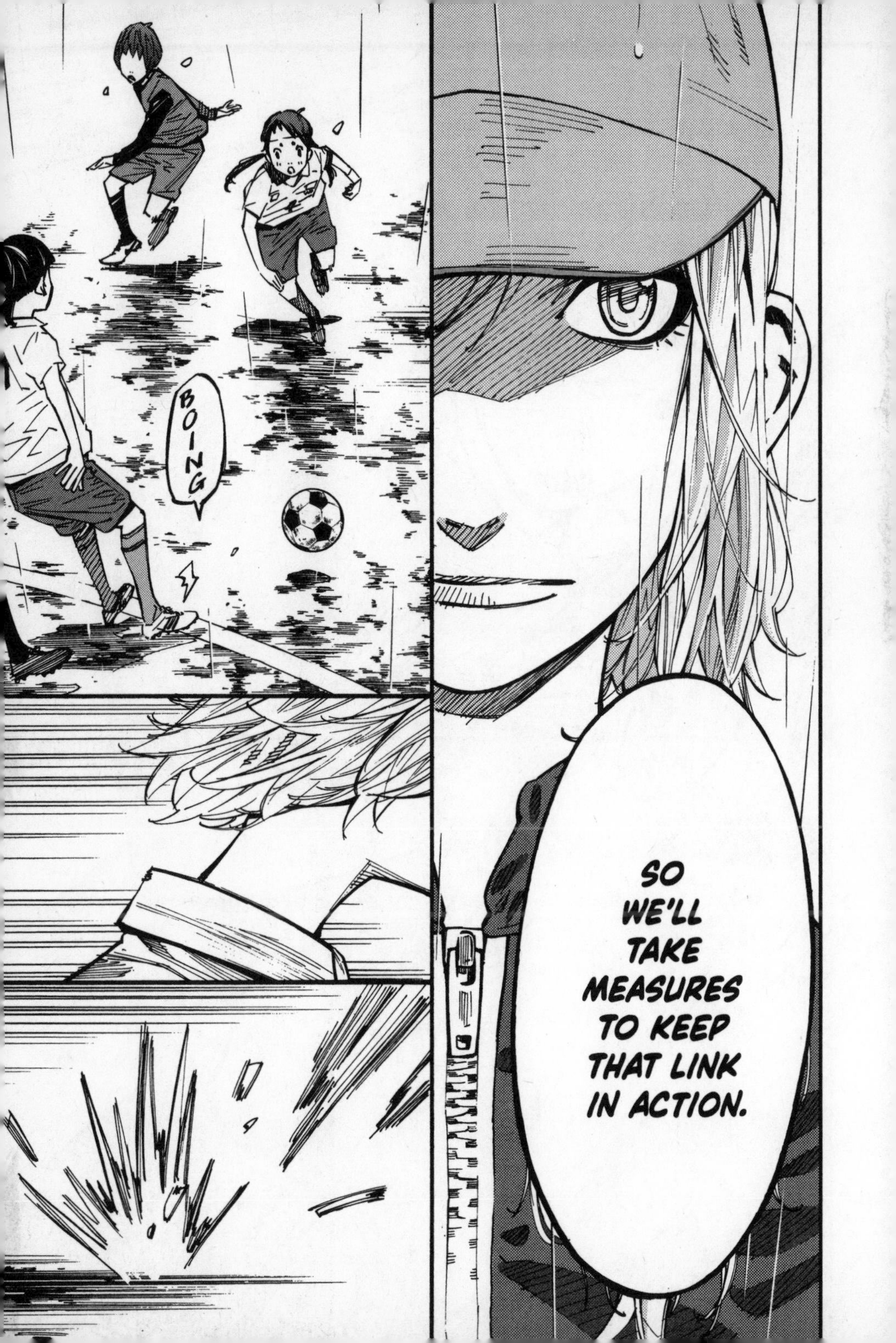
SO WE'LL TAKE MEASURES TO KEEP THAT LINK IN ACTION.
BOING

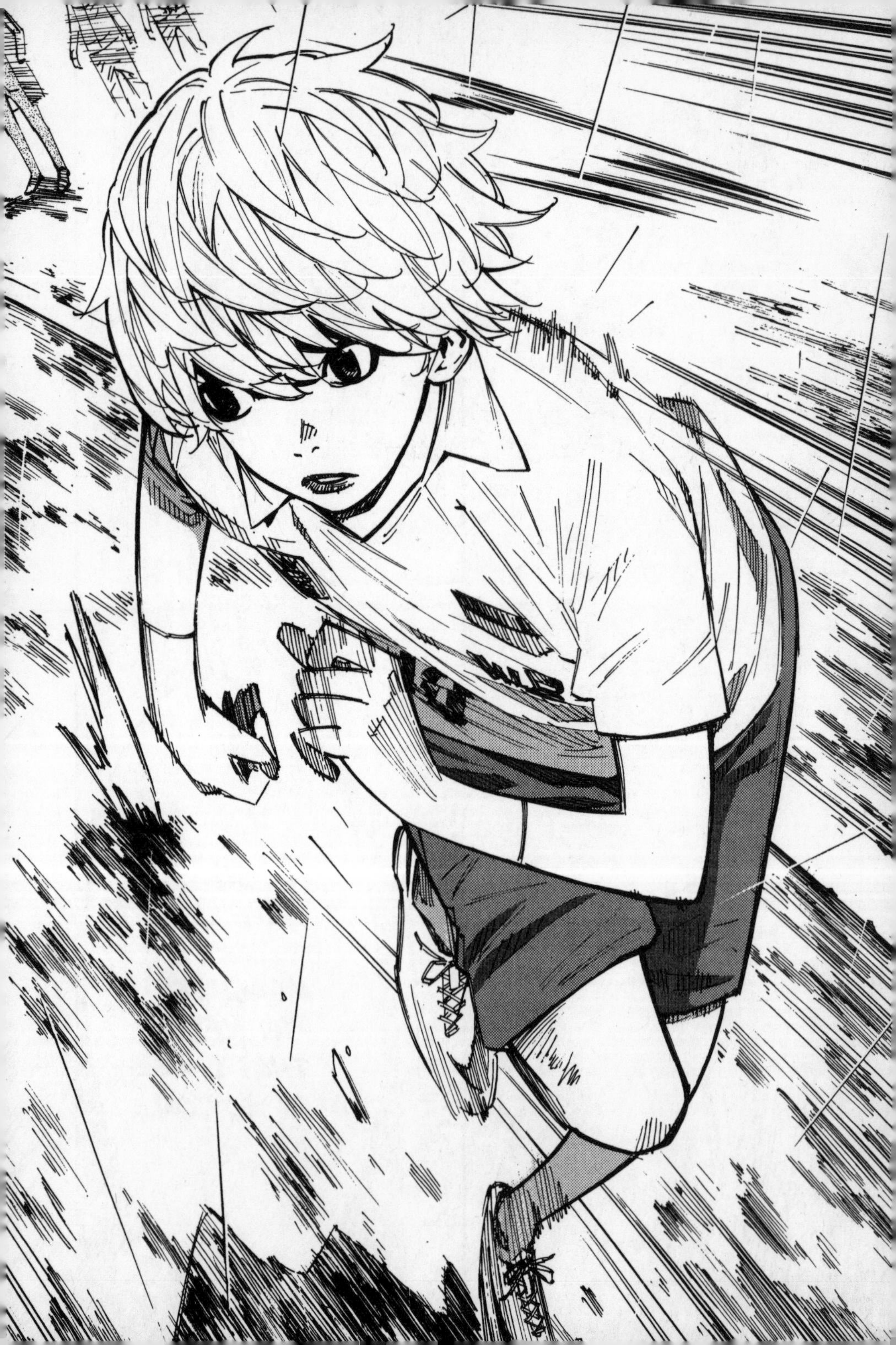

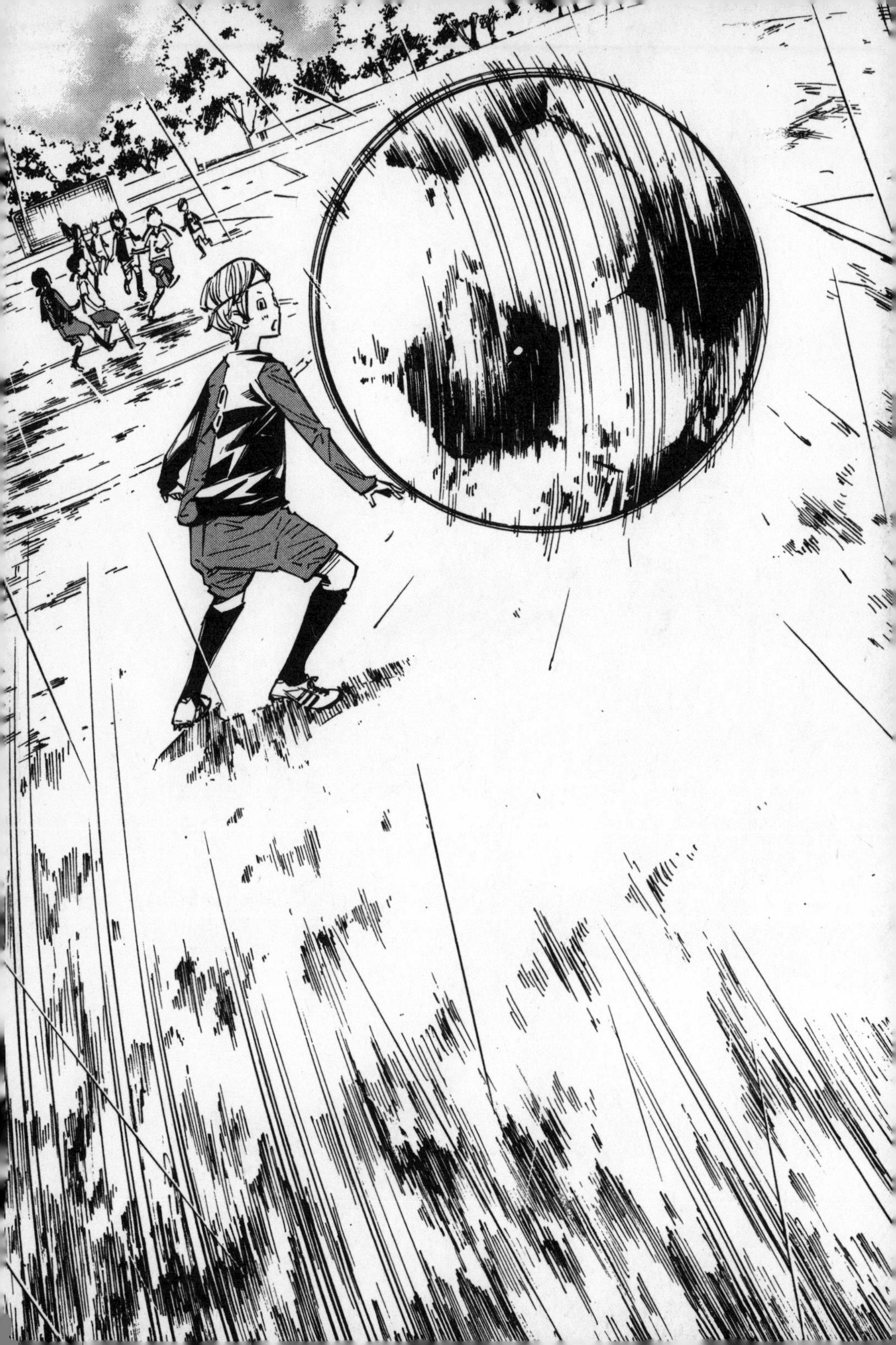

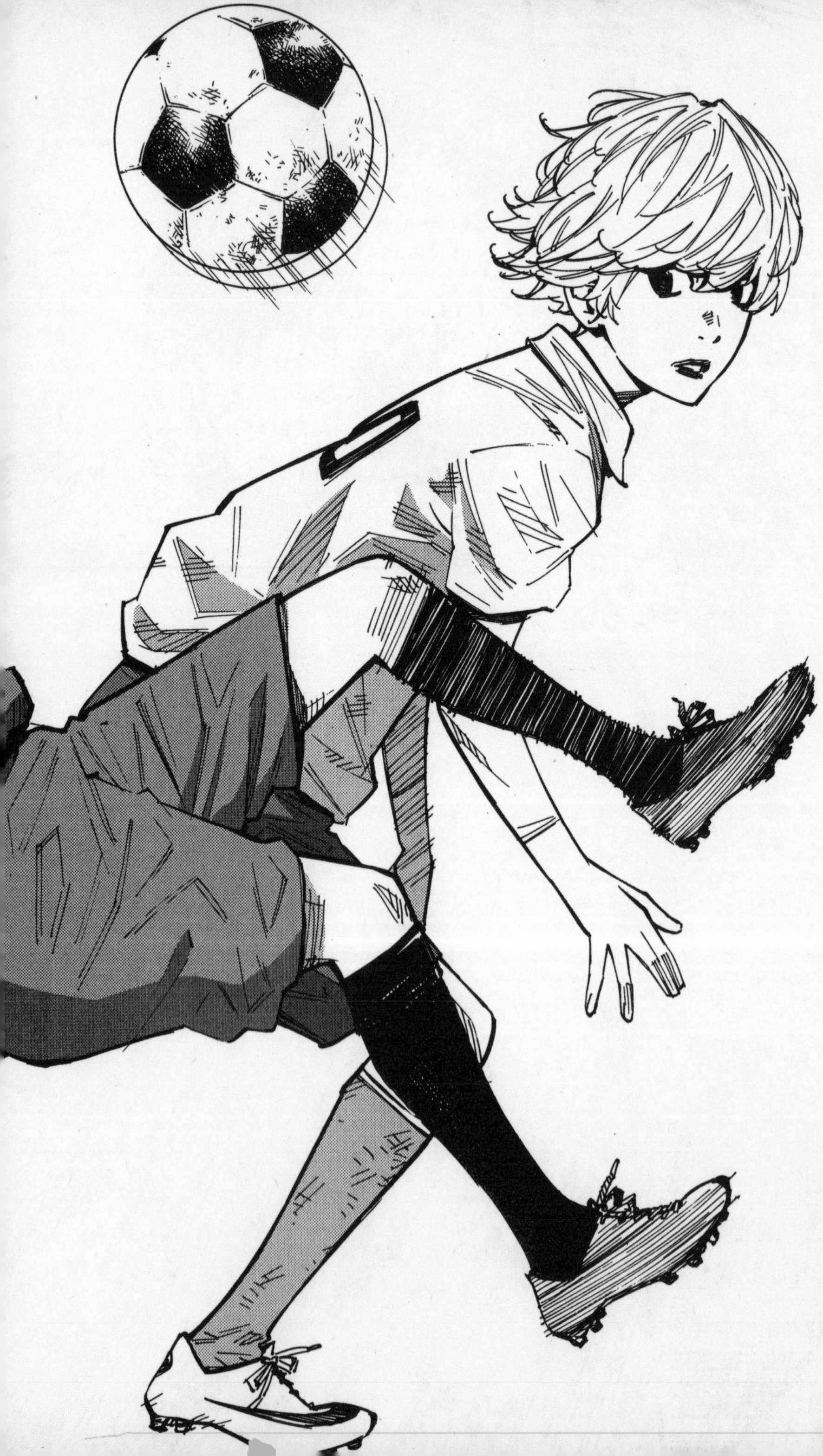

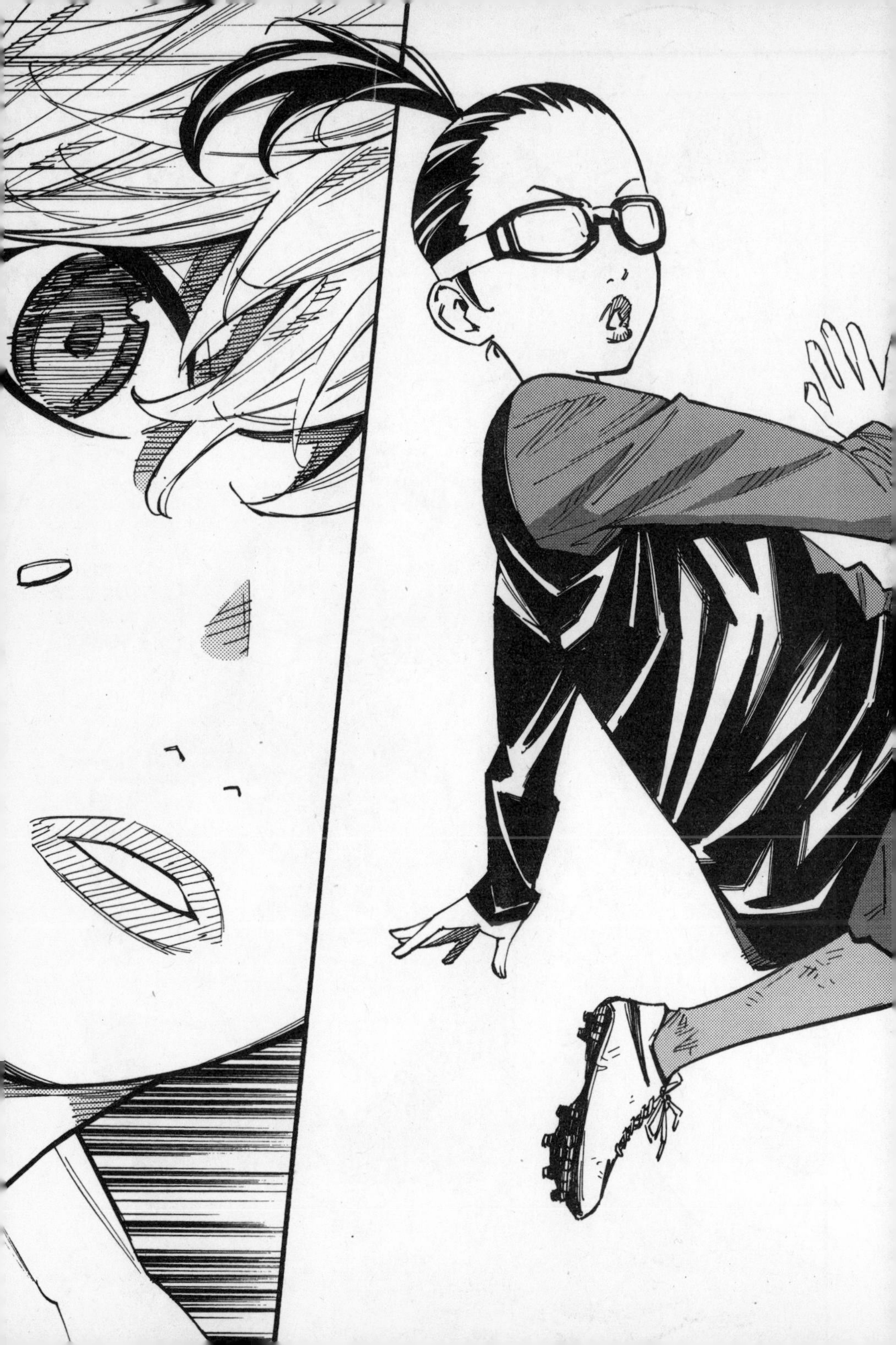

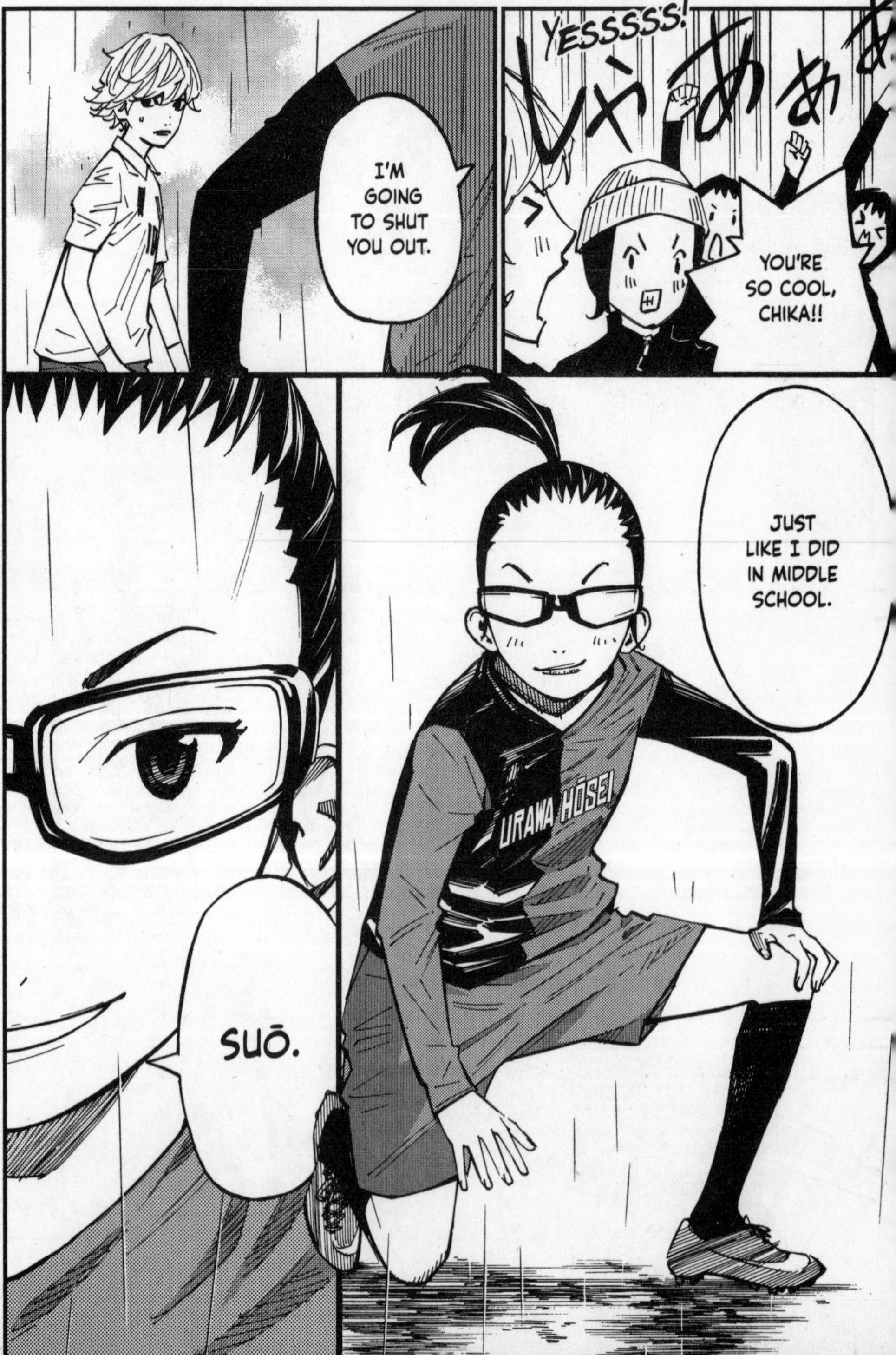
YESSSSS!
YOU'RE SO COOL, CHIKA!!
I'M GOING TO SHUT YOU OUT.
JUST LIKE I DID IN MIDDLE SCHOOL.
SUŌ.

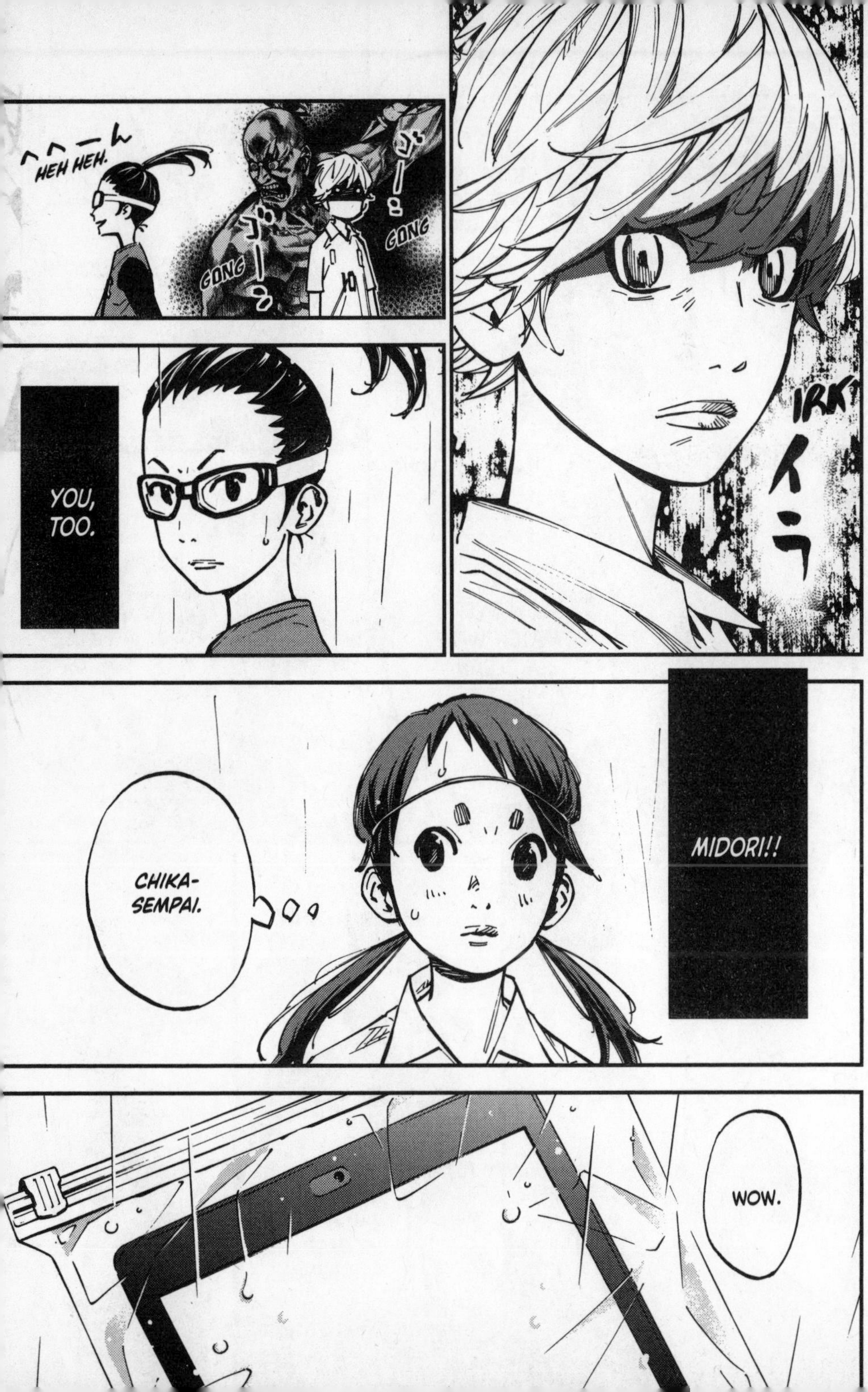
IRK
イラ
ゴーン
GONG
へへーん
HEH HEH.
ゴーン
GONG
YOU, TOO.
MIDORI!!
CHIKA-SEMPAI.
WOW.

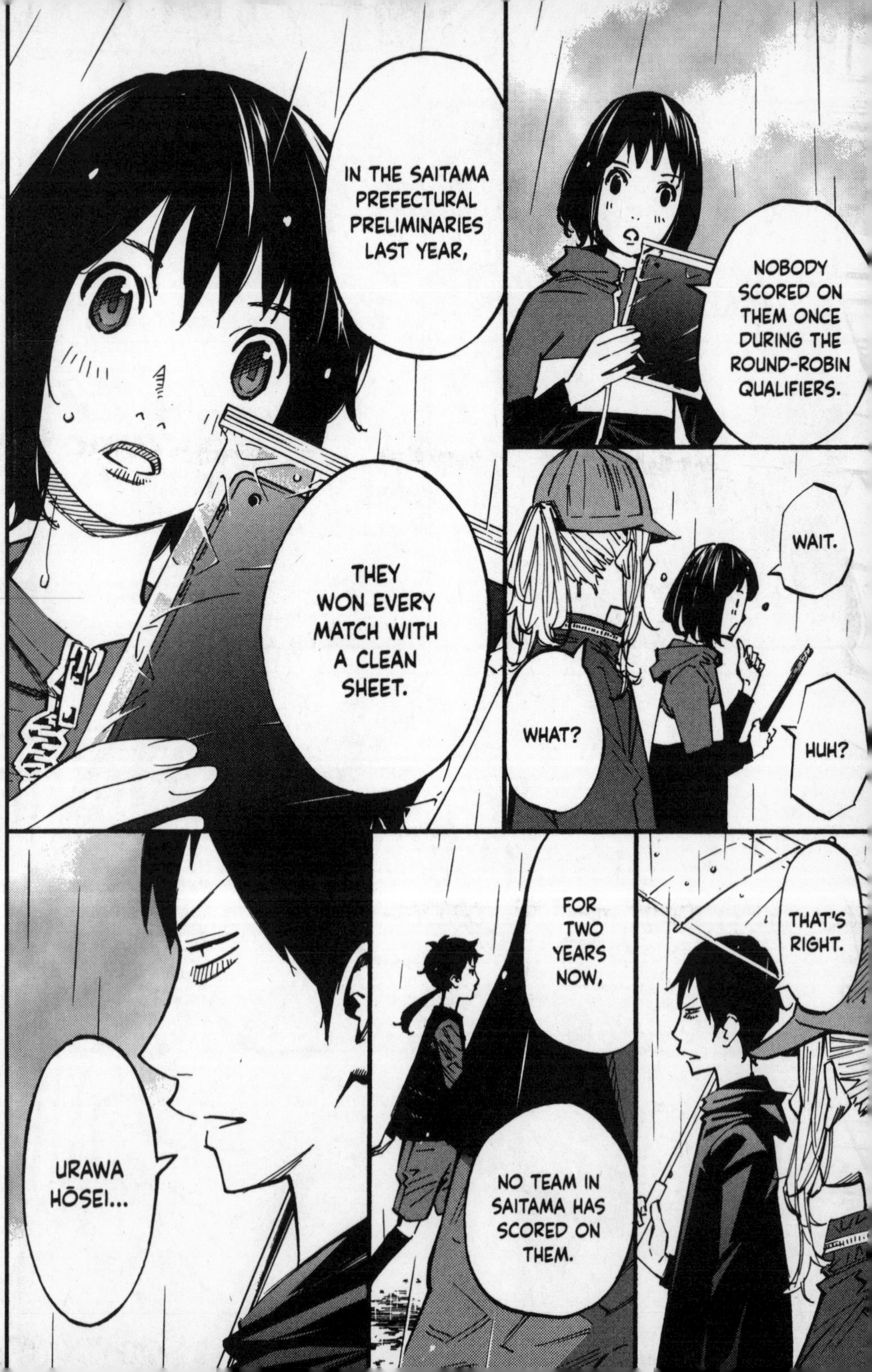
NOBODY SCORED ON THEM ONCE DURING THE ROUND-ROBIN QUALIFIERS.
WAIT.
HUH?
WHAT?
IN THE SAITAMA PREFECTURAL PRELIMINARIES LAST YEAR,
THEY WON EVERY MATCH WITH A CLEAN SHEET.
THAT'S RIGHT.
FOR TWO YEARS NOW,
NO TEAM IN SAITAMA HAS SCORED ON THEM.
URAWA HŌSEI...

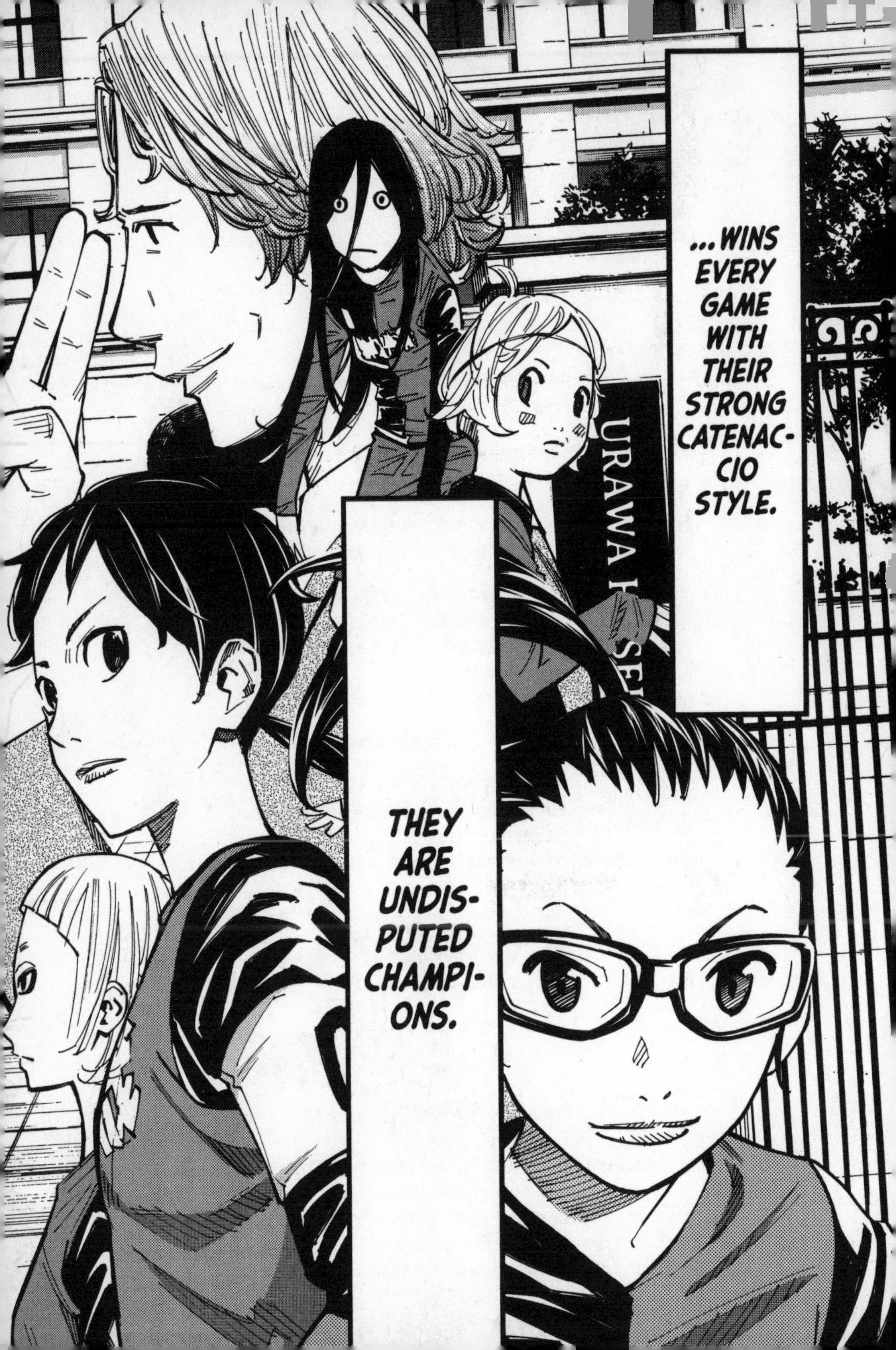
...WINS EVERY GAME WITH THEIR STRONG CATENACCIO STYLE.
URAWA
THEY ARE UNDISPUTED CHAMPIONS.

A Kodansha Comics Trade Paperback Original
Sayonara, Football 5 copyright © 2017 Naoshi Arakawa
English translation copyright © 2021 Naoshi Arakawa

© Nike © Adidas Japan © Puma Japan K.K.

Published in the United States by Kodansha Comics, an imprint of Kodansha USA Publishing, LLC, New York.

Publication rights for this English edition arranged through Kodansha Ltd., Tokyo.

First published in Japan in 2017 by Kodansha Ltd., Tokyo as *Sayonara watashi no Cramer*, volume 3.

ISBN 978-1-64651-099-3

Original cover design by Asakura Kenji

Printed in the United States of America.

www.kodanshacomics.com

9 8 7 6 5 4 3 2 1
Translation: Alethea and Athena Nibley
Lettering: Nicole Roderick
Kodansha Comics edition cover design by Adam Del Re

Publisher: Kiichiro Sugawara

Director of publishing services: Ben Applegate
Associate director of operations: Stephen Pakula
Publishing services managing editors: Alanna Ruse, Madison Salters
Assistant production managers: Emi Lotto, Angela Zurlo
Logo and character art ©Kodansha USA Publishing, LLC